The Pedagogy of Economic, Political and Social Crises

Crises have been studied in many disciplines and from diverse perspectives for at least 150 years. Yet recent decades have seen a marked increase in the crisis literature, reflecting growing awareness of crisis phenomena from the 1970s onwards.

Responding to this mainstream literature, this edited collection makes six key innovations. First, it distinguishes between crises as event and crises as process, as well as crises as accidental events or as the result of system-generated processes. Second, it distinguishes crises that can be managed through established crisis-management routines from crises of crisis management. Third, it focuses on the symptomatology of crisis, i.e., the challenge of moving crisis symptoms to understanding underlying causes as a basis for decisive action. Fourth, it goes beyond the cliché that crises are both threat and opportunity by distinguishing valid accounts of the origins and present nature of a crisis, from more speculative accounts of what potentially exists. Fifth, it explores how crises can disorient conventional wisdom, thus provoking efforts to interpret and learn about crises and draw lessons after a crisis has ended. Finally, the sixth element is the move away from the conventional focus on executive authorities and disaster management agencies, instead turning attention towards how other social forces construe crises and attempt to learn from them.

Offering important insights into the pedagogy of crisis throughout, this collection will offer excellent reading to both researchers and postgraduate students.

Bob Jessop is Distinguished Professor of Sociology and Co-Director of the Cultural Political Economy Research Centre at Lancaster University, UK. He is best known for his contributions to state theory, critical political economy, the analysis of comparative welfare regimes, critical governance studies, and cultural political economy.

Karim Knio is Associate Professor in International Political Economy and Governance at the Institute of Social Studies, The Hague, Netherlands. He is also the current Associate Managing Editor of *European Political Science Review (EPSR)*. His research focuses on the intersection between international political economy, governance and public policy.

Routledge Frontiers of Political Economy

For more information about this series, please visit: www.routledge.com/books/series/SE0345

The Pedagogy of Economic, Political and Social Crises

Dynamics, Construals and Lessons

Edited by Bob Jessop and Karim Knio

 Routledge
Taylor & Francis Group

LONDON AND NEW YORK

First published 2019
by Routledge
2 Park Square, Milton Park, Abingdon, Oxon OX14 4RN

and by Routledge
52 Vanderbilt Avenue, New York, NY 10017, USA

First issued in paperback 2020

Routledge is an imprint of the Taylor & Francis Group, an informa business

British Library Cataloguing-in-Publication Data
A catalogue record for this book is available from the British Library

Library of Congress Cataloging-in-Publication Data
Names: Jessop, Bob, editor. | Knio, Karim, editor.
Title: The pedagogy of economic, political and social crises : dynamics, construals and lessons / edited by Bob Jessop and Karim Knio.
Description: Abingdon, Oxon ; New York, NY : Routledge, 2019. |
Series: Routledge frontiers of political economy ; 250 |
Includes bibliographical references and index.
Identifiers: LCCN 2018030853 (print) | LCCN 2018032475 (ebook) |
ISBN 9781315161587 (Ebook) | ISBN 9781138062504 (hardback : alk. paper)
Subjects: LCSH: Crises. | Crisis management.
Classification: LCC HN13 (ebook) | LCC HN13 .P4185 2019 (print) |
DDC 303.48/4–dc23
LC record available at https://lccn.loc.gov/2018030853

ISBN 13: 978-0-367-58389-7 (pbk)
ISBN 13: 978-1-138-06250-4 (hbk)

Typeset in Bembo
by Integra Software Services Pvt. Ltd.

Contents

PART VI
Conclusions **263**

Illustrations

Figures

Tables

Contributors

Editors

Bob Jessop is Distinguished Professor of Sociology and Co-Director of the Cultural Political Economy Research Centre at Lancaster University. He is best known for his contributions to state theory, critical political economy, the analysis of comparative welfare regimes, critical governance studies, and cultural political economy. His most recent books comprise: *Beyond Cultural Political Economy: Putting Culture in its Place in Political Economy* (with Ngai-Ling Sum, 2013, Edward Elgar); *The State: Past, Present, Future* (Polity 2015); *Cultures of Finance and Crisis Dynamics* (co-edited with Brigitte Young and Christoph Scherrer, 2014, Routledge); and *Transnational Capital and Class Fractions: The Amsterdam School Perspective Reconsidered* (co-edited with Henk Overbeek, 2018, Routledge).

Karim Knio is Associate Professor of International Political Economy and Governance at the Institute of Social Studies (ISS) of Erasmus University Rotterdam. He is the current Associate Managing Editor of European Political Science Review (EPSR). His research focuses on the intersection between international political economy, governance and public policy. He has research interests in the literatures on varieties of capitalism, institutional analysis, politics of crisis management, EU democracy promotion programs and Lebanese politics. He is the author of *The European Union's Mediterranean Policy: Model or Muddle? A New Institutionalist Perspective* (Palgrave Macmillan 2013), *and The South China Sea and Asian Regionalism: A Critical Realist Perspective* (with Thanhdam Truong) (Springer 2016).

Contributors

Robert Boyer is Emeritus Professor of Economics at Institut des Ameriques, France.

David Chandler is Professor of International Relations at the University of Westminster, UK.

Andrew Gamble is Professor of Politics at The University of Sheffield, UK.

Des Gasper is Professor of Human Development, Development Ethics and Public Policy at the International Institute of Social Studies, Erasmus University, The Netherlands.

Jeff Handmaker is Senior lecturer in Law, Human Rights and Development at the International Institute of Social Studies, Erasmus University, The Netherlands.

Wil Hout is Professor of Governance and International Political Economy at the International Institute of Social Studies, Erasmus University, The Netherlands.

Zuzana Novakova is a PhD researcher at the International Institute of Social Studies, Erasmus University, The Netherlands.

Magnus Ryner is Professor of International Political Economy at King's College London, UK.

Matthew Watson is Professor of Political Economy at the University of Warwick, UK.

Angela Wigger is Associate Professor in Political Science at Radboud University, Netherlands.

Preface

This book is a product of the research initiative on Crisis, Continuity and Change (C3) sponsored by the research group on Governance, Law and Social Justice (GLSJ) at the Institute of Social Studies (ISS) of Erasmus University Rotterdam. In the process of developing this book, we have accumulated an immense array of personal, practical and intellectual debt to a number of colleagues and friends.

We would like to express our gratitude to GLSJ and ISS for providing the financial and logistical support behind the organization of the Development Research Seminar Series in 2014 and the C3 workshops held in 2015. These events were key for forging both the intellectual stimulation and identity for this collective endeavour. We also would like to thank Anna Jungen, Aleksandra Piletic, Amy Austin and Rhiannon Lambe for their research and editorial assistance. This volume could not have been completed without their help.

Bob Jessop also benefitted from a sabbatical term from Lancaster University, during which time he worked on his chapters and engaged in editorial work on other contributions to the volume. Some of his ideas and arguments derive from a Professorial Research Fellowship funded by the UK's Economic and Social Research Council in 2010-2013 (Grant: RES-051-27-0303). The ideas on the pedagogy of crisis were developed at different times in association with JI Joo Hyoung, Mathis Heinrich and Amelie Kutter and the broader cultural political economy approach was co-developed with Ngai-Ling Sum, who also tolerated the hours devoted to completing this publishing project.

At Routledge, we are grateful to Anna Cuthbert, Andy Humphries and Laura Johnson for their enthusiastic support and patience.

Bob Jessop
Karim Knio
Lancaster and den Haag,
4 June 2018

Abbreviations

BDI	Bundesverband der Deutschen Industrie e.V. (Federal Association of German Industry)
CJ	Critical juncture
CR	Critical realism
CPE	Cultural political economy
DSGE	Dynamic Stochastic General Equilibrium
ECB	European Central Bank
ECOSOC	Economic and Social Council (United Nations)
EMU	European Monetary Union
ENP	European Neighbourhood Policy
ERT	European Round Table of Industrialists
ETUC	European Trade Union Confederation
EU	European Union
G7	Group of Seven
G20	Group of Twenty
GDP	Gross Domestic Product
GTI	Great Transition Initiative
HI	Historical institutionalism
IMF	International Monetary Fund
ICC	International Criminal Court
IPPC	Intergovernmental Panel on Climate Change
LRA	Lord's Resistance Army
MDGs	Millennium Development Goals
MEDEF	Mouvement des entreprises de France (Movement of Enterprises of France)
NCAR	National Centre for Atmospheric Research
NGOs	Non-Governmental Organizations
OECD	Organization of Economic Cooperation and Development
QE	Quantitative Easing
RUF	Revolutionary United Front
SDGs	Sustainable Development Goals
SVS	Savages, Victims and Saviours
SYRIZA	Synaspismós Rizospastikís Aristerás (Radical Left Party, Greece)

TPP	Trans-Pacific Partnership
TTIP	Transatlantic Trade and Investment Pact
UK	United Kingdom
UN	United Nations
UNDP	United Nations Development Programme
US	United States of America
USSR	Union of Soviet Socialist Republics
WWII	World War II

Part I

Introducing some key themes

1 Introduction

Organizational perspectives on crisiology and learning

Karim Knio and Bob Jessop[1]

Crises have been studied in academia in many disciplines and from diverse perspectives for at least 150 years. However, recent decades have seen a marked increase in the crisis literature, primarily due to the pervasiveness of crises throughout the 1970s, 1980s, and onwards, and an associated inflation in crisis discourses. The 1970s witnessed a range of political and economic crises – the Nixon Shock, the 1973 oil crisis, stagflation, and intensified class struggles as well as the emergence of new social movements – which contributed to the electoral victories of Ronald Reagan and Margaret Thatcher in the US and the UK, respectively. The 1980s in turn witnessed high-profile commercial, industrial, and technological disasters (e.g., the Bhopal disaster, Chernobyl, the Challenger explosion, and the Exxon Valdez oil spill) that reignited interest in disasters as well as crises and how to prevent, manage, or resolve them. A further major boost came with the 9/11 attacks on the World Trade Center and the Pentagon in 2001. Indeed, this led to greatly increased funding and efforts to enhance coordinated research and planning. Thus, as Boin, McConnell and 't Hart point out, this has triggered efforts to unify "a disjointed, segmented set of niches within the social sciences" concerned with crises (2008, p. 6).

The newly rediscovered terror threat in the "homeland", the eruption of the 2008 global financial crisis in the "heartland" of finance-dominated neoliberal accumulation, and the rise of new forms of instability and popular resistance accentuated by the economic and political turmoil consequent upon the 2008 financial crisis, have all contributed to a diversification of the study of crises. One current is preoccupied with the cause and nature of crises, another focuses on crisis management, and a third on learning and lesson-drawing processes post-crisis. These currents may overlap. As Shrivastava notes, the "expansion of crisis research and practice is undeniably impressive"; however, "there is no single paradigm guiding research" and there are "many different disciplinary voices, talking in different languages to different issues and audiences" (1993, p. 33). This is reflected in crisis research in the fields of organizational studies, economics, political science, public policy, and sociology, as well as international relations. A plurality of perspectives and approaches is appropriate to complex phenomena because each may reveal what others cannot see. However, without serious efforts at synthesis and at rendering commensurable different paradigms and perspectives, the result can be a mosaic with contrasting impulsions and problematiques, creating a 'tower of Babel' effect, leading to "difficulties in communication of research results within the research community" (ibid.). It can also lead to serious questioning about what gets lost or overlooked if crisis narratives and an inflationary use of the concept of crisis marginalize other ways of examining recent events and social processes that challenge established inherited routines and experiences (cf. Roitman, 2015; see also Chapter 3). In this sense, while crisis and critique have been closely coupled in the modern era (cf. Koselleck, 1988), it may be time to critique a one-sided concern with crisis at the expense of other ways of construing and explaining significant and/or disruptive events in the modern world.

To offer some guidance through this literature, we distinguish crisis from other forms of disruption, identify a key distinction between two broad kinds of crisis, highlight the challenge of symptomatology when it comes to interpreting the nature and significance of crises, and, as the special contribution of this collection, explore different aspects of what we call the pedagogy of crisis.

1. We distinguish disasters from crises in terms of the more accidental nature of disasters, which have the character of one-off events even if they occur regularly or frequently, and the more systemic and recurrent nature of crises, rooted in systemic processes of individual systems and/or the patterned interaction among a plurality of systems. This is reflected in two different, if overlapping, kinds of literature, concerned respectively with the prevention and management of disasters and the regulation of crisis tendencies and challenges of crisis management (see Chapter 3).

2. Following Claus Offe (1976), although in more nuanced ways, we also distinguish normal from exceptional crises – with the former being susceptible to routine crisis management and the latter requiring extraordinary measures to overcome a crisis of crisis management (on these distinctions, see Chapters 2 and 3).

3. This pair of distinctions raises the issue of symptomatology, i.e., how actors set about deciphering the opaque relationship between the symptoms of a disaster or crisis and their underlying causes, and, hence, address the challenge of intervening into these causes to manage or resolve the resulting crisis (on symptomatology, see Jessop, 2015; and Chapters 3 and 14). Indeed, this is also the site of struggles over how to construe the immediate symptoms of an extraordinary event or process and to politicize or depoliticize how they are construed, explained, and managed.

4. A fourth aspect concerns the pedagogy of crisis over different spatiotemporal horizons. Here we distinguish between the challenge to past lessons and current perceptions of how the world works that is induced by disasters and crises, the attempt to decipher their character when they first emerge on the basis of immediate empirical symptoms, efforts to

identify and make sense of their underlying causes through trial-and-error experimentation based on efforts to respond to, manage, or resolve these phenomena, and, fourth, possibly, efforts to learn lessons from a disaster or crisis to improve capacities (elsewhere and/or in the future) to prevent, address, manage, or overcome similar events or processes (cf. Ji, 2006; Jessop, 2015). This last aspect is of special interest for the pedagogy of crisis. An important example is the role of commissions or other organized inquiries to draw lessons from recent crises for the future (the basis for societal and organizational learning and the refinement of expertise and resilience) or, alternatively, perhaps, to obfuscate causes, depoliticize crises, and avoid or divert blame (e.g., Boin, 't Hart, Stern and Sundelius, 2005).

5. Regarding the last of these possibilities – but linked to struggles over how to construe symptoms – is the use of past lessons to interpret current crises (as events and/or processes) to guide crisis management. This can be interpreted as the first-order use of the past to remake the present or as the reflexive use of history to make history (or historicity) (cf. Brändström, Bynander and 't Hart, 2004; and Chapter 14 below).

6. Combining these different topics and fields of inquiry invites us to investigate the difference that alternative modes of crisis response make to crisis management for different kinds of crises (see below).

The contributions to this book therefore propose different but complementary ways to analyse crises and, on this basis, indicate ways to develop a new cartography of crisis. They range across different fields in which crises occur, adopt different disciplinary and trans-disciplinary perspectives, and explore different levels of social relations from individual leadership, through organizations and inter-organizational relations and, further, institutions and institutional orders, up to social formations and their crises. Each of these levels is significant because it has distinctive forms of embeddedness and kinds of emergent properties that can serve as the basis for interpreting crisis symptoms based on direct experience or capacities for collective reflection, as the basis for crisis prevention and/or management through access to distinctive and complementary institutional capacities and resources and developing capacities for higher-order metagovernance, and as the basis for learning through and from crisis based on critical self-reflection of different kinds of actor in different settings.[2] Thus, in addition to the problems of interpersonal trust and networking, inter-organizational cooperation depends on finding ways to secure the internal cohesion and adaptability of individual organizations; and in making compatible through inter-organizational negotiation their respective operational unities and independence with their *de facto* material and social interdependence on other organizations and reliance on specific resources that each controls. This can be especially challenging where different organizations are primarily anchored in institutional orders (e.g., economic, juridical, political, scientific, religious) with different organizational logics; this is reinforced when crisis construal, crisis management, or crisis lessons require cooperation among self-organizing systems with their own codes, programmes, institutional logics, and interests in self-reproduction. Here it is important that organizations from different institutional orders or functional systems seek to reduce 'noise' in inter-systemic communication by enhancing mutual sensitivity to the autonomous logics or rationales of complex autonomous systems and thereby promote mutual understanding; and try to engage in negative coordination, i.e., take account of the possible adverse repercussions of their own actions on third parties or other systems and exercise self-restraint as appropriate. This may then provide the basis for specific inter-organizational partnerships oriented to the positive coordination of relevant activities around specific objectives.

These different sites and forms of social relation can be involved in *tangled hierarchies* in so far as lower levels are constrained by higher levels yet simultaneously help to shape the latter. For example, interpersonal trust may ease inter-organizational negotiation and/or help build less personalized, more 'generalized trust' as collective actors are seen to sacrifice short-term interests and reject opportunism (cf. Luhmann, 1979, pp. 20–22). In turn, inter-organizational dialogue eases inter-systemic communication and thereby permits 'systemic trust' (in the integrity of other systems' codes and operations) by promoting mutual understanding and stabilizing expectations as the basis of self-binding actions in the future. These are important mechanisms for reaching shared understandings about the nature of crises, developing agreed responses, and acting on any lessons learnt.

Unsurprisingly, then, a common thread across all the studies is the important mediating role of social organizations and movements as key sites of social construal and crisis response even if organizations are not themselves the specific site at which crisis dynamics operate and crisis eruption. Thus, this introduction takes the opportunity to provide a critical commentary on the organizational literature on crises and organizational learning before other chapters widen the scope of crises analysis and learning by adding further features corresponding to their specific objects of inquiry. Our conclusions will then reconnect these various literatures by showing how the pedagogy of crises necessitates a deeper analytical treatment of symptomatology. Accordingly, the next section delves deeper into the multifaceted mosaic of literature, mostly concerned with organizations that deal with crises, the second section then identifies some of the innovations and contributions of this introduction, while the final section considers how each of the authors contribute to the overall aim of this book.

The mosaic of crisis literature

Crises as events or processes? trends in the literature

The crisis management literature is prone to conceive crises in binary fashion as **events** or as **processes** (Forgues and Roux-Dufort, 1998; Jaques, 2010). The event approach tends to treat crises as "incidents or accidents", i.e., "contingent and/or peculiar events as opposed to routines, regularities and experience" (Forgues and Roux-Dufort, 1998, p. 4). Thus, event-based approaches typically focus on how a given event triggers a distinct crisis that "may be isolated in space and time" and "has often quite distinguishable origins" (ibid., p. 5). Conversely, the process-based approach explores the transformative phenomena that unfold over space-time and, through their interaction, caused the onset of crisis (ibid.). Whether these phenomena are sequential or systemic, they nonetheless combine a "series of different familiar or unfamiliar stakeholders, issues and resources resulting in a destructing effect on the organization and its stakeholders" (ibid.). The same distinction can be usefully applied to crises outside the field of organizational studies.

More generally, Tony Jaques has argued that the event-based approach tends to obscure some of the more enduring trends that provide the background to the triggering of a crisis (2010, p. 470). This argument is also relevant to the distinction that we introduced above between disasters and crises – for, in Jaques' terms, disasters may result from more systemic underlying trends. Therefore, the process-based approach, although less widely used and less developed, has been more successful in focusing attention on the "continuum of activity" that underlies the occurrence of the crisis event (ibid.). The latter approach is illustrated by Denis Smith, who insists the "configuration of individual crisis events can be seen. . .as a function of the interactions between a number of smaller events which conspire to generate the main crisis event" (1990, p. 265).

Much mainstream work relies more on an event over a process-oriented approach, both theoretically and in practice (Roux-Dufort, 2005; Jaques, 2010, p. 470). This is largely rooted in the fact that crises were initially treated as unexpected/accidental phenomena, hence, in our language, more like disasters than crises. As Rosenthal comments, until the mid-1990s, "the crisis agenda was rather thin" and mainstream social science and public administration had "some reason to marginalize crisis research" (2003, p. 131). Generally speaking, the demise of the Soviet Union and economic prosperity in the Western hemisphere "created an optimistic atmosphere" (ibid.). Crises were therefore seen as "incidental disturbances that should not and did not disturb the dominant mood. Whenever a crisis occurred, the watchword was getting 'back to normal'" (ibid.). As a result, mainstream crisis management theory inherently prioritized "quickly containing accidents or unexpected events and in deploying mechanisms to handle the urgency and the destabilization" (Roux-Dufort, 2005, p. 5). However, increasing economic instability, as well as the September 11 attacks, caused a fundamental paradigm shift, forcing scholars to recognize the "inability to anticipate, and the accumulation of weaknesses and ignorance that made these acts possible" (ibid.). This reoriented the mainstream study of crises and crisis management towards a more process-based approach. To understand the evolution of the understanding of crises, the two conceptualizations will be elaborated.

Crises as events

The crisis-as-event literature conceptualizes crises as irregularities or accidents that stand out in relation to the normal state of affairs. Consequently, this type of understanding had come to view crises as "low-probability, high-impact events" (ibid., p. 6, Pearson and Clair, 1998, p. 60). They are also unanticipated and very frequently contain an element of surprise (Forgues and Roux-Dufort, 1998, p. 6). The triggering event could be a "piece of information, a perturbation, a trouble, a tension that disrupts the fragile balance of the organization" and "has often quite distinguishable origins" (Forgues and Roux-Dufort, 1998, pp. 4–5). Thus, defined as irregularities and damaging or harmful disruptions, crises as events necessarily acquired negative connotations, implying a need for rectification and reversion to a prior state of stability (ibid.).

This is why crisis management is frequently confounded with risk management in advance and with disaster management after the event, with risk management employing probabilistic methods to assess risks (ibid.).

Crises as processes

More recently, crises have come to be understood as "the result of a long period of incubation which bluntly occurs through the influence of a triggering event" (Forgues and Roux-Dufort, 1998, p. 6). They are now understood to be manifest in phases. A typical periodization in this kind of "natural history" approach to crises comprises: (1) the pre-crisis or warning phase; (2) the triggering event; and (3) the post-crisis, or amplification and resolution phase (ibid.; Fink, 1986; Smith, 1990; Mitroff and Pearson, 1993; Kovoor-Misra, 1995; Roux-Dufort, 2005). Within the field of crisis management, analysts have therefore reoriented their study of crises to "grasp the full context of the conditions, characteristics, and consequences" that surround them (Quarantelli, 1998; Rosenthal, 2003). This has numerous consequences. As opposed to the event-based interpretations, process-based views do not adopt an inherently negative view of crises. Rather, they view crises as having "revealing properties and uncover[ing] hidden factors that the organization would not have been aware of if the crises had not occurred (Roux-Dufort, 2005, p. 9). In addition, the triggering event is no longer seen as the solitary manifestation of the crisis but, rather, as the factor that "reveals a pre-existing dynamic of crisis" (ibid.). So, crises are "the ultimate moment of a continuous cumulative process of organizational failures" (Bowonder and Linstone, 1987; Forgues and Roux-Dufort, 1998).

Furthermore, crises as processes are believed to be "normal" and to arise as a result of the intrinsic nature of systems that are inherently chaotic and prone to failure (Hearit and Courtright, 2003, p. 83; Roux-Dufort, 2005, p. 11). As we indicated above, this is a productive approach but even more so when combined with the distinction between normal crisis management responses and crises of crisis management. This is because crises are the "result of the interaction of complex systems and faulty decisions by those who manage them" (Hearit and Courtright, 2003, p. 83). Therefore, Hearit and Courtright conclude that crises are not only "inevitable and unavoidable", but also "just as likely to emanate from within the organization as without" (ibid.). So, what conditions underlie the formation of crisis tendencies? The three-phase, sequential model mentioned above (pre-crisis/triggering event/post-crisis) is generally posited in the literature, with some variations:

1. Pre-crisis phase

The pre-crisis phase was initially developed by the early organizational sciences pioneer Barry A. Turner (1976), who proposed the concept of "incubation" defined as "the accumulation of an unnoticed set of events which are at odds with the accepted beliefs about hazards and the norms of their avoidance" (as cited in Jaques, 2010, p. 470). Similarly, Kovoor-Misra understands the pre-crisis phase as the "phase during which signals are emitted" (1995, p. 145). As Jaques points out, over the past three decades, the notion of "failure of foresight through the incubation period has come to be one of the distinguishing features of scholarship on the critical pre-crisis phase" (ibid.).

Roux-Dufort elaborates on this notion by pointing out that "[a]dopting a chaos and a system view of the organization is a first step towards understanding organizations as a generator of imperfections" (2005, p. 11). These types of imperfections, as well as the degree of their severity, are then able to give us a better idea of the "development of the crisis ground" (ibid.). In particular, he hypothesizes four different degrees of imperfections: **anomalies, vulnerabilities, disruptions** and ultimately **crisis** (ibid., p. 12). Anomalies and vulnerabilities form the lowest level of imperfections (ibid., pp. 12–13). While anomalies take the form of "negligence, errors or whatever unexpected events linked to the natural move of organizations" and can effectively "remain invisible", vulnerabilities represent the accumulation of anomalies and are "produced by an accumulation and a combination of unmanaged or mismanaged organizational anomalies" (ibid.). Disruptions, on the other hand, are "the end result of a process of accumulation of vulnerabilities that have developed over time throughout the organization;" they should be regarded as "a crisis catalyst" because they take the form of a "non-return point" (ibid., p. 13). Roux-Dufort emphasizes that a "crisis should not be confused with its triggering event and the scope of a crisis should not be related to the scope of the triggering event" considering that "the ground in which it takes root will determine whether or not a situation will turn into a crisis" (ibid.). Finally, as a result of the disruptions, when crises occur "the internal vulnerabilities are abruptly made visible" (ibid., p. 14).

Smith echoes this idea in the phase that he calls "crisis of management" (1990, p. 271). He argues this phase of the crisis very often passes unnoticed as "[m]any of those working within the organization fail to see the significance of the 'ways in which they do things' in terms of their impact on crisis generation" (2005, p. 312). As a result, Smith defines this phase as that "in which the actions (or inactions) of management can promulgate the development of an organizational climate and culture within which a relatively minor triggering event can rapidly escalate up through the system and result in a catastrophic failure" (1990, p. 271). Moreover, management plays a "major, but often neglected, role" in the production of "those crises that it will subsequently have to manage" (Smith, 2005, p. 312). This can be seen as a precursor to crises of crisis management, as an early warning sign of subsequent problems.

2. Triggering event/full-blown crisis

For Smith, this phase is one where the organization is "in the throes of an *operational crisis situation*" (1990, p. 271). It is inherently chaotic in nature as the organization tries to cope with the initial shock of the crisis event and struggles against time (ibid.). Moreover, because of the threat posed to the organization, "its dominant internal environment becomes one of support, rather than departmental bickering or buck passing" (ibid.). The aim during this phase is therefore basic – to prevent a worsening of the situation (ibid.).

3. Post-crisis phase

The post-crisis phase is understood in different ways. Jaques differentiates the understanding of post-crisis in the literature as either the period focused on "tactical response objectives" or as the "prospective view" where the post-crisis is seen as "the core of the crisis in political or institutional terms" (2009, pp. 6–7). Therefore, the first segment of the literature tackles post-crisis communication as "what to say and do" after a crisis in order to ameliorate the status quo, or understands it as a period of "post-mortem, assessment, learning and constitution of new understandings of risk and risk avoidance" (ibid., p. 37). In contrast, the other segment of the literature refers to what 't Hart and Boin call "the crisis after the crisis", which they assert can often be "every bit as intense, intractable, and potentially debilitating as the 'CNN part,' i.e., the acute stage of the crisis" (2001, p. 28).

However, 't Hart and Boin proceed to argue that the notion that "crises are events clearly marked in time and space" should be abandoned along with the traditional pre-crisis-crisis-post-crisis trichotomy (ibid.) Rather, what is needed is a "differentiated, contingent view of crises" which essentially assumes that "critical moments, turning points, and strategic choices shape the process" such that the aftermath/post-crisis phase "may actually be the core of the crisis in political and institutional terms (ibid.). We now turn to the different ways in which crisis management models are conceptualized.

Models of crisis management

Coombs notes that two of the historically most influential models of crisis management are Fink's (1986) classic four-stage and Mitroff's (1994) five-stage model (2012, p. 7). Fink's model was, according to Coombs, one of the first to treat a crisis as an extended event and postulate that warning signs exist before the trigger event. He identifies four stages in the crisis life cycle: (1) the prodromal phase, (2) crisis breakout or acute phase, (3) the chronic phase and

(4) resolution. The prodromal phase occurs when signs of an impending crisis begin to emerge; this is the stage at which crisis managers must be *proactive* to "know and read the warning signs" (ibid., p. 7). On the other hand, phases (2), (3), and (4) are *reactive* – they entail a triggering event, the "effects of the crisis that linger as efforts to clean up the crisis progress", and a final resolution stage that signals that the crisis is over (ibid., p. 8). In terms of the pedagogy of crisis of interest in the present volume, Fink concludes that "different stages of the life cycle require different actions from the crisis manager" (ibid.).

Using the same "natural history" type of approach, Mitroff's model distinguishes five phases: "(1) signal detection: new crisis warning signs should be identified and acted upon to prevent a crisis, (2) probing and prevention: organization members search known crisis risk factors and work to reduce their potential for harm, (3) damage containment: a crisis hits and organization members try to prevent the damage from spreading into uncontaminated parts of the organization or its environment, (4) recovery: organization members work to return to normal business operations as soon as possible, and (5) learning: organization members review and critique their crisis management efforts, thereby adding to the organization's memory" (ibid., p. 8). As Coombs points out, despite similarities in approach, whereas "Mitroff's model emphasizes how the crisis management team can facilitate the recovery, ... Fink's model simply documents that organizations can recover at varying speeds" (ibid., p. 9). In addition, Fink's model is linear, simply noting that resolution "occurs when a crisis is no longer a concern" (ibid, p. 9) and implies, as Jaques notes, that issues or crises present themselves one at a time and each is resolved before the next emerges or irrupts (Jaques, 2007, p. 148). In contrast, Mitroff's later model is cyclical (Coombs, 2012, p. 9) and, as such, his approach inherently includes the capacity for learning from crises and, hence, for management teams to prepare for the next issue or crisis.

Fink's and Mitroff's models can fit into the standard "common-sense" approach and widely used three-stage conceptualization of crisis management considered in the previous section. The two models already indicate an important distinction in the standard model, namely, between linear and non-linear approaches. Indeed, Jaques notes that this distinction involves two divergent foci in crisis management research (2009, p. 38). For Falkheimer and Heide (2006, p. 182), this distinction traces the divide between studies that are practitioner-oriented and those that adopt a more theoretical perspective. Practitioner-oriented literature tends towards a "sequential, tactical conception of crisis management" (Jaques, 2009, p. 38) and construes crisis management as "the process of business continuity management", emphasizing the study of crisis response teams, drafting strategies and damage control (Smith, 2005, p. 312). Conversely, theoretical approaches are non-linear and highlight the multifaceted nature of the crisis management process (Jaques, 2009, p. 38).

One classic practitioner-oriented model was formulated by Smith (1990). It comprised three phases plus a feedback loop, which indicated that learning had occurred or could occur; but it retained the the assumption that crises followed each other one at a time. This model is paradigmatic in the the more linear, orthodox crisis management literature. The three phases reflect the threefold differentiation among crisis of management, operational crisis and crisis of legitimation. While the first phase focuses on the organisational culture in the "period leading up to the crisis event in which the organization fails to take account of an impending situation", the second concerns institutional support and coping. Finally, phase three involves efforts to win or regain external confidence in the organisation's system via a politics of scapegoating and culpability. Smith notes that this phase is often associated with government intervention (all references from Smith, 1990, p. 271).

According to Smith, much of the previous literature focused on phases two and three, i.e., how an organization managed the crisis and the wider politics of its aftermath. However, to reduce the frequency of crises, more attention should be directed to the first phase. It was essential "to look at the culture of the organization and assess its effect on crisis generation" (ibid, p.274). This is where feedback loops were needed to shift an organization's culture to prevent rather than simply manage crises (ibid.).

Conversely, a more sophisticated practitioner-oriented model was developed by Kovoor-Misra (1995) in that she proposed a non-linear approach to crisis management that explores the interaction among *six* dimensions. Her systemic approach asserts that "the causes, types, and consequences of crises are rooted in the technical, human [and] social, economic, political, legal, and ethical dimensions of organizations" (ibid.). She notes that, while her account is inspired by the models posited by Fink and Mitroff, it "differs from these frameworks in that it focuses on *specific* organizational dimensions and addresses the relationship of crises to these dimensions" (ibid.: p. 144). For crises "emerge from or affect" the different organizational dimensions mentioned above (ibid., p. 148). Thus, while it acknowledges the interactions across the pre-crisis, crisis, and post-crisis stages, it "recommends the use of integrating mechanisms" to ensure that all six dimensions are addressed across the organization as a whole and not compartmentalized in silos (ibid.). She therefore concludes that "to be prepared for crises, technical organizations must address the causes of crises that are rooted in each of their dimensions, the consequences of crises that affect their different dimensions, and the types of crises to which they are susceptible" (ibid.). As noted, this requires an integrated approach.

Another group of scholars proposes a spiral model whereby the process progresses through a loop, starting from the trigger and then passing through a series of phases of observation, choice, interpretation, and dissemination (Hale, Dulek and Hale, 2005, p. 123; Jaques, 2009, p. 38). Hale et al. hypothesize the existence of a "series of sequential communication activities…iteratively throughout the crisis response phase" (2005, p. 122). The number of iterations changes on a case-by-case basis, depending on the complexity of the triggering event and the types of choice articulated (ibid.). Observation is therefore initially concerned with "whether to label an event a crisis", whereas later iterations "involve trying to gain greater understanding regarding the impact of previously enacted responses" (ibid.). Interpretation and choice involve an iterative evaluation of the status quo, as well as the selection of a method of action. Dissemination finally spreads the crisis response to actors and stakeholders in relevant segments and the goal is "to mitigate direct damages and terminate cascading effects" (ibid., p. 123). Hale et al. therefore point out that the emerging model asserts that crisis response is "both cyclical and linear within a single iteration through the cycle" (ibid., p. 130).

Jaques' (2007) reformulation of the linear, three-phase conceptualization echoes John Penrose's (2000) claim: "the past, pre- and post-crisis actions have not been consolidated as one integrated unit... These activities do cluster together and should be considered in aggregate rather than as separate sets of activities" (as cited in Jaques, 2007, p. 150). In other words, Jaques insists that crisis management phases should be understood in a holistic manner.[3] Such an approach posits that:

> crisis prevention and crisis preparedness are just as much parts of the overall process as the tactical steps to take once a crisis strikes. Furthermore, that the post-crisis cluster of activities has a critical function looping back to preparing for and managing future crises.
>
> (2007, p. 150)

An important aspect of this model is that it combines the typical tactical concern of crisis-management literature with the more strategic approach to issue-management, i.e., how to anticipate and identify issues that are ripe for resolution (Jaques, 2007). He therefore proposes to develop a "relational model of crisis management" that "emphasizes that the elements should be seen as 'clusters' of related and integrated disciplines, not as 'steps' to be undertaken in a [linear] sequential fashion" (ibid.). While the pre-crisis and crisis management *phases* must be kept analytically distinct, individual elements may either overlap or even occur simultaneously. For instance, crisis prevention and crisis preparedness most often do happen simultaneously. Therefore, he claims, the relational model successfully incorporates the non-linear and temporal elements of crisis management, while also addressing "both trigger events and underlying causes" (ibid., p. 151). It can also illustrate the "interdependence between issue management, crisis management and the related activities", thereby addressing some of the weaknesses of previous frameworks (ibid.).

Denis Smith (2005) drew upon his earlier model to propose a framework that assumes that the various stages of crisis management are "not strictly linear and often become complicated and more ill-defined over time" (p. 312). He suggests that crisis management should be understood as a "spiral that is stretched over a timeline;" and within this spiral, organizations move quickly through some phases and linger in others such that in some cases "the process can take place over many years and will span different periods of leadership" (ibid.). It is here that managers play an important role – crises are difficult to manage unless they are constantly addressed (ibid.). Indeed, in revising his own basic model (p. 312), he explicitly introduces the scope for organizational learning and also identifies important barriers to learning. Thus, in Smith's revised model, crisis management should attempt "both to prevent damaging incidents from taking place and also to mitigate the impacts of such events when prevention fails" (ibid.). This shows how both theorists as well as practitioners (here managers) can learn from systematic observation of crises as events and, especially, processes that evolve unevenly in time and space.

Organizational learning

As indicated in Denis Smith's changing models, the process of organizational learning has become an integral part of the crisis management model. In Pearson and Clair's (1998) account, an analysis of the outcomes of the crisis is said to form part of the crisis management process. Namely, Pearson and Clair propose that "any crisis process results in relative degrees of success *and* failure" (1998, p. 67). The understanding of success/failure is situated on a continuum such that, while in one aspect the organization might have failed, in others it might have proved successful (ibid.). On the other hand, some lessons are not learned at all, leading organizations to repeat the same mistakes over and over again (Crandall, Parnell and Spillan, 2014, pp. 13–14). This success/failure understanding of crises has contributed to the expansion of the field of study related to organizational learning, which has sought to conceptualize the methods learning can employ to stave off/prevent crises. Organizational learning has come to be understood as the process whereby "experience systematically alters behavior or knowledge" (Schwab, 2006, p. 233). We turn next to the understanding of *what* is learned, *when* learning occurs, as well as what *types* of learning exist within the scope of the organizational learning literature.

What is learned?

The most influential categorization of organizational learning is Argyris and Schön's (1978, 1996) distinction between "single- and double-loop learning" (Deverell, 2009, p. 181). Namely, single-loop learning is said to occur when organizational members alter divergences and flaws without "inquiring into basic organizational premises and norms" (ibid.). This tends to occur most frequently when the external environment does not exert pressure on the organization, or when the organizational premises are not in immediate conflict (ibid.). Double-loop learning, on the other hand, occurs at a deeper level and entails more fundamental structural changes whereby "organizational norms, strategies and assumptions associated with those norms" are challenged (ibid.). This means that "old understandings are discarded as new ones are added" (ibid.). Later accounts have come to theorize triple-loop learning as well; this type of learning has sought to account for a wider shift encompassing more general cultural adjustments (Veil, 2011, p. 133). Bartunek and Moch (1987) for instance claim that triple-loop learning occurs when the members of the organization themselves become their "own diagnostician, decision maker, and expert", thereby enacting internally-driven change. Third-order change is therefore the most difficult because, before organizations try new ideas, "they must unlearn old ones by discovering their inadequacies and then discarding them" (Nystrom and Starbuck, 1984; as cited in Veil, 2011, p. 133).

When does learning occur?

As to *when* learning occurs, Veil notes that "where included, learning is the last step in the crisis model and not an ongoing aspect of the crisis management process" (2011, p. 118). Namely, within the literature, learning is most frequently incorporated into models as a "process of improving the crisis response after the crisis has occurred" (ibid., p. 119). This is seen as a rigid understanding of learning, relying on an inherently linear and sequential model. Moreover, placing learning at the end of the crisis management process also sometimes causes the problem of 'hindsight bias' whereby "the use of knowledge about outcomes to edit reconstructions of the antecedents of those outcomes, should lead people to learn the wrong things" (Weick and Ashford, 2001, p. 726, as cited in Veil, 2011, p. 119). In addition, most models fail to provide an explanation for why warning signals are sometimes overlooked (ibid.). Boin et al. suggest that crisis recognition depends on "both the capacity of individuals operating (parts of) these systems" and "the organizational 'designs' for early crisis detection" (2005, p. 19). Thus, even though occasional 'check-ups' may help to spot "emerging vulnerabilities", they argue that it is "virtually impossible to predict with any sort of precision when and where a crisis will strike" (ibid.).

In order to conceptualize how organizations are inhibited from recognizing warning signals and the potential for crisis throughout the learning model, (Veil 2011) contrasts two models of learning. The first is the Learning Barrier Model, which highlights cognitive barriers to noticing warning signals that are rooted "in our rhetorical understanding of the world": She identifies that rhetorical barriers of "*classification with experience, reliance on success,* and *trained mindlessness* provide paths that lead to failure or crisis before providing an opportunity to learn" (ibid., p. 121). While *classification with experience* denotes "the inability to see past our own experiences to recognize crisis warning signals" (ibid, p.124), *reliance on success* notes how "success can hinder future success by blinding the organization to potential failure" (ibid, p. 125). *Trained mindlessness* on the other hand refers to the insensitivity which occurs when individuals follow the same routine (ibid, p. 125). Thus, the failure to anticipate crises means learning only occurs, if at all, in the face of the recalcitrance of a crisis (ibid., p. 122).

The second model is the Mindful Learning Model. This highlights the contribution of "a mindful culture that recognizes warning signals and learns from them to prevent failure and crisis" (Veil, 2011, p. 135). This culture focuses on a contextual understanding of crises rather than working with a "preconceived notion of what the outcome should be" (ibid., p. 134). In other words, by "taking into account the contexts, environment, and perspectives surrounding a situation and welcoming new information, mindfulness allows us to reframe the situation" (ibid., p. 135). This reframing and "attentiveness to signals that something does not look or feel right" suggests that there exists a continual cycle of recognizing warning signs and learning from them to adapt to the routine process (ibid., p. 136). Making a transition from the Learning Barrier Model to the Mindful Learning Model is said to constitute a third-degree change (or full cultural readjustment) as it requires "more than simple adjustments to processes and policies" (ibid., p. 137). In the terms introduced above, then, it is a form of double loop learning, concerned with learning how to learn – in a mindful way.

What types of learning exist?

Bennett and Howlett note that writers on this topic conceive organizational learning in diverse ways with the result that "many of the fundamental elements of such learning remain conceptually unclear" (1992, p. 276). Consequently, the entire phenomenon of experience-induced policy change "remains difficult to operationalize" (ibid.). Thus, the literature has seen an increasing drive to make a distinctive typology of learning processes. Notably, Claudio Radaelli builds upon existing efforts (e.g., Heclo, 1974; Etheredge, 1981; Bennett and Howlett, 1992; Sanderson, 2002) and distinguishes *instrumental learning, cross-national emulation*, and *political learning* (Radaelli, 2009, p. 1149). Instrumental learning operates by updating existing beliefs "on the basis of evidence about policy"; and is based upon rational policy-making and triggered by analyses of changing information sets on "what seems to work" (Radaelli, 2009, pp. 1149, 1148). In turn, cross-national emulation works via networks and multi-level fora, such as the EU, as well as through bilateral exchange and/or informal networking mechanisms. It is based upon shifting ideas on "what seems to provide legitimacy" (Radaelli, 2009, p. 1149). Finally, political learning involves "evidence and conjectures pursued about the strategies pursued by other actors" (ibid.). However, in his own case study of regulatory policy learning, Radaelli concedes there is evidence of political learning only in the Netherlands and the UK (ibid., p. 1157).

Plan of the book

In addition to this introduction, Part One includes chapters by the editors that propose novel theoretical perspectives on crisis, crisis construals, and crisis lessons. Knio builds on the arguments in the introduction, developing the distinction between crises as events and processes and summarizing some recent institutional accounts of crisis and recent literature on organizational learning, especially in the policy field. He shows how the parallel development of these two disparate literatures – institutional and organizational respectively – can be exploited fruitfully to distinguish two contrasting types of lesson about crises, crisis construals, and crisis lessons. The first reads crises as trigger events that are construed by policy makers as stimuli to remedial action; the second regards crises as nodal points that can indicate the possibility of more or less radical transformation depending on how they come to be construed through a contested politics of framing and on the prevailing balance of forces. While these two approaches provide interesting accounts of key themes of this book, Knio also employs critical realism to show how they can be related in an analysis of the crisis-learning nexus.

Jessop develops his earlier arguments, inspired by critical realism and also building on Régis Debray's analysis of the politics of time in normal and crisis conjunctures, about the objective overdetermination and subjective indeterminacy of crises and explores this further through the concept of symptomatology. The challenge of deciphering the significance of apparent crisis symptoms (in the double sense of potential symptoms of a crisis and symptoms of one or another kind of crisis) corresponds well to the etymology and diverse fields of application of the concept of crisis, with its connotations of judgement, decision, and critique. After elaborating this metaphor and its relevance to the challenges of symptomatology, Jessop then advances two further important arguments. The first is that there is a radical ontological and epistemological difference between the practices involved in explaining the objective over-determination of crises (if such, indeed, they be) and deciding (*krinein*) on the appropriate course of action, in the form of a speculative bet on the future and how it might be shaped in more or less complex conjunctures in which diverse other social agents and forces are also seeking to shape the future. The second is that part of the overall process of symptomatology involves the pedagogy of crisis, with different kinds of learning processes and different lessons being feasible at different (analytically) distinct stages of crisis from initial eruption through to, perhaps, an eventual resolution. The examples are drawn from macro-economic and political crises in advanced capitalism, but the arguments transcend this particular context.

Part Two explores the distinction between "crises in/crises of" relative to contemporary capitalist social formations and also makes important contributions to *Zeitdiagnostik* (here, analysis of the changing nature of modernity). Specifically, whereas Andrew Gamble focuses on continuities in the dynamic of capitalism over 350 years, whilst recognising discontinuities in different periods, David Chandler suggests that, rather than crisis being seen as evidence of pathologies, as it was during modernity, it is now being used as a means of governance in the guise of discourses and practices of resilience. Thus, in Chapter 4, Andrew Gamble describes how the 2008 crisis relates to capitalist crises of the past as well as how the neoliberal order has been exceptional in relation to prior capitalist periods. He notes how the North Atlantic financial crisis led to crisis responses that ran counter to neo-liberal principles and aimed to rescue "too-big-to-fail" banks. This was based in part on lessons drawn from the experience of the Great Depression. Gamble also offers a periodization of the crisis. The fact that the economic and financial crisis was not accompanied by a political or ideological crisis was crucial for economic and political elites to be able to rescue financial interests – albeit without the financial rescue attempt did not work as the authorities expected and created the conditions for right-wing populist backlashes and, in the UK context, the referendum vote for Brexit. He also assesses the heuristic value of the distinction between "crises in" and "crises of" a system regarding how neoliberalism and its crises have unfolded in the US and the UK over the past decade.

In Chapter 5, David Chandler suggests that, in the discourses of modernity, crises were regarded normatively as threats and temporally as one-off events. Yet they have now become central to governing rather than an exception to it, thereby leading to the normalizing of crisis discourse in governance. Prominent among modes of governance that seek to include (and govern through) crises is the resilience approach. Chandler's chapter reflects on how the understanding of crisis has become transformed in this process, particularly linking this transformation to the radical appreciation of contingency and of the limits to instrumental cause-and-effect approaches to rule. Focusing on the work of Ulrich Beck and Bruno Latour, this chapter engages with the 'ontological turn' in crisis theorising. This shift is also seen in new approaches to risks, especially anthropogenic understandings of environmental threats, which were once seen as 'natural. Chandler thereby echoes Gamble's concern with the distinction between 'crises in/of' and reinforces this by identifying the specificities of the status quo in perpetuating and normalizing a sense of crisis.

The next section explores forms of learning and non-learning in neo-classical economics, economic and juridico-political policy prescriptions, and heterodox economics.

Specifically, in chapter six, Matthew Watson explores non-learning in asking why the 2008 financial crisis has not translated into a crisis of mainstream economics, which has retained its enduring focus on General Equilibrium theory, Dynamic Stochastic General Equilibrium models, and rational expectations assumptions not only to analyse the (capitalist) market economy in the abstract but also to make policy recommendations, either explicitly or by implication. He draws on Schumpeter's reflections on the ideological bias of economists resulting from their 'preanalytic visions' and investigates mainstream economists' inability to learn from the 2008 financial crisis. His analysis illustrates, for the mainstream economics profession, Karl Deutsch's aphorism that power conveys the ability not to have to learn from one's mistakes (1963, p. 111). In this case, this can be related to the claim that it is not economists' task to make predictions and, even if it were, the financial crisis was a singular event from which no lessons can be drawn about economic theory or economic policy.

In the next chapter, Magnus Ryner applies critical political economy to the economic crisis in the Eurozone and how this relates to the functioning of democracy in the European Union. He assesses the scope for a democratic solution to the triple European crises of financialization, neoliberal austerity, and the democratic deficit. He investigates the crisis construals proposed by left federalists and left intergovernmentalists and their transformative potential in the face of the growing trend towards an authoritarian neoliberal state. For different reasons, he finds both approaches phantasmagoric as well as phantastic. He emphasizes the need to be able to diagnose long-term crisis tendencies and their manifestation in the current conjuncture, to propose organic solutions based on a realistic analysis of the past and present – which requires the identification of causes, the formulation of feasible reforms, a serious analysis of the agents or agencies that might deliver these reforms and, crucially, recommendations on how the balance of forces could be reorganized at different sites and scales to deliver these reforms. In short, economic analysis must be combined with political analysis because economic reforms occur within specific political forms and are pursued by specific political agencies. This is where the two left currents that he considers are deficient. For the analysis of the objective overdetermination of crises should be combined with phantastic but rigorous analysis of what exists *in potentia* in a crisis conjuncture and how this could be achieved.

In the final chapter in Part III, Robert Boyer provides a magisterial regulationist perspective on economic crises. He provides a taxonomy of economic crises and notes the difficulties of drawing lessons from crisis, especially when elites resort to different kinds of magical thinking that lead them to believe or assert that "this time is different. Drawing on regulation theory, he explains how different forms of Fordist economic model in post-war Europe and the United States experienced different forms of crisis that converged in legitimising a return to the liberal theory of efficient, self-regulating markets. Yet neo-liberalism eventually met a similar fate in a crisis of finance-led growth regimes, prompting several lessons about these regimes and proposals to reinvigorate a pragmatic approach to state intervention for the purposes of crisis management and economic policy that heeds some of the lessons from the history of past crises so the next one can be anticipated and, if it cannot be prevented, crisis management can be based on lessons about what measures work. On this basis, he identifies important lessons from the financial crisis and seeks to revive and adapt lessons from the Fordist-Keynesian period and deliver social justice and reduce environmental damage. These lessons recognize the unprecedented extent of world market integration and the new threats to ecological, economic, political, and social order and their implications for the interdependence of policy regimes.

The two chapters in Part Four provide contrasting examples of fetishistic and reflexive learning in two contrasting substantive fields. First, Angela Wigger explores the EU's approach to crisis management post-2008, focusing on the EU's industrial policy scheme introduced in 2014. Rather than transcending the neoliberal tenets on which the EU is resting, Wigger argues that the new common industrial policy with its package of crisis-management solutions actually deepens these tenets. The discourses and policies for industrial policy revive previous policies and claim to have learnt from previous experiments in promoting competitiveness and to have adapted them to the current economic conjuncture in the European Union. However, this is fantasy learning in the sense that the lessons involve magical thinking and will fail in ways similar to earlier attempts to promote competitiveness.

Next, Jeff Handmaker examines the institutions of international criminal litigation, especially the institutions created to enforce international criminal justice: national courts and their principal jurisdictional complements; the International Criminal Court (ICC) and ad hoc tribunals. These have all recently experienced a major legitimacy crisis that challenges their liberal underpinnings. Drawing on Jessop's analysis of crisis construals and crisis management, Handmaker comments on how lawyers can engage in reflexive learning to address this legitimacy crisis. More specifically, drawing on the rule of law, Mutua's critical characterization of the "human rights corpus" and a reflexive learning approach, it analyses different proposals to address this crisis by ending impunity through cases before the ICC and other institutions involved in prosecuting international crimes. Handmaker concludes with reflections on the potential for legal learning as well as on potential future directions for international criminal litigation.

The contributions in Part Five explore the limits to learning and the scope for overcoming these limits in the field of development studies. In Chapter 11, Des Gasper emphasizes the multi-dimensional nature of the multiple crises that now threaten humankind and planet earth. This complexity places severe cognitive limits on crisis construal because the processes that generate these crises are veiled and contestable. But he also notes that "the growth imperatives of capitalism, techno-optimism and market theology, plus nationalist loyalties, ambitions and rivalries mean that denial, inattention and non-preparation prevail" (p. 00). He illustrates these general propositions from crisis anticipation, preparation, and responses regarding the Rio+20 process, the 2012 global summit on sustainable development, and the 2015 Agenda for Sustainable Development. He argues that these institutional frameworks give us both hope and anxiety about tackling crisis tendencies in the future. The optimism is grounded in the scientific consensus on the challenges of climate change; the pessimism is grounded in the asymmetric distribution of risks and eventual harms – disproportionately affecting the poor and marginal, both inter- and intra-nationally, with the result that, in the short-term at least, ruling elites typically largely carry on regardless, not learning from accumulating disasters and crises.

In the following chapter, Wil Hout investigates the paradox that the perceived crisis in development that has prompted development assistance, most recently in the form of the millennium development goals (MDGs) and sustainable development goals (SDGs), has itself shown signs of crisis during most of its existence. In this regard, crisis does not so much designate a turning point, a critical moment for decisive intervention, as an enduring catastrophe or impasse. Accordingly, Hout explores the *permanent crisis of development aid* and the failure of its promoters and practitioners to learn from this crisis. Rather than tackling the legitimacy of aid in a reflexive way, the aid industry limits its understanding of the crisis by focusing on actual symptoms (and corresponding empirical indicators) rather than digging beneath symptoms to underlying real causes – and then formulates its responses on the basis of its changing construal of the symptoms. This explains why, despite spending several trillions of USD in aid, poverty has risen globally, millennium goals are still far from being achieved, and sustainable development remains a pipe dream.

In the final chapter in Part Five, Zuzana Novakova examines the pedagogy of crisis in relation to the EU's response to the governance and security crisis in Ukraine. She takes this as an example of problems in the European Neighbourhood Policy, which is the most ambitious EU external governance project and has, indeed, already been reviewed four times in response to these problems. In other words, this is a good example of a recurrent crisis of crisis management. Novakova then explores the underlying causes that prevent lesson drawing and the challenging of the common sense that is at the heart of the prevailing policy paradigm. She illustrates this through a critical analysis of the discourses on EU policies as different social forces attempt to reinforce or reassess the currently hegemonic foreign policy wisdom (and its legitimating public philosophy), the prevailing policy paradigm, and particular policies. This contestation is an inherently political process but, as this case study shows, it is harder to challenge high level common sense than specific policies. This sets limits to the scope for lesson drawing from crises and policy failures and, hence, the extent of policy change. Based on this case, the chapter ends with some general observations on the pedagogy of crisis.

Part Six comprises the concluding chapter by the editors. It returns to some of the distinctions introduced in their previous joint or individual chapters and relates them to the lessons on crisis theories, specific crises, crisis construals, and crisis lesson-drawing elaborated in other contributions. After a summary of the main points made in Part One, the editors offer three sets of comments based on the contributions in the individual contributions. These comments concern: (1) the nature of crises, (2) the challenge of symptomatology, and (3) the pedagogy of crisis. The chapter concludes by highlighting and reaffirming the distinctive features of the approach to crisis, crisis construals, and crisis lessons that have informed the analyses in this volume and can be further developed on the basis of the contributions presented below.

Notes

1 The non-alphabetic listing of authors reflects the fact that the bulk of this chapter, namely, the analysis of the mosaic of crisis literatures, derives from Karim Knio's investigations, which are further elaborated in Chapter 2.

2 The arguments in this paragraph and the next paragraph draw heavily on Jessop (1997, 2011). Note that they presuppose a collective effort to resolve and learn from crises. In later chapters, this presupposition is qualified as different contributors identify sites of conflict, rivalry, and contradiction as social forces with rival or antagonistic interests seek to define, manage, or resolve crises and draw lessons from them that serve their particular interests. The range of approaches is indicated in our later summaries of individual chapters.

3 Jaques' relational model (Jaques, 2007) distinguishes between pre-crisis management and crisis management. The former phase consists of two sub-phases: Crisis Preparedness (planning processes, system manuals and training simulations) and Crisis Prevention (early warning scanning, issue and risk management and emergency response). The latter phase (Crisis Management) also has two sub-phases: Post-Crisis Management (evaluation modification, post-crisis issue impacts and recovery, business resumption) and Crisis Incident Management (crisis management, system activation/response and crisis recognition). All (sub-) phases are dynamically interrelated. (Jaques, 2007, p. 152).

References

Argyris, C. and Schön, D.A. (1978) *Organizational Learning: A Theory of Action Perspective.* Reading, MA: Addison-Wesley.

Argyris, C. and Schön, D.A. (1996) Organizational Learning II: Theory, Method, and Practice, Volume 2. Reading, MA: Addison-Wesley.

Bartunek, J.M. and Moch, M.K. (1987) 'First-order, second-order, and third-order change and organization development interventions: A cognitive approach'. *The Journal of Applied Behavioral Science* 23(4), pp. 483–500.

Bennett, C.J. and Howlett, M. (1992) 'The lessons of learning: Reconciling theories of policy learning and policy change'. *Policy Sciences* 25(3), pp. 275–294.

Boin, A., 't Hart, P., Stern, E. and Sundelius, B. (2005) *The Politics of Crisis Management: Public Leadership Under Pressure.* Cambridge: Cambridge University Press.

Boin, A., McConnell, A. and 't Hart, P. (2008) 'Governing after crisis', in A. Boin, A. McConnell, and P. 't Hart (eds.), *Governing After Crisis: The Politics of Investigation, Accountability and Learning.* Cambridge: Cambridge University Press, pp. 3–30.

Bowonder, B. and Linstone, H. (1987) 'Notes on the Bhopal accident: Risk analysis and multiple perspectives'. *Technological Forecasting and Social Change* 32, pp. 183–202.

Brändström, A., Bynander, F. and 't Hart, P. (2004) 'Governing by looking back: Historical analogies and crisis management'. *Public Administration* 82(1), pp. 191–210.

Coombs, W.T. (2012) *Ongoing Crisis Communication: Planning, Managing, and Responding.* London: SAGE.

Crandall, W.R., Parnell, J.A. and Spillan, J.E. (2014) *Crisis Management: Leading in the New Strategy Landscape.* London: SAGE.

Deutsch, K.W. (1963) *The Nerves of Government. Models of Political Communication and Control.* New York: Free Press.

Deverell, E. (2009) 'Crises as learning triggers: Exploring a conceptual framework of crisis-induced learning'. *Journal of Contingencies and Crisis Management* 17(3), pp. 179–188.

Etheredge, L.S. (1981) 'Government learning: An overview', in S.L. Long (ed.), *The Handbook of Political Behavior,* Vol. 2. Oxford: Pergamon.

Falkheimer, J. and Heide, M. (2006) 'Multicultural crisis communication: Towards a social constructionist perspective'. *Journal of Contingencies and Crisis Management* 14(4), pp. 180–189.

Fink, S. L. (1986) *Crisis Management: Planning for the Inevitable*. New York: Amacom.

Forgues, B. and Roux-Dufort, C. (1998) Crises: Events or processes? Paper presented at the Hazards and Sustainability Conference, Durham, May, pp. 26–27.

Hale, J.E., Dulek, R.E. and Hale, D.P. (2005) 'Crisis response communication challenges: Building theory from qualitative data'. *Journal of Business Communication* 42(2), pp. 112–134.

't Hart, P. and Boin, R.A. (2001) 'Between crisis and normalcy: The long shadow of post-crisis politics', in U. Rosenthal, R.A. Boin, and L.K. Comfort (eds.), *Managing Crises: Threats, Dilemmas and Opportunities*. Springfield, IL: Charles C. Thomas, pp. 28–46.

Hearit, K.M. and Courtright, J.L. (2003) 'A social constructionist approach to crisis management: Allegations of sudden acceleration in the Audi 5000'. *Communication Studies* 54(1), pp. 79–95.

Heclo, H. (1974) *Modern Social Politics in Britain and Sweden: From Relief to Income Maintenance*. New Haven, CT: Yale University Press.

Jaques, T. (2007) 'Issue management and crisis management: An integrated, non-linear, relational construct'. *Public Relations Review* 33, pp. 147–157.

Jaques, T. (2009) 'Issue management as a post-crisis discipline: Identifying and responding to issue impacts beyond the crisis'. *Journal of Public Affairs* 9, pp. 35–44.

Jaques, T. (2010) 'Embedding issue management as a strategic element of crisis prevention'. *Disaster and Prevention Management* 19(4), pp. 469–482.

Jessop, B. (1997) 'The governance of complexity and the complexity of governance: Preliminary remarks on some problems and limits of economic guidance', in A. Amin and J. Hausner (eds.), *Beyond Markets and Hierarchy: Interactive Governance and Social Complexity*. Cheltenham: Edward Elgar, pp. 111–147.

Jessop, B. (2011) 'Metagovernance', in M. Bevir (ed.), *Handbook of Governance*. London: SAGE, pp. 106–123.

Jessop, B. (2015) 'The symptomatology of crises, reading crises and learning from them: Some critical realist reflections'. *Journal of Critical Realism* 14(3), pp. 238–271.

Ji, J. H. (2005) *Learning from Crisis: Political Economy, Spatio-Temporality, and Crisis Management in South Korea, 1961–2002*. PhD thesis. Lancaster University.

Koselleck, R. (1988) *Critique and Crisis: Enlightenment and the Pathogenesis of Modern Society*. Oxford: Berg <1959>.

Kovoor-Misra, S. (1995) 'A multidimensional approach to crisis preparation for technical organizations: Some critical factors'. *Technological Forecasting and Social Change* 48, pp. 143–160.

Luhmann, N. (1979) *Trust and Power: Two Essays*. Chichester: John Wiley & Sons.

Mitroff, I.I. and Pearson, C.M (1993) *Crisis Management*. San Francisco: Jossey-Bass.

Mitroff, I.I. (1994) 'Crisis management and environmentalism: A natural fit. *California'. Management Review* 36(2), pp. 101–113.

Nystrom, P.C. and Starbuck, W.H. (1984) 'To avoid organizational crises, unlearn'. *Organizational Dynamics* 12, pp. 53–65.

Offe, C. (1976) 'Crisis of crisis management'. *International Journal of Politics* 6(3), pp. 29–67.

Pearson, C.M. and Clair, J.A. (1998) 'Reframing crisis management'. *Academy of Management Review* 23(1), pp. 59–76.

Penrose, J. (2000) 'The role of perception in crisis planning'. *Public Relations Review* 26 (2), pp. 155–171.

Quarantelli, E.L. (1998) *What Is a Disaster? Perspectives on the Question*. London: Routledge.

Radaelli, C.M. (2009) 'Measuring policy learning: Regulatory impact assessment in Europe'. *Journal of European Public Policy* 16(8), pp. 1145–1164.

Roitman, J. (2015) *Anti-Crisis*. Durham, NC: Duke University Press.

Rosenthal, U. (2003) 'September 11: Public administration and the study of crises and crisis management'. *Administration & Society* 35(2), pp. 129–143.

Roux-Dufort, C. (2005) 'A passion for imperfections: Revisiting crisis management', in C.M. Pearson, C. Roux-Dufort, and J.A. Clair (eds.), *International Handbook of Organizational Crisis Management*. Thousand Oaks, CA: SAGE, pp. 221–252.

Sanderson, I. (2002) 'Evaluation, policy learning and evidence-based policy making'. *Public Administration* 80(1), pp. 1–22.

Schwab, A. (2006) 'Incremental organizational learning from multilevel information sources: Evidence for cross-level interactions'. *Organization Science* 18(2), pp. 233–251.

Shrivastava, P. (1993) 'Crisis theory/practice: Toward a sustainable future'. *Industrial & Environmental Crisis Quarterly* 7(1), pp. 23–42.

Smith, D. (1990) 'Beyond contingency planning: Towards a model of crisis management'. *Industrial Crisis Quarterly* 4, pp. 263–275.

Smith, D. (2005) 'Business (not) as usual: Crisis management, service recovery and the vulnerability of organizations'. *Journal of Services Marketing* 19(5), pp. 309–320.

Turner, B.A. (1976) 'The organizational and interorganizational development of disasters'. *Administrative Science Quarterly* 21(3), pp. 378–397.

Veil, S.R. (2011) 'Mindful learning in crisis management'. *Journal of Business Communication* 48(2), pp. 116–147.

Weick, K.E., and Ashford, S.J. (2001) 'Learning in organizations', in F.M. Jablin and L.L. Putnam (eds.), *The new handbook of organizational communication: Advances in theory, research, and methods*. Thousand Oaks, CA: Sage, pp. 704–731.

2 The diversity of crisis literatures and learning processes

Karim Knio

Like many phenomena explored in the social sciences, crises have multiple dimensions and can be defined in various ways. As Colin Hay has aptly maintained, "crises may be singular, exceptional, recurrent or periodic; momentary, ephemeral, enduring or eternal; linear or cyclical; destructive or creative; underdetermined or overdetermined; inevitable or contingent; pathological or regenerative; organic or inorganic; paralyzing or liberating; immanent, latent or manifest" (Hay, 1999, p. 318). To this empirical complexity and heterogeneity, we can add the variability that different approaches to theorizing about crises can generate. How one chooses to characterize and represent crises is clearly connected to the observer's ontological and epistemological tenets. Indeed, as Janet Roitman (2014) notes, even to treat a given event or process as a crisis as opposed to some other kind of phenomenon involves specific theoretical and normative judgments. Likewise, Rahm Emanuel's proposition that "you never want to let a serious crisis go to waste" (2008)[1] suggests that crises have *at least* a dual significance. Besides signalling a more or less significant rupture in established systemic, institutional, organizational, or behavioural routines, crises also provide opportunities for change and, perhaps, improvement. This indicates the importance of considering the subjective as well as objective features of crisis and, in particular, the importance of whether and, if so, how different kinds of social agent interpret, respond to, and learn about natural and social phenomena that come to be characterized as crises.

Theoretical contributions to the study of crises within political economy and mainstream economics are remarkably diverse. Among the usual theoretical suspects here are (Neo-)Marxist, (Post-)Keynesian, Neo-Gramscian, Neo-Institutional/Evolutionary, Real Business Cycle and Efficient Market Hypothesis approaches.[2] These have contributed in diverse ways to the study of the nature and significance of economic, political, and socio-cultural crises. A parallel body of work, mostly in organization studies, communication studies, policy analysis, public administration, conflict management, and cognate fields is more concerned with crisis management and policy learning. Unsurprisingly, given the breadth of these topics and/or disciplines, the scope of this literature extends far beyond crises in the political economic field. This chapter will focus on organizational and cognate disciplinary analyses that bear directly on the kind of crises discussed in this collection and, in this context, on contributions that address the extent, scope and conditions of learning in, about, and from crises. In the light of Pearson and Clair's observation that "any crisis process results in relative degrees of success *and* failure" (1998, p. 67), a key issue in this regard concerns the factors that shape the understanding of crises and abilities to anticipate, prevent, or, at least, manage them successfully. This is where the literature on organizational learning can contribute much, directly and by extension, to work on the pedagogy of crisis.

The aim of this chapter is to study the intersection between the literatures on the nature/meaning of different types of crises and on organizational and policy learning around crisis management. These two disparate literatures have developed in parallel and explicit theoretical links between them in the main-stream literature are relatively rare and weak. For example, the literature on the nature/meaning of crises tends to be more abstract and largely reflects a thematic organization of the topic (Castree, 2010 illustrates this) and/or a given author's preferred theoretical perspective. Conversely, the literature on policy/organizational learning in crisis management is more concrete – reflect-ing the concerns of specific sets of actors – and is oriented to practical lessons. Here one can distinguish managerial and organizational concerns with coping with crisis (functional challenges such as prevention, preparedness, decision making, coordination and communication responses) and the more political and strategic dimension of crisis management (impact of crisis on political elites and institutions and general problems of leadership)[3] (Brand, 2013; t' Hart and Sundelius, 2013).

To explore potential links between these two relatively distinct fields of investigation, I suggest two ways in which crisis and learning may be linked, depending on whether the crisis literature deepens the analysis of learning, or vice versa. In the first approach, the learning literature adds much to these analyses of crisis. It treats *crises as triggering events* pertaining to moments of temporal or intertemporal uncertainty and fluidity (such as critical junctures or paradigm shifts) and, based on this definition, highlights how policy-makers construe these events and moments as a guide to action (Weick, Sutcliffe, and Obstfeld, 2005). At its best, this approach incorporates insightful agency-based explanations oriented to different spatial and temporal horizons into historical and conjunctural analyses of crisis dynamics. The second approach complements the first because a nuanced crisis literature deepens the understanding of learning. This way of linking the two literatures treats crises as nodes of potential transformation where outcomes are influenced by the politics of framing (Boin, t' Hart, and McConnell, 2009; cf. Stone, 2001). It thereby teases out the relation between chronocentrism (hereafter also presentism) – i.e. the "tendency to concentrate upon the present moment and, in so doing, to remove that moment from its historical context" (Hay, 2002, p. 112) – and the historically specific. This approach is illustrated by different kinds of thick and thin constructivism and cognate currents in historical materialism.

After presenting these two types of linking crisis and learning literatures, this chapter seeks to transcend their respective emphases by developing an integrated account of crises as processes that unfold through rival attempts to manage them. Following Régis Debray, I define crises as "objectively over-determined moments of subjective indeterminacy" (Debray, 1973, p. 113). Thus, regarding their objective over-determination, I draw on critical realism (hereafter CR), which sees crises as processes characterized by ontological depth and emergent properties. Here, this involves treating crises as emergent results of the interaction among the necessary and the contingent; the historical and chronocentric; and the contextual with the historically cumulative. Regarding their subjective indeterminacy, I relate this to the challenge of the "symptomatology" of crises and learning – which implies that actors must look beyond symptoms to underlying causes and decide on courses of action in their light. This approach avoids the analytical elision between causality and symptoms of crises evident in contemporary academic and policy making debates (see further, Jessop, 2015; and this chapter).

Two possible ways of dealing with the crisis-learning nexus

Category 1: crises as trigger events or moments of time uncertainty

This category represents crises as **trigger** events or moments that threaten the stability of previously organized contexts and conducts. As such, they oblige actors to attribute sense and meaning to the observed disruption of old routines. However, crises as trigger events need not open pathways towards social change. Two alternatives to the dominant approach within the broad paradigm known as Historical Institutionalism (HI) illustrate this category. The dominant approach tends to treat historical development in terms of "punctuated equilibria" and to see crises as exogenous shocks that trigger the disruption of self-reinforcing, self-equilibrating "natural" state of a system and create space for radical change (Krasner, 1984). The two variants considered here reject this account of crisis. After describing how each one departs from the dominant HI paradigm, I show how different aspects of the learning literature complement their respective analyses.

Variant I: crises and critical junctures

Critical Juncture (CJ) literature focuses on the (re)production of legacies. Crises, or cleavages in this lexicon, sit between antecedent conditions and critical junctures. While the *antecedent conditions* represent the "base-line" of institutional continuity, an emergent *cleavage/crisis* departs from the "base-line" and triggers the critical juncture (Collier and Collier, 1991, p. 29). The latter is "a period of significant change, which typically occurs in distinct ways in different countries (or in other units of analysis) and which is hypothesized to produce distinct legacies" (ibid., p. 29). During these critical junctures, the structural influences on political action are said to be "significantly relaxed" so that "the range of plausible choices open to powerful political actors expands substantially" and their decisions have greater impact upon the institution's further development (ibid., p. 343). This fluid time poses a break in causality[4] between (1) antecedent conditions and cleavages (crises) and (2) the (re) production of legacies. The CJ literature presents a non-deterministic interplay between deep-seated historically cumulative factors and crisis-triggered contextual developments and thereby opens significant space for powerful actors to make a difference by virtue of how they articulate interests and preferences. James Mahoney refines this agential turn when he observes that, "critical junctures are moments of relative structural indeterminism when wilful actors shape outcomes in a more voluntaristic fashion than normal circumstances permit," arguing that "these choices demonstrate the power of agency" (Mahoney, 2002, p. 7). This is echoed by Daren Acemoglu and James Robinson in *Why Nations Fail* (2012), which operationalizes this agential framework and remarks that events during critical junctures have contingent outcomes whereby the "exact path of institutional development during these periods depends on which one of the opposing forces will succeed, which groups will be able to form effective coalitions and which leaders will be able to structure events to their advantage" (2012, p. 274).

Variant II: crises and "paradigm shifts"

Peter Hall's (1993) pioneering work on social learning in policy-making explored the mediating role of ideas in constructing crises. His model emphasizes that policymakers customarily work within a framework of ideas and standards that specifies not only the goals of policy and the kind of instruments that can be used to attain them, but also the very nature of the problems they are meant to be addressing. (ibid., p. 279)

He calls this ideational framework, with interrelated cognitive and normative aspects, a "policy paradigm"[5] and suggests that crisis can lead to "paradigm shifts" (ibid.).

Following Thomas Kuhn's model of scientific paradigm shift, Hall distinguishes three increasingly significant orders of change, concerning, respectively: (1) the policy paradigm, (2) the research programme, and (3) the worldview. Thus, the policy paradigm comprises policies and policy solutions proposed by policy makers; the research programme involves a more general frame of reference allowing agents (or observers) to situate these policies; and the worldview (*Weltanschauung*) consists in public philosophies that organize ideas, values and principles of knowledge and society. While the three levels are always interrelated, worldviews undergird the other two levels, often simply as unarticulated background knowledge (Hall, 1993, pp. 281–287). In these terms, Hall's model conceptualizes crises as triggering moments that occur when previously dominant ideas and assumptions about an economic and political reality are exhausted and can no longer solve new problems. New solutions backed up by a new set of ideas are articulated[6] through various channels and confront each other in political contests where rival parties fight for control over policy (ibid., p. 289).

Michael Oliver and Hugh Pemberton propose a critical revision of Hall's approach to crises. They characterize the three levels of change as: (1) "changes to the setting of existing instruments"; (2) "adoption of new instruments"; and (3) "goal alteration" (Oliver and Pemberton, 2004, p. 417). While the first order displays the features of "incrementalism, satisficing and routinized decision-making," the second leads to the development of new policy instruments that "may move one step beyond in the direction of strategic action" (ibid.). In contrast, third order change encompasses rare events that result in substantial divergences in both ideational, and consequently institutional, orientations. Building on these distinctions, Oliver and Pemberton conclude that "paradigmatic change is both less clean and more contingent than Hall allows" (2004, p. 2). Unlike Hall, who views crises as largely endogenous, they maintain that an exogenous shock plays a vital role in the triumph of the new policy paradigm (ibid., p. 416). In addition, this triumph is contingent on "the preparedness of interest groups to adopt it, on their ability to promote the new idea and to secure its endorsement by those in power, and on its subsequent adoption by the institutions of economic policy" (ibid.). These contingencies imply that sometimes – even when an old paradigm and its underlying ideas and assumptions have been depleted – there exist cases when an acceptance of a new paradigm will not occur (ibid.).[7]

Organizational and policy learning in crisis management

Critical conjunctures and paradigm shift accounts of crisis correlate well with the literature on organisational and policy learning in crisis management that treats crises as triggering events. Of particular interest here is how this literature analyses the timing of these triggers. Permutating the interplay between threat, time, and surprise, Charles F. Hermann (1998) and Christophe Roux-Dufort (2005), offered alternative criteria for classifying crisis from an actor's perspective in terms of the threat level (high, moderate, low), time (short, extended), and surprise (anticipated vs. no advance warning). Twelve possible combinations of these criteria can be generated; for Hermann, a crisis exists where there is a situation of high threat, short time and surprise (Hermann, 1972, p. 193). Note that what matters here is not a disinterested observer's view of the situation but the actors' (or decision-makers') perception.

When a crisis occurs, the decision-making process differs from all other cases. In crisis, decision-making processes engage more individuals and the number of alternative solutions identified is reduced while the rate of internal (within agencies) and external (with international actors) communication will increase.

t' Hart and Sundelius (2013) developed this research agenda by considering the *stages* of crisis response. They distinguished between:

- Sense-making (managing radical uncertainty)

    - Making sense of the crisis occurs as events and phenomena are noticed, interpreted, and reacted to *as crisis events* (Gephart, 2007, p. 127). There are two main types of interruptions that trigger sense-making and changes in cognition: a new event that is not expected and/or an expected event that does not occur (Gephart, 2007).

    - Sense-making and "labelling": imposing labels on interdependent events in ways that suggest plausible acts of managing, coordinating, and distributing...as an organized activity that provides actors with a given set of cognitive categories and a typology of actions (Tsoukas and Chia, 2002, p. 573, cited in Weick, Sutcliffe, and Obstfeld, 2005).

    - Sense-making as a primary site where meanings materialize, inform, and constrain identity and action (Mills, 2003, p. 35 in Weick, Sutcliffe, and Obstfeld, 2005, p. 409).

- The steering and synthesizing stage (scaling/coordinating response action), largely based on the sense-making that serves as a springboard to action ("what's the story?" as a basis for asking "now what?").

- Adapting or managing the process of post-crisis recovery, inquiry, and debates. Strategically, this stage involves clarifying causes/responsibilities, defining the form of crisis inquiry, blame management (and avoiding blame-games), and potentially adaptive change.

- Public inquiries and hearings often form part of this process, with the aim to both re-legitimate key institutions and to assign responsibility for the incidents (Gephart and Pitter, 1993). Thus, inquiry discourse is oriented at interpreting events, and both legitimating and critical interpretations are commonly produced[8] (Gephart, 2007).

In a nutshell, the common thread in this category consists of defining crises as triggering events followed by time fluidity as policy makers construct sense and meaning in response to these events (Weick, Sutcliffe, and Obstfeld, 2005). As such, this category can offer a nuanced analytical relation between the historically cumulative and the contextual. The historically cumulative part speaks to the non-contextual and lingering legacy of antecedent factors, while the contextual lays within the immediate response to the triggering event (crisis), followed by a time fluidity where agents embark on a variety of possible pathways of action. Both the historically cumulative and the contextual levels of analysis, however, can be seen as opening greater space for agency in shaping crisis responses and dynamics. The historically cumulative (antecedent conditions in CJ; the *Weltanschauung* in paradigm shifts) and the contextual layer (the concept of critical junctures; policy and research programmes in paradigm shifts) do not have unambiguous, predetermined effects in shaping the crisis because agency makes a difference through its role in articulating interests and preferences during crises moments. This is where the corresponding literature on organizational and policy learning in crisis management can deepen such historical institutionalist analyses by addressing how agency is impacted by the distinctive historical and conjunctural features of the crisis. For example, following Hermann (1998) and Roux-Dufort (2005), one might ask how actors' responses are shaped by their perception of threat level, length of time, and level of surprise in defining the crisis. Or, following t' Hart and Sundelius (2013), one might identify various stages of crisis response in relation to different periods of time within moments of crises themselves. In short, the learning literature can deepen the treatment of agency in this category by specifying the multiple dimensions of actors' responsiveness to crises.

Category 2: crisis as nodal points of transformation

While the previous category treats crises as triggering moments followed by time fluidity, this one regards crises as nodal points for transformative intervention. Examples include thick and thin variations of constructivism (see below) along with certain currents within historical materialism that emphasize the key role of ideas in mediating structure-agency relations. Nonetheless, as one might expect, these approaches diverge in their analytical treatment of ideas within the nodal point of transformation. For constructivists, ideas are not just auxiliary instruments used by agents in conditions of uncertainty. Instead, they are the repertoire of meaning through which actors filter their intra- and inter-subjectivities which are always structurally embedded. Hence it is ideas that drive or mediate the transformative effects of crisis and crisis management. For thin constructivism, the interpretation of a crisis that comes to fruition through contestation is directly path-shaping. In contrast, thick constructivism adds that the influence of discourse (ideas) is mediated and overdetermined within institutional contexts. In consequence, constructed moments of crises here give meaning, re-meaning and post-meanings to the events that happen in the aftermath (this will be elaborated below).

The relevant historical materialist positions echo such arguments but reject an idealist account of how ideas shape history. They are interested in the forms of mental production, the materiality of ideational transmission, the material foundations of ideational resonances, and the conditions in which actors and observers attribute excessive (or insufficient) attention to the role of intellectuals, ideas, and argumentation. In short, if we accept the terms of this debate, they claim the "material" both shapes and is shaped by "ideas" (Bruff, 2008). Thus, in contrast to constructivism, the construction of meaning is not only regarded as inter- and intra-subjective, but also anchored in and selected through sedimented, layered, unstable and unequal material contexts. In other words, the nodal points of transformation in these positions refer to the anchoring of meaning-making processes within materially specific social relations of production.

This said, all three perspectives regard crises as nodal moments. They emphasize the mutual constitutiveness of episteme and practice andthe organic interaction between thought and practice that becomes crystallized in institutions. I now present these perspectives and then link them with the literature on organizational and policy learning.

Crises as analysed in "thin" constructivism

One variety of constructivist/constructivist-institutionalism examines the social construction of ideas during crisis. Mark Blyth argues that historical institutionalists (including Hall) reduce ideas to a "filler" such that they represent a "solution to prior theoretical problems inherent in an already existing research program" rather than treating them "as objects of investigation in their own right" (2002, pp. 229–231).[9] Thus Blyth develops Hall's approach by giving an important independent causal role to ideas, explores how ideas may be used to demobilize existing patterns of collective action and to develop new ones.

In his *Great Transformations*, Blyth argues that economic crises involve what he calls "Knightian" uncertainty; they are regarded by agents as unique events where they are uncertain about their interests andhow to realize them in a world that cannot be directly observed (2002, p. 9). Crisis resolution entails the restoration of a more "normal" condition of "Knightian certainty" – in which actors' interests are once again made clear and transparent to them. (Blyth, 2002, cited in Hay, 2004, p. 207). Faced with uncertainty, which excludes quasi-algorithmic translation of self-evident interests into action, ideas become fundamental to explain why actors did what they did. This has two aspects. On the one hand, actors contest whether there is a crisis and, if so, its nature and significance; and, on the other hand, they reflect on how best to act to pursue their values and interests. This makes ideas about crisis and appropriate courses of action critical to the explanation of crisis construals and responses. They become important causal factors in the path-shaping role of instititutions in critical conjunctures. Under this conceptualization, crises themselves are not self-evident phenomena but rather events or progesses whose meaning must be argued over, diagnosed and ultimately constructed. Once this meaning is agreed upon, "collective action to resolve the uncertainty facing them can take any meaningful institutional form" (ibid.). As structures "do not come with an instruction sheet," ideas become crucial in diagnosing both "what has gone wrong" and "what is to be done" (ibid., p. 10). In other words, "ideas allow agents to reduce uncertainty, propose a particular solution to a moment of crisis, and empower agents to resolve that crisis by constructing new institutions in line with these new ideas" (ibid., p. 11).

The thin constructivist model proposed by Blyth speaks to the notion that "crises cannot be reduced to material forces or socialization, but *are what agents make of them*" (Widmaier, Blyth, and Seabrooke, 2007, p. 757, emphasis added). This research programme focuses on "how moments of change are framed," that is, on the competing problematizations and the persuasion techniques used to put forth a particular interpretation of the crisis that has occurred (ibid., p. 753). Widmaier, Blyth and Seabrooke argue for "a greater focus on persuasion as intersubjective contestation among both elite and mass public agents" (ibid., p. 754). Analytically, they distinguish four levels: (1) "the interplay of inter-subjective tensions and interpretive struggles," whereby persuasion is articulated as an ongoing process of contestation between elites, as well as elites and the general public, on "what's to be done;" (2) "institutional and rhetorical norms which guide efforts to frame particular events" which stress the impact institutional contexts have on social constructions; (3) "mass-elite persuasive interactions," i.e. the political climate dominant among the general public which dictates the ability of elite attitudes to be accepted/rejected; (4) "subsequent debates over the 'lessons of history'," i.e. the reinterpretation of past crises through the lens of present events (ibid., pp. 754–755). According to this research framework, then, crises are "moments where elite and mass public agents attempt to persuade each other over 'who they are' and 'what they want'" (ibid., p. 756). Such understanding downplays the conjunctural specificities in favour of available ideas. Crises are turning points "not because of changes in material structures *per se*, but because of transformations in broader inter-subjective understandings" (ibid., p. 757). This implies that the developmental trajectory or outcome of a crisis is highly contingent upon the ideational contestation *during* the crisis (Hay, 2010, p. 208). In short, to understand institutional change, "we must acknowledge the independent causal and constitutive role of ideas" (ibid., p. 207).

Crises as analysed in "thick" constructivism

Colin Hay's work calls for a strategic-relational account of crisis that takes discourse (ideas) seriously. One should examine how far – through normalization and institutional embedding – ideas become established and codified and thereby serve as cognitive filters through which actors come to interpret signals from their environment and conceive of their interests in this context (Hay, 2011). At stake here is how crisis constructions have been presented and framed in relation to particular social positions, and not just in ideational terms. Hay's strategic-relational conceptualization goes well beyond ideational bias to a context that is strategically selective, favouring some strategies over others. The existing manifestations of structure and agency are relational (mutually constitutive) and dialectical (not reducible to one set of factors) (Hay, 2002, p. 127). In other words, the discursive construction of crises is embedded within the aspirations of strategic actors in strategically selective contexts (Hay, 2002, p. 128). In this sense, his work represents a thicker variation of the role of ideas.

Reacting to Blyth's conceptualization of crises, Hay argues that "[i]deational factors certainly need to be given greater attention, but surely not at the expense of all other variables" (2006, p. 72). One of the major pitfalls of Blyth's conceptualization of crises, Hay points out, is the claim that "actors' conduct is not a (direct) reflection of their material interests, but, rather, a reflection of particular *perceptions* of their material interests" (ibid., p. 68). Interests are therefore referred to as "social constructs that are open to redefinition through ideological contestation" (Blyth, 2002, p. 271, as cited in Hay, 2006, p. 69). This becomes important in times of crisis, when "bouts of intense ideational contestation" are unleashed and actors' perceptions of their own self-interest are said to become blurred (ibid., pp. 67–69). Hay identifies two problems in Blyth's position here: first, it is not self-evident that interests become blurred during moments of crisis, and second, such an understanding of crises implies an uneven ontology (ibid., pp. 69–70).

On the first problem, he notes that, while crises arguably "provide focal points around which competing political narratives might serve to reorient actors' sense of their own self-interest," interests nevertheless cannot be said to be unclear or blurred (ibid.). Rather, it is more likely that moments of crisis would precipitate a "vehement reassertion, expression, and articulation of prior conceptions of self-interest – often in the intensity of political conflict" (ibid.). In relation to the second problem, the indeterminacy of interests during moments of crisis (i.e. "Knightian uncertainty") causes an analytical conundrum – if interests are unknown, then whose interests are ultimately being advanced (ibid., p. 70)? In his analysis, Blyth calls upon "influential opinion formers with access to significant resources" to resolve this problem (ibid.). Surely, then – Hay argues – if "access to material resources is a condition of successful crisis narration," does this not imply a "slippage towards a residual materialism" (ibid.)? To provide a successful constructivist account of crises, Hay argues that we need to know more about the "determinants (material and ideational), internal dynamics, and narration of the crisis itself" (ibid.).

Unlike the moments of "Knightian uncertainty," Hay does not view crises as moments when ideas have a determining, path-shaping role, but rather as strategic moments of structural transformation (ibid., p. 331), where ideas are involved both in strategic context analysis – construing the conjuncture and balance of forces – and in the strategic imaginaries oriented to economic, political, cultural, and other modes of potential transformation. In other words, "the struggle to impose discursively a new trajectory upon the structures of the state is won and lost *not* in the wake of the crisis moment but in the very process in which the crisis is constituted" (ibid., p. 335). Thus, there is no such thing as a "moment of crisis" – it cannot be isolated, neutralized or recognized as a definite milestone as it is "part of the new process that is growing out of it" (ibid.); crisis becomes the transformation moment and not the moment itself.

So, how is this decisive intervention mediated and narrated? Hay points out that the struggle to narrate the crisis takes place within a "strategically selective context, favouring the strategies of certain interests over others" (ibid., p. 336). Naturally, "a multiplicity of conflicting narratives of crisis" is sustained and such narratives "compete in terms of their ability to find resonance with individuals' and groups' direct, lived experiences, and not in terms of their 'scientific' adequacy as explanations for the conditions they diagnose" (Hay, 1996, p. 255). He argues that the ability to articulate certain strategies depends on four factors: "(i) access to the means of dissemination; (ii) the nature of the contradictions and failures themselves; (iii) information and knowledge of such contradictions and the experiences to which they give rise; and (iv) the association of those presenting themselves as the organic intellectuals of a new hegemonic project with the 'symptoms' of the crisis themselves" (Hay, 1999, p. 336). Once constructed, crisis discourses then "operate by identifying minor alterations in the routine texture of social life, recruiting such iterative changes as 'symptomatic' of a generic condition" (Hay, 1996, p. 255). Eventually, a dominant construction may emerge after which the crisis "becomes lived in these terms" (ibid.).

Crises as analysed in historical materialism

Certain currents of historical materialism also exemplify the treatment of crises as nodal moments of transformation. These currents are more sensitive to the role of subjectivity, agency, contingency and the ideational alongside the "material." They critique the approach to crisis of both forms of constructivism. For instance, Andreas Bieler and Adam Morton argue that, while Blyth implicitly links the emergence of new ideas to material relations in moments of crisis, he does so in an ad hoc manner because he has an "underdeveloped conceptualization of the social relations of production" (Bieler and Morton, 2008, p. 108). They argue that Blyth adopts a "dualistic view of material structure and ideas that are always-already separated as variables that are then combined in their external relationship to one another" (ibid.). He is therefore oblivious to the "importance of material structural conditions in their *internal* relation to ideas" (ibid., emphasis added).

This understanding of production is rooted proximately in the work of Robert W. Cox, who drew on the work of Antonio Gramsci, to relate material production to the "production and reproduction of knowledge and of the social relations, morals and institutions that are prerequisites to the production of physical goods" (Cox, 1989, p. 39). This involves a comprehensive analysis of the social relations of production, encompassing "the totality of social relations in material, institutional and discursive forms that engender particular social forces" (Bieler and Morton, 2004, p. 87).

It leads Cox to examine the *what* of production, asserting that "[p]roduction creates the material basis for all forms of social existence, and the ways in which human efforts are combined in productive processes affect all other aspects of social life" (Cox, 1987, p. 1). The second half of the phrase opens the door to the simultaneous *how* of production, referring to the way in which production is "organised through the ideas that respond to ...the need for such production" (Bruff, 2009, p. 346). Consequently, it is through the persistent interaction of the *what* and *how* of production over time, that there arises an "institutionalization in a mode of production which constitutes the material basis for existence – 'the objective world' for those living in it" (Cox, 1996, p. 514). This is reminiscent of the chapter on Feuerbach in *The German Ideology* (Marx and Engels, 1976) and, more recently, Gramsci's argument that the humanly objective is actually the historically or universally subjective (Gramsci, 1971, p. 445).

Thus, through the analytical primacy of social relations of production and reproduction, historical materialists can account for both the destructive and creative role of material practices, as well as the role of ideas as both intersubjective meanings and collective images. Ideas as intersubjective meanings is a point of convergence with constructivists; but the second, ideas as collective images, brings divergence. Historical materialists' view of ideas as collective images invokes an anchoring into social positions, thus accounting to a greater degree for the material. It is precisely this point that speaks to the *how* of production, opening the door to the significance of form arising from the variety of ways ideas interact with matter.

This understanding enables an analysis of how common sense secures the reproduction of the social relations of production. For Gramsci, two points matter here:

1. All humans are philosophers because everybody holds conceptions about the world, or common sense, no matter how fragmented and uncritical.
2. These conceptions of the world are embodied in all human social practice (Bruff, 2008, p. 8, referencing Gramsci, 1971, pp. 323, 344, 357).

Developing Gramsci's points and noting that common sense is inherently cultural, Bruff argues "in all aspects of life, common sense is the basis for how humans make sense of the situation they find themselves in" (Bruff, 2008, p. 47). Specifically, he suggests common sense involves not only "the conglomeration of each person's thoughts about the world" as their own version of common sense, but also the necessary synthetization "embodied in present *collective* patterns of human activity and thought" (ibid., pp. 8–9). This implies common senses are reducible to ideational collectivities but are dialectically related with the material. Thus, as Huw Macartney claims, "the material and ideological realms are inextricably and dialectically interwoven" (2011, p. 35). An important corollary is that "hegemonic common senses become institutionalized in material social processes" (ibid., p. 157).

Unlike some "economic" thinkers, theorists and activists who maintain that economic crises automatically induce change, Gramsci argued: "It may be ruled out that immediate economic crises of themselves produce fundamental historical events; they can simply create a terrain more favourable to the dissemination of certain modes of thought, and certain ways of posing and resolving questions involving the entire subsequent development of national life" (1971, p. 184). This statement highlights the importance of the discursive-cum-political mediation of response to crisis. A historical materialist understanding of crises based on this approach largely develops a Neo-Gramscian understanding of social and economic change that contends "organic (material-economic) crises fuel changes in accumulation strategy, precipitating the role of ideas" (Macartney, 2008, p. 433).[10]

However, historical materialists endure continuing critiques from both the idealist and materialist sides of the ontological spectrum, despite obvious errors in interpretation. On the one hand, from "social constructivists and post-structuralists who perceive the embedded materialism. . . as evidence of economism," and on the other, accusations of "pluralist-idealism" from Marxists responding "to the prominence of ideas and the under-theorization of formal categories" such as class, capital and labour (Macartney, 2011, pp. 160–161). In response, Macartney illustrates the need to "walk the fine line between over-contingency and over-determinism," highlighting "the unavoidable role of ideas and discourses through a conception of contested common senses" (ibid., p. 161).[11]

Likewise, as Bieler and Morton note, ideas are dialectically connected to material social processes, which allows for a "non-deterministic understanding of structural change" (2008, p. 117). This, as Bruff notes, "is very different from postulating a deterministic economism which seeks to explain all human activity with recourse to material conditions (which postmodernists and others accuse historical materialism of doing)" (2008, p. 51).

Therefore, moving from the analytical primacy of social relations of production and reproduction through the construction of common senses that are inextricably embedded within the material, such historical materialist positions offer a perspective on crises as nodal moments of transformation that deepens the historically cumulative dimension by not only highlighting what is specific about the historical, but also by providing significant contributions to explaining the various questions of *why* in relation to crises. Through a renewed reading of Gramsci, historical materialists can attribute to the potential of crises as nodal moments of transformation, yet also explain the nuances of why such opportunities may be missed.

To begin with, while Ian Bruff confirms Colin Hay's assertion that perception of crisis is necessarily subjective, he adds that Hay "neglects the fact that the conceptions themselves are saturated with references to the material basis for existence" (Bruff, 2008, p. 103). He concludes that it is necessary to "elucidate why such awareness emerged *in the first place*, which enables us to identify its social content" (ibid). Similarly, within crises as particular nodal moments of transformation, Bruff argues that it is important to consider "*why* certain ideas became truths about the economy and others did not" (ibid., p. 106). Through studying the economic crisis of the early 1980s in the Netherlands, Bruff finds it "not only generated a collective perception of crisis but also a perception that the crisis should be resolved collectively," yet by elucidating the material underpinnings in the construction of common senses during this time, he is able to explain why, despite the perception of collectivity, "the resulting reforms were much closer to the capital's than the labour's interest" (ibid., pp. 92–93).

Another recent direct application of these debates on crises is Huw Macartney's work, which articulates common sense with the analysis of fractions of capital. His articulation of impulsions (or tendencies)- agency-common sense suggests that "crises *only* provide *utile* windows [of transformation, emphasis added] if collective agency and alternative common sense are sufficiently mature in their development" (Macartney, 2011, p. 161, capitalization in original). He demonstrates how "[t]he 2007–09 crisis was a missed opportunity" due to "the relative lack of an organized working-class movement; the ubiquity of the neoliberal consensus; and the institutionalization of neoliberalism" (2011, pp. 161, 157). He argues the 2007–09 crisis "came at exactly the right stage of neoliberal common senses' development – when it had reached relative maturity across the political economies of the West – in order for capital to survive and reinforce its hold through state aid" (Macartney, 2011, p. 161).

Thus, for Macartney, while "crises provide unique conditions for struggles over future paths of development represented in alternative common senses," it is equally important to consider "the historically specific conditions for accumulation and expansion are embedded within common sense frames of reference" (ibid.). Thus, through a re-reading of Marx and Gramsci which brings a renewed emphasis on the tendencies (impulsions) of capitalism, Macartney can account for "a more abstract understanding of the expansionary impulsions which tend to generate crises, the requirement to shift the burden of crises through devaluation, and the shift to expand finance and credit as means to offset crises in surplus value production" (ibid.). Macartney provides an historically situated analysis of the failure of the 2007–09 crises to serve as a nodal moment of transformation, concluding with the hope that "the next time round ought not to be so" (ibid.).

Crisis management and organizational learning (in crisis as nodal points)

Compared with the first category, the relevant literature on crisis and organizational learning for this second category recognizes that crisis management must be understood in light of the contest over which interpretive frame prevails and gains majority support in relevant formal political arenas "processing" the crisis (e.g. Stone, 2001; Boin, t' Hart, and McConnell, 2009). In framing contests, the actors need to convince policy makers to consider/ support their particular crisis frame (Boin, t' Hart and McConnell, 2009). In this vein, the literature on positioned knowledge production deserves a mention - highlighting that knowledge is not apolitical. Knowledge organizations usually push forward a particular frame, or even engage in a form of "indirect coercive transfer" of policy solutions (Stone, 2001). Hence, knowledge construction is a form of power in crisis governance.

Any theory of crisis exploitation needs to capture the emergence of new frames as well as how the clash between them produces particular types of political and policy consequences (Boin, t' Hart, and McConnell, 2009). These contests largely determine attribution of meaning to the events, "allocation" of credit and blame within system, and what "lessons" are drawn moving forward (Brändström, Bynander, and 't Hart, 2004; Boin, t' Hart, and McConnell, 2009; Hood, 2011). Therefore, it is not only the framing imperative at stake here, but the political nature that accompanies the framing. Sense-making and knowledge production in general are characterized by unequally strong position(s) to influence the construction of social reality (Mills, 2003, p. 153 quoted in Weick, Sutcliffe, and Obstfeld, 2005), to power expressed in acts that shape what people accept, take for granted, and reject (Pfeffer, 1981). According to Weick, Sutcliffe, and Obstfeld, such shaping occurs through influence at various dimensions of sense-making: the social relations that are encouraged and discouraged, the valued or derogated identities, the accepted or discredited retrospective meanings, the highlighted or suppressed cues, the encouraged or discouraged updating, the accurate or plausible standard of accuracy to which conjectures are held, and the approval of proactive or reactive action as the preferred mode of coping (2005, p. 418).

Boin, t' Hart, and McConnell (2009) distinguish two spheres of crisis exploitation: political game (between government and opposition) and policy game (between proponents of regulatory and administrative status quo and proponents of change). They claim most research to date (as of 2009) has looked at the managerial dimension of coping with crisis, that is the functional challenges (such as prevention, preparedness, critical decision-making, coordinating responses, communication and the media), while the more political and strategic dimension to crisis management – such as the impact of crisis on political elites (and institutions), their policies and leadership - remained largely ignored (Cf. 't Hart, 2008; 't Hart and Sundelius, 2013). On the other hand, Daniel Beland (2006), distinguishes between high- and low-level setting of learning in politics. In the former, a highly politicized topic gets debated in the public limelight, with importance of actors ranked as follows: politicians, civil servants, experts, mass media. In the latter, a less politicized topic gets discussed in the shadow of bureaucracy, with civil servants, experts, politicians and policy clientele and community being the important actors. These settings influence the motivation of main actors, the goals, style, critical assessment and learning.

Across these differences, the learning game presupposes space for safe critical self-interrogation, hence "blameless" crises generate more reflective forms of policy change then "shameful" crisis. Crises become "shameful" when the dominant opposition asserts they were due to avoidable failures within one or more of the key organizations involved (media, political and legal struggles become major obstacles to policy-oriented learning) ('t Hart, 2013). Moreover, crises that fit within existing risk catalogues and fit known patterns usually receive less contentious scrutiny and stimulate learning processes that boil down to more of the same, boosting strategies/resource claims of existing risk management coalitions ('t Hart, 2013). Furthermore, is not automatically the case that learning will institutionalize in the programs and policies of international organizations or governments (Stone, 2001) and learning from a crisis cannot be correlated with policy improvement. Learning may not lead to policy changes because of the intensity of resource conflicts and vested interests or the incommensurability of value structures (Sabatier and Jenkins-Smith, 1999; Böcher, 2007 in Biegelbauer, 2011).

Unlike the first category, the literature on the nature and meaning of crises enriches in so many ways the learning literature in this category through the deepening of the relation between presentism and historicism. As just presented, the learning literature stresses the political nature of knowledge production during crises (Stone, 2001), highlighting the unequally strong positions which influence framing and sense-making (Mills, 2003, p. 153 quoted in Weick, Sutcliffe, and Obstfeld, 2005). The literature also juxtaposes the political sphere with the policy sphere in relation to crisis exploitation, highlighting that most research addresses the latter pertaining to the managerial dimension of coping with crisis.

The literature on the nature of crises nonetheless serves to deepen the explanation in relation to all of this through first understanding that crises arise only when events or processes are interpreted as such. For example, examining the social construction of ideas during moments of crisis, thin constructivists focus on "*how* moments of change are framed" (Widmaier, Blyth, and Seabrooke, 2007, p. 753, emphasis added), thereby accounting for "the independent causal and constitutive role of ideas" during moments of crisis (Hay, 2010, p. 207). Thick constructivists then bring in an emphasis on how these crisis constructions have been presented and framed through particular social positions, thereby illuminating the strategic selectivity of particular strategies by actors according to their aspirations (Hay, 2002, p. 128).

While constructivists strengthen the chronocentric nature of explanation, historical materialists strengthen the historically specific through their understanding of the ideational as always embedded within the material. Bruff argues it is necessary to "elucidate why such awareness emerged *in the first place*" (Bruff, 2008, p. 103), and Macartney highlights the importance of "understanding of the expansionary impulses which tend to generate crises" (Macartney, 2011, p. 161). Therefore, taking this seriously leads to a more intensive conceptualization of the deeper mechanisms implicated in crisis, thus provoking the need to account for the role of the state as a "social relation with power-shaped selectivities" (Brand, 2013, p. 425). Leubolt stresses how the concept of selectivities enables an analysis of the state which "highlights the differentiated and unequal possibilities of different actors to influence policies" (2014, p. 312). Through providing a more thorough understanding of the historically specific nature of the context's unevenness during moments of crisis, "the consideration of selectivities enables analyses to highlight structural constraints and possibilities for different groups of actors," thereby deepening the explanation of framing, sense-making and other related phenomena during moments of crises (ibid., p. 313).

Towards a critical realist treatment of crisis and learning

The presented literature has demonstrated a deepening in both approaches to the crisis-learning nexus, namely: crises as triggering events, and crises as nodal moments of transformation. In category one, it is evident that the learning literature can teach more to literature on the nature of crisis; whereas, in crises as nodal moments of transformation, it is the other way around. Thus, while the historically specific legacies and present conjunctures have been deepened within this cartography of crises and policy learning, I echo Jessop's symptomatology argument (see previous chapter), which stresses the potential that Critical Realism (hereafter CR) has in further explaining the nature of crisis, crisis management and crisis lessons. The promise of CR manifests itself through the refined yet complex combination it proposes between (1) the historically specific and the chronocentric, (2) the contextual and the historically cumulative, and (3) the necessary and the contingent via the concepts of stratification and emergence. While the two categories presented in this chapter extensively cover various dimensions within 1 and 2, a rigorous differentiation between subjective and objective dimensions of crises- as noted earlier in this chapter- requires a distinct yet relational interplay between what is necessary and what is contingent (possible) for the overall analysis of crises and learning. In this way, a CR-led analytical treatment of crises juxtaposes 1 and 2 against the background of 3 by positing crises as processes characterized by tendential stratifications and emergent properties. The thematic translation of this implies crises are processes that unfold through the various attempts at managing them. I will first unpack the conceptual version before I delineate the thematic one. This should pave the ground for linking the nature of learning in relation to crises.

Crises are tendentially stratified because the ontological distinction between the real, actual, and empirical is always made in tandem with the tendencies that particular relational entities exhibit (I will explain these terms further as I go along). Bhaskar succinctly stated, "tendencies may be possessed unexercised, exercised unrealized, and realized unperceived (or undetected)" (2008, p. 7). In this vein, the real concerns the realm of objects where their powers and structures are either contingently juxtaposed to each other (but resistant to change) and/or triggered but relatively resistant to these triggering forces (possessed unexercised, exercised unrealized). The actual denotes the level where the tendencies, counter-tendencies, powers, and liabilities associated with real mechanisms interact and are activated (actualized). Actualization does not entail that these phenomena are perceived or detected. This is associated with the empirical realm, i.e., the domain of observation and experience.

Its emphasis on this stratified reality allows CR to offer a distinctive account of the articulation of the necessary and the contingent across different levels of the natural and social world. While the real denotes a combination of necessary *and* contingent relations, the actual posits a combination of necessary *or* contingent (possible). The regularities often expressed in the empirical realm are purely contingent in relation to the ontological layers preceding them. This is precisely why CR problematizes any effort to construct causal explanations couched within the empirical domain (Sayer, 2000).

Crises have emergent properties because the nested nature of these tendential ontological layers explained above does not necessarily preclude social agents from drawing conclusions from the present situation they find themselves in (the historical and the chronocentric). This is the vexing yet promising challenge of the concept of emergence in CR. Emergence is generally defined as the "situations in which the conjunction of two or more features or aspects gives rise to new phenomena, which have properties irreducible to those of their constituents, even though the latter are necessary for their existence" (ibid, p. 2000). While some CR scholars primarily focus on the synchronic nature of emergence (relation between the whole and its part is specific in time, see Elder-Vass, 2010 for example), a "Higher Realism," as Archer (2012) notes, necessarily requires the linking between synchronic and diachronic emergence (relation between whole and parts in time- synchronic- and over time- diachronic). This means the relation between a lower stratum and an upper one is always contingently necessary while the relation between the upper strata and the lower ones are always necessarily contingent (the actual is contingently necessary to the empirical, while the empirical is necessarily contingent to the actual). This is why learning about crisis at the empirical level cannot be similar to the learning conducted at the actual level even though the two are intrinsically related.

The thematic translation of this conceptual version implies that crises are processes that unfold through the various attempts at managing them. The word process denotes a certain motion in time and space taking a variety of contextual forms without necessarily evoking a linear or teleological temporal sequencing. These space-time configurations however must correspond to natural or social reference points called objects in CR. These reference points are both relative (intra subjective) and relational (inter subjective) but nonetheless objective, meaning their existence must be independent from how we perceive them, otherwise the mere possibility of perceiving and even disagreeing over them would simply not exist (distinction between the in/transitive dimensions of knowledge in CR). A financial crisis for instance can symbiotically be represented as an environmental one depending on how it is perceived and by whom. But if one cannot disentangle the reference points speaking to what is specifically financial or environmental, then the risk of analytical conflation is highly evident.

The phrase "various attempts" implies the involvement of social agents: the structural positions they occupy, the social imaginaries that animate them, the meaning system they are embedded in, and the strategic deployment at their disposals (see the variation-selection-retention movement in Jessop's immediately following chapter). "Managing them" on the other hand highlight the crucial differentiation between crisis management and crisis of crisis management (see Jessop again).

The crisis management attempts posit par excellence an amalgam of actual-empirical type of tendential stratification. These attempts primarily occur at the level of the actual and later manifested at the empirical level. Responding to certain triggers that have thwarted the relative stability of systemic regularities, policy makers will attempt to solve these problems in relation to the available repertoire they have at their disposal and independent of the causes that might have triggered these thwarting moments or events (actual). Whether these systemic solutions solve, partially solve or do not solve the crisis, the effects of these interventions definitely appear in the empirical realm. Hence, learning in crisis is associated with crisis management attempts couched at the actual level whereas learning from crisis is associated with crisis management attempts at the empirical level.

Crisis of crisis management attempts, on the other hand, are an emergent property of crisis management. They denote the unresponsiveness of crisis management routines and hence appear at the empirical level. Due to the profound nature of their existence, they evoke a certain learning about crisis in an attempt to unravel the hidden, passive and unmarked structures and powers of what the social agents in question subjectively view as the reference points or objects related to the crisis.

Put differently, this has two important implications. First, both crisis management (actual and empirical levels) and crisis of crisis management (empirical level) exist against the background of objects or reference points pertaining to the nature of crisis (the real) that are transcendentally ever present throughout all these processes. Second, crisis management attempts by definition will always absent the real dimension of crisis (no need for learning about crisis). Crisis of crisis management attempts, however, de facto open a window for reform or transformation. This depends on whether the dominant social agents treat the level of the real as a necessary background for knowing more about the crisis (reform), or whether the detection and articulation of that real will be at the heart of future policy reforms (transformation). This is where the learning aspect of crisis becomes extremely important.

In sum, contemporary literatures on crisis and policy learning can build upon the analytical advances provided by CR. If crises are processes characterized by tendential stratifications and emergent properties, then the learning construals associated with such stratifications and emergence can provide us with a promising methodology to disentangle the complex and interwoven dimensions of crisis.

Notes

1 A remark made on the Bloomberg television channel in November 2008 in his capacity as transition manager for President-elect Barack Obama.
2 For (Neo-)Marxist literature, see Roberts (2016); Heinrich (2013); Clarke (2012); Dunn (2011); Harvey (2010); Mavroudeas and Ioannides (2006); Fine, and Saad-Filho, (2004); Clarke, (1993); Lebowitz (1982); and Weisskopf (1979). For (Post-)Keynesian literature see the work of Stockhammer (2015); Kates (2000); Jonsson (1995); Minsky (1992). For the (Neo-)Gramscian literature see Overbeek and Van

Apeldoorn (2012). For Neo institutional/evolutionary literature see Acemoglu and Robinson (2012); Robinson (2006); Mahoney (2002); Baumgartner and Jones (1993); Krasner (1984). For real business cycle literature, Nason and Tallman (2015); and Hale (2012). For the Efficient Market Hypothesis, Ball (2010).

3 For the literature on the stages of crisis response, see Boin, t' Hart, and McConnell (2009); t' Hart (2008); Weick, Sutcliffe, and Obstfeld (2005). For the literature on the situational factors in which crisis response unfolds and learning takes place see Biegelbauer (2011); 't Hart (2008); Beland (2006); Hermann (1972). On crisis as framing contests, see Hood (2011); Boin, t' Hart, and McConnell (2009); Bränd-ström, Bynander and 't Hart (2004). On knowledge production in general, see De Guevara (2014); Böhling (2011); Weick, Sutcliffe, and Obstfeld (2005); Child and Heavens (2001); Stone (2001).

4 This can be contrasted with the punctuated equilibrium model which proposes the persistence of a contextually transcendent deep-seated causality (i.e., where no break in causality occurs.

5 So policy paradigms have path dependency – ideational as well as structural.

6 They often pre-exist and are pre-positioned.

7 Baker (2013) echoes these views by pointing out difficulties with achieving consistency in the "ordering and sequencing" of change as outlined by Hall (1993 p. 128).

8 A simplified model utilized by Weick, Sutcliffe, and Obstfeld (2005) concentrates these stages into three phases of sense-making, organizing and enactment. This sequential model is similar to the variation-selection-retention model found in other evolutionary approaches (see also Sum and Jessop, 2013).

9 In particular, Blyth notes that, while Hall's treatment offers does award ideas a sort of ontological primacy, they are insufficiently fleshed out methodologically and "analyses of them remain very impressionistic" (Blyth, 1997, p. 236). Attributing "a change in behaviour to a change in ideas is tenable only if it is counterfactually demonstrated that the change could not have occurred without the ideas" (ibid.).

10 Although it must be acknowledged that there is certainly a distinction between the Gramscian understanding of crisis and various neo-Gramscian understandings of crisis, even though they draw on Gramsci's thought (Jessop and Sum, 2006).

11 For more on Gramsci's own understanding the distinction between voluntarism and superdeterminism, see Jessop and Sum (2006, pp. 348–373).

References

Acemoglu, D. and Robinson, J.A. (2012) *Why nations fail: The origins of power, prosperity and poverty*. New York, NY: Crown Publishers.

Archer, M.S. (2012) *The reflexive imperative in late modernity*. Cambridge: Cambridge University Press.

Baker, A. (2013) 'The new political economy of the macroprudential ideational shift'. *New Political Economy* 18(1), pp. 112–139.

Ball, R. (2010) 'The global financial crisis and the efficient market hypothesis: What have we learned?'. *Journal of Applied Corporate Finance* 21(4), pp. 8–16.

Baumgartner, F.R. and Jones, B.D. (1993) *Agendas and instability in American politics*. Chicago, IL: University of Chicago Press.

Beland, D. (2006) 'The politics of social learning: Finance, institutions, and pension reform in the United States and Canada'. *Governance* 19(4), pp. 559–583.

Bhaskar, R. (2008) *A realist theory of science*. London: Routledge.

Biegelbauer, P. (2011) 'Learning through and about policies in politics: How much politics is there in policy learning?', Paper presented at the ECPR Joint Sessions 2011. St. Gallen, Switzerland: ECPR.

Bieler, A. and Morton, A.D. (2004) 'A critical theory route to hegemony, world order and historical change: Neo-Gramscian perspectives in International Relations'. *Capital and Class* 28, pp. 85–113.

Bieler, A. and Morton, A.D. (2008) 'The deficits of discourse in IPE: Turning base metal into gold?'. *International Studies Quarterly* 52, pp. 103–128.

Blyth, M. (1997) '"Any more bright ideas?" The ideational turn of comparative political economy'. *Comparative Politics* 29(2), pp. 229–250.

Blyth, M. (2002) *Great transformations: Economic ideas and institutional change in the twentieth century.* Cambridge: Cambridge University Press.

Böhling, K. (2011) 'Symbolic knowledge at work: Learning from experts in EU public policy', Paper presented at ECPR Joint Session 2011. St. Gallen, Switzerland: ECPR.

Boin, A., 't Hart, P. and McConnell, A. (2009) 'Crisis exploitation: Political and policy impacts of framing contests'. *Journal of European Public Policy* 16(1), pp. 81–106.

Brand, U. (2013) 'State, context and correspondence: Contours of a historical-materialist policy analysis'. *Austrian Journal of Political Science* 42(4), pp. 425–442.

Brändström, A., Bynander, F. and 't Hart, P. (2004) 'Governing by looking back: Historical analogies and crisis management'. *Public Administration* 82(1), pp. 191–210.

Bruff, I. (2008) *Culture and consensus in European varieties of capitalism: A 'common sense' analysis.* London: Palgrave Macmillan.

Bruff, I. (2009) 'The totalisation of human social practice: Open Marxists and capitalist social relations, Foucauldians and power relations'. *British Journal of Politics and International Relations* 11(2), pp. 332–351.

Castree, N. (2010) 'The 2007-09 financial crisis: Narrating and politicising a calamity'. *Human Geography* 3(1), pp. 34–48.

Child, J. and Heavens, S. (2001) 'The social constitution of organizations and its implications for organizational learning', in Dierkes, M., Berthoin Antal, A., Child, J. and Nonaka, I. (eds.), *Handbook of organizational learning and knowledge.* Oxford: Oxford University Press, pp. 308–326.

Clarke, S. (2012) 'Crisis theory', in Fine, B., Saad-Filho, A. and Boffo, M. (eds.), *The Elgar companion to Marxist economics.* Cheltenham, UK: Edward Elgar, pp. 90–95.

Clarke, S. (1993) *Marx's theory of crisis.* London: Macmillan.

Collier, R.B. and Collier, D. (1991) *Shaping the political arena.* Princeton. NJ: Princeton University Press.

Cox, R. (1987) *Production, power and world order: Social forces in the making of history.* New York, NY: Columbia University Press.

Cox, R. (1989) 'Production, the state and change in world order', in Czempiel, E.-O. and Rosenau, J.N. (eds.), *Global changes and theoretical challenges: Approaches to world politics for the 1990s.* Toronto: Lexington Books, pp. 37–50.

Cox, R. (1996) 'Multilateralism and world order', in Cox, R. (ed.), *Approaches to world order.* Cambridge: Cambridge University Press, pp. 494–523.

De Guevara, B.B. (2014) 'Studying the international crisis group'. *Third World Quarterly* 35, pp. 545–562.

Debray, R. (1973) *Prison writings.* London: Allen Lane.

Dunn, B. (2011) 'Marxist crisis theory and the need to explain both sides of capitalism's cyclicity'. *Rethinking Marxism* 23(4), pp. 524–542.

Elder-Vass, D. (2010) *The causal power of social structures: Emergence, structure and agency.* Cambridge: Cambridge University Press.

Emanuel, R. (2008) 'Video Interview'. *Wall Street Journal*, 9 November. Available at https://www.youtube.com/watch?v=_mzcbXi1Tkk

Fine, B. and Saad-Filho, A. (2004) *Marx's capital.* London: Pluto.

Gephart, R.P. (2007) 'Crisis sensemaking and the public inquiry', in Pearson, C.M., Roux-Dufort, C. and Clair, J.A. (eds.), *International handbook of organizational crisis management.* Thousand Oaks, CA: SAGE, pp. 123–160.

Gephart, R.P. and Pitter, R. (1993) 'The organizational basis of industrial accidents in Canada'. *Journal of Management Inquiry* 2(3), pp. 238–252.

Gramsci, A. (1971) *Selections from the prison notebooks.* London: Lawrence and Wishart.

Hale, G. (2012) 'Bank relationships, business cycles, and financial crises'. *Journal of International Economics* 88(2), pp. 312–325.

Hall, P.A. (1993) 'Policy paradigms, social learning, and the state: The case of economic policymaking in Britain'. *Comparative Politics* 25(3), pp. 275–296.

Harvey, D. (2010) *The enigma of capital: And the crises of capitalism.* Oxford: Oxford University Press.

Hay, C. (1996) 'Narrating crisis: The discursive construction of the "winter of discontent"'. *Sociology* 30(2), pp. 253–277.

Hay, C. (1999) 'Crisis and the structural transformation of the state: Interrogating the process of change'. *British Journal of Politics and International Relations* 1(3), pp. 317–344.

Hay, C. (2002) *Political analysis: A critical introduction.* Basingstoke, UK: Palgrave Macmillan.

Hay, C. (2006) 'Constructivist institutionalism', in Rhodes, R.A.W., Binder, S.A. and Rockman, B.A. (eds.), *The Oxford handbook of political institutions.* Oxford: Oxford University Press, pp. 56–74.

Hay, C. (2010) 'Ideas, interests and institutions in the comparative political economy of great transformations'. *Review of International Political Economy* 11(1), pp. 204–226.

Hay, C. (2011) 'Ideas and the construction of interests', in Beland, D. and Cox, R.H. (eds.), *Ideas and politics in social science research.* Oxford: Oxford University Press, pp. 65–82.

Heinrich, M. (2013) 'Crisis theory, the law of the tendency of the profit rate to fall, and Marx's studies in the 1870s'.*Monthly Review* 64, p. 11.

Hermann, C.F. (1972) 'Threat, time and surprise: A simulation of international crisis group', in Hermann, C.F. (ed.), *International crises: Insights from behaviour research.* New York, NY: Free Press, pp. 187–214.

Hermann, M.C. (1998) 'Leadership, value conflict and crisis management', in Newlove, L.M. (ed.), *Coping with value conflict and institutional complexity* (Vol. 4). Stockholm: International Conference on National Crisis Management in an International Perspective, pp. 65–72.

Hood, C. (2011) *The blame game.* Oxford: Oxford University Press.

Jessop, B. (2015) 'The symptomatology of crises, reading crises and learning from them: Some critical realist reflections'. *Journal of Critical Realism* 14(3), pp. 238–271.

Jessop, B. and Sum, N-L. (2006) *Beyond the regulation approach: Putting capitalist economies in their place.* Cheltenham, UK: Edward Elgar.

Jonsson, P.O. (1995) 'On the economics of Say and Keynes' interpretation of Say's law'. *Eastern Economic Journal* 21(2), pp. 147–155.

Kates, S. (2000) 'The Malthusian origins of the general theory or how Keynes came to write a book about Say's law and effective demand', in Wood, J.C. and Kates, S. (eds.),

Jean-Baptiste say: Critical assessments of leading economists, Vol. 5. London: Routledge, pp. 131–146.

Krasner, S.D. (1984) 'Review: Approaches to the state: Alternative conceptions and historical dynamics'. *Comparative Politics* 16(2), pp. 223–246.

Lebowitz, M.A. (1982) 'The general and the specific in Marx's theory of crisis'. *Studies in Political Economy* 7, pp. 5–25.

Leubolt, B. (2014) 'History, institutions, and selectivities in historical-materialist policy analysis: A sympathetic critique of Brand's *State, context and Correspondence*'. *Austrian Journal of Political Science* 43(3), pp. 309–318.

Macartney, H. (2008) 'Articulating particularistic interests: The organic organizers of hegemony in Germany and France'. *British Journal of Politics and International Relations* 10(3), pp. 429–451.

Macartney, H. (2011) *Variegated neoliberalism: EU varieties of capitalism and international political economy*. London: Routledge.

Mahoney, J. (2002) *The legacies of liberalism: Path dependence and political regimes in Central America*. Baltimore, MD: Johns Hopkins University Press.

Marx, K. and Engels, F. (1976) *The German ideology*. Moscow: Progress Publishers.

Mavroudeas, S. and Ioannides, A. (2006) 'Henryk Grossman's falling rate of profit theory of crisis: A presentation and a reply to old and new critics'. *Indian Development Review* 4 (1), pp. 69–91.

Mills, J.H. (2003) *Making sense of organizational change*. London: Routledge.

Minsky, H.P. (1992) 'The financial instability hypothesis', Working Paper No. 74, Jerome Levy Economics Institute.

Nason, J.M. and Tallman, E.W. (2015) 'Business cycles and financial crises: The roles of credit supply and demand shocks'. *Macroeconomic Dynamics* 19(4), pp. 836–882.

Oliver, M.J. and Pemberton, H. (2004) 'Learning and change in twentieth-century British economic policy'. *Governance* 17(3), pp. 414–441.

Overbeek, H. and Van Apeldoorn, B. (eds.) (2012) *Neoliberalism in crisis*. Basingstoke: Palgrave Macmillan.

Pearson, C.M. and Clair, J.A. (1998) 'Reframing crisis management'. *Academy of Management Review* 23(1), pp. 59–76.

Pfeffer, J. (1981) *Power in organizations*. Marshfield, MA: Pitman.

Roberts, M. (2016) *The long depression: Marxism and the global crisis of capitalism*. Chicago, IL: Haymarket.

Robinson, S.E. (2006) 'Punctuated equilibrium models in organizational decision making', in Morcol, G. (ed.), *Handbook on human decision-making*. Boca Raton, FL: CRC Press, pp. 133–149.

Roitman, J. (2014) *Anti-crisis*. Durham, NC: Duke University Press.

Roux-Dufort, C. (2005) 'A passion for imperfections: Revisiting crisis management', Paper submitted to the Academy of Management Meetings, 5-10 August 2005.

Sabatier, P. and Jenkins-Smith, H.C. (1999) 'The advocacy coalition framework: An assessment: Theories of the policy process', in Sabatier, P. (ed.), *Theoretical lenses on public policy*. Boulder, CO: Westview Press, pp. 117–166.

Sayer, A. (2000) *Realism and social science*. London: SAGE.

Stockhammer, E. (2015) 'Rising inequality as a cause of the present crisis'. *Cambridge Journal of Economics* 39(3), pp. 935–958.

Stone, D. (2001) 'Learning lessons, policy transfer and the international diffusion of policy ideas', CSGR Working Paper No. 69/01.

Sum, N.L. and Jessop, B. (2013) *Towards a cultural political economy. Putting culture in its place in political economy*. Cheltenham: Edward Elgar.

't Hart, P. (2008) 'Governing after crisis', in 't Hart, P., Boin, A. and McConnell, A. (eds.), *Governing after crisis: The politics of investigation, blame and learning*. Cambridge: Cambridge University Press, pp. 3–32.

't Hart, P. (2013) 'After Fukushima: Reflections on risk and institutional learning in an era of mega-crises'. *Public Administration* 91(1), pp. 91–104.

't Hart, P. and Sundelius, B. (2013) 'Crisis management revisited: A new agenda for research, training and capacity building within Europe'. *Cooperation and Conflict* 48(3), pp. 444–461.

Tsoukas, H. and Chia, R. (2002) 'On organizational becoming: Rethinking organizational change'. *Organizational Science* 13(5), pp. 567–582.

Weick, K.E., Sutcliffe, K.M. and Obstfeld, D. (2005) 'Organizing and the process of sensemaking'. *Organization Science* 16(4), pp. 409–421.

Weisskopf, T.E. (1979) 'Marxian crisis theory and the rate of profit in the postwar U.S. economy'. *Cambridge Journal of Economics* 3, pp. 341–378.

Widmaier, W.W., Blyth, M. and Seabrooke, L. (2007) 'Exogenous shocks or endogenous constructions? The meaning of wars and crises'. *International Studies Quarterly* 51, pp. 747–759.

3 Valid construals and/or correct readings? On the symptomatology of crises

Bob Jessop

To posit or not to posit crises?

The Chinese ideogram for crisis combines two characters: *danger* and *opportunity*. This indicates the duality of crisis and suggests several important issues for current and future analyses of crisis, crisis construals, and crisis lessons. First, the ideogram signifies that crises have both objective and subjective aspects corresponding to danger and opportunity respectively. Building on Régis Debray, we can say that, objectively, crises occur when a set of social relations (including their ties to the natural world) cannot be reproduced (cannot "go on") in the old way. Subjectively, crises tend to disrupt (even "shock") accepted views of the world and create uncertainty on how to "go on" within it. For they threaten established views, practices, institutions, and social relations, calling into question theoretical and policy paradigms as well as everyday personal and organizational routines. Second, in this sense, crises do not have predetermined outcomes: how they are resolved, if at all, depends on the actions taken in response to them. They are potentially path-shaping moments with performative effects that are mediated through the shifting balance of forces competing to influence crisis construal, crisis management, crisis outcomes, and possible lessons to be drawn from crisis. Third, without the objective moment, we have, at worst, deliberately exaggerated or even manufactured "crises," at best, unwarranted panic based on mis-perception or mis-recognition of real world events and processes.[1] Sometimes, crises may be manufactured or, at least exaggerated, for strategic or tactical purposes not directly related to immediate events or processes. Agents may, for "political" motives, broadly interpreted, conjure crises from nowhere or exaggerate the breadth, depth, and threat of an actual crisis (Mirowksi, 2013). After all, "you never want to let a serious crisis go to waste" (cf. Rahm Emanuel's comment, made on the Bloomberg television channel in November 2008 in his capacity as transition manager for President-elect Barack Obama).[2] A rigorous analysis of crises, crisis construals, and crisis management must be able to distinguish these alternatives or it could fall into a simplistic form of constructivism. Fourth, without the subjective moment, while disinterested *observers* may perceive a crisis developing either in real time or after the "event," the crisis will have insufficient resonance for relevant *participants* to spur them into efforts to take decisive action. Yet the notion of critical moment and turning point is a key feature of crises as conventionally understood. Fifth, from this perspective, then, crises are complex, objectively overdetermined moments of subjective indeterminacy, where decisive action can make a major difference to the future (Debray, 1973, p. 113; see also pp. 99–100, 104–105).

However, cautioning against too-easy an adoption of this kind of perspective, Janet Roitman (2014, p. 41) notes that, while positing a given situation as a crisis makes certain questions possible, it also forecloses other kinds of question and lines of investigation. In other words, an over-reliance by participants or observers on interpreting specific symptoms as evidence of a continuing crisis or yet another crisis can create a blind spot that sidelines alternative descriptions, diagnoses, prognoses, and potential courses of action. Taking crisis *for granted* as a starting point means that the nature of crisis as an explanandum is left unexamined and therefore directs attention to the search for the best explanation (or, at least, some explanation). So, rather than asking whether X (an event or process) does or does not constitute a crisis, treating it in an unquestioned, unreflective manner as a crisis, of whatever kind, short-circuits its analysis and, hence, decision-making about suitable responses. Although Roitman directs her criticism against historical narratives shaped by the interpretive couplet of crisis critique that is allegedly characteristic of modernity since the eighteenth century (cf. Koselleck, 1988; Festl, Grosser, and Thomä, 2018), her arguments are also very apt for the inflation of crisis diagnoses and discourses in recent decades as mentioned in Chapter 1.

Indeed, the more crisis discourse expands, the greater the risk that crisis becomes an empty concept. This is especially true where crisis is employed counter-intuitively, as is often the case nowadays, to describe an *enduring condition* rather than, as implied in its original meaning, to identify a *moment for decisive action* that might restore the *status quo ante* or lead to more or less radical social transformation. This risk can be remedied on condition that the durability of crises is related to *contingent* conditions that block a resolution that might otherwise occur. This is compatible with the general principles of critical realism and is analysed by Gramsci, for example, in terms of a "catastrophic equilibrium of forces" (1971: 219-23, 300; cf. 1975: Q13, §27; Q14, §23; Q22, §10;[3] for a discussion in relation to the crisis in Europe, see Keucheyan and Durand, 2015). These contingencies are illustrated in Chapter 4, where Andrew Gamble refers to the impasse of the British state or economy, which he regards as structural and deep-seated, leading to inertia, deadlocks or catastrophic equilibria. Likewise, Will Hout notes the permanent crisis in development assistance and explains this in terms of a failure to look beyond symptoms to deeper causes of poverty, inequality, and unsustainable development. In a different context, more related to crisis construals than the objective overdetermination of crisis, enduring crises are especially likely where repeated critiques serve as substitutes for transformative action, which is an obvious temptation of intellectuals, and can lead to fatalism, cynicism, or stoicism (cf. Thomä, Festl, and Grosser, 2015, p. 17; Hindrichs, 2015).

In contrast, writing four decades earlier than Janet Roitman, Edgar Morin (1993 [1976]) advanced a transcendental argument about crises as an appropriate theoretical object for a full-fledged "crisiology" (in French, *crisologie*), i.e., a *sui generis* theory of crisis. Whereas Roitman disputes the validity of crisis as an object of knowledge, Morin insists it can be. But this requires the crisiologist to locate crises in a precise theoretical framework in order to develop a general theory of crisis and corresponding praxis of crisis management.

> If one wants to move beyond conceiving crisis as perturbation, test, rupture in equilibrium, it is necessary to conceive society as a system capable of having crises, i.e., to pose three orders of principles, the first systemic, the second cybernetic, the third negative-entropy, without which the theory of society is inadequate and the notion of crisis inconceivable .
> (Morin, 1993 [1976], p. 149, my translation; cf. 1993 [1976], p. 142)

In this respect, Morin's complements Roitman's critique of the naturalization of crisis. He insists that to talk of crisis entails quite specific theoretical and real-world conditions. This can be related to the distinction noted in Chapter 1 between crises as "accidental" events (which can also be described as "disasters") and crises as systemically generated events or processes based on specific structural contradictions, vulnerabilities, and crisis tendencies. Both perspectives reviewed above are pertinent to a critical crisiology. For, whereas Roitman cautions against *unreflective categorization and explanation* of surprising or anomalous events and processes as "crises", Morin aims to specify the conditions in which it would be *theoretically appropriate* to categorize them as crises and seek to explain them as such. However, as we shall see, it is one thing to posit the abstract possibility of particular types of crisis or even the abstract possibility of a general crisiology; it is another thing entirely to explain the concrete form, substantive features, location, timing, and so forth, of specific crises.

This said, assuming that it makes sense to posit crisis as a valid object of inquiry in certain circumstances, one must recognize that crisis is a polysemic *word* and a problematic *concept*. It denotes multi-faceted phenomena that invite analysis from different entry points and standpoints. Hence, the theoretical significance of crisis depends on how it is articulated into a broader set of (preferably commensurable) concepts and on the sort of meta-theoretical framework in which the concept is embedded. Karim Knio explored the issue of the theoretical compatibility of different sets of concepts in Chapter 2. For example, constructivist accounts emphasize the constitutive role of discourse in identifying and shaping responses to crisis. Empiricist accounts analyse crises in terms of superficial features based on obvious external feature of crises, such as their sectoral, regional, financial, fiscal character, their intensity or duration or on statistical differences (e.g., crises with V-shaped, W-shaped, or L-shaped recoveries, i.e., a sharp drop and quick recovery, double-dip crises, and secular stagnation respectively.)[4] This approach is then used to generate taxonomies, produce empirical generalizations about different taxa, or even to develop invariant laws of cause and effect. Another approach can be described, in critical realist terms, as "actualist". This tends to associate particular (sets of) symptoms with particular (sets of) causes. In the case of economic crises, for example, these causes might be irrational exuberance, excessive state interference with market forces, Minsky's financial instability hypothesis (1982), the real business cycle, etc. In contrast with critical realism, then, actualism starts from crisis symptoms and moves directly to explain them in terms of corresponding prior sequences of events or causal processes. This is often associated with a chronological narrative approach or simplistic cause-effect analyses. In contrast, critical realist analyses start from symptoms and then inquire systematically into potential underlying real causal mechanisms, complete with their respective tendencies and counter-tendencies, and ask how these interacted in specific initial conditions to generate these particular symptoms as their contingently necessary outcome (see Sayer, 1992).

Once more: crisis, what crisis?

Critical realism is an appropriate meta-theoretical framework for analysing the objective overdetermination of crises as events or processes. But it does not provide the specific conceptual and theoretical tools for exploring specific cases of crisis (cf. the argument in Jessop, 2015). For there is no crisis in general or general crisis: only particular crises of particular sets of social relations and, perhaps, the totality of crises in a given conjuncture. This requires specific critical realist theoretical frameworks with corresponding substantive concepts rather than a general invocation of the virtues of critical realism in general vis-à-vis alternative meta-theoretical approaches.

Crisis is also an inherently *temporal concept* with spatial connotations. The concept implies that time unfolds *unevenly*, with continuities and discontinuities, transition points and ruptures, with scope for irreversible change rather than simple iteration, hence scope for path-shaping alongside path-dependence. "[T]ime moves faster in periods of crisis, and stagnates in times of regression" (Debray, 1973, p. 90). This indicates an important uncertainty in the crisis concept: is it a *single event* (and, if so, how would one identify its beginning and its conclusion), a *contingent series of events distributed in time and space* that are connected, if at all, because of earlier crisis responses that could have taken a different turn with different effects, or a series of events with an underlying tendential logic that therefore unfold as *a relatively predictable process* (if only from the perspective of informed observers)?[5]

A crisis is never a purely objective, extra-semiotic event or process that automatically produces a definite response or outcome. Crises do not generate their own resolution, even where trusted crisis-management routines exist; on the contrary, crises *of* given sets of social relations, especially where form-determined, often need relatively long, discursively, institutionally, technologically (in a

Foucauldian sense), and agentially mediated search processes before a new, relatively durable order based on new institutional and spatio-temporal fixes allows movement beyond such a crisis. Without subjective indeterminacy, there is no crisis – merely chaos, disaster, or catastrophe and, perhaps, fatalism or stoicism in the face of the inevitable. In this sense, crises are a potential moment of decisive intervention, where, rather than muddling through, resolute action may repair broken social relations, promote piecemeal adaptation, or produce radical transformation.

In the light of these remarks, it is useful to classify crises on two dimensions (cf. Chapter 1). The first concerns their aetiology. On the one hand, some crises appear "accidental," that is, are readily (if sometimes inappropriately) attributable to natural or "external" forces (for example, a volcanic eruption, tsunami, crop failure, invasion). When these have significant effects, they may be termed "*disasters*" (Quarantelli, 1988). This distinguishes them from crises rooted in crisis tendencies or antagonisms grounded in specific structural forms (for example, profit-oriented, market-mediated capital accumulation). In other words, they result from the inherent crisis potentials and crisis tendencies of a given social form and may have corresponding patterns of crisis management. This may require attention to systemic contradictions, structurally grounded antagonisms, and social conflicts without assuming every crisis derives there-from. This distinction does not imply that accidental crises lack causes – just that these are so varied, individually or in their interaction, that they are harder to recover in a systematic manner. This said, external, coincidental, incidental causes may trigger structural or systemic crises by working "through the intermediary of the internal, structural, essential causes that constitute the determining element in society's crises" (Debray, 1973, pp. 101–102). In this regard, they would not be accidental because they have a primary causal mechanism that is expressed in very diverse ways. This poses interesting empirical challenges to identify this mechanism amid a wide and disparate range of circumstantial factors.

The second dimension concerns the significance of crises in terms of their potential impact on the simple or expanded reproduction of the relevant "order" or "system," including its typical modes of reproduction, its conditions of existence, and its relative embedding in a wider social formation. Such reproduction in the social world depends on the reproduction of the social relations that support the relevant "order" or "system" – relations that can be contradictory, conflictual, or antagonistic (the capitalist mode of production is an obvious example). On the one hand, crises "*in*" are normal (expected). They occur within the parameters of a given natural environment and/or set of social arrangements. There are also well-developed routines for dealing with accidental crises, reducing subjective indeterminacy. These are reflected and systematized in a large practical literature on how to respond to accidents and emergencies, whether these be natural disasters, large-scale accidents, or reputational damage to companies, organizations, and governments (Faraz-mand, 2001). Indeed, repeated observation of "normal" disasters, accidents, and crises, leaning *about* and *from* recurrent crises may encourage monitoring, risk management, disaster education and preparedness, rehabilitation, and the sharing of best practice (Kirschenbaum, 2004; Pinkowski, 2008) such that subjective indeterminacy is reduced. This could mean that crisis management has become so routinized that a "crisis" no longer exists even when objective crisis symptoms are present because there is no subjective moment since the symptoms merely trigger a "here we go again" response. Instead the basic features of disturbed arrangements are routinely restored through internal adjustments and/or shift crisis effects into the future, elsewhere, or onto marginal and vulnerable groups. This is exemplified in alternating phases of unemployment and inflation in the post-war advanced capitalist economies and their treatment through countercyclical economic policies.[6]

Crises "*of*" are less common. They occur when there is a crisis of crisis management (that is, normal responses no longer work) and efforts to defer or displace crises encounter growing resistance. Crisis of crisis management is a term introduced by Claus Offe (1984) to denote potential second-order effects of established economic crisis-management routines, manifested in the displacement of crisis tendencies from the economic into extra-economic spheres (e.g., fiscal crisis, administrative crisis). Habermas advances similar ideas (1975) regarding rationality, legitimation and motivational crises. This displacement implies crisis tendencies remain incompressible but have different forms of appearance linked to different institutional and spatio-temporal fixes and to different crisis-management routines. This is a heuristically insightful notion and deserves broader use in dealing with crisis dynamics. For example, an additional factor in crises of crisis management is shifts in the balance of forces that may intensify crisis tendencies by weakening or resisting established modes of crisis management.

One reason why crises of crisis management occur is that crises result from the interaction of different crisis tendencies in complex conjunctures, so no crisis in all its complex overdetermination is ever identical with the previous actualizations of the same crisis tendency. Thus, previously successful crisis-management routines may no longer be effective in different circumstances. For, whatever the universal features of crisis tendencies in any given system (e.g., the capitalist mode of production), the particular features of any particular set of crisis tendencies associated with a particular type of crisis (e.g., overproduction, underconsumption, disproportions, tendency of the rate of profit to fall, credit crisis, fiscal crisis, sovereign debt crisis), no algorithm, even if based on learning in, about, and from crisis, would be cognitively adequate in the face of the *singularity* of the crisis, which, therefore, remains subjectively indeterminate.

Crises of crisis management are more disorienting than crises "in" specific structures or systems, indicating the breakdown of previous regularities and an inability to "go on managing crises in the old way." In certain regards, one might consider these as crises in/of crisis management. The prepositional ambivalence of "in/of" reflects the prospective as opposed to retroductive character of crisis construal, with the latter more suited to scientific analysis, the former more dependent on speculative bets about the future and, a *fortiori*, whether crisis-management routines are irretrievably broken or open to piecemeal reform. This reflects the open nature of social systems and the scope for human agency (as well as the non-linear interaction of non-agential causal mechanisms) to make a difference to the future. This opens space for strategic interventions to significantly redirect the course of events rather than "muddling through" until the crisis is eventually resolved or hoping the "business as usual" can be restored through emergency measures (see below). This poses a whole series of counterfactual epistemological problems about crisis construal and the asymmetry, emphasized in critical realism, between explanation and prediction. More generally, crises of crisis management can cause social stasis or regression, attempts to restore the old system by *force majeure*, fraud, or corruption; efforts at more radical social innovation for good or ill, leading in some cases to temporary states of emergency or more enduring exceptional regimes (for example, military dictatorship, fascism), or to efforts to break the power of such regimes.

This classification could be misleading if it were to one-sidedly highlight the objective aspect of crisis. A crisis is never a purely objective, extra-semiotic event or process that automatically produces a definite response or outcome. The objective moment of crisis becomes socially and historically relevant through the moment of subjective indeterminacy. This denotes the absence of an algorithm that unambiguously identifies the correct response to the crisis on the basis of its objective features, i.e., the absence of a self-evident way to restore simple or expanded reproduction or to move smoothly to another stable "order" or "system." The subjectively indeterminate response set includes non-decision or non-intervention – which, given the objective nature of crisis, also has system-relevant effects and is therefore a mode of decision and intervention. Ideas and imaginaries[7] shape the interpretation. A rigorous analysis of crises, crisis construals, and crisis management must be able to distinguish these alternatives or fall into a simplistic form of constructivism.

The importance of subjective indeterminacy also poses the question of the resonance of crisis construals and responses, on the one hand, and, on the other hand, their material adequacy to the objective character of the crisis, multiple crises, or interaction among different kinds of crisis. This is a source of massive practical as well as theoretical problems in analysing and managing crises. A crisis is also a moment for contestation and struggle to construe it and inform individual and collective responses. Interpretations can range from denial ("nothing to see here") through claims of a major break ("tipping" or "turning" points) to a more radical rupture ("revolutionary moment").

Symptomatology

The relationship between objective overdetermination and subjective indeterminacy poses the question of how to interpret or construe crisis symptoms.

This is the challenge of symptomatology, i.e., of establishing the contingently necessary relation between actual symptoms and underlying causal mechanisms. I relate this to disputes over the nature of crises, especially whether they are crises "in" a relevant order or crises "of" that order, which would require fundamental change. Another key feature of the subjective indeterminacy of crises concerns "what is to be done?" Here I distinguish between situations where established crisis-management routines can plausibly overcome challenges and restore order and those where a crisis in crisis management requires a rethinking of crisis-management approaches or more radical change in the relevant system, complex, or social configuration. This is related to the asymmetry between attempts to develop an adequate account of the objective overdetermination of a crisis (if such it be) and the challenge of reading what exists *in potentia* in a crisis conjuncture and could be realized through appropriate strategies. For crisis management and crisis reactions often involve speculative bets on an indeterminate future such that crisis construals and responses are performative – creating as yet unrealized possibilities or, conversely, aggravating contradictions, antagonisms, and conflicts. This has important implications for whether crises are managed to restore something resembling the *status quo ante* or seized as an opportunity "not to be wasted" for social transformation.

Discussion of crises often invokes the medical metaphor of crisis symptoms and the scope for decisive interventions into the course of an illness to cure it or, at least, minimize its effects. The key question is "what must the patient's mind-body (and her world) be like for these symptoms to appear?" Such retroductive questions are characteristic of critical realism. In the social world, the corresponding question is "what must the social (and natural) world be like for these crisis symptoms to appear?" This is an almost too-easy comparison. However, less attention is paid to how actors and observers can decipher the causes of a non-medical crisis based on its symptoms and, where relevant, decide on whether, when, and how to intervene. To address this question, I employ a cultural political economy (CPE) approach that is informed by critical realism and shaped by a concern with the emancipatory potentials (as well as with the negative and often repressive consequences) of crisis (for the general approach, see Sum and Jessop, 2013). CPE integrates research on sense- and meaning-making into the analysis of the basic features of capital accumulation, including its contradictions, crisis tendencies, and crisis dynamics. But its general approach to the differential articulation of semiosis and structuration can be applied far beyond the critique of political economy. The dual character of crisis means that struggles over crisis construal shape the nature and relative success, if any, of efforts at crisis management, depending on whether or not the construals are substantively adequate to dealing satisfactorily with complex crises (typically by providing suitable ways of reducing their complexity as a basis for decisive action rather than waiting for more information at the risk of things getting worse or, perhaps, waiting optimistically for "something to turn up") and, consequently, providing suitable responses for at least some key actors affected by the crisis. An important aspect of this process is the nature of learning in, through and from crisis, whether from previous crises, which might guide adequate responses to current crises, or during current crises in real time with possible lessons for future crisis events or processes.

This raises the question of how to distinguish among the *phenomenal forms* of crisis and underlying causes and causal connections, the *contingent trigger* events – often external – that reveal crisis, and the more internal, structural factors that make crisis *necessary*. The disjunction between objective and subjective aspects also has implications about the *longue durée,* secular crisis tendencies, and the immediacy of crisis "events". In particular, it suggests a tendency to focus on immediate symptoms rather than causes that have operated over longer-term time and/or more extensive socio-spatial horizons. These are often entangled and require correspondingly complex periodizations in terms of interwoven temporalities and/or complex socio-spatial analyses reflecting the substantive causal mechanisms at play. This also reveals the Janus-faced nature of crisis – that is, the possibility (and necessity) of interpreting their historically overdetermined aetiology for the purposes of diagnosis and evaluating current possibilities of intervention with a view to prognosis and potentially decisive intervention to change the future in terms of conjunctural possibilities.

While crises become visible through symptoms, these have no one-to-one relation to crisis tendencies and specific conjunctures. This explains the subjective indeterminacy that attends the objective overdetermination of crisis. Thus economic "symptomatology" challenges the interpretive capacity of social agents just as medical symptoms challenge the knowledge and skills of physicians and surgeons. In both cases, of course, there are competing schools and interpretive paradigms (on competing schools in medicine, see Jessop, 2015). This is why crises are moments of profound cognitive and strategic disorientation. They disturb inherited expectations and practices; challenge dominant paradigms and produce radical uncertainty; undermine faith in past lessons and ways of learning; open space for new lessons and ways of learning; and provide the context for struggles over the right way forward.

One way to address the challenge of symptomatology is to appropriate (and transform) the distinction, introduced by St Augustine in *De Doctrina Christiana* (Augustine of Hippo, 389 AD, 1995), between *signa data* and *signa naturalia*. He writes that "a sign is something which, offering itself to the senses, conveys something other to the intellect."[8] In this context, *signa data* largely comprise words, that is, the conventional linguistic relationship explored by Saussureans and social constructivists in terms of *signum* (sign) and *signans* (signifier). *Signa data* (sign-signifier relations) are used intentionally to convey a particular meaning.[9] In contrast, *signa naturalia* are natural, indexical signs that can be interpreted as symptoms of something beyond the *signum-signans* relation. Thus, St Augustine writes: "Natural signs are those which, apart from any intention or desire of using them as signs, do yet lead to the knowledge of something else, as, for example, smoke when it indicates fire" (389 AD, Book 2, Chapter 1). They are symptoms of an underlying reality, outward manifestations of some other fact, internal condition, quality, or overall state of affairs (cf. Favareau, 2006). Other examples of natural signs he gives are animal tracks and an angry or sorrowful countenance (insofar as it is an unintended expression of inner feelings). Elsewhere he interprets some events as natural signs of the impending end of the world (Dyson, 2005, p. 46). The same temptation is found, of course, in contemporary catastrophist readings of crisis symptoms. To St Augustine's examples we can add symptoms of disease in medical diagnosis (linked to the medical notion of crisis) and those of economic crisis (and the attendant problems of interpreting their causal link to economic crisis tendencies). Having mentioned these examples, St Augustine focuses on conventional signs and the hermeneutic problems of scriptural interpretation. This is where we must part company with him and return to *signa naturalia*.

St Augustine posits an objective relationship (or causal nexus) that connects an invisible entity to the visible signs that it produces. Nonetheless this relationship is not immediately transparent or self-evident but requires interpretation because there is no one-to-one relation between event and symptom. It is underdetermined. No algorithm can establish *the* cause (though expert systems with fuzzy logic may attempt to narrow down possible causes) and this poses a whole series of problems about causal interactions, infinite regress in time and infinite egress in space, and issues of attribution (including blame and responsibility). If we read symptoms as signifiers, then we can ask what is being signified and what is its referent? In these terms, crises can be seen as stratified. Adopting critical realist language, we can say they are generated by real mechanisms, they are actual events or processes, and they have evidential symptoms. This invites the question: what must the real world be like for this event to have occurred and/or these symptoms to exist? Thus, the challenge is to relate the empirical symptoms, actual crisis, and underlying mechanisms as a basis for possible decisive interventions. This is the field of "symptomatology." It is based on trial-and-error observation and construal that draws on past experience but may also require forgetting as a basis for "correct" intervention.

Scientific validity

Moving beyond these remarks and thinking about crisis construal more generally, construals can be assessed in three ways. The first is in terms of their *scientific validity*, i.e., their conformity with prevailing scientific procedures and rules of evaluation. The second is in terms of the *narrative plausibility* of a given construal in identifying and explaining the (symptoms of) crisis relative to the prevailing discourses in circulation among relevant social forces. The third is in terms of the *pragmatic correctness* of construals, i.e., their ability to read a conjuncture, discern potential futures, provide a plausible narrative, and guide action that transforms the conjuncture (Lecercle, 2006).

In a crude way, these distinctions correspond to the explanation of past events and processes leading to the present conjuncture, a narrative account that builds on a specific construal of the past to describe the present and draw conclusions for the future; and a speculative prediction coupled with prescriptions for action about what might be achievable when crisis is taken as an opportunity. These criteria involve different epistemological judgements. Scientific validity depends on specific protocols of investigation and acknowledges that conclusions may be fallible. Narrative plausibility depends on rules of argumentation oriented to persuasion rather than apodictic truth. In this context, while scientific argument has its rhetorical features, these should be subordinate to scientific analysis; conversely, the plausibility of crisis narratives may be enhanced by reference to facts, but these are selected to lend credibility to the overall narrative with the result that the factual elements are less rigorous and comprehensive and will often screen out inconvenient details.[10] Pragmatically correct construals are epistemologically different again because they involve what currently exists (if at all) only in potentia, may never be actualized, and cannot therefore be analysed in the same ways as the past and present. At stake here, then, is the distinction between the *explanation* of past and present events, processes or conjunctures and the *prediction* of the future of *open systems* where development depends on the strategic and tactical choices of diverse actors and social forces. Here prediction is related not just to the objective indeterminacy of the future but also – crucially – to the agents' differential capacity to shape their future through actions and inactions.

The validity of scientific explanation depends on scientific procedures and rules of evaluation according to specific scientific programmes and paradigms. At stake here is crisis considered as an external, objective phenomenon that is subject to first-order observation by third parties of its origins, course, and potential resolution. Crisis construals may address a more or less broad range of questions. This involves, among other issues, delimiting the origins of a crisis in space-time and its uneven spatio-temporal incidence and development; identifying rightly or wrongly purported causes (agential, structural, discursive, and technical) at different scales, over different time horizons, in different fields of social practice, and at different levels of social organization from nameless or named individuals through social networks, formal organizations, institutional arrangements, specific social forms, or even the dynamic of a global society; determining its scope and effects, assessing in broad terms whether it is a crisis "*in*" or "*of*" the relevant arrangements; reducing its complexities to identifiable causes that could be targeted to find solutions; charting alternative futures; and promoting specific lines of action for socially identified forces over differently constructed spatio-temporal horizon.

Scientific validity does not require a full explanation of an overdetermined event or process. Provided they have some basis in the objectively overdetermined nature of the crisis, different scientific readings may reduce its complexity by selectively identifying some aspects of its objective features as important, while others are marginalized, ignored, or remain invisible. The objective overdetermination and subjective indeterminacy create a space for *plausible* alternative *contested* readings of a crisis *within specific limits*. This does not imply that scientific accounts are always accurate. Scientific inquiries are distorted by scientists' own ideological assumptions. Thus, in addition to the cognitive limits related to the scientific legibility of a crisis for differently situated observers using different methods of investigation, construals may also reflect specific ideal and material interests of these observers as revealed through the critique of ideology and/or domination. This is, of course, a standing criticism of the attempts of orthodox economists to explain the recurrence of economic crises (see, for example, Matthew Watson's arguments in Chapter 4).

Narrative plausibility

Scientific explanations have their logic but may lack narrative plausibility for those directly or indirectly affected by "the crisis" or charged with responding to it. Narratives have a different structure and purpose from scientific explanations. They emplot selected past events and forces in terms of a temporal sequence with a beginning, middle, and end in the form of a story that embodies causal and moral lessons. The plausibility of narratives and other construals and their associated crisis-management solutions (including inaction) depends on their resonance with (or capacity to reinterpret and mobilize) key social forces. For example, neo-liberals narrated how trade union power and the welfare state undermined economic growth in the 1970s and called for more market, less state. The Tea Party and Occupy Wall Street movements offer different narratives about the recent crisis and reach radically different conclusions. Narratives play a key role in strategic action because they can simplify complex problems, identify simple solutions, connect to common sense and mobilize popular support. To be effective in the long run, however, they should correspond to the objective conditions and the real possibilities of action. Yet strategies based on "inorganic" narratives, however, can have adverse path-shaping effects, making recovery from a crisis harder or shifting its forms and consequences.

Although many plausible narratives may be advanced, their narrators will not be equally effective in conveying their messages and securing support for the proposed solutions. Powerful resonance does not mean these construals and solutions should be taken at face value. All narratives are selective, appropriate some arguments, and combine them in specific ways. So, we must also consider what goes unstated or silent, repressed or suppressed, in specific discourses. Interpretive power depends on the "web of interlocution" (Somers, 1994) in different fields and its discursive selectivities, the organization and operation of the mass media, the role of intellectuals in public life, and the structural biases and strategically selective operations of various public and private apparatuses of economic, political, and ideological domination. This is mainly an issue of political contestation, broadly interpreted.

An important distinction here concerns interpretive power and interpretive authority (cf. Heinrich and Jessop, 2014). The former refers to differences in the ability of social forces to identify and construe urgent social problems and translate these into policies, successful or not, intended to address maintain or transform the world. This is not so much a question of having the best scientific analyses and most persuasive arguments as it is one of having the capacities to act upon a given interpretation, which also involves access to key decision-making structures, the availability of appropriate governmental technologies, and the ability to mobilize sufficient support to make a difference in a particular conjuncture. Interpretive authority is narrower in scope but sometimes more significant in practice. It refers to the legal instance or authority with the legal right to interpret the law in a given juridico-political context and translate that interpretation into policy. This is especially important regarding the right to declare a state of emergency (e.g., military, political, or economic) and authorize exceptional crisis-management measures. More generally, this distinction shows the limits of a purely constructivist approach to crisis management that somehow forgets that institutions matter too.

Pragmatic correctness

Whereas scientific validity concerns the genealogy of the crisis as an event and/or continuing process, pragmatic correctness is judged in the light of future developments, including counterfactual analysis, and depends on social agents' ability to read present and future conjunctures in terms of what exists *in potentia* and how it might be realized. I now elaborate these remarks. Plausible narratives are typically an important moment of pragmatic correctness.

It is one thing to identify the *real* causes of *actual* crisis symptoms as a basis for crisis management intended to restore the status quo ante and/or to stabilize the situation. It is another to decide on possible courses of more radical transformative action in response to crisis. This requires moving beyond a strictly scientific programme to consider the emancipatory (or other) potentials present in a given crisis conjuncture, which involves thinking crisis in counterfactual terms. This brings us to the moment of pragmatic correctness. This aspect is mediated through language as well as through social practices and institutions beyond language. Indeed, since the development of print media at least, crisis construal is heavily mediatized, depending on specific forms of visualization and media representations, which nowadays typically vary across popular, serious, and specialist media. Pragmatic correctness depends on: (1) the strategically selective limits to action set by the objectively overdetermined form of a crisis conjuncture; (2) the interpretive and mobilizing power of crisis construals and strategic perspectives – notably its ready communicability to relevant audiences – which affects the capacities of strategic forces to win hegemony; and (3) the balance of forces associated with different construals or, at least, the ability of some forces to impose their preferred construals, crisis-management options, and exit solutions (Lercercle, 2006, pp. 40–41; Debray, 1973, pp. 106–107; and, on the analysis of the first limit, Patomäki, 2008).[11]

Considered in these terms, to paraphrase Gramsci, "there is a world of difference between conjunctural analyses [he writes of ideologies] that are arbitrary, rationalistic, and willed and those that are organic" (1971, pp. 376–377; cf. Gramsci, 1975, Q7§19, p. 868). The former analyses misconstrue the crisis – minimizing or exaggerating its scale and scope and its system-threatening qualities – and misidentify necessary or feasible solutions. An organic analysis is an at least minimally adequate analysis of the objective dimensions of the crisis and its manageability or transformability in terms of a possible attenuation of crisis symptoms, muddling through, displacement or deferral, etc., and in terms of the correlation of forces and the strategic horizons of action of the social forces whose ideal and material interests it represents. This raises the key issue of the (always limited and provisional) fit between imaginaries and real, or potentially realizable, sets of material interdependencies in the real world. Proposed crisis strategies and policies must be (or seen to be) effective within the spatio-temporal horizons of relevant social forces in a given social order.

In all cases, how a crisis is managed has path-shaping effects: responses affect the manner in which subsequent crises will develop. This corresponds to the idea that crises are moments where a decisive intervention can mark a turning point in the progress of a disease or other critical conjuncture. Furthermore, even scientifically invalid and/or conjuncturally incorrect construals, when translated into responses, will have constitutive or constructive effects. In many cases what is "correct" organically and chronologically (being first to resonate and/or to impose agreed reading) matters more in *selection* than "scientific truth".

Indeed, a "correct" reading creates its own "truth-effects" and may then be *retained* thanks to its capacity to shape reality. Getting consensus on an interpretation about which of different aspects of a crisis or, alternatively, which of several interlocking crises matters is to have framed the problem (variation). Nonetheless this consensus must be translated into coherent, coordinated policy approach and solutions that match objective dimensions of the crisis (selection). Effective policies adapt crisis-management routines and/or discover new routines through trial-and-error experimentation and can be consolidated as the basis of new forms of governance, meta-governance, and institutionalized compromise (retention). Only crisis construals that grasp key emergent extra-semiotic features of the social world as well as mind-independent features of the natural world are likely to be *selected* and *retained*. Effective construals therefore also have constructive force and produce changes in the extra-semiotic features of the world and in related (always) tendential real mechanisms and social logics.

These diverse complexities mean that, those affected by crisis typically disagree both on their objective and subjective aspects because of their different entry points, standpoints, and capacities to read the crisis. The system-specific and conjunctural aspects of crises have many spatio-temporal complexities and affect social forces in quite varied ways. The lived experience of crisis is necessarily partial, limited to particular social segments of time-space. So, it is hard to read crises. Indeed, if spatiotemporal boundaries are uncertain, if causes and effects are contested, can we speak of THE CRISIS? As Gramsci noted, writing on the Great Depression:

> Whoever wants to give one sole definition of these events, or what is the same thing, find a single cause or origin, must be rebutted. We are addressing a process that shows itself in many ways, and in which causes and effects become intertwined and mutually entangled. To simplify means to misrepresent and falsify. … When did the crisis begin? This question is bound up with the first since we are dealing with a process and not an event … It is hard in real terms to separate the economic crisis from the political and ideological ones, etc.
>
> (1995, p. 219; cf. Gramsci, 1975, Q15, §5;)[12]

Resolving a crisis into one essential crisis, let alone one with one main cause, involves at best *strategic essentialism*[13] rather than rigorous scientific practice. This said, simplifications may be necessary to begin to respond to a crisis when its character is as yet unclear, but its immediate effects are serious and wide-ranging. Actors do not always have the luxury of postponing action until the nature of the crisis becomes evident – even refusing to act could alter its dynamic as process (as opposed to event) and a judicious "wait-and-see" approach, considered or nonchalant, may well enable others to fill a strategic, political, or policy void with path-shaping consequences. Thus, simplifications may be correct in the circumstances – they may help to create suitable conditions to learn lessons and take effective action. This is why a critical realist, CPE approach needs to consider how different actors or social forces learn in, about, and from crisis – especially as the symptoms and causes of crisis (not the CRISIS) will affect them differently in space-time as well as in relation to identities, interests, and values.

Often, wider ideational and institutional innovation going beyond the economy narrowly conceived is needed, promoted and supported by political, intellectual and moral leadership. Indeed, as Milton Friedman put it hyperbolically but tellingly: "[o]nly a crisis produces real change. When that crisis occurs, the actions that are taken depend on the ideas that are lying around" (1965, p. 32). It follows that preparing the ground for crisis-induced strategic interventions helps to shape the nature and outcome of crisis management and crisis responses. Inadequate preparation (for whatever cause) makes it harder to influence struggles over crisis construal and crisis management, even if the eventual crisis construal is "organic". Magnus Ryner's chapter in this volume illustrates the problems that arise when crisis construals are more fantasmagoric than organic; and Angela Wigger demonstrates this in her chapter regarding EU industrial policy strategies, where previous lessons on competitiveness strategy went unheeded.

The pedagogy of crisis

Another important aspect of crisiology is the pedagogy of crises, i.e., learning in and from crises and drawing lessons for future crises. This provides the basis for a fourfold distinction between past lessons being thrown into crisis, learning in crisis, learning about crisis, and learning from crisis (see Ji, 2006; Sum and Jessop, 2013; Jessop, 2015; and Table 3.1). In brief, the first term indicates the disorienting effects of crisis on expectations and routines, rooted in past lessons. The others merit more extended but still necessarily limited discussion. This implies crises are moments for critical reflexion that lead to unlearning past lessons together with learning *in, about* and *from* crisis and, in this context, for theoretical, policy, and practical innovation. These processes affect different actors or social forces in different ways and are often deeply contested and different actors and social forces may traverse these analytical distinct (but potentially overlapping) stages in different ways. This occurs in part because the crisis affects them differently in space-time as well as in relation to their different identities, interests, and values.

Learning can be instrumental (including successful muddling through), critical (or counter-critical), or emancipatory. Its goals and potentially transformative effects matter especially for policy and strategic learning in the face of crises (including crises of crisis management). Just as medical diagnosis requires knowledge about the relation between symptoms and underlying causes based on careful observation, trial-and-error experimentation, and successful retroduction (i.e., asking what the world must be like for "x" to happen), so does the correct diagnosis of crisis symptoms in the social world and their translation into effective "treatment" of the crisis or, at least, useful lessons for future attempts at crisis management. For, while crises become visible through their symptoms, the latter have no one-to-one relation to crisis tendencies and specific conjunctures. Thus, both social and medical crises, the relation between symptom and generative mechanisms is grounded in a causal nexus

Table 3.1 The pedagogy of crisis

Learning *into* crisis	Crisis throws past lessons into confusion and may disrupt established modes of learning, making it harder to learn, and leading to false, "fantastic", simplistic, partial, incoherent, or contradictory lessons
Learning *in* crisis	Occurs through actors' direct experience of the *phenomenal* forms of crisis. This will vary across persons, groups, organizations, *or*
	For "outsiders", occurs through real time observation of *phenomenal* forms of crisis – often mediated through diverse forms of representation
Learning *about* crisis	Occurs when actors learn about deeper causes and dynamics (often discovered through efforts at crisis management) *or*
	Occurs when "outsiders" focus on real causes, dynamics, effects and observe actors' trial-and-error attempts to solve or shape crisis
Learning *from* crisis	Learning from a directly experienced crisis after "it" ends
	Learning from a crisis that one has observed in real time after "it" ends
	Both may re-enter learning process through "historicity"

Source: Based on arguments in this chapter

that connects an invisible entity to the visible signs it produces. This explains the subjective indeterminacy that attends the objective overdetermination of the crisis.

The following remarks distinguish for analytical purposes between those affected directly or indirectly by the crisis as it unfolds and those who are not so affected, either because they are studying *past* crises to draw lessons for the present or future and/or because they are motivated by disinterested curiosity in the nature of past or present crises (for example, to compare and contrast crisis dynamics in different contexts for scientific purposes in order to understand and explain crisis tendencies as neutral observers).

Learning in crisis occurs in the immediacy of crisis, considered as a moment of profound disorientation, and is oriented to the phenomenal forms of crisis. For those directly affected, it occurs via direct experience (*Erlebnis*) of its *phenomenal* forms. Lived experience will vary across persons, groups, organizations. Thus, the first phases of a crisis generally prompt massive *variation* in construals. Many early accounts disappear in the cacophony of competing interpretations or lack meaningful connections to the salient phenomenal forms of the crisis. This holds for religious readings of the crisis as signs of divine retribution for moral degeneration, for example, and for the equally fanciful claim that the terminal crisis of capitalism had arrived. Significant shifts can also occur in hegemonic imaginaries. Alan Greenspan, former Chair of the US Federal Reserve, for example, famously conceded that the North Atlantic Financial Crisis had led him to identify "flaws" in the operating ideology that he had used to steer the US economy: namely, the efficient market hypothesis (Greenspan, 2008). For those not directly affected, learning in crisis occurs through real time observation of the *phenomenal* forms of crisis. This is often mediated through diverse forms of representation (serious and tabloid journalism, statistics, charts, econometric models, reports, etc.) and can be highly mediatized. In neither case does such learning dig beneath surface phenomena to deeper causes, crisis tendencies, etc.

Learning in crisis occurs in the immediacy of crisis, considered as a moment of profound disorientation, and is oriented to the phenomenal forms of crisis. For those directly affected, it occurs via direct experience of its *phenomenal* forms. Lived experience varies across persons, groups, organizations. How a person experiences and understands his/her world(s) as real and meaningful depends on their subject positions and standpoint. Organizations also have specific modes of calculation that reflect their specific interests. For those not directly affected by a current crisis, *learning in crisis* occurs through real time *observation* of the relevant phenomenal forms. This is often mediated through diverse forms of representation (serious and tabloid journalism, statistics, charts, econometric models, reports, etc.) and can be highly mediatized (Tetlock, 2007 MacKenzie, 2009; Engelen et al., 2011; Pahl, 2011; on mediatization, Hajer, 2011). Specific forms of visualization and media representations typically vary across popular, serious, and specialist media. In no case, by definitional fiat, does learning in crisis dig below surface phenomena to deeper causes, crisis tendencies, and so on.

Learning about crisis occurs with lags in real time as a crisis unfolds, often in unexpected ways, and as the routine crisis-management measures resorted to by actors prove (or seem to be) inadequate or inappropriate. Common sense and/or instituted social imaginaries typically ignore key features of the actually existing natural and social world. In capitalist economies, for example, these features include: contradictions, dilemmas, crisis tendencies and counter-tendencies; important extra-economic conditions of existence and effects of economic practices and institutions; and the uneven links across different scales of economic action and their embedding in broader spatio-temporal frameworks. These features operate even when they are unacknowledged by first-order social agents (and/or are denied by observers) and, because of their interaction in specific contexts and conjunctures, may generate crisis tendencies or otherwise disorient agents and observers, prompting the occasion for learning more about the facticity of the natural and social worlds. For those directly affected, this occurs when attention turns from phenomenal forms to deeper causes and dynamics and their bearing on crisis management. Trial-and-error experimentation through efforts at crisis management is a key element of learning about the nature of the crisis. In financial crises, for example, this is possible for those directly tasked with crisis management (e. g., central bankers, international financial institutions, key figures in the political executive, and regulators) and/or those able to guide the official approach to crisis management, whether by reinforcing hegemonic or dominant paradigms or reviving, reinventing, or relaying plausible alternatives. These lessons are rarely purely technical or instrumental but are also shaped by the changing political conjuncture (broadly defined) in which efforts to manage the crisis occur (cf. Poulantzas, 1979; for an application of Poulantzas to the politics of austerity, Seymour, 2014).

For those without the power to translate construals directly into policy, key mediating roles in the process of *learning about crisis* are played by financial, economic, and political journalists alongside such "usual suspects" as research institutes, think tanks, vested economic interests, lobbies, and academics. Not all actors or observers move to this stage because it involves not only interpretive power but also the capacity to translate construals into authoritative action. An interesting example of this is Hyman Minsky's analysis of the role of speculative and Ponzi finance in financial crises, leading him to ask whether "it" can happen again (Minsky, 1982). Without the authority to translate his observations into policy, the role of Ponzi finance in particular had to be relearnt in the North Atlantic Financial Crisis, when policy-makers and commentators rediscovered the "Minsky moment" (for further discussion, see Rasmus, 2010). Learning about crisis may also occur among those who seek to resist, subvert or redirect official responses and/or to develop alternative approaches that do not rely on access to the "official" levers of power, including the ability to resort to "exceptional" measures. In either case, such learning is typically highly selective, partial, and provisional as well as mediated and mediatized. Finally, for retrospective learning *about* crisis, whether interested or disinterested, lessons may well draw on contemporary accounts.

The "unmarked" and "unobserved" take their revenge on those who ignore them, and this leads to crisis or other system failures. This is where learning *about* crisis and its roots in the unacknowledged matter. For in this analytically distinct (but not necessarily sequentially distinct) phase of crisis construal and management, these processes are more experimental as actors seek to make sense of the crisis not merely at the phenomenal level but also in terms of underlying mechanisms and crisis dynamics. For those directly affected, this occurs when attention turns from phenomenal forms to deeper causes and dynamics and their bearing on crisis management. For "outside" observers, it occurs when they focus on real causes, dynamics, effects and monitor actors' trial-and-error attempts to solve crisis and/or how other "outsiders" seek to shape its course, costs, outcome. Not all actors or observers can or do move to this stage and it is typically highly selective, partial, and provisional as well as mediated and mediatized.

Learning from crisis occurs later, as crisis-management efforts succeed, or recovery takes place for other reasons, and actors reflect on the crisis and its import for future crises and crisis management. Whether one has directly experienced the crisis or "merely" observed it in real time, learning from crisis occurs after "it" ends. Learning from a crisis can also occur through institutionalized inquiries, based on reports from those who experienced it, observed it, and tried to describe, interpret, and explain it. This is an important mechanism of policy learning for future crisis prevention and crisis management. In contrast to learning in and about crisis, learning from crises may happen much later based on lessons drawn from other times and/or places. Such studies may be limited to iconic, high profile, or benchmark crises or aim to be more comprehensive. Relevant comparators and appropriate lessons are often disputed, as demonstrated by the continuing debate on the 1930s Great Depression, the genealogy and impact of which is regularly contested, revisited, and revised because of the changing interests at stake.

Learning from crisis may shape policies and individual and collective strategies in two ways. First, lessons learnt by those directly affected can be conveyed in more or less codified terms to others who experience similar crises. This may lead to fast policy and/or strategy transfer, whether appropriate or not. Because learning and normal politics both "take time", crises create pressure to act based on unreliable information, narrow or limited consultation and participation. Calls for quick action lead to shorter policy development cycles, fast-tracking decision-making, rapid programme rollout, continuing policy experiments, institutional and policy Darwinism, constant revision of guidelines, and so on. An emphasis on speed affects the choice of policies, initial policy targets, sites where policy is implemented, and the criteria adopted for success. It also discourages proper evaluation of a policy's impact over various spatio-temporal horizons, including delayed and/or unintended consequences and feedback effects.

Second, lessons drawn by "outside" observers may be conveyed to those directly affected as more or less codified guidance for managing future crises. However, there is many a slip between the discursive resonance of old, reworked, or new imaginaries in a given conjuncture and their translation into adequate policies, effective crisis-management routines, durable new social arrangements, and institutionalized compromises to support renewed accumulation. Indeed, codification of knowledge can backfire where it is followed too rigidly without regard to the tacit knowledge and improvisation that also shaped crisis management. The one-size-fits-all lessons of bodies such as the IMF illustrate this and can be contrasted with the very different lessons drawn from Iceland's handling of its disastrous liquidity and solvency crises – and, indeed, with the recent admission by the IMF that it had underestimated the impact of austerity on debt-default-deflation dynamics. Very different lessons can be drawn from how Iceland handled its financial crises against IMF advice (Sigfússon, 2012); and the IMF has admitted that it had underestimated austerity's impact on debt-default-deflation dynamics (Blanchard and Leigh, 2013).

Lessons from the past can be invoked in all three types of learning. Sometimes this involves seeking good historical parallels to guide crisis responses in real time – with the risk of drawing false analogies and/or missing novel features. Even clear parallels may not alert policy-makers to the risks involved in following failed policies. Thus Boyer (this volume) notes that the Baltic States repeated the errors that contributed to the 1997 East Asian crises by incurring large debts in foreign currency. Lessons from the past can also be deliberately invoked to steer crisis construal toward one rather than another set of crisis measures (on historical parallels, see Samman, 2013).

Reflections on learning in, about, and from crises has spawned a huge literature on crisis management, intervention, and communication. But this adopts a mainly instrumental position with limited implications for developing the critique of political economy. On this last point, it is worth recalling Karl Deutsch's aphorism that power is the ability not to have to learn from one's mistakes (1963, p. 111). In other words, elites may try to impose the costs of their mistakes onto others as well as to shape learning processes and, in particular to control ex post inquiries into crises and lessons drawn therefrom. For, given asymmetrical power relations, crises may also lead to the re-assertion of old ideas and values, policy paradigms, and routines (traditionalism, reaction, restoration). This remark highlights structural and strategic asymmetries that might influence both policy and political learning. Learning may not be translated into new policies: "identifying lessons" is not the same as "acting on them" and many factors can interfere here. Agents may lack the capacity (technologies, suitable leverage points, or access to power) to act on lessons learnt; the powerful may block action where they believe it might hurt their interests. There are many other causes of learning failure. These include drawing simplistic conclusions, fantasy lessons, falsely generalized lessons, turbulent environments that quickly render lessons irrelevant, rhetorical learning, limits on learning due to prior political or policy commitments, politicized learning that reflects power relations, and ideological or social barriers that block active learning. In addition, as noted above, codified lessons miss tacit, implicit lessons/practices.

Conclusions

Crises are potentially path-shaping moments that provoke responses that are mediated through semiotic-cum-material processes of variation, selection, and retention. A critical realist approach to crises that takes seriously their duality – objectively overdetermined, subjectively indeterminate – must combine structural and semiotic analyses. It would examine: (1) how crises emerge when established patterns of dealing with structural contradictions, their crisis tendencies, and strategic dilemmas no longer work as expected and, indeed, when continued reliance thereon may even aggravate matters; (2) how contestation over the meaning of the crisis shapes responses through processes of variation, selection, and retention that are mediated through a changing mix of semiotic and extra-semiotic mechanisms. This approach opens space for studying the variation, selection, and retention of crisis construals and policy lessons as crises develop. Crisis construals establish "truth effects," i.e., the hegemonic or dominant meanings of crisis result from power relations. They are not the outcome of a co-operative language game with fixed rules but of a political struggle with variable rules and contested stakes (Lercercle, 2006, p. 98). In this sense, construals are not simple *linguistic (re-)descriptions* of a conjuncture but, when backed by powerful social forces, involve *strategic interventions* into that conjuncture.

The mechanisms of variation, selection, and retention that privilege some crisis construals over others and some crisis lessons over others produce particular "modes of crisis management" that are not dictated solely by the objective overdetermination of the crisis nor by "arbitrary, rationalistic, and willed" construals of this, that, or another social force. At stake here is the production of "truth effects" that are not so much scientifically valid as pragmatically correct in specific conjunctures. In other words, these construals offer a sound objective analysis in terms of the correlation of forces as well as underlying causes and can gauge and guide the strategic horizons of action, organizing effective action and disorganizing opposition. In general, then, learning in, about, and from crises is relevant to the critique of political economy, to strategic and policy learning on how to prevent and/or manage crises, and to political learning.

Notes

1 On the important distinction between crises as events or processes, see Forgues and Roux-Dufort (1998).
2 In foreign and military affairs, "false flag" operations are attempts to manufacture crises and provide a *casus belli*. Analogous activities occur in other fields.

3 In references to Gramsci, Q designates the Quaderno (notebook) and § denotes the paragraph.
4 Rasmus (2010) offers an excellent criticism of such empiricist approaches.
5 For a less complex, but still important (and widely-cited), discussion of crisis as event vs crisis as process, see Forgues and Roux-Dufort 1998.
6 In practice, however, counter-cyclical policies were often badly executed, proved /pro-cyclical, and, over time, led to stagflation.
7 Imaginary refers here to sets of cultural elements common to a given social group (or groups) that shape "lived experience" and help to reproduce social relations.
8 "*Signum ... est res praeter speciem quam ingerit sensibus, aliud aliquid ex se faciens in cogitationem venire*" (cited Favareau, 2006, p. 4)
9 There is some debate about the appropriate translation of signa data regarding whether the emphasis is on the *intention* behind the use of the sign or its conventional linguistic character (see Jackson, 1968, pp. 13–15). For present purposes, this is irrelevant because my focus is on signa naturalia, where intention is absent.
10 This is analogous to the distinction drawn by Wallis and Brian Dollery (1999, p. 5) between scientific and policy paradigms: "In essence, policy advisers differentiate policy paradigms from theoretical paradigms by screening out the ambiguities and blurring the fine distinctions characteristic of theoretical paradigms" (1999, p. 5).
11 "The study of possible futures must be grounded on the analysis of causally efficacious geo-historical layers of reality – agency, structures and mechanisms" (Patomäki, 2008, p. xiii).
12 The whole note is interesting because it distinguishes empirical features, the crisis as event and process, and its underlying causes considered as crisis-tendencies and counter-tendencies.
13 This notion was introduced by Gayatri Chakravorty Spivak (1987), who uses it to describe the discursive construction of an "essential unity" among heterogeneous groups as a basis for strategic political action in relation to nationalities, ethnic groups, gender politics and other movements. It can be generalized to other forms of though and action oriented to strategic interventions.

References

Augustine of Hippo (389 AD) (1995) *De doctrina christiana*. Oxford: Oxford University Press.

Blanchard, O. and Leigh, D. (2013) *Growth forecast errors and fiscal multipliers*. IMF Working Paper WP 13/1. Washington, DC: International Monetary Fund.

Debray, R. (1973) *Prison writings*. London: Allen Lane.

Deutsch, K.W. (1963) *The nerves of government. Models of political communication and control*. New York: Free Press.

Dyson, R.W. (2005) *St Augustine of Hippo. The christian transformation of political philosophy*. London: Continuum.

Engelen, E., Ertürk, I., Froud, J., Johal, S., Leaver, A., Moran, M., Nilsson, A. and Williams, K. (2011) *After the great complacence: Financial crisis and the politics of reform*. Oxford: Oxford University Press.

Farazmand, A. (2001) *Handbook of crisis and emergency management*. New York: Marcel Deker.

Favareau, D. (2006). 'The evolutionary history of biosemiotics', in Barbieri, M. (ed.), *Introduction to biosemiotics: The new biological synthesis*, Berlin: Springer, pp. 1–67.

Festl, M.G., Grosser, F., and Thomä, D. (eds) (2018). *Über Krise und Kritik. Crise et critique. Studia Philosophica*, Vol.74, Basel: Schwabe.

Forgues, B. and Roux-Dufort, C. (1998) 'Crises: Events or processes?' Paper presented at Hazards and Sustainability Conference, Durham, UK, 26-27 May.

Friedman, M. (1965) *Capitalism and freedom.* Chicago, IL: University of Chicago Press.

Gramsci, A. (1971). *Selections from the prison notebooks.* London: Lawrence and Wishart.

Gramsci, A. (1975) *Quaderni del carcere.* Turin: Einaudi.

Gramsci, A. (1995) *Further selections from the prison notebooks.* London: Lawrence and Wishart.

Greenspan, A. (2008) *Evidence given on 23 October 2008.* Washington, DC: House Committee on Oversight and Government Reform.

Habermas, J. (1975) *Legitimation crisis.* London: Hutchinson.

Hajer, M.A. (2011) *Authoritative governance: Policy making in the age of mediatization.* Oxford: Oxford University Press.

Heinrich, M. and Jessop, B. (2014). 'The crisis in the EU from a cultural political economy perspective: Crisis interpretations and their translation into policy', in Jessop, B., Young, B., and Scherrer, C. (eds), *Cultures of finance and crisis dynamics,* London: Routledge, pp. 278–293.

Hindrichs, G. (2015) 'Reflexionsverhältnisse der Krise', in Festl, M.G., Grosser, F., and Thomä, D. (eds), *Über Krise und Kritik. Crise et critique. Studia Philosophica,* Vol. 74, Basel: Schwabe, pp.22–38.

Jackson, B.D. (1968). 'The theory of signs in St. Augustine's *De doctrina christiana'. Revue des études augustiniennes* 15(1–2), pp. 9–49.

Jessop, B. (2015). 'The symptomatology of crises: Reading crises and learning from them. Some critical realist reflections'. *Journal of Critical Realism* 14(3), pp. 238–271.

Ji, J.H. (2006) Learning from crisis: Political economy, spatio-temporality, and crisis management in South Korea, 1961-2002. PhD Thesis, Lancaster University.

Keucheyan, R. and Durand, C. (2015). 'Bureaucratic caesarism: A Gramscian outlook on the crisis of Europe'. *Historical Materialism* 23(2), pp. 23–51.

Kirschenbaum, A. (2004) *Chaos organization and disaster management.* New York: Marcel Dekker.

Koselleck, R. (1988). *Critique and crisis: Enlightenment and the pathogenesis of modern society.* Cambridge, MA: MIT Press.

Lercercle, J.J. (2006) *A Marxist philosophy of language.* Leiden/Boston: Brill.

MacKenzie, D.J. (2009) *Material markets: How economic agents are constructed.* Oxford: Oxford University Press.

Minsky, H.P. (1982) *Can "it" happen again? Essays on instability and finance.* New York: M.E. Sharpe.

Mirowksi, P. (2013). *Never let a serious crisis go to waste. How neoliberalism survived the financial meltdown.* London: Verso.

Morin, E. (1993 [1976])). 'For a crisiology'. *Organization and Environment* 7(1), pp. 5–22.

Offe, C. (1984) *Contradictions of the welfare state.* London: Hutchinson.

Pahl, H. (2011). "Die Wirtschaftswissenschaften in der Krise: Vom massenmedialen Diskurs zu einer Wissenssoziologie der Wirtschaftswissenschaften'. *Swiss Journal of Sociology* 37(2), pp. 259–281.

Patomäki, H. (2008) *The political economy of global security: War, future crises and changes in global governance.* London: Routledge.

Pinkowski, J. (ed.) (2008) *Disaster management.* New York: CRC Press.

Poulantzas, N. (1979). 'The political crisis and the crisis of the state', in Freiburg, J.W. (ed.), *Critical Sociology: European Perspectives,* New York: Halsted, pp. 373–393.

Quarantelli, L (1988). 'Disaster crisis management: A summary of research findings'. *Journal of Management Studies* 25(4), pp. 373–385.

Rasmus, J. (2010) *Epic recession*. London: Pluto.

Roitman, J. (2014) *Anti-crisis*. Durham, NC: Duke University Press.

Samman, A. (2013) Re-imagining the crises of global capital. PhD Thesis, Birmingham University, UK.

Sayer, A. (1992). *Method in social science. A realist approach*. 2nd edition. London: Routledge.

Seymour, R. (2014). *Against austerity: How we can fix the crisis They Made*. London: Pluto.

Sigfússon, S. (2012) We reacted immediately to symptoms of crisis (Interview with Iceland's Economy Minister). *Der Spiegel*, 26 November. http://www.spiegel.de/international/europe/icelandic-economy-minister-explains-reaction-to-finance-crisis-a-869351.html, accessed 31 January 2013.

Somers, M. (1994). 'The narrative constitution of identity: A relational and network approach'. *Theory and Society* 23(5), pp. 605–649.

Spivak, G.C. (1987). *In other worlds: Essays in cultural politics*. London: Routledge.

Sum, N.L. and Jessop, B. (2013) *Towards a cultural political economy: Putting culture in its place in political economy*. Cheltenham: Edward Elgar.

Tetlock, P.C. (2007). 'Giving content to investor sentiment: The role of media in the stock market'. *Journal of Finance* 60(3), pp. 1139–1168.

Thomä, D., Festl, M.G. and Grosser, F. (2015) 'Einstimmung: Vier Etappen der Geschichte von Kritik und Krise', in Festl, M.G., Grosser, F., and Thomä, D. (eds), *Über Krise und Kritik. Crise et critique. Studia Philosophica*, Vol. 74, Basel: Schwabe, pp. 11–18.

Wallis, J.L. and Dollery, B.E. (1999) *Market failure, government failure, leadership and public policy*. London: Macmillan.

Part II

Resilience in and through crises

4 The 2008 crisis and the resilience of the neo-liberal order

Andrew Gamble

The 2008 crisis stands out as one of the greatest crises of the capitalist era, an era that has now lasted in its modern form for more than 350 years. Although there were important antecedents, this era is roughly as old as the Bank of England, which received its charter in 1694. It has been the most dynamic and productive form of economy the world has known. This owes much to the conflict and cooperation among states, markets and households, both within bounded national communities and between them. Capitalism was an international system from the beginning, characterized by its remorseless drive to privatize gains and socialize losses, as well as by its tendency to combine ever greater economic connectedness and interdependence with political fragmentation, leading to continual competition and conflict.

Capitalism has always been plagued by two major risks to its continued order and prosperity; wars and financial crises. Both have punctuated the progress of capitalist society. A third major risk is now looming on the horizon: environmental catastrophe (Gough, 2011). Financial crises and their wider economic and political consequences are the focus below. It is a matter of observation and historical record that capitalism has suffered from periodic crises, which always take a financial form, although their consequences often go far beyond finance. There is no need to resort to reductionist or mechanistic or cyclical explanations of such crises. The term crisis as it has been used in the capitalist era has had diverse meanings, but two have been particularly prominent. As Karim Knio and Bob Jessop argue in Chapters 1 and 2, a key distinction is between crisis as event and crisis as process. The first is the idea of crisis as a moment of danger, suspense, or emergency. When a situation is critical, urgent action is required to defuse it and resolve the problem. This usage freely employs analogies drawn from medicine and drama. The second meaning is crisis as an impasse, which is structural and deep-seated, leading to inertia, deadlocks or catastrophic equilibria. Politics becomes, in Weber's phrase, 'boring of hard boards' (Weber, 1946, p. 128). Sometimes the endless war of position is interrupted by sudden shocks and emergencies, like flashes of fire at the top of volcanoes that do not lead to a major eruption. Such crises can last decades before they are fully resolved.

In the last century, capitalism has experienced three major economic and financial crises. The first was the depression of the 1930s, signalled by the crash of 1929 and the collapse of the gold standard in 1931. The second was the ending of the Bretton Woods system in 1971 and the lengthy period of stagflation and reconstruction that followed. The third is the present period, signalled by the financial crash of 2008 and marked by a new form of stagnation, leading to the notion of secular stagnation (Cowen, 2011; Summers, 2014) rather than the deflation that characterized the 1930s depression or the stagflation that characterized the crisis in the late 1960s and 1970s. There is broad agreement that these are the three major crises episodes of the last 100 years, but some disagreement as to whether the 1970s crisis is on the same level as the other two. But one can also to argue, as Wolfgang Streeck does, that the 2008 crash is only the latest in a long sequence of political and economic disorders that began with the end of post-war prosperity in the mid-1970s (Streeck, 2016).

The way these three crises have been framed, the political responses to them, and the consequent outcomes have been very different. Nonetheless, they do have some common features. All involved a crisis in how the international market order is governed; all involved a crisis over growth; and all involved a fiscal crisis. In the first two cases, a prolonged period of economic, social and political restructuring eventually issued in a new era of general prosperity and increased integration in the circuits of North Atlantic capitalism. The first period, *les trente glorieuses*, associated with the Keynesian welfare national state (KWNS), was more substantial in many ways than the second, the globalization era, associated in parts of the North Atlantic region with a Hayekian market state. Its success in developing a new governance formula was real, and that must be recognized to understand its current resilience. Nothing is guaranteed by the past and, although there is clearly the potential for a new era of prosperity and progress, the obstacles to achieving it are large. The impasse of the 1930s was only broken by a world war. The international market order had been destroyed, the world had split into rival currency and trading blocs that became military blocs covetous of territory and resources.

In most modern accounts of capitalism, the 1930s produced a series of events that should never be allowed to happen again. The lessons learnt from the 1930s would inoculate capitalism against a repeat. The reconstruction of the international market order after 1945 would guarantee this in advanced capitalist societies (Kindleberger, 1987). It was aided by the exceptional dominance of one state, the United States, which used its power to establish a new system of global governance and international institutions, at the same time isolating its only significant rival – the USSR – through military alliances. The initial impulse to punish the defeated powers rapidly gave way to a determined effort to reconstruct them. Western Europe and Japan were the beneficiaries and the western world as a whole (including its post-colonial southern outposts in Australia and New Zealand) entered an era of rapid economic growth, full employment, low inflation, mixed economies, welfare states, and expanded democracies. This was John Ruggie's 'embedded liberalism' (Ruggie, 1998) and Seymour Martin Lipset's 'good society in operation' (Lipset, 1960). It certainly appeared to be a reformed capitalism, in which national states had considerable autonomy in choosing levels of spending, redistribution and welfare (Shonfield, 1966). Many followed a form of Keynesianism that allowed discretionary economic management, a much larger public sector, and a state with greater capacity and more policy levers at its disposal.

The success of the KWNS appeared to disprove the argument, very common in the 1930s, that capitalism and democracy were incompatible. The rise of socialist movements and their potential to command electoral majorities threatened to deprive owners of their property and, to defend themselves, they were prepared to finance authoritarian movements to stop these threats. This was a class struggle with high stakes. The brief flowering of democracies in the 1920s was quickly followed by their rapid contraction or overthrow in the 1930s (and sometimes earlier as in the case of Italian fascism). But, in the 1950s and 1960s, more durable democracies were created, based on a compromise between capital and labour and their respective catch-all parties, which although often uneasy, generally held. Moreover, after the collapse of the Soviet Union in the 1990s, there the number of democracies increased again so that, by 2000, there were more states judged to be democracies than ever before.

All was not well, however, because the new wave of democratization was much less securely based than the earlier one, partly because it was not underpinned by Keynesian welfare national states, which had come under sustained attack during the various crises of the 1970s. The international monetary system broke down amidst accelerating inflation, fiscal crisis, and the first generalized recession since 1945. This led to heightened distributional conflict and fears about excess spending, overloaded government, and trade union militancy. Once again, many could be found debating whether democracy and capitalism were in fact compatible.

The political and economic crisis of the 1970s was eventually resolved to the advantage of capital, thanks to the framing of the crisis in particular ways by the new right and the triumph of right wing coalitions, initially in the US and the UK, and then more broadly. Led by the US, new rules for the governance of the international market order were gradually elaborated. Inflation was prioritized over unemployment, taxes were lowered, spending was cut, the economy was restructured away from manufacturing towards services, and trade union power was severely weakened. Neo-liberal doctrines promoted a new common-sense, giving priority to markets and market solutions, although it was noticeable how active (and extended) states remained. This conforms to the neoliberal principle of the free market and the strong state (Gamble, 1988).

The 1970s and 1980s were periods of heightened class and distributional conflict in western capitalist societies that substantially weakened the post-war political settlement between capital and labour on which post-war prosperity and social peace had been based along with the boost to productivity and profits that came from a broad transition to Fordist mass production and mass consumption. For a time, it looked as though the attempt to solve the impasse of the 1970s by new right policies might precipitate a breakdown not only of international order but also of democracy. But this was avoided. Parties of the left gradually adjusted to the new dispensation and, when the Soviet Union collapsed, the western capitalist democracies still operating under the leadership of the United States appeared vindicated and, indeed, invincible (Fukuyama, 1993). It inaugurated a new wave of optimism and an era of significant economic expansion and prosperity in the 1990s and 2000s, even if, as noted above, it was not as significant as the les trente glorieuses, especially in western Europe. Yet, from a wider international perspective, the economic upswing was as marked and, in certain respects, much greater. Its most important feature in the 1990s and 2000s was the entry of major, high population countries such as China, India, and Brazil into full participation in the international market economy. These emerging market economies as the IMF and World Bank called them were also rising powers. Their rates of growth transformed the international economy, shifting the centre of economic gravity and modifying the hierarchy of states – which had, until then, endured substantially unchanged since the start of the capitalist world system.

Since 1945, we have moved from national protectionism to globalization and from Keynesianism to neo-liberalism, but what has been constant, even during the troubled 1970s and 1980s, has been continued US leadership and commitment to maintaining the conditions for security and economic prosperity (Ikenberry, 2011). But, from the perspective of the period since 2008, it is clear that the neo-liberal solution to the pathologies of Keynesianism has failed and has developed its own pathologies. Yet neo-liberalism remains firmly in place. It has been discredited but not dislodged. The inertia of ideas and frameworks and policy solutions is one of the features of the present impasse (Schmidt and Thatcher, 2013).

Peter Jay diagnosed the pathologies of the Keynesian political economy in the 1970s, arguing that it had become a quadrilateral of unstable forces. It had set out to achieve full employment, price stability, free elections and free collective bargaining, but the way these had come to interact made it impossible to achieve all four simultaneously, and the political economy had started to produce perverse outcomes, accelerating inflation, declining growth and fiscal crisis (Jay, 1976). At least one and perhaps two of the core principles had to be sacrificed. These principles turned out to be full employment and free collective bargaining. Neo-liberal political economy aimed at free movement (of capital, finance and people), flexible labour markets, free elections and monetary targets to control inflation. The outcomes have been deflation, rising inequality, weak productivity and stationary living standards for the majority. The basic promises of capitalism, that it can deliver rising living standards to the majority and that each generation will be better off than its predecessor, have been cast into doubt. In this way, the crisis in the system has become a crisis of the system.

This requires the recent crisis or set of crises to be analysed on several levels. The very dramatic financial crash of 2008 led to the near meltdown of the entire financial system, with the supply of credit or liquidity drying up, and the major networks of production and exchange paralysed. Unimaginably severe social repercussions were averted by swift and concerted action by governments, which proved very successful in the short-run in stabilizing the economy and restoring a minimal level of confidence thanks to exceptional measures that contradicted the basic principles of the neoliberal economic project. Governments broke many neo-liberal rules, nationalizing banks, dropping interest rates close to zero, embarking on huge programmes of quantitative easing (QE), covertly helping to rebuild the capital base of distressed banks, and, in some cases, fiscal stimulus. The state acted as it had always done in the past, as the guarantor of last resort of the capitalist order. While the manner and extent of intervention solved several of the most pressing immediate problems, it created many new ones. It ushered in a period of severe recession followed by stagnation, to which governments responded by implementing major programmes of austerity, with cuts focused on the welfare state, which disproportionately affected the poor. Conversely, while the assets of the rich initially took a hit, they were subsequently protected by QE, which fuelled a boom in asset prices.

The resilience of the neo-liberal order

There are many ways to explain the cataclysm of 2008 and the events that followed. Actors at all levels struggled to make sense of these events and what they mean for how households, companies, and government agencies should respond. At the beginning, there was little agreement as to how the crash should be characterized. Was it just a blip, a one-off episode, a unique financial crash with little lasting significance? Many in the financial markets wanted to believe so. There had been many financial crises before during the neo-liberal era. In 1988, for example, there had been a sudden plunge in stock markets world-wide that some commentators interpreted as heralding a major economic downturn. But it turned out just to be a blip, and the markets quickly recovered with no other major effects. There had also been other big financial bubbles arising in the increasingly interconnected, 24-hour financial markets, that eventually burst, such as the Asian financial crisis in 1997 or the collapse of the dotcom bubble in 2000–2001. Alan Greenspan had suggested that these bubbles were to be expected and even welcomed. They were a sign of the natural exuberance of the financial markets and, with light touch regulation, they could be safely defused without broader damage to the international economy. Some people would lose money, others would profit, but that was part of the healthy competitive process by which capitalism renewed itself. Later, at the height of the financial bubble that eventually led to the 2008 crash, he answered those who feared the process was running out of control by arguing that the markets had greater wisdom than any regulator could possibly possess and that, however excessive the prices in the markets appeared, investors could be confident that the markets were pricing in all risks and there would be no crash.

Greenspan later admitted he had been mistaken (Greenspan, 2008). Markets were very good at spotting and pricing in particular risks but not at understanding systemic risk (Bell and Hindmoor, 2015). But there were still hopes that the financial crash of 2008 would be no more lasting in its effects than the Asian financial crisis. Some of the early evidence seemed to point that way. When the authorities glimpsed the scale of the meltdown that appeared imminent after the refusal to bail out Lehman Brothers in September 2008, they reacted with great urgency, sweeping aside political and administrative obstacles. The financial system was rescued, and, although the crash was followed by a severe recession, the fall-out was much less than might have been predicted at the end of September. The crisis was successfully managed and there was no slump as had happened after 1929. Despite thirty years of neo-liberalism, the authorities still knew enough to avert a disaster through improvisation in response to an unexpected crisis rather than forward planning.

This also meant that an air of calm and normality, if not quite business as usual, quickly returned. There were some changes of the party or parties in government. The timing of the crash helped Barack Obama win the US presidency, for example; but there were no regime crises, no overthrow of established elites or challenges to the established consensus, apart from Iceland. There was much talk of the need to learn lessons and implement reforms, in particular, to make new regulations for finance. But few signs of radicalism emerged. There was no bloc of business interests seeking an alternative to the discredited policy regime, no appetite in the political class across the western democracies for radical experiment. Neo-liberalism suffered a loss of prestige but there were few moves to dethrone it. Some spoke of the return of Keynesianism and belief in an active state, but it quickly became clear that what most of the political class and the business class wanted was as rapid a return as possible to the world as it existed immediately before 2008. The status quo was staunchly defended, and many reasons offered as to why this was not the time for radical change. The austerity programmes that governments introduced were aimed at paying for the costs of the bank bailouts and the recession by loading the costs onto the public sector (Blyth, 2013). These responses were highly orthodox and new thinking was officially discouraged.

The problem with characterizing the crisis in this way is that, if it were true, we should not be continuing to talk about the crisis in 2018. The OECD and IMF and former Governors of the Bank of England should not be warning us that another crisis is highly likely. Having saved the banking system with some unorthodox policies, the authorities went on to orchestrate a broadly orthodox policy response to the problem of public debt that arose because of the bank bailout and the recession. But the orthodox policy set did not work. The recovery did not come. Governments expected that, as with all other recessions since 1945, the recession would be short-lived, 18 months at most, after which the economy would rebound and growth return. But it took much longer for states to regain the level of output they enjoyed before the crash, and the recovery, when it came, even for the best performers, proved sluggish and below average. The mountain of debt overhanging economies, and the poor prospects for trade and growth meant central banks continued with their record low interest rates, still in force in most countries eight years after the crash. Only in the United States in early 2017 had there been an upward movement, and then only small. The zero-interest rate policy, unprecedented in the history of capitalism, was needed because of the fragility of confidence and the need to maintain liquidity. Even with interest rates at such low levels and many companies with large financial reserves, it did not lead to an investment boom. QE was needed on a massive scale to prop up asset prices.

The slowness of the recovery and the macroeconomic policies put in place were signs that the financial crash was not a one-off episode and indicated much deeper problems which had not been resolved by the bank bailout and austerity programmes. This confirmed some earlier views that the crisis was possibly the opening step of a major political and economic restructuring of the international economy and international politics, a process which might last two decades. Such views of the crash have argued that there is no going back. The neo-liberal order cannot be put back together again, and the crash is a watershed in capitalist development (Kaletsky, 2010). The evidence for this is also compelling. The slow recovery marks the arrival of a new kind of stagnation, repeating the experience of secular stagnation in Japan in the 1990s and 2000s when it struggled to deal with deflationary pressure (Koo, 2009). Such deflation pressures are now spreading to the US and the EU. At the same time, the crash has highlighted the major shift in the balance of the international economy with the rise of China, India and Brazil. The continued growth of these countries in 2009–2010, as other economies entered recession, appeared to underline their new weight and importance. The US recognized this when it convened the G20 rather than the G7 to discuss the impact of the crisis and how it should be managed – hoping in part to draw on China's reserves and reflationary programmes to support Western debt and boost global demand (Thompson, 2010). It led to new authority being given to the central banks and the setting up of a Financial Stability Board to regulate international finance and propose reforms so as avoid future financial crises (Mackintosh, 2014).

This view of the financial crash is not obviously wrong. However, although the crisis was a major shock, it is hard to deny the immediate crisis was successfully contained. Most of the economic, political, and ideological challenges to the neo-liberal order were defused. Minsky was rediscovered and the return of Keynes was heralded – but then there was silence. The Occupy movement, with its sloganeering on behalf of the 99% against the 1% enjoyed a brief flowering but, like many mass movements, failed to maintain momentum. Centre-Left and socialist parties lost support, and when they were successful, like SYRIZA in Greece, their success was either short-lived or they were forced to submit to neo-liberal conditionalities (Varoufakis, 2016). The financial system and the economy of the neo-liberal order seemed fragile, but the political system and the ideological system proved very resilient. The deep structural contradictions in the neo-liberal regime, such as rising inequality and stagnant real wages, the use of QE to keep the banks afloat and asset prices high, the need for government intervention to rescue markets despite the denial that it was needed, were clear enough, but there were no clear agencies of change to press for reform, and an absence of alternatives, both political and ideological, which carried any weight. That is not surprising. It can take a long time for a practical alternative to the established order to emerge. The calm in the first few years after the crash was deceptive. The crisis was not over, only postponed, displaced into other areas. At first the crisis had been focused in the financial heartlands of Anglo-America (including Ireland but not, for example, Canada or Australia); but, in the second phase, the epicentre became the eurozone, as the banking crisis became a sovereign debt crisis. The eurozone applied much more stringent austerity policies on its members, which led to very high unemployment and huge drops in output in the southern periphery of the zone, particularly in Greece, Spain and Portugal. The severity of the clampdown brought a wave of support for left wing anti-establishment parties, SYRIZA and Podemos. The third phase of the crisis after 2013 saw problems spreading to the rising powers. They had become overextended and overindebted in seeking to keep their own economies going when the western economies faltered, and now experienced a sharp deceleration in growth, as a result of falling commodity prices and falling demand for their exports. Brazil was most seriously hit, India least. China saw its growth rate decline but then stabilise. China was most active of the three in seeking to rebalance its economy and develop new initiatives to support its continued growth, such as the 'One Belt One Road' programme first unveiled in 2013.

In 2016, a fourth phase opened in the crisis, and from an unexpected quarter. The political resilience of the neo-liberal order suddenly developed cracks. The victory of the Leave campaign in the EU Referendum in the UK in June 2016 was followed by the victory of Donald Trump in the US presidential election in November. Brexit dealt a blow to the cohesion of the western democracies and to the ideals of multilateral institutions and cooperation that had been so important in building the post-war international market order, by weakening one of its pillars; the EU. The UK did however propose to stay within the international system, falling back if necessary on WTO rules and bilateral trade deals with other countries. The Trump victory was potentially much more serious, however, because he ran for the presidency on a platform of economic nationalism, threatening to disrupt many of the alliances and institutions the US had fashioned since 1945 to defend its interests. He called, instead, for the scrapping of multilateral trade deals like TPP and TTIP and aimed to replace them with bilateral deals that would place 'America first' and start disengaging from the role the United States had played for seventy years (Laderman and Simms, 2017).

It is uncertain how much Trump will either be willing or able to follow through his campaign rhetoric. There are already signs the results may be less radical than some fear. He has already softened his position on NATO, for example. But the uncertainty that this first major victory of the national-populists of the right have secured, has made the political as well as economic order much more fragile. This is at a time when many international bodies, including the IMF, the OECD, the World Economic Forum, and the Bank for International Settlements are warning of the risk of another major crisis (Inman, 2017). In short, little has changed since 2008. Inequality remains high and is expected to start rising again. Finance has regained its dominance and its confidence, and bubbles are inflating. Meanwhile living standards for the majority continue to stagnate, and the burden of personal and public debt remains high and growing. The Trump administration plans a massive fiscal stimulus, through tax cuts and higher spending on defence and infrastructure, while threatening to force US companies to break up their supply chains, end outsourcing, and bring jobs back to the United States. The risk of trade and currency wars and major economic dislocation are high. Trump's supporters think that the fiscal stimulus is the way to break the impasse and return to much higher levels of growth. There may be some short-term success, but the disruption to the international market order on which US prosperity has been based for so long could be very costly.

Structural dilemmas

The western democracies that have sustained the international market order for so long are facing difficult dilemmas on how to revive it; and they seek to develop a new formula for political economic governance to replace neo-liberalism that has become exhausted. The first dilemma concerns global governance. One of the issues any new formula must address is how to reach agreement on rules for the international economy, international security, and increasingly the ecological management of the planet, in a situation where there is no sovereign but fragmented political jurisdictions. Any such agreement must find a way to involve China, India, Brazil and other rising powers, as well as older powers such as Russia, in helping to shape and enforce rules. The new profile for the G20 and the establishment of the Financial Stability Board were steps in that direction. But since 2010 these initiatives have stalled. No further agreements have emerged, and the US has downgraded the G20, refocusing attention on the G7, to which neither China or India belong. The US Senate delayed modest proposals to acknowledge the importance of China by changing the voting weights on the IMF and only finally agreed in December 2015. Similarly, reform of the membership of the UN Security Council is urgent, but none of the alternatives command agreement. There are also deadlocks in many other areas, such as the WTO. In the UN Climate Change conference there was some limited progress at the 2015 Paris summit, but that looks in jeopardy because the Trump administration carried through its threat to withdraw from the agreement.

Previous eras of generalized prosperity and economic and social progress have depended on the establishment of rules for the international market order, and some means of upholding them. The US is still the world's dominant economic and military power, but it is weaker than it was and, even before Trump, was no longer so willing to play the leadership role it once did. Trump signals a more rapid disengagement. Without the United States, it is hard to see how a new cooperative form of international governance can be established; and, without it playing such a role, the prospects of conflict between blocs over trade and resources will grow. China is gradually establishing a sphere of interest in East Asia and Latin America (also Africa – where there is a growing US military presence too). Russia is doing the same in its neighbourhood. The EU is beset with major challenges, particularly over the future of the euro and immigration. With the US turning inwards too, it seems the world may well be moving into a much more nationalist phase. If true, this will entrench the impasse, and make resolution of the crisis more difficult. The events that could change this trajectory are not obvious.

The second dilemma is over economic growth. A successful governance formula needs to ensure rising productivity and living standards as well as an economy that is sustainable and able to reproduce itself. One of the biggest threats to recovery is the secular stagnation gripping the western democracies. There is debate as to whether this is caused primarily by supply or demand factors. Is it the result of a vanishing of investment opportunities despite the ever-increasing pace of technological change, or is it the result of growing distributional inequality and the falling labour share which has depressed wages and boosted returns to capital (Perraton, 2017)? There are advocates of both, but what is apparent is that no government has many good ideas about how to reverse the fall in labour's share and the rapid rise in inequality, or how to overcome the drying up of significant economic innovations. There are some interesting debates around whether artificial intelligence will allow a big spike in productivity, and if so, whether the wealth it generates can be captured by taxation to fund basic income schemes. All other past foundations for growth, such as population growth, immigration or an inexhaustible natural environment all appear weaker or no longer politically possible. None of the orthodox policies appear to be working, so governments and societies are gradually adjusting to a low growth economy.

The third dilemma is over legitimacy, maintaining consent for economic, social, and governance arrangements both internationally and within national communities. The difficulty of devising a growth model which works or constructing a new framework of rules for the international market order are both directly related to this. The new hard times of stagnant living standards, cuts in public services, higher unemployment, and still very high levels of personal debt have brought sharper struggles over distribution, and the targeting of certain groups such as the disabled and welfare recipients for disproportionate cuts. Welfare states have once again come under sustained attack. As in all such periods, the state comes under pressure to spend more and cut back at the same time. Major challenges have emerged around affordability and competitiveness (Gamble, 2016). There is a renewed fiscal crisis because governments are finding it hard to maintain an adequate fiscal base in the face of the growth of tax avoidance and tax evasion by companies and the rich, and resistance by citizens to paying higher taxes. At the same time, costs of providing public services continue to rise more steeply than costs in other parts of the economy, and expectations and entitlements of citizens are rising too. The competitiveness challenge arises because capital has become increasingly international through outsourcing and global supply chains, while labour remains largely tied to nation-states. Globalization has weakened organized labour and destroyed the full employment regime of the Keynesian welfare national state (Rodrik, 2011). This has created anxiety about a possible race to the bottom, in which labour, welfare and environmental standards would be sacrificed to keep the economy competitive and strip out unnecessary costs.

The political backlash

The political events of 2016, particularly Brexit and Trump, raise the issue of whether the political resilience of the neoliberal regime can be maintained indefinitely, or whether it could implode. The period of phoney war seems to be over, and more contestation of issues of fundamental principle are now arising. The main challenge to neoliberalism has so far come mainly, not from a revived left, but from a revived economic nationalist and populist right. There are many variations in the parties and movements that comprise this new political trend, but they all share a rejection of the liberal political and business establishment. They are against globalization, regional forms of government like the EU, and free movement of goods, capital, and people. Many are also socially illiberal.

This phase of the crisis is rapidly becoming a crisis of democracy. The evidence for this lies in the many signs of disengagement and disaffection, creating a crisis of representation and the hollowing out of democratic institutions such as political parties, trade unions, the civil service, and parliaments. A growing number of institutions, such as central banks, are now organized outside the formal mechanisms of political accountability. Trust in politics, politicians, and belief that voting might make a significant difference to people's lives have all declined. Turnout and support for mainstream parties have both suffered. A new category of voters has been identified: those who are left behind who tend to be older, poorer, less educated, and unskilled are more prone to the politics of fear, insecurity, and uncertainty (Ford and Goodwin, 2014). The contrast with the liberal cosmopolitan elite is stark and is the main source for the rise of national-populism across Europe and North America.

There is a great deal of momentum behind economic nationalism since the votes for Brexit and Trump, but it is doubtful it will provide stability or a new formula for political and economic governance. It is more likely to disrupt further and help disintegrate the key pillars of the neo-liberal order. This would be a highly destructive and potentially dangerous phase for the western democracies, and some of them might not remain democracies. This would lead to further fragmentation and conflict. Economic nationalism will seek to create self-sufficient national blocs. Regional associations will collapse. But the threats to try and reverse globalization, if successful, are likely to prove costly in terms of both jobs and trade.

Eight years after the crash, a political challenge to neoliberalism has finally emerged, not just on the periphery but in the heartland of the neo-liberal order; the United States. It is an open question how far this nationalist revolution will go, and whether it may trigger the kind of systemic crisis that has been avoided until now, and whether that will spark other political responses. Some observers, like Wolfgang Streeck, are pessimistic. He argues that although lower growth, higher inequality, and rising debt are not indefinitely sustainable, there are no signs, apart from the national populists, of an opposition or resistance emerging able to formulate and implement an alternative. Capitalism has succeeded in disorganizing not only its own systems, but also the opposition to it, to such a degree that it is no longer a self-reproducing, sustainable, predictable, or legitimate social order. Instead it will become increasingly disordered because of stagnation, redistribution of resources to an oligarchic elite, the continued plundering of the public domain, and the growth of corruption and global anarchy. The prospect is for a capitalism that lacks the means to restore itself internally, and has destroyed all the institutions and opposition movements which might have rescued it externally (Streeck, 2016).

Streeck's analysis is powerful and bleak, but he may underestimate the forces of resistance that are still latent in the system and are showing some signs of re-emerging. One example is surge of support in the UK election in 2017 for a left social democratic programme, protesting against continuing austerity and rising inequality. The course of large structural crises is highly uncertain, and the past gives only a limited guide to what may happen. The unexpected and the contingent have been powerful shapers of the course of this crisis so far and will continue to be so in the future. Democracy is under serious challenge, and the task of renewing it will depend on finding political answers to the three dilemmas of governance which reflect the deep contradictions of neoliberal political economy that the crisis has revealed. The powers of renewal in capitalism are formidable, but not limitless. It may well be, as Streeck argues, that capitalism can no longer save itself (Streeck, 2016). Whether there are still other forces in the democracies which can rescue it and reconstruct it is a more open question.

References

Bell, S. and Hindmoor, A. (2015) *Masters of the universe, slaves of the market: banking and the great financial meltdown.* Cambridge, MA: Harvard University Press.
Blyth, M. (2013) *Austerity: the history of a dangerous idea.* Oxford: Oxford University Press.

Cowen, T. (2011) *The great stagnation*. New York: Dutton Press.

Ford, R. and Goodwin, M. (2014) *Revolt on the right: explain support for the radical right in Britain*. London: Routledge.

Fukuyama, F. (1993) *The end of history and the last man*. London: Penguin.

Gamble, A. (1988) *The free economy and the strong state: the politics of Thatcherism*. London: Macmillan.

Gamble, A. (2016) *Can the welfare state survive?* Cambridge: Polity.

Gough, I. (2011) *Climate change and public policy futures*. London: British Academy.

Greenspan, A. (2008) 'Testimony of Dr. Alan Greenspan to the Committee of Government Oversight and Reform', 23 October. Available at: https://democrats-oversight. house.gov/sites/democrats.oversight.house.gov/files/migrated/20081023100438.pdf (Accessed 19 April 2018).

Ikenberry, J. (2011) *Liberal Leviathan: the origins, crisis and transformation of the American world order*. Princeton, NJ: Princeton University Press.

Inman, P. (2017) Financial markets could be overheating, warns central bank body. *The Guardian*, 3 Dec. Available at: https://www.theguardian.com/business/2017/dec/03/financial-markets-overheating-financial-crisis-bis (Accessed 13 May 2018).

Jay, P. (1976) *Employment, inflation and politics*. London: Institute of Economic Affairs.

Kaletsky, A. (2010) *Capitalism 4.0*. London: Bloomsbury.

Kindleberger, C.P. (1987) *International capital movements*. Cambridge: Cambridge University Press.

Koo, R. (2009) *The Holy Grail of macroeconomics: lessons from Japan's great recession*. Chichester: Wiley.

Laderman, C. and Simms, B. (2017) *Donald Trump: the making of a world view*. London: Endeavour Press.

Lipset, S.M. (1960) *Political man*. London: Heinemann.

Mackintosh, S. (2014). 'The global financial and economic crisis and the creation of the Financial Stability Board', *World Economics*, 15(3), pp. 103–120.

Perraton, J. (2017). 'Secular stagnation: the new normal for the UK?', in C. Hay and T. Hunt (eds.), *The coming crisis*, Palgrave-Macmillan, pp. 95–102.

Rodrik, D. (2011) *The globalisation paradox*. Oxford: Oxford University Press.

Ruggie, J. (1998) *Constructing the world polity: essays on international institutionalization*. London: Routledge.

Schmidt, V. and Thatcher, M. (eds.) (2013) *Resilient liberalism in Europe's political economy*. Cambridge: Cambridge University Press.

Shonfield, A. (1966) *Modern capitalism: the changing balance of public and private power*. Oxford: Oxford University Press.

Streeck, W. (2016) *How will capitalism end? Essays on a failing system*. London: Verso.

Summers, L. (2014) 'Washington must not settle for secular stagnation', *Financial Times*, January 8.

Thompson, H. (2010) *China and the mortgaging of America*. London: Palgrave Macmillan.

Varoufakis, Y. (2016) *And the weak suffer what they must? Europe, austerity and the threat to global stability*. London: The Bodley Head.

Weber, M. (1946) 'Politics as a vocation', in H.H. Gerth and C.W. Mills, eds., *From Max Weber: Essays in Sociology*. New York: Oxford University Press, pp. 71–128.

5 Crises are the new normal

Governing through resilience

David Chandler

Introduction

For modernist discourses of power, crises were one-off exceptions to the norm: although considered to be unavoidable, they were to be "bracketed" off (in the terminology of Carl Schmitt, 2003) and treated differently, as "exceptions" or "accidents". Risk insurance is a classic modernist form of the bracketing of crises: ensuring that they are to be compartmentalized through a separate mode of calculus and regulation, dissipating responsibility for securing systems of production and exchange.[1] On the other hand, for discourses of modernist critique, crises – from economic crisis to social breakdown and international conflict – were far from arbitrary or accidental but seen as revealing the systemic or inner contradictions of capitalist social relations. It was the interconnection of forms of crisis with forms of rule that was crucial to critique, which sought to materially ground alternatives through bringing awareness of these connections to the surface.[2]

In the sphere of international politics, since the 1990s, the relationship between governance and crisis has been transformed through the inclusion of crises into governance as part of the new normal. In fact, crises have increasingly come to be seen as enabling governance rather than as a barrier to it. In 2009, the United Nations renamed Natural Disaster Day (12 October) as Disaster Day to intentionally emphasize that crises previously seen as "natural" were to be governed rather than seen as unpredictable or accidental exceptions, thus extending the sphere of governance. Crisis management has been mainstreamed, increasingly woven into the heart of policy-making itself. Policy-makers have come to live with crises, so much so that discourses of resilience – the science of turning crises into assets and opportunities that enable governing – are now central to every international and domestic policy concern.

This chapter analyses how crises came to be central to governing, morphing from being a pressing concern or threat to being grasped as processes revealing new and enabling opportunities. The following section illustrates how, rather than excluding crisis, dominant policy understandings of resilience have sought, in diverse ways, to govern with and through crises, extending hegemonic frameworks of control and regulation. The next section considers radical approaches, which have included crises as a worry or concern for policy-making through emphasizing risk and contingency in a world where traditional modernist binaries, particularly those between culture and nature, are no longer fixed and clear; focusing on the work of Ulrich Beck and Bruno Latour. The chapter concludes with a consideration of how immanent, process-based, perspectives have increasingly enabled crises to be positively incorporated into governance, analysing emergent understandings of disasters, which take on broad post-epistemic assumptions and tend to lack the modernist causal framings that enabled crises to be part of the lexicon of critique.

Resilience: governing through crisis

The conceptualizations that best reflect the rapid integration of crises into governance are those developed in resilience approaches which seek to include unintentional feedbacks and unexpected changes of context. Resilience conceptions demarcate a break:

> with modernist conceptions of social protection that are based upon knowing and protecting against the future through statistically derived forms of insurance, resilience positively embraces uncertainty and the ultimate unknowability of the future. An organism, an individual, an eco-system, a social institution, an engineered infrastructure, even a city – in fact, anything that is networked, evolving or "life-like" in some way – is now said to be resilient in so far as it able to absorb shocks and uncertainty, or reconfigure itself in relation to such shocks while still retaining its essential functionality.
>
> (Duffield, 2011, p. 3)

Resilience approaches seek to govern through crises, to enable a constant process of monitoring, adaptation, and improvement. The more ways in which crises can be conceived the more efficient and responsive new forms of governance are held to be. To illustrate this, I will take three, quite different, representative examples. In no case is an effort made to govern by excluding or separating crises from the norm or by submitting them to a different calculus. The dynamic is the opposite: to include crises as an enabling resource or opportunity, making them integral to governance. Perhaps one could say that, rather than seeking to govern crises by developing mechanisms and techniques of exclusion that isolate them as threats with potential contagion effects, there is now a desire to let crises govern policy-making processes through developing mechanisms and techniques for their inclusion.

The first example is a news report on civil engineering for climate extremes, which highlights how crises and catastrophic failure have become key to thinking about the management of hazards and risks (Smith, 2015). The starting assumption, as stated by Mari Tye, a scientist based at the National

Centre for Atmospheric Research (NCAR), is that: "Failure isn't if but when and how badly" (Smith, 2015). The "solution" or way of responding to the inevitability of such a crisis was to intentionally design systems for "graceful failure". The scientist argues that the potential for crises to arise must be built into design rather than excluded: "Resilient systems account for a range of scenarios and are designed to recover in a controlled way from hazards, with an acceptable level of impact" (Smith, 2015). Not building in the possibility of crisis would only lead to increased exposure to negative impacts according to senior scientist Greg Holland, who co-leads the Engineering for Climate Extremes Partnership. The understanding that good governance must reckon with the inevitability of crises rather than attempt to manage and reduce risks is increasingly dominant within resilience thinking.[3]

The second example is the stated need to build the possibility of crisis into agricultural planning (Hargrave, 2015). Here, focusing on unknown and unpredictable risks and contingencies – from extreme weather to water shortages and pest infestations – can help farmers "be more efficient and get the biggest yields possible and use the least amount of agrochemicals" (Hargrave, 2015). Here, new forms of technological and analytical capacities are deployed based on seeing crises as emergent processes, which can be seen and responded to through the analysis of open data culled from a plurality of sources and the development of alternative forms of management. Tim Holmes, head of technical solutions at the Centre for Agriculture and Biosciences International's Plantwise Knowledge Bank, suggests organizing around the potential for crisis promises more than sticking to success. He states:

> The service offers a traffic light warning system with advice on what farmers can do for each different threat level, starting with good farming practice – such as pruning trees and bushes and keeping the farm clean – right up to the last resort of applying a particular insecticide.
>
> (Hargrave, 2015)

The promise of open data is that crises, risks, and contingencies, can be constantly adapted to in their real-time emergence.

Key is that these resilience approaches do not organise governance upon traditional binary understandings of crisis and the norm, where crisis is an inevitable outlier on the margins, but through a new framework, which includes crises at the centre of its calculations. Crises are thus not something that can be minimized on the assumption that they can be treated as distinct or separate from normal governance operations; this would be seen as hubristic. Still less can crises be seen as problems in need of purely preventive measures. In fact, the Stockholm Resilience Centre, a leading policy influencer in this area, has popularized the concept of "coercive resilience" to problematise attempts to govern out crises through preventive means rather than by seeking to accept and organise around them (Stockholm Resilience Stockholm Resilience Centre, 2014). As highlighted in the first example, excluding the possibility of crisis is understood to undermine adaptive capacities and result in more disastrous long-term consequences. Similarly, resilience approaches increasingly do not seek to merely respond reactively to a crisis – to "bounce back" afterwards (Haas, 2013, 2015). This would not address the problems, still attempting to deny rather than welcome crises and therefore mean being unable to respond through real time adaptive measures (Pelling, 2011; Tierney, 2014). Welcoming crises and enfolding them into governance is counter-intuitively seen to be a way of minimizing negative impacts (Walker and Salt, 2006; Rodin, 2015). The message is that crises are inevitable, but their consequences are highly contingent on the levels of adaptability and resilience a society possesses.

The third example is the Government of Rwanda's launch of its National Risk Atlas. This was widely billed "as the first-ever comprehensive risk profile developed in Africa" (Habib, 2015). In collaboration with the United Nations Development Programme (UNDP), the World Bank and the European Union, the National Risk Atlas was developed through a comprehensive risk assessment to provide guidance in national planning and policy-making on disaster risk. In the language of the risk planners, the potential for crises was to be mainstreamed into development planning so that "evidence-based" and "risk informed" policy-making would ensure that the awareness of contingency shaped governance strategy. UNDP Assistant Administrator and Director of the Bureau for Policy and Programme Support, Magdy Martínez Solimán, argued that responding to crises had to be kept at the forefront: "We will never successfully eradicate poverty or achieve sustainable development so long as we continue to marginalize disaster risk reduction" (ibid.). Here, the goals that would have been instrumentalized and used to shape governance in the past – ending poverty and furthering development – have become secondary by-products of focusing upon the world as it is: the real-time adaptation to the world in its becoming.

> Risks are dynamic owing to rapid changes in the country's demographic, social, and economic processes. Therefore, risk assessment should also be dynamic so as to keep up with these changes. In order for the National Risk Atlas to remain relevant, useful, and sustained, it is recommended that it be updated every 5 years. This aligns with Rwanda's strategic plans... This will enable the use and integration of the assessment findings in the analysis and planning.
>
> (ibid., p. 166)

Increasingly, the process of continually adapting to crises as they emerge seems to be displacing other frameworks for seeing how governance and urban planning could be managed or legitimized.[4] Noticeable here, of course, is how it is the possibility of crisis that drives innovation and new accounting technologies – not views of governments as initiators of projects of change and transformation. It seems clear that the integration or enfolding of crises into the heart of governance constructs a new discourse of internationally managed programmes of good governance as resilience, understood as the efficient and non-disruptive adaptation to changing relationships, flows, and interactions.[5] It is little surprise, then, that bringing crises into hegemonic discourses of power seems only to intensify the levels of international regulative intervention and control. If crises open possibilities for new ways of thinking, it would appear that these definitely do not stretch to challenging the dominant concerns of the maintenance and strengthening of the system that currently exists.

The ontologization of crisis

The opening up of the globalizing and interconnected world in the 1990s and the rise of concerns of environmental degradation and global warming enabled critical "crisis" discourses to take what could be called a "complexity" turn (Urry, 2003; Smith and Jenks, 2006; Bryne and Callaghan, 2014; Chandler, 2014). These radical approaches, sought to include crises, indeterminacy, and risk as inherent in the postmodern, complex and interdependent world. In this framing, crises – while still problematic – became linked less to capitalism as a social system of production and more to what were now seen as narrow or reductionist liberal or modernist modes of understanding. Crises were not a product of capitalism per se but the by-product of technological developments, which were held to have constituted the world in new and interconnected ways. Thus, crises were the ontological product of complex feedback loops and systemic interactions that could not be predicted or foreseen in advance. Crises, through becoming ontological, thereby called for new ways of thinking and governing: ways that went beyond modernist linear, cause-and-effect assumptions and that could cope with unexpected, unknown and unintended effects.

Probably the leading theorist of these 1990s' approaches was Ulrich Beck, who argued the risk of crisis could no longer be bracketed off, compartmentalized or excluded in the Second Modernity (Beck, 1992). Beck built crises into policy-making as a result of globalization and interconnectivity, suggesting the boundaries of liberal modernity – between the state and society and between culture and nature – were increasingly blurring. Crises could no longer be treated as the exception, to be quantified and insured against. The radical inclusion of the possibility of crisis into policy-making, as articulated by Beck, was as a problem to be addressed, and potentially minimized, through governing under the "precautionary principle".[6] Thus the inclusion of crises began to integrate contingency into modernist forms of governance. Further, despite the world lacking its cause-and-effect linearity, the human subject still stood external to the world and able to contemplate the potential outcomes of this interconnectedness.

Beck's precautionary principle still posited a knowing and controlling subject but, as the assumptions of modernity ebbed away, this subject had to act more humbly and cautiously, testing and experimenting rather than assuming cause and effect modalities.[7] Problematically, Beck focused on the prevention of crises through predicting or imagining the consequences of human actions, which seemed logically impossible to foresee. For example, even if scientists reached consensus before its application on the safety of a new procedure or initiative, scientific experimentation in the laboratory cannot produce the same results in real, differentiated and complex life. This led critics, like Bruno Latour, to convincingly argue that, once included, crises could not be prevented or minimized through precautions but had to be followed through "all the way" (Latour's thesis is considered further below) (2011, p. 27).

Towards the end of his life, Beck (in line with the times) shifted the presentation of his approach, articulating the appreciation of crises as enabling governance rather than merely constraining it (2015, p. 79). There were positive side-effects of the entanglements of culture and nature which were exposed through crises, indicating the need to adapt to and to adequately understand the new anthropogenic manufacture of risks – such as global climate change. Thus, the awareness of catastrophic crisis in dealing with climate change and other risks could be seen to be potentially positive (ibid., p. 76). For Beck:

> Anthropological shocks provide a new way of being in the world, seeing the world and doing politics. The anthropological shock of Hurricane Katrina is a useful example…Until Hurricane Katrina, flooding had not been positioned as an issue of environmental justice – despite the existence of a substantial body of research documenting inequalities and vulnerability to flooding. It took the reflection both in the publics and in academia on the devastating but highly uneven "racial floods" of Hurricane Katrina to bring back the strong "Anthropocene" of slavery, institutionalized racism, and connect it to vulnerability and floods. This kind of connecting the disconnected is the way the cosmopolitan side effects of bads are real, e.g. the invisibility of side effects is made visible.
>
> (ibid., p. 80)

The flooding of New Orleans was a crisis with the side-effect of enabling us to know the connection between risks we thought were natural or external with racial, social, and economic inequalities we thought were purely social. The side-effect of this crisis was held to be the bringing together of the world in its realisation that the natural and the social were intermingled and that the politics of race was not disconnected from the politics of ecology.[8] Likewise, the natural and social sciences needed to be brought together in rethinking how to engage with the world beyond this posited culture/nature divide. For Beck, this:

> Metamorphosis is not social change [it]… is a mode of changing the mode of change. It signifies the age of side effects. It challenges the way of being in the world, thinking about the world and imagining and doing politics.
>
> (Beck, 2015, p. 78)

A new form of governance thus emerges from the inclusion of crises: the understanding of crises and disasters as no longer natural but as social products:

Verwandlung or metamorphosis then also means that the past is reproblematized through the imagination of a threatening future. Norms and imperatives that guided decisions in the past are re-evaluated and questioned through the imagination of a threatening future. From that follow alternative ideas for capitalism, law, consumerism, science (e.g. the IPCC), etc.

(ibid., p. 83)

"The age of side effects" nicely encapsulates how crises have been captured and incorporated into governance under discourses of resilience. This approach has also been applied to re-examine the past, as Beck advocated. In fact, Kathleen Tierney argues that disasters throughout history have had social roots, being products of human decision-making and non-linear path dependencies.[9] International organizations such as the UN, the World Bank and the IMF have been central to the process of bringing disaster into good governance regulations.[10] In 2005, the Hygo Agreement was signed encouraging all states to take disaster risk measures. In 2015, the Sendai Agreement was much clearer in terms of bringing disasters into mainstream governmental planning processes, very much along the lines of Beck's precautionary principle. Bringing crises and disasters into everyday governmental planning allowed them to be included rather than excluded on the basis of the need to think less linearly about planning, development and construction, education, social welfare and other measures, which previously had not taken into account the unintended consequences of their approaches.

One of the most interesting aspects of the Sendai preparations was the argument that disaster risk reduction was itself problematic and that, instead of risk reduction, policy-thinking should shift to the proper recognition and integration of disaster: the paradigm of disaster risk management (Lavell and Maskrey, 2014, p. 278; UNISDR, 2014). However, these frameworks assumed governance could work through re-evaluating past actions on the basis of present experience, and could not deal so well with problems that were unexpected. Beck had not much more to offer than that the "imagination of a threatening future" would focus attention on the ways in which governance and failure interacted.

Bruno Latour aimed to go beyond the limits of Beck's work in this area, seeking to trace the effects of human actions in real time feedback loops; requiring less of the imagination and more of science and technology. Latour has deployed the radical discourse of crisis as enabling, having long waged war on modernist binary understandings, particularly that of the separation of culture and nature. For Latour, just as humanity has become more entangled with nature than ever before, ecologists have sought to emphasise the need for separation to protect "nature" and modernist science aspires to know the world/"nature" as somehow a separate and fixed reality.[11] Therefore, along similar lines to Beck's later work, global warming signifies not so much the crisis of modernity but serves to enable new forms of governing. The unknown and unintended consequences of humanity's historical footprint on the planet could only be construed as a "crisis" in modernist terms if people still bought into modernity's linear fantasy of "progress" (Latour, 2011, p. 25). Instead, the inclusion of crises reveals the entanglements of humanity and the environment and is a critical wake up call to radically reorganise the governance of the planet on the basis of a more inclusive understanding that "nature" cannot just be left alone, but must be "even more managed, taken up, cared for, stewarded, in brief, integrated and internalized into the very fabric of policy" (ibid.).

Crucial for Latour's project of enfolding the possibility of crises into the everyday practices of governance is the ability of the human subject to follow the unintended consequences of their actions "all the way". This ability to govern reflexively based on an understanding of causal chains of interaction, presupposes that modernist forms of governing are still possible, that in fact, the enfolding of crises into governance adds to the existing knowledge of a knowing and governing humanity acting as a controlling and directing force. Latour thus enthuses:

> the principle of precaution, properly understood, is exactly the change of *Zeitgeist* needed: not a principle of abstention – as many have come to see it – but a change in the way *any action* is considered, a deep tidal change in the linkage modernism established between science and politics. From now on, thanks to this principle, unexpected consequences are *attached* to their initiators and have to be followed through all the way.
>
> (ibid., p. 27)

Latour's subject is the initiator of actions and thereby responsible for the interactive consequences of this initiation.[12] For Latour, and for other thinkers, seeking to integrate crises, the consequences of human actions are capable of forming the basis of governing better, through feedback loops which impact upon human understanding.[13] This sense of acquiring knowledge and governing power through recognising feedbacks and interconnections also drives the debates on the Anthropocene as enabling new, more progressive processes of governance and the calls for greater sensitivity to the everyday feedbacks that enable a recalibration of thinking.[14] For some authors, crises such as extreme weather events or blight and pestilence are seen as products of process-based feedback loops revealing the errors of past forms of governance; for example, the linkages between carbon use and global warming or the industrialization of agriculture and the reduction of bio-genetic diversity leading to the global spread of viruses and microbial mutations and the vulnerability of the human immune system.[15]

Crises become more enabling the more feedbacks as reverse causal connections can be established or imagined and the more "radical" or "political" these authors become in their normative advocacy. These complex and intricate feedback loops also call for greater technological insights, such as those described in the resilience policy prescriptions discussed above, a technical task that, according to Latour:

> can only be accomplished by crisscrossing their [the loops'] potential paths with as many instruments as possible to have a chance of detecting in what ways they are connected... laying down the networks of equipment that render the consequences of action visible to all the various agencies that do the acting... "[S]ensitivity" is a term that applies to all the agencies able to spread their loops further and to feel the consequences of what they do come back to haunt them... but only as long and as far that it [humanity] is fully equipped with enough sensors to feel the feedbacks.
>
> (Latour, 2013, p. 96)

Latour's framework seems to be a highly modernist one,[16] involving the interventionist technology and regulatory mechanisms necessary to "trace and ceaselessly retrace again the lines made by all those loops" with a "strong injunction: keep the loop traceable and publically (*sic*) visible" so that "whatever is reacting to your actions, loop after loop... weighs on you as a force to be taken into account" (ibid., p. 135). Highly regulatory forms of governance are given a material political form as a new set of political competencies and responsibilities are established: "Such an accumulation of *responses* requires a responsible agency to which you, yourself, have to become in turn *responsible*" (ibid.). This sounds very much like a technocratic modernist nightmare where, with the reintroduction of reductionist understandings of feedbacks and responsibilities, radical perspectives of including crises seem to chime perfectly with policy shifts. Despite the claims of the end of the "Modernist Constitution" and of the dispersion of agency through a myriad forms of complex life, the traditional modernist framing of governance as regulatory control seems alive and well in Latour's world.

Conclusion: immanence as a form of governance

Beck and Latour both suggest and intimate the need to develop immanent or emergent approaches to crisis management – without the transcendental legacies of policy goals or claims to causal knowledge, networked connections, and predictive capacities.[17] Latour, in the "Facing Gaia" lectures, suggests Nature has to be understood in "post-epistemological" terms (Latour, 2013, p. 26). By this he means that modernist forms of representation, reduction, abstraction, and exclusion cannot know a world that is plural, lively and interactive. This is post-epistemological because knowledge can no longer be extracted from its concrete context of interaction in time and space. In this framing, knowledge, to be "objective" – to be real – has to be plural, fluid and concrete (ibid., p. 49). This is very similar to Donna Haraway's understanding of "situated epistemology", which rejects modernist drives to extract knowledge, i.e. to turn knowing into abstractions from real emergent processes through methods of scaling up, generalizing and universalizing, fixing knowledge apart from its plural, changing and overlapping context of meaning (Haraway, 1988, pp. 575–599). In this way of rethinking knowledge, the modernist divisions between subjective and objective and qualitative and quantitative are dissolved.[18] The multiple concrete of emergence articulates a different ontology from that examined above. Here, there can be no feedback loops circling the globe, allocating responsibilities and instantiating new ethical forms of governance based on extensive self-reflexivities. As Latour implies, in a world of unknowable contingencies "it is the *what is* that obstinately requests *its due*" (2013, p. 126).

This "empirical" displacement of causal understandings can also be intimated from Beck's later work. He imagined the development of real time empirics as able to evade both the dangers of critical immanent approaches, which tended to reproduce the knowledge scepticism of postmodernism, and the hubristic knowledge claims of transcendental frameworks of cause-and-effect. Thus, the world could be governed in its complex emergence, enabling failure to be the dynamic for adaptation.

> Seen this way, climate change risk is far more than a problem of measures of carbon dioxide and the production of pollution. It does not only signal a crisis of human self-understanding. More than that, global climate risk creates new ways of being, looking, hearing, and acting in the world – highly conflictual and ambivalent, open-ended, without any foreseeable outcome. As a result, a compass for the 21st century arises. This compass is different from the postmodern "everything goes" and different from false universalism. This is a new variant of critical theory which does not set the normative horizon itself but takes it from empirical analyses. Hence, it is an empirical analysis of the normative horizon of the self-critical world risk society.
>
> (Beck, 2015, p. 83)

The focus on empirical analysis as enabling real-time responsiveness allows immanent understandings to discursively frame governance without an external subject "setting the normative horizon". This new "normative horizon" is one imagined as set by the world itself – in which crisis and norm are indistinguishable from each other – and accessed through the development of new mechanisms and techniques sensitized and responsive to the world in its emergence. Therefore, to refer back to the three examples presented above, governance can increasingly be rationalized and legitimated without a "dimension supplementary to the dimensions of the given", enabling the "what is"-ness of the world to be finally given its due. Discourses of resilience enable generalized understandings of emerging and changing risks to inform governance – from architectural engineering to developments in agricultural productivity right up to national development plans – on the basis that the tasks of governing, as a continuous process of adaptation, are always and already given through the capacity to sense and respond to the emerging nature of life itself.

The integration of crises into policy-making, understood as policy-process opportunities rather than as exceptions and threats, presupposes the acceptance of contingency and unknowability. In this respect, the transformation of the relation between crises and governance reflects the decline of transcendental approaches, setting the human up as separate to the world, able to know, direct and increasingly transform its circumstances. Today, it seems that the world of crisis as the norm – understood in terms of the vitality of matter, the agency of Gaia, the flat ontology of assemblage theory, the immanent power of emergence, or the feedback loops of complexity – is emancipating humanity from its modernist aspirations. However, there is a real danger that this "emancipation" will be even more problematic than those that have gone before. The posthuman world of crisis and contingency sets no "normative horizons" beyond obedience to the external appearances of the world: the necessity of continuous adaptation to the world in its emergence.

Notes

1 There is a rich collection of Foucault-inspired work on insurance as a modernist attempt to compartmentalize, explain away, and exclude crises. As François Ewald argued: "Insurance, through the category of risk, objectifies every event as an accident" (1991, p. 199). Thus, responsibility for crises (from natural disasters to war and financial losses) is removed from social, political or economic agencies and becomes a blameless, "accidental", statistical regularity that can be insured against. See further, Defert (1991) and Dillon (2008).
2 See, for example, Lenin (1975); Marx (1983).
3 See, for example, Sheffi (2015) who argues that supply chain failures are inevitable, meaning that risk reduction needs to be supplemented by resilience mechanisms for coping with crises.
4 Janet Roitman (2013), in considering how crises are constituted as objects of knowledge, argues that viewing phenomena in terms of crisis leads to blind-spots about alternative ways of reading these phenomena.
5 Deborah Cowen (2014) excellently highlights how resilience has become the new guide to security, life and logistics.
6 He argued: "If we anticipate catastrophes whose destructive potential threatens everybody, then the risk calculation based on experience and rationality breaks down. Now all possible, to a greater or lesser degree improbable, scenarios must be taken into consideration; to knowledge drawn from experience and science we must add imagination, suspicion, fiction and fear" (Beck, 2009, p. 53).
7 For the critics of the principle, which has been taken up in a number of ways in international policy documents, the problem was the paralysing aspects of "possibilistic" thinking. See, for example, Sunstein (2002–2003).
8 See also the analysis of Hurricane Katrina in Protevi (2009, pp. 163–183).
9 For Tierney, Beck is mistaken in linking the social production of crises to late modernity. "In contrast, the position taken here is that the consequences of all types of disasters, both historical and contemporary, arise from decision making by organisations, political groups, and other powerful actors" (Tierney, 2014, p. 36). She makes the point that as early as the 1775 Lisbon earthquake and tsunami, Marquis de Pombal sought to rebuild through instituting new earthquake resistant urban design and building practices and that civil engineering works to mitigate natural perils can be dated much earlier to ancient and premodern societies.
10 See, for example, The United Nations and the World Bank (2010); GFDRR (2015).
11 See, for example, Latour (1993); Latour (2004).

12 Exemplified by Frankenstein's failure to care for his creation, which then turned into a tragic monster, Latour (2011).

13 See, for example, Clark (2011) or Klein (2014, pp. 1–3), which opens with the ironies of anthropogenic feedback loops, for example, when extreme hot weather, caused by the profligate burning of fossil fuels, melted the tarmac and grounded aircraft at Washington DC in the summer of 2012.

14 Latour (2013, pp. 94–95); see also, Connolly (2013), Bennett (2010). Latour echoes Connolly and Bennett on the cultivation of sensitivity: "To become sensitive, that is to feel responsible, and thus to make the loops feedback on our own action, we need, by a set of totally artificial operations, to place ourselves *as if we were* at the End of Time" (2013, p. 112).

15 See, for example, Haraway (2015); Tsing (2015, pp. 37–43); Gillings (2015).

16 As Gilles Deleuze and Felix Guattari note, tracing causal loops could only be a "selective", "artificial" and "restrictive" procedure, "overcoding" and reproducing its starting assumptions in a transcendent manner (2013, pp. 11–22).

17 Deleuze nicely captures the difference between transcendent and immanent approaches in his suggestion that transcendent approaches introduce a "dimension supplementary to the dimensions of the given"; i.e. ideas of goals, direction and causal connections, which separate the human subject from the object of governance. Whereas, on the plane of immanence: "There is no longer a subject, but only individuating affective states of an anonymous force. Here [governance] is concerned only with motions and rests, with dynamic affective charges. It will be perceived with that which it makes perceptible to us, as we proceed" (Deleuze, 1988, p. 128).

18 See further, Venturini and Latour (2010).

References

Beck, U. (1992) *Risk society: Towards a new modernity*. London: SAGE.

Beck, U. (2009) *World at risk*. Cambridge: Polity Press.

Beck, U. (2015) 'Emancipatory catastrophism: What does it mean to climate change and risk society?' *Current Sociology* 63(1), pp. 75–88.

Bennett, J. (2010) *Vital matter: A political ecology of things*. Durham, NC: Duke University Press.

Bryne, D. and Callaghan, G. (2014) *Complexity theory and the social sciences: The state of the art*. London: Routledge.

Chandler, D. (2014) *Resilience: The governance of complexity*. London: Routledge.

Clark, N. (2011) *Inhuman nature: Sociable life on a dynamic planet*. London: SAGE.

Connolly, W.E. (2013) *The fragility of things: Self-organizing processes, neoliberal fantasies, and democratic activism*. Durham, NC: Duke University Press.

Cowen, D. (2014) *The deadly life of logistics: Mapping violence in global trade*. Minneapolis: University of Minnesota Press.

Defert, D. (1991) '"Popular life" and insurance technology', in Burchell, G., Gordon, C. and Miller, P. (eds.) *The Foucault effect: Studies in governmentality*. Chicago, IL: University of Chicago Press, pp. 211–233.

Deleuze, G. (1988) *Spinoza: Practical philosophy*. San Francisco: City Lights.

Deleuze, G. and Guattari, F. (2013) *A thousand plateaus*. London: Bloomsbury.

Dillon, M. (2008) 'Underwriting security'. *Security Dialogue* 39(2–3), pp. 309–332.

Duffield, M. (2011) 'Environmental terror: Uncertainty, resilience and the bunker', Working Paper, no. 06-11. School of Sociology, Politics and International Studies (SPAIS), University of Bristol.

Ewald, F. (1991) 'Insurance and risk', in Burchell, G., Gordon, C. and Miller, P. (eds.) *The Foucault effect: Studies in governmentality*. Chicago, IL: University of Chicago Press, pp. 197–210.

Gillings, M. (2015) 'Comment: How modern life has damaged our internal ecosystems', *SBS News*, 12 October. Available at: http://www.sbs.com.au/news/article/2015/10/09/comment-how-modern-life-has-damaged-our-internal-ecosystems (Accessed 25 April 2018).

Global Facility for Disaster Reduction and Recovery (GFDRR) (2015) *Managing disaster risks for a resilient future: A work plan for the global facility for disaster reduction and recovery 2016–2018*. Washington, DC: World Bank.

Haas, M. (2013) *Beyond bouncing back: A roundtable on critical transportation infrastructure resilience*. Washington, DC: US Department of Transportation.

Haas, M. (2015) *Bouncing forward: Transforming bad breaks into breakthroughs*. New York: Enliven.

Habib, M.M. (2015) 'Rwanda launched national risk atlas, the first-ever comprehensive risk profile developed in Africa'. *Newshour*, 11 September.

Haraway, D. (1988) 'Situated knowledges: The science question in feminism and the privilege of partial perspective'. *Feminist Studies* 14(3), pp. 575–599.

Haraway, D. (2015) 'Anthropocene, capitalocene, plantationocene, chthulucene: Making kin', *Environmental humanities*. Vol. 6, pp. 159–165.

Hargrave, S. (2015) 'Can open data prevent a global food shortage? With the world's population set to grow to nearly 10 billion by 2050, pioneering farmers look to open data for eco-friendly solutions', *The Guardian*, 2 September.

Klein, M. (2014) *This changes everything: Capitalism vs. the climate*. New York, NY: Simon & Schuster.

Latour, B. (1993) *We have never been modern*. Cambridge, MA: Harvard University Press.

Latour, B. (2004) *Politics of nature: How to bring the sciences into democracy*. Cambridge, MA: Harvard University Press.

Latour, B. (2011) 'Love your monsters'. *Breakthrough Journal* 2, pp. 21–28.

Latour, B. (2013) *Facing Gaia: Six lectures on the political theology of nature*. Edinburgh: Gifford Lectures on Natural Religion. 18–28 February (draft version 1 March 2013).

Lavell, A. and Maskrey, A. (2014) 'The future of disaster risk management'. *Environmental Hazards* 13(4), pp. 267–280.

Lenin, V. (1975) *Imperialism, the highest stage of capitalism*. Moscow: Progress Publishers.

Marx, K. (1983) *Capital: A critique of political economy*. Vol. 1. London: Lawrence & Wishart.

Pelling, M. (2011) *Adaptation to climate change: From resilience to transformation*. London: Routledge.

Protevi, J. (2009) *Political affect: Connecting the social and the somatic*. Minneapolis: University of Minnesota Press.

Rodin, J. (2015) *The resilience dividend*. London: Profile Books.

Roitman, J. (2013) *Anti-crisis*. Durham, NC: Duke University Press.

Schmitt, C. (2003) *The nomos of the Earth: In the international law of the Jus Publicum Europaeum*. New York: Telos Press.

Sheffi, Y. (2015) *The power of resilience: How the best companies manage the unexpected*. Cambridge, MA: MIT Press.

Smith, J. (2015). 'Engineering for disaster: New NCAR collaboration strives to bolster weather, climate resilience', *AtmosNews*, 29 September. Available at: http://www2.ucar.edu/atmosnews/in-brief/17219/engineering-for-disaster (Accessed 25 April 2018).

Smith, J. and Jenks, C. (2006) *Qualitative complexity: Ecology, cognitive processes and the re-emergence of structures in post-humanist social theory*. London: Routledge.

Stockholm Resilience Centre (2014) The hidden cost of coerced resilience. Available at: http://www.stockholmresilience.org/research/research-news/2014-11-29-the-hidden-cost-of-coerced-resilience.html (Accessed 25 April 2018)

Sunstein, C. (2002–2003) 'The paralyzing principle'. *Regulation* 25, pp. 32–37.

Tierney, K. (2014) *Social roots of risk: Producing disasters, producing resilience*. Stanford, CA: Stanford University Press.

Tsing, A.L. (2015) *The mushroom at the end of the world: On the possibility of life in capitalist ruins*. Princeton, NJ: Princeton University Press.

UN Office for Disaster Risk Reduction (UNISDR) (2014) *Progress and challenges in disaster risk reduction: A contribution towards the development of policy indicators for the post-2015 framework on disaster risk reduction*. Geneva: UNISDR.

The United Nations and the World Bank (2010) *Natural hazards, unnatural disasters: The economics of effective prevention*. Washington, DC: World Bank.

Urry, J. (2003) *Global complexity*. Cambridge: Polity Press.

Venturini, T. and Latour, B. (2010) 'The social fabric: Digital traces and quali-quantitative methods', in Chardronnet, E. (ed.) *Proceedings of futur en Seine 2009: The digital future of the city*. Paris: Cap Digital, pp. 87–101.

Walker, B. and Salt, D. (2006) *Resilience thinking: Sustaining ecosystems and people in a changing world*. Washington, DC: Island Press.

Part III

Non-learning, fantasy learning, and potential learning

6 Vision and ideology in economic theory

The post–crisis persistence of mainstream general equilibrium macroeconomics

Matthew Watson

It is generally agreed – at least outside mainstream macroeconomics – that the community of academic economists had a bad global financial crisis. This agreement involves more than simply repeating the well-worn observation that most of them failed to see the crisis coming. As most economists would deny that prediction is their main job, this is hardly a reason for deep introspection on their part. Of course, there were several macroeconomists who can justifiably claim to have sounded the alarm. However, they come from the margins of mainstream macroeconomics and find it hard to gain the ear of their more orthodox-minded colleagues. Thus, although Wynne Godley, Nouriel Roubini, Steve Keen, Dean Baker, Randall Wray, Michael Hudson, Karl Case and Marc Lavoie have substantial followings, they cannot speak on behalf of the entire profession (Bezemer, 2009).

What should be more unsettling for mainstream macroeconomists than their failure to anticipate the crisis is that it first broke out in financial markets where orthodox economics assumptions about how markets work had fundamentally guided valuation techniques. These assumptions informed the dominant class of macroeconomic models that existed as the symptoms of crisis first attracted public concern. They posited it was possible to identify the structure of risks inherent in financial institutions' increasingly over-sized personal loan books and to manage them through financial arbitrage. This justified the bundling of household debt repayment schedules into securities with different risk profiles on the assumption that all these risks could then be arbitraged away through trading the resulting securities on secondary markets. Instead of the promised risk-free financial environment, however, the global financial crisis revealed that securitization created something akin to the proverbial house of cards. Given this congruence between mainstream economics and crisis-generating financial practice, it is hardly surprising that the economists who did predict the global financial crisis were working with models that differed markedly from mainstream opinion (Keen, 2013; Quiggin, 2013).

This has been the primary cause of discomfort for academic economists as they have attempted to navigate their way through the aftermath of the crisis (Kates, 2011). It creates a predicament about what to do next. Should they double down on the assertion that prediction is simply not their business and attempt to ride out the storm? Or should they accept the demands from critics about the need for more realistic assumptions to undergird their future macroeconomic modelling? Those who have chosen the former route out of the predicament continue to regard the global financial crisis as a singular moment that has now passed and belongs to a freak type of event that is statistically highly unlikely to recur. Those opting for the latter route must again question the first principles that inform macroeconomic theorizing. This particularly concerns the Dynamic Stochastic General Equilibrium (DSGE) models that for some time have constituted mainstream macroeconomics. These models attribute internal laws of motion to the economy that ensure its operations are self-correcting and hence self-stabilizing. For those who double down, the global financial crisis was not seen before it arrived because it was a fundamentally unseeable singular event; conversely, for those who choose to walk back from the original assumptions, it is a category mistake to conflate the factually unseen and the inherently unseeable.

My contribution to this volume adopts the latter perspective. I contextualise the role of mainstream macroeconomics in the global financial crisis through Joseph Schumpeter's methodological writings on economists' preanalytic "vision". He first explicitly outlined this notion in his 1948 Presidential Address to the American Economic Association, "Science and Ideology", and filled in the details in his posthumously published classic, *History of Economic Analysis* (see, respectively, Schumpeter, 1949, 2009 [1954]). His use of the notion of preanalytic vision implies a plea to his fellow economists to think seriously about what phenomena might inadvertently be removed from their line of sight by their starting assumptions. To commit oneself to a given vision, he argued, necessarily restricts the type of real-world relationships about which economic theory could speak. Any preanalytic vision produces its own subsequent analytic blind spots such that it cannot see what it cannot see. Reflecting on a preanalytic vision in these terms requires a critic to consider not only what it deems to be worth observing in the real world but also how this theoretical lens confines resulting observations to those things, events, processes or relations that are intuitively most seeable on this basis. Both moments are important in Schumpeter's methodology. Vision remains the indispensable "preanalytic cognitive act that supplies the raw material for the analytic effort" (Schumpeter, 2009 [1954], p. 41). However, because this vision can be burdened by its articulation with ideological baggage, empiri-cally-oriented analytic efforts are required to assist in the eradication of ideological elements and improve the abstract theoretical model. Using the initial vision one-sidedly, unreflexively and, hence, uncritically to adjudicate findings (selecting only corroborating evidence) confirms rather than elim-inates ideological bias. This is not just a question of initial assumptions but also of the bias inscribed in specific methods or techniques of investigation (see below). Rigorous empirical testing is essential to preserve what is theoretically valuable in the underlying vision and to purge its ideological aspects both methodologically and substantively.

The practice of mainstream economic theorists both pre- and post-global financial crisis suggests that Schumpeter's methodological optimism was misplaced. We know now, a decade on, that the global financial crisis has not produced a transformation in the theoretical assumptions or ideological commitments of most academic economists. The global financial crisis generated lots of new facts, almost all of which might have been expected to prove disconcerting to mainstream macroeconomics. But this largely failed to occur. This suggests the economists' vision and their ideology remain blinkered. It is important here to note that Schumpeter employed ideology in two distinct senses. First, his American Economics Association Presidential Address is clearly focused mainly on the ideology of technique such that methods and techniques are employed that are likely to confirm a preferred line of argument. In the present case, for example, DSGE models have been widely criticized for their reliance on so-called calibration tests. These provide parameter estimates constructed judiciously from those bits of the historical data that the model can replicate whilst acting as if the rest of the data were absent (Bhidé, 2010). However, such selective data matching does not constitute a serious test of the model (Danielsson, 2011). Second, Schumpeter's discussion in the *History of Economic Analysis* also refers at several points to the corrupting influence of political values. Especially vivid in this regard was his insistence that "the garb of philosophy is removable ... in the case of economics" (Schumpeter, 2009 [1954], p. 31). It seems that this has not occurred in the case of DSGE models. Indeed, their creators have been consistently criticized for trying to pass off as purely technical model parameters what are actually their normative preferences for pro-market macroeconomic policies (Engelen et al., 2011).

The problem facing mainstream macroeconomics is that competitive pricing dynamics are now treated as the norm on both sides of the Schumpeterian divide between vision and ideology. It is the assumption of competitive pricing dynamics that makes DSGE models thinkable in the first instance – it is, so to speak, their methodological condition of possibility. Yet this same assumption now routinely informs policy recommendations from DSGE modellers on how best to manage economic relations. What might originally have been merely a set of tools to guide attempts to make sense of the world in abstract terms has since become increasingly difficult to disentangle from the assertion that competitive pricing is essential to the efficient allocation of scarce resources in the modern economy. Initially, the assumption of continuous market-clearing dynamics was just a means of making the mathematics of a purely hypothetical general equilibrium model operable. Increasingly, however, this same assumption is invoked to justify remaking economic institutions and attitudes so the world operates just like the model.

Schumpeter's objective of cleansing preanalytic visions of ideological bias appears to remain a distant utopia in light of the practices of contemporary mainstream macroeconomists. Given that methodologists of economics writing much later dismissed the idea of an easy separability between the two (e.g. Blaug, 1992), perhaps Schumpeter's goal was always destined to be utopian. Yet even if his prescriptions are more aspirational than practical, they still serve to show just how far mainstream macroeconomics remains from his ideal situation. Most academic economists appear to have learnt little from previous financial crises about how orthodox economic theory contributed to creating the systemic tendencies that generated them. They also seem no better placed to learn anything in this regard from the global financial crisis. Schumpeter's methodological reflections therefore remain instructive at the very least as a guide to what *could* be learnt.

Schumpeter on vision and ideology

Vision seems to be Schumpeter's substitute for the more traditional philosophical notion of epistemology. It arises from the need to create some sort of bridge between practical insight and economic intuition (Redman, 1997, p. 316). Social reality is never revealed to the observer in all its complexity in real time, if ever (cf. Sum and Jessop, 2013). Nobody ever sees every aspect of anything, let alone everything. Schumpeter's concept of vision can be usefully located in this context. He introduced it in the *History of Economic Analysis* by noting that "to be able to posit to ourselves any problems at all, we should first have to visualize a distinct set of coherent phenomena as a worthwhile object of our analytic efforts" (Schumpeter, 2009 [1954], p. 41). Thus, his notion of vision serves to tell economists whether they have recognised the presence of something worth the initial effort invested in looking for it. It follows that it is an expected shape of reality and not reality itself that guides the observation of events and allows those events to be depicted as either typical or atypical.

There is a distinct order for Schumpeter, then, in which economic theorizing occurs: "analytic effort is of necessity preceded by a preanalytic cognitive act" (Schumpeter, 2009 [1954], p. 41). What the eventual analytic effort will consist of turns crucially around an initial "perception of a set of related phenomena" (Schumpeter, 1949, p. 350), where that perception might relate, for example, to claims regarding allocative efficiency, the logic of contract underpinning exchange relations or, for the purposes of this chapter, coordination of economic activity through competitive pricing dynamics. Schumpeter described this perception as "a prescientific act [that] must be performed in order to give our minds something to do scientific work on" (ibid.). The preanalytic and the prescientific are thus distinguishable, because the "object of research ... must be recognized as having some meaning or relevance that justifies our interest". The prescientific understanding of what counts as a valid area of investigation usually comes from the sense – that is, the professionally socialized sense – of working within an established theoretical tradition. One economist's prescientific act therefore follows from other economists' prior analytic efforts.

This relationship could easily collapse into purely self-referential theoretical pursuits. Attempting to avoid such an outcome, Schumpeter (2009 [1954], p. 37) suggested economic theory should only be treated as "true" where there is a distinct verisimilitude to repeated empirical observations. This epistemological approach requires continuing consistency between the chosen vision of what it is important to study and resulting observations (cf. Allen, 1991, p. 103). Because models might always bear the imprint of residual ideological bias, the underlying theory can never be proved "right" per se. However, for Schumpeter, aggregating repeat observations becomes the empirical means of driving out a bad model and replacing it with a better one. This requires that only modest claims can be made on behalf of economic theory: it is merely "designed to give convenient expression to certain facts of the world in which we live" (Schumpeter, 2009 [1954], p. 41). Much therefore depends on what is meant by "facts" and whether "the world in which we live" refers to the heterogeneous and contested realm of everyday experience in all its complexity or to the simplified, homogeneous and uncontested relationships that economic theory finds it far easier to posit.

Schumpeter's studies in the history of economic thought tend to focus more on successive theoretical models than on supporting evidence, so they leave the reader wondering whether these models are based on something more than self-referential claims. By contrast, his methodological studies give the impression that only the presentation of corroborating facts will allow theoretical models to resonate beyond the theorists' self-made worlds. For Schumpeter the methodologist, a theoretical model without facts is difficult to differentiate from ideology. Moreover, the whole point of carefully constructing and refining a theoretical model is to purge the initial underlying vision of those ideological elements that inevitably accompanied and shaped its original articulation (Schumpeter, 1949, pp. 346, 351, 356). As all economists are likely to have personal commitments to both academic technique and political values, this is ideology in both of its senses as deployed by Schumpeter across his work.

Schumpeter (ibid., p. 358) made it clear just how difficult he thought it was to eliminate bias or even to be fully conscious that the process of eliminating bias had been successfully started. This is because ideologically-inflected statements "are truthful statements about what a man thinks he sees" (ibid., p. 349). This element of selective sight is, he wrote, inescapable. Nonetheless, ideology is tameable, and its effects can be lessened, because theoretical models can always be subjected to testing, where the practice of testing appears to escape the intrusion of ideology in a way that theoretical model-building does not. This, in many ways, represents the crux of Schumpeter's philosophy of science. There is an important distinction that runs throughout his methodological work between the process of discovery and the process of justification, and it is in keeping these two processes apart that ideology can allegedly be removed from the findings of economics. The purely theoretical aspect of economists' endeavours concludes with the final articulation of a fully fleshed out model, because this is when the moment of discovery is complete. At that point, the attention turns to the accumulation of facts that help justify commitment to a particular model world.

Yuichi Shionoya has gone further than anyone in recovering the influences that underpin Schumpeter's account of the research process. He attributes Schumpeter's thinking on the distinction between discovery and justification to the work of Hans Reichenbach (1938). The basic idea is to distinguish between, on the one hand, the setting of problems and their subsequent formulation as theoretically-oriented puzzles and, on the other hand, the creation of explanatory frameworks and their appraisal as functioning windows on the world. The former pair belongs to Schumpeter's realm of vision and the latter to the process through which attempts are made to allow vision to stand alone shorn of ideology (Shionoya, 1997, p. 60). Discovery allows for the identification of possible facts that might shed light on what is considered to be of interest, but it is justification that shows whether those facts provide support for the chosen theoretical model (Shionoya, 1997, p. 58).

As I hope to show now, discovery has always dominated justification in the general equilibrium tradition that has, as its legacy, today's leading dynamic stochastic general equilibrium (DSGE) macroeconomic models. Yet we are further away than ever before from striking the sort of balance between the two that Schumpeter took as evidence of good economics. It is the lack of attention to the justificatory stage that allowed orthodox economics opinion to unite around the claim that the global financial crisis does not signify or entail a crisis of economics. Theoretical models deserve to be recognised as genuinely scientific models, according to Schumpeter (2009 [1954], p. 570), only when "factual and 'theoretical' analysis [are placed] in an endless relation of give and take" (see also Schumpeter, 2009 [1954], p. 42). It is the "factual" side of this relationship that seems to be most obviously missing from the practices that reproduce the dominance of DSGE models in contemporary macroeconomics. Thus, Schumpeter's (1949, p. 358) characterization of ideologies as "creeds which for the time being are impervious to argument" seems to be especially appropriate here.

Seeing through the Arrow–Debreu lens

Schumpeter believed that one phenomenon above all others had captured economists' trained imagination: competitive pricing dynamics (Schumpeter, 2009 [1954], p. 39). He was quick to lavish praise on Léon Walras's (1984 [1954]) *Elements of Pure Economics* for shaping his fellow economists' prescientific sense of the significance of market prices for the coordination of economic activity. Indeed, for this reason, he called it "the only work by an economist that will stand comparison with the achievements of theoretical physics" (Schumpeter, 2009 [1954], p. 827). He saw within it a series of questions relating to proofs for the existence of general equilibrium that "are in logic although not always in fact neutral to ideology" (Schumpeter, 1949, p. 352). Walras's vision, he was saying, may or may not ultimately withstand systematic testing but, from the viewpoint of the philosophy of science, its importance lies elsewhere. The equilibrium construct provides for economists a basic way of seeing their own self-made model world that might eventually lose all ideological presentiments.

It was left to others to flesh out the Walrasian vision in a burst of creative theoretical activity in the years immediately following Schumpeter's death in 1950. This initial development of a general equilibrium tradition seems to meet Schumpeter's demands for the constant interaction between theoretical and factual analysis, at least as far as it was built around a series of "if-then" statements that *if* certain assumptions were to hold *then* a related set of effects should make themselves available for observation (Starr, 2011, p. xvi). Yet these "if-then" statements never went beyond working out as a matter of logic the type of results that general equilibrium models should imprint on the theorist's imagination if a certain class of assumptions was to be deemed acceptable in its own terms (Clower, 1995, p. 314). At no stage did the pioneers claim they were describing the economic world as it is (i.e. a Schumpeterian vision with its accompanying ideology eradicated) or even that they were describing the economic world as they would like it to be (i.e. where Schumpeterian vision and ideology continue to collide). They were clear they were working with thought experiments designed solely to elaborate the vision of a functioning economic system bounded by market prices alone.

The most important pioneering works written in this tradition are those by Kenneth Arrow and Gérard Debreu (Arrow, 1951, 1959; Arrow and Debreu, 1954; Arrow and Hurwicz, 1953; Debreu, 1959). One of Arrow's students, Ross Starr (2011, p. xxiii) has described the effects on the field of accepting Arrow-Debreu visualization techniques as truly "revolutionary: It fundamentally changes your way of thinking. Once you see things this way, it is hard to conceive of them otherwise". In the conversation between competing model worlds for general equilibrium theorists, the Arrow-Debreu approach appears to have won hands-down, and this *despite* its evident limitations. It is what tells economists about the things they might care to look for in their self-made model world of pure theory, what tells them their professional vision remains unimpaired, and what tells them, most crucially, what "the economy" is. It provided economists with "a new line of argumentation" (Scarf, 1986, p. 117), with the image of what they "ought to aim for as modern scientists" (Blaug, 2002a, p. 37), and with "the 'benchmark' model" for seeing the world "as it is" (Sonnenschein, cited in Starr, 2011, p. xxi).

Arrow and Debreu did nothing to try to replace what Schumpeter said had always been the underlying vision of analytic economics: namely, the organization of the market environment through competitive price dynamics. The art of discovery remained fundamentally as it ever was. All that was changed was how to evaluate the facts that the underlying vision could make known. Arrow and Debreu simply attempted to rid economics of one means of theorizing "the optimality of competition" so that another means could be introduced to replace it. Simple mathematics thus gave way to more complex mathematics, in the hope that the greater technical demands subsequently being made of economists would lead to enhanced abstract precision in understanding the condition of equilibrium (Warsh, 2006, p. 162). Pretty much everything that can be said through the prism of mathematical general equilibrium theory results from the use of convex sets to promote a particular image of what we might be looking at when imagining the economy (Carter, 2001, p. 387). Convex set theory allowed the classic two-dimensional demand-and-supply diagram to be overwritten as the dominant way of imagining how markets come to be coordinated into an equilibrium state. The classic approach was replaced by an *n*-dimensional mapping of shapes that was seeable in mathematical logic but fundamentally unseeable to the human eye (Watson, 2018, pp. 26-8, 97-8).

What, then, are we to make of the achievements associated with elaborating the core characteristics of the Arrow-Debreu world in which general equilibrium economics and DSGE macroeconomic models now reside? From a Schumpeterian perspective at least, further steps are necessary before concluding the economic meaning associated with relationships in that world are attributable to something more than giving economic-sounding names to the internal properties of convex sets. The Arrow-Debreu world is constructed mathematically on the assumption that any two points in the set of all possible points can be joined by a straight line that never once passes through a point that lies outside the set of all possible points. This is the mathematical property of convexity (Florenzano, 2003). It is used to model an economic world of continuous demand, continuous supply and, therefore, continuous market-clearing potential, because every possible combination of demand and supply falls within the set of all possible points. Yet it takes a substantial leap of faith to assume that the economy mirrors in actuality the continuities provided by the assumption of convexity (Düppe and Weintraub, 2014). Proof-making in Arrow-Debreu terms thus follows the structure of mathematical assumptions and not empirical investigations of the way in which market demand and market supply actually interact in given situations. However, discovering a logical proof that one has set out specifically to discover is little different in Schumpeter's terms to seeing only what one chooses to see when accepting the insights of the prevailing "creed". The something else required here is what Schumpeter had in mind when writing of the constant "give and take" between factual and theoretical analysis. However, it is far from clear whether results arising from Arrow-Debreu proofs are genuinely testable in the classic Popperian sense of falsifiability (Garry, 1995, p. 7).

The purely axiomatic structural models of general equilibrium theory are so remote from the information required for any individual to reliably navigate their way through everyday economic life that doubts must persist over the availability of data that would allow economists to re-specify their DSGE models in a more appropriate manner. Economics in the Arrow-Debreu tradition might therefore forever be confined to what Deirdre McCloskey (1994, p. 133) has called "the blackboard", where the problems under discussion are those of economists' own creation rather than being related to how people perceive the struggles of day-to-day living (see also Blaug, 2002b, p. 35). This is in stark contrast to Schumpeter's notion of constant feedback between factual and theoretical analysis. Yet only through testing their theories properly might economists become fully aware of the "ideological burden" in their underlying vision (McCloskey, 1994, p. 177). Other ways of proceeding risk elevating the form of economists' self-made model world over its function or, worse still from Schumpeter's perspective, allow ideology to crowd out vision. If the former charge seems most applicable to the first generation of Nobel Prize-winning general equilibrium economists, the final section of this chapter argues that the latter applies more readily to the second.

Arrow's approach used the idealization of a free market economy to show the adverse effects of allowing market institutions to encroach into ever more aspects of social existence. He compared the egalitarian nature of the behavioural axioms of general equilibrium economics – everyone had to have both the same capabilities and the same opportunities to act upon those capabilities if the mathematics of convex set theory was to work – with the deeply inegalitarian outcomes produced through actual markets. The test that Arrow had in mind as an equivalent to Schumpeter's notion of the constant "give and take" between factual and theoretical analysis was a purely subjective one: how much observable inequality should be permissible in a civilised society? If this is Schumpeterian ideology speaking to problems that are imaginable in the first place only through commitment to a Schumpeterian vision of price-competitive markets, Arrow's egalitarian instincts suggest that the vision is most useful for drawing attention to the real-life limits that should be imposed on such markets. The Schumpeterian ideology that speaks through the work of a later generation of general equilibrium theorists gives voice to what appears to be a different political priority.

Vision, ideology and the second generation of general equilibrium Nobel Laureates

The most important analytical distinction between the first two generations of general equilibrium Nobel Laureates is that the latter brought the theory of rational expectations into economics. They continued to inhabit the same vision of what it might mean to think of the economy in terms of the auto-corrective principles of price competition, but this shifted the ideological basis of the vision away from Arrow's concern for demonstrating the logic of market failure to a new concern for demonstrating the fallibility of government intervention (LeRoy, 1995, p. 249). The class of DSGE models arising from the rational expectations revolution is notable for the absence of what Arrow (cited in Klein, 2013, p. 277) has called the realm "beyond the province of private business". Every problem is thus modelled as if it has a potential market solution, thus repositioning government as an unnecessary inconvenience within the economy. Ray Canterbery (2011, p. 288) has alluded to "the smart bomb of rational expectations", which, in the hands of Nobel Prize winners Robert Lucas and Thomas Sargent in particular, laid waste to previous assumptions about the effectiveness of targeting increases in the social welfare function (Snowdon, 2002, p. 136).

All rational expectations models derive their impetus from a single source: the so-called Lucas Critique. Lucas argued that policy-making models had parameters that would vary with the policy itself and, because of this, they would be unable to capture the dynamic path of behaviour in any predictive sense (Lucas, 1976, p. 41). The most that could be achieved with any degree of certainty was to understand the logical properties of combining price-competitive behaviour with the ability to know all future states of the economy. As a result, the real economy was rendered entirely autonomous of all expected stabilizing policy interventions (Frisch, 1983, p. 136). This is not a change of vision in itself, because all articulations of an Arrow-Debreu world place a similar emphasis on the economy finding its equilibrium position through the influence of market institutions. What is different about rational expectations models is that the market necessarily performs this coordinating mechanism not only well but far better when left alone than when competing against other forms of allocative decision-making. The theory of rational expectations is therefore destructive of the notion of policy *choice* (Mishkin, 2007, p. 3). Any anticipated policy intervention is likely to be counter-productive and, at the very best, can only leave intact the outcomes that market institutions would have produced on their own.

The clearest account of this way of thinking can be found in the policy ineffectiveness proposition as asserted by Thomas Sargent and Neil Wallace (1975, p. 241). They were still working with the same visualization techniques as those employed by Arrow and Debreu, seeking to ascertain what would happen in their hypothetical economy under the assumption of continuous market-clearing dynamics (Gordon, 2004, p. 228). Policy gets in the way in this perspective because it necessarily introduces discontinuities into pricing activities if it is to successfully steer the economy towards a new path (Marin, 1992, pp. 90–93). Arrow and Debreu ruled out the presence of such disconti-nuities for the sake of giving the mathematical expressions in their general equilibrium model some degree of pseudo-economic meaning. Arrow was concerned merely to make the mathematics operable so the price-competitive vision could be seen in its own terms prior to comparing the resulting hypothetical economy with actually observed economic outcomes. Sargent and Wallace, by contrast, asserted a continuous structure of market-clearing prices for reasons that seem difficult to attribute to vision per se. They appear much more interested in being able to advance the deeply political argument that technocratic economic management conducted in line with clear policy rules is always preferable to government discretion, declaring the debate amongst economists on this issue to be long since over (Sent, 2006, p. 54). What is a palpable expression of Schumpeterian vision in Arrow and Debreu's hands therefore looks much more like Schumpeterian ideology in Sargent and Wallace's. The policy ineffectiveness proposition is, after all, merely a list of things policy-makers should prevent themselves from doing (Gottschalk, 2005, p. 98). The image of a creed thus rears its head.

It is noteworthy that both Lucas and Sargent are eager to stress that there is nothing other than scientific endeavour motivating their work. Lucas (1984, p. 54): "I don't like talking about how big government should be". Sargent (cited in Sommer, 2011): "[Political opinions] really don't matter in my research". Sargent might well be talking for the whole cohort of contemporary general equilibrium theorists when saying, "I'm not really interested in politics. This rational expectations stuff is clearly not politically motivated" (cited in Klein, Daza and Mead, 2013, p. 572). Yet this is to miss Schumpeter's point. Much more pertinent to his concern is Sargent's admission in his Nobel Lecture that "broad insights from [rational expectations] models shape virtually everything I see in the fiscal and monetary history of my country" (Sargent, 2012, p. 9). Placing boundaries around what might be seen runs in parallel to looking for what is hoped might be shown to be there. This is the territory that Schumpeter (2009 [1954], p. 33) equated explicitly with ideology, where vision subsequently tells the economist not only how the world might look but how it needs to be made to seem if economic theory is to pursue a particular purpose.

The only antidote to such a situation, according to Schumpeter (ibid., p. 562), is to submit the underlying vision to rigorous testing designed to weed out the distortions associated with ideology. It is here, however, that the rational expectations-informed policy ineffectiveness proposition falls down most obviously. Critics have lined up for many years now to highlight its failure to survive adequate testing (Buiter, 1989; Gordon, 1989; Sheffrin, 1996). Model justification, from Schumpeter's perspective, requires the sort of descriptive content that model discovery does not. Yet this is precisely what models built upon rational expectations theory lack. They can show with attendant mathematical proofs that any economy whose internal features are commensurable with the models' assumptions will always and everywhere produce the models' results (Starr, 2008, p. 237). But what sort of economy will this be?

To see whether it is one that belongs only to economists' self-made model world we need merely look at the questions asked of it. The economics of equilibrium have shifted from an interest in how prices adjust within markets to an interest in the unique set of prices that must arise under the assumption of continuous market-clearing dynamics across the whole of the economy (Blaug, 2002a, p. 37). In other words, it has shifted from a position in which descriptive content is possible along the lines of model justification to a position in which descriptive content is sacrificed in the interests of a purer process of model discovery.

A new class of tests called calibration tests has been devised in an attempt to provide apparent descriptive content to rational expectations models in the DSGE tradition. However, they carefully handpick strictly limited parts of the available data because it is known that these parts best fit the models' specified results. This is quite different from having demonstrated the models' robustness and representativeness (Gregory and Smith, 1991, p. 297). When attempting the latter through reference to anything other than strategically selected data, rational expectations models of a price-competitive economy have always been found wanting. This is unsurprising, as they rely on a symmetrical relationship between output and prices that simply cannot be found in the data (Gordon, 2004, p. 229). Price changes do not respond automatically to cancel out anticipated policy interventions, and therefore there is no evidence in real life of markets ever clearing continuously (Gottschalk, 2005, p. 99).

This is an example of the market failure that Arrow's commitment to mathematizing the market coordination problem was designed to illustrate. He set up continuities in mathematical space as a means of highlighting their frequent absence in economic space. In comparison, the rational expectations assumption of perfect market-clearing dynamics due to inherent price continuities feels like argument by assertion. Schumpeter (1949, p. 358) had warned that when "ideologies crystallize ... they find defenders whose very souls go into the fight for them". Is this what we see here? Even if this is to push the critique of Lucas and Sargent slightly too far, it still raises serious doubts about whether the work of the second generation of general equilibrium Nobel Laureates has ever proceeded beyond the Schumpeterian level of model discovery at which ideology is unavoidable.

Conclusion

Schumpeter appears to have used his methodological reflections to launch a pre-emptive strike against the second generation of general equilibrium Nobel Laureates and their insistence that scientific endeavour alone motivates their work. He worried that most economists "do not admit that [ideological bias] is an inescapable curse and that it vitiates economics to its core" (Schumpeter, 1949, p. 349). "There is little comfort", he concluded his address as President of the American Economic Association, "in postulating, as has been done some-times, the existence of detached minds that are immune to ideological bias and *ex hypothesi* able to overcome it" (Schumpeter, 1949, p. 358). Thus viewed, perhaps it is more than coincidence that those who have done most to deny the ideological content of Dynamic Stochastic General Equilibrium theory are those who have been most adamant that orthodox economics opinion is not in crisis in the wake of recent traumas in financial pricing functions. Lucas (2009) and Sargent (2010) have often been the public faces of the counterattack on behalf of the practices that produced macroeconomic models cast in the DSGE mould.

Two possible interpretations follow for understanding how the global financial crisis has not also translated into an accompanying crisis of mainstream macroeconomics. There is still a puzzle to explain here, because the collapse of the financial pricing structure that destroyed huge stocks of social wealth occurred within the context of mainstream macroeconomic models blithely predicting continuing conditions of stability. The first potential explanation revolves around the claim that economics in its orthodox guise simply affirms the implications of working with price-competitive models. This would be to insist that vision can always stand alone in a pristine state and that economists should not be blamed when other people read more into their models than those models can actually say. However, this defence sits uncomfortably with the extent to which orthodox economics opinion has been imbued with social authority. Economists have become the expert commentators of choice over recent generations, but only on the basis of their prior credentials as theoretical model builders. The relationship between the model world and what lies beyond it therefore seems substantially blurred. Thus, a second reading appears more appropriate. The insistence that DSGE models by definition are non-ideological closes theorists' minds to the need to try to purge their models of ideology in Schumpeter's justification stage. It is often the case, of course, that it is difficult to gain awareness of the ideological bias contained within one's professional vision if one's professional peers are routinely making the same assumptions (Norgaard, 2003, p. 25). And one's professional peers are more likely to reflect back one's own assumptions in a subject field like economics in which so much deference is paid to the field's acknowledged "stars". Lucas and Sargent, Nobel Laureates both, clearly belong in such exalted company.

These divergent interpretations offer different views of what mainstream macroeconomists might learn in the aftermath of the global financial crisis. The first, which asserts that economists have never had any intention of commenting beyond the sphere of their own self-made model world, suggests they have nothing to learn. They are only interested, from this perspective at least, in thought experiments concerned to flesh out their own hypothetical visions, and they have no desire for their opinions to be acted upon. The second, more realistic, view is that, whilst the proponents of orthodox economics opinion have plenty to learn, they are likely to ignore their own culpability in the global financial crisis and so choose to learn nothing. They have told themselves for so long that their vision of a price-competitive economy is neutral with respect to both policy choice and distributional consequences that this has been turned into a mantra of faith. Anyone who thinks otherwise is therefore likely to continue to be dismissed as a non-believer in the creed.

The success of Lucas and Sargent in restating the case for orthodox economics opinion has certainly been helped by the political redefinition of the crisis. What was once a meltdown of financial markets that began life as experiments in blackboard economics has now been repositioned as evidence of a social malaise that results when governments give out false hope that they can take care of people's futures (Watson, 2014, p. 11). DSGE models were rendered silent about the impending implosion of financial markets, because their ideological assertion of continuous market-clearing dynamics made such an event fundamentally unseeable within the confines of the relevant model world. However, that model world is constructed specifically to facilitate commentary on the perils of state largesse and the self-defeating nature of sacrificing budgetary balance to target enhancements of the social welfare function. A crisis fundamentally unseeable in one political narration thus becomes only too predictable in another. In these circumstances (but in these circumstances alone) the proponents of orthodox economics opinion might once again be able to hide their ideology from themselves (if not from other people). By changing the questions asked of them, mainstream macroeconomists' models have restored the deceit that they are non-ideological and simply describe the world as it is.

References

Allen, R.L. (1991) *Opening doors: The life and work of Joseph Schumpeter, volume 1: Europe.* New Brunswick, NJ: Transaction Publishers.

Arrow, K. (1951) *Social choice and individual values.* New York: John Wiley & Sons.

Arrow, K. (1959) 'Toward a theory of price adjustment', in Abramovitz, M. (ed.) *The allocation of economic resources: Essays in honour of Bernard Francis Haley.* Palo Alto, CA: Stanford University Press, pp. 41–51.

Arrow, K. and Debreu, G. (1954) 'Existence of an equilibrium for a competitive economy', *Econometrica*, 20(3), pp. 265–290.

Arrow, K. and Hurwicz, L. (1953) *Hurwicz's optimality criterion for decision-making under ignorance.* Technical Report Number 6, Department of Economics and Statistics. Palo Alto, CA: Stanford University.

Bezemer, D. (2009) *"No one saw this coming": Understanding financial crisis through accounting models.* SOM Research Reports 09002, University of Groningen. Available at: http://www.rug.nl/research/portal/en/publications/no-one-saw-this-coming-understanding-financial-crisis-through-accounting-models(b2851c5e-ffd3-4d3d-b840-9780e63725c4).html.

Bhidé, A. (2010) *A call for judgment: Sensible finance for a dynamic economy.* Oxford: Oxford University Press.

Blaug, M. (1992) *The methodology of economics: Or how economists explain.* 2nd edn. Cambridge: Cambridge University Press.

Blaug, M. (2002a) 'Ugly currents in modern economics', in Mäki, U. (ed.) *Fact and fiction in economics: Models, realism and social construction.* Cambridge: Cambridge University Press, pp. 35–56.

Blaug, M. (2002b) 'Is there really progress in economics?', in Boehm, S., Gehrke, C., Kurz, H. and Sturn, R. (eds.) *Is there progress in economics? Knowledge, truth and the history of economic thought.* Cheltenham: Edward Elgar, pp. 21–41.

Buiter, W. (1989) *Macroeconomic theory and stabilization policy.* Manchester: Manchester University Press.

Canterbery, R. (2011) *A brief history of economics: Artful approaches to the dismal science.* 2nd edn. Singapore: World Scientific.

Carter, M. (2001) *Foundations of mathematical economics.* Cambridge, MA: MIT Press.

Clower, R. (1995) 'Axiomatics in economics', *Southern Economic Journal*, 62(2), pp. 307–319.

Danielsson, J. (2011) *Financial risk forecasting: The theory and practice of forecasting market risk.* Hoboken, NJ: John Wiley & Sons.

Debreu, G. (1959) *Theory of value: An axiomatic analysis of economic equilibrium.* New Haven, CT: Yale University Press.

Düppe, T. and Weintraub, R. (2014) *Finding equilibrium: Arrow, Debreu, McKenzie and the problem of scientific credit.* Princeton, NJ: Princeton University Press.

Engelen, E., Ertürk, I., Froud, J., Johal, S., Leaver, A., Moran, M., Nilsson, A. and Williams, K. (2011) *After the great complacence: Financial crisis and the politics of reform.* Oxford: Oxford University Press.

Florenzano, M. (2003) *General equilibrium analysis: Existence and optimality properties of equilibria.* Boston, MA: Springer.

Frisch, H. (1983) *Theories of inflation.* Cambridge: Cambridge University Press.

Garry, B.D. (1995) 'Society and political change', in Kaushik, S.L. and Patnayak, R. (eds.) *Modern governments and political systems, Volume 4.* 1st edn. New Delhi: Mittal Publications, pp. 1–20.

Gordon, R. (1989) 'Symposium on macroeconomics 1: Fresh water, salt water, and other macroeconomic elixirs', *Economic Record,* 65(2), pp. 177–184.

Gordon, R. (2004) *Productivity growth, inflation, and unemployment: The collected essays of Robert J. Gordon.* Cambridge: Cambridge University Press.

Gottschalk, J. (2005) *Monetary policy and the German unemployment problem in macroeconomic models: Theory and evidence.* New York: Springer.

Gregory, A. and Smith, G. (1991) 'Calibration as testing: Inference in simulated macroeconomic models', *Journal of Business and Economic Statistics,* 9(3), pp. 297–303.

Kates, S. (ed.) (2011) *The global financial crisis: What have we learnt?* Cheltenham: Edward Elgar.

Keen, S. (2013) 'Predicting the "global financial crisis": Post-Keynesian economics', *Economic Record,* 89(2), pp. 228–254.

Klein, D. (2013) 'Kenneth J. Arrow', *Econ Journal Watch,* 10(3), pp. 268–281.

Klein, D., Daza, R. and Mead, H. (2013) 'Thomas J. Sargent', *Econ Journal Watch,* 10(3), pp. 570–576.

LeRoy, S. (1995) 'On policy regimes', in Hoover, K. (ed.) *Macroeconometrics: Developments, tensions, and prospects.* Norwell, MA: Kluwer Academic Publishers, pp. 235–252.

Lucas, R.E. (1976) 'Econometric policy evaluation: A critique', *Carnegie-Rochester Conference Series on Public Policy, Elsevier,* 1(1), pp. 19–46.

Lucas, R.E. (1984) 'Interview [with Arjo Klamer]', in Klamer, A. *Conversations with economists: New classical economists and their opponents speak out on the current controversy in macroeconomics.* Totowa, NJ: Rowman & Allanheld, pp. 29–57.

Lucas, R.E. (2009) 'In defence of the dismal science', *The Economist,* 6(August), p. 67.

Marin, A. (1992). *Macroeconomic policy.* London: Routledge.

McCloskey, D. (1994) *Knowledge and persuasion in economics.* Cambridge: Cambridge University Press.

Mishkin, F. (2007) *Monetary policy strategy.* Cambridge, MA: MIT Press.

Norgaard, R. (2003) 'Passion and ecological economics: Toward a richer coevolution of value systems and environmental systems', in Dovers, S., Stern, D. and Young, M. (eds.) *New dimensions in ecological economics: Integrated approaches to people and nature.* Cheltenham: Edward Elgar, pp. 23–34.

Quiggin, J. (2013) 'The state of economics in 2012: Complacency amid crisis', *Economic Record,* 89(S1), pp. 23–30.

Redman, D. (1997) *The rise of political economy as a science: Methodology and the classical economists.* Cambridge, MA: MIT Press.

Reichenbach, H. (1938) *Experience and prediction: An analysis of the foundations and the structure of knowledge.* Chicago, IL: University of Chicago Press.

Sargent, T. (2010) 'Modern macroeconomics under attack', *Minneapolis Federal Reserve*, September 2010, Available at: https://www.minneapolisfed.org/publications/the-region/interview-with-thomas-sargent (Accessed: 2 May 2018).

Sargent, T. (2012) 'Nobel lecture: United States then, Europe now', *Journal of Political Economy*, 120(1), pp. 1–40.

Sargent, T. and Wallace, N. (1975) ''Rational' expectations, the optimal monetary instrument, and the optimal money supply rule', *Journal of Political Economy*, 83(2), pp. 241–254.

Scarf, H. (1986) 'Testing for optimality in the absence of convexity', in Heller, W., Starr, R. and Starrett, D. (eds.) *Social choice and public decision making: Essays in honour of Kenneth J. Arrow, Volume 1.* Cambridge: Cambridge University Press, pp. 117–134.

Schumpeter, J. (1949) 'Science and ideology', *American Economic Review*, 39(2), pp. 345–359.

Schumpeter, J. (2009 [1954]) *History of economic analysis.* London: Routledge.

Sent, E.-M. (2006) *The evolving rationality of rational expectations: An assessment of Thomas Sargent's achievements.* Cambridge: Cambridge University Press.

Sheffrin, S. (1996) *Rational expectations.* 2nd edn. Cambridge: Cambridge University Press.

Shionoya, Y. (1997) *Schumpeter and the idea of social science.* Cambridge: Cambridge University Press.

Snowdon, B. (2002) *Conversations on growth, stability and trade: An historical perspective.* Cheltenham: Edward Elgar.

Sommer, J. (2011) 'The slogans stop here', *New York Times*, 29 October.

Starr, R. (2008) 'Arrow, Kenneth Joseph (Born 1921)', in Durlauf, S. and Blume, L. (eds.) *The new Palgrave dictionary of economics.* 2nd edn. Basingstoke: Palgrave Macmillan, pp. 232–241.

Starr, R. (2011) *General equilibrium theory: An introduction.* 2nd edn. Cambridge: Cambridge University Press.

Sum, N.-L. and Jessop, B. (2013) *Towards a cultural political economy: Putting culture in its place in political economy.* Cheltenham: Edward Elgar.

Walras, L. (1984 [1954]) *Elements of pure economics: Or the theory of social wealth.* Translated by W. Jaffé. Philadelphia, PA: Orion Editions.

Warsh, D. (2006) *Knowledge and the wealth of nations: A story of economic discovery.* New York: W.W. Norton and Company.

Watson, M. (2014) *Uneconomic economics and the crisis of the model world.* Basingstoke: Palgrave Macmillan.

Watson, M. (2018) *The market.* Newcastle: Agenda Publishers.

7 The crisis in democracy and authoritarian neoliberalism after the Eurozone crisis

Fantastic debates and power as affording not to learn from mistakes

Magnus Ryner

Introduction

This chapter asks whether the crisis in Europe today has a dialectical quality. Drawing on ideas from Jürgen Habermas's classic text, *Legitimation Crisis* (1975), to characterize the crisis, it posits that the European system lacks the "self-healing powers that are necessary for a recovery" and that its subjects find themselves, like the *dramatis personae* in classical tragedy, at the "turning point in a fateful process". This already challenges the generally benign readings of the progressive, self-reforming nature of the European Union, through which each positive step in European integration is a successful response to a new crisis. It then asks whether they can "summon up the strength to win back their freedom by shattering the mythic power of fate through the formation of new identities" (Habermas, 1975, p. 2). At stake here is the scope for a democratic solution to the triple European crises of financialization, neoliberal austerity, and the democratic deficit. This involves two sets of issues: first, the ability to diagnose these crises and the current conjuncture, propose organic solutions based on a realistic analysis of the past and present that not only identifies causes; and, second, proposals about feasible reforms as well as the agents or agencies that might deliver them, and indicate how the balance of forces can be reorganized at different sites and scales to deliver these reforms. In short, economic analysis must be combined with political analysis because economic reforms occur within specific political forms and are pursued by specific political agencies.

A *prima facie* case for posing this question is that the loss of self-healing powers signified in the dark clouds of Eurozone crisis seems to contain the silver-lining of a rich pan-European heterodox debate over possible alternative futures. In seeking a dialectical answer to the question above, this chapter draws on Friedrich Engels's contrast, in *Socialism: Utopian and Scientific* (1880 [1986], p. 403), between (1) utopian visions based on the elucubrations of great minds in response to moral disquiet about current conditions and (2) a scientific analysis based on a materialist analysis of the emerging contradictions of contemporary capitalism and their role in preparing the ground for its practical transcendence. Engels thereby directs us to consider whether the solutions proposed in the aforementioned debate are merely the more or less refined "phantasies" of "this or that ingenious brain", that may nonetheless contain "stupendously grand thoughts and germs of thought that … break out through their phantastic covering" but need to be reworked to reveal their transformative potential, or are based on compelling diagnoses of the historical-economic conditions in which the EU and attendant social forces find themselves today. This in turn poses important questions about crises, their construal, the scope for learning from utopian or phantastic diagnoses of the crisis and the corresponding solutions, and the challenges of developing a valid account of the crisis and a correct reading of the potential for transformation in the light of the complexity of the crisis and the balance of forces (on these distinctions, see the introduction by Jessop and Knio).

In addressing this question, I examine the respective diagnoses, and the debates within and between, two alternative visions of how to overcome European disciplinary neoliberalism. In broad terms, this heterodox economic debate is one between left-federalists (or as I call them, *federalist Kaleckians*), who envisage radical reform of EU structures, and *left intergovernmentalists* who envisage a fundamental break, where the immediate conjuncture entails a return to struggles in the field of the nation state and inter-state relations. Whilst these visions are grounded in economic analysis, they both raise the question of whether the EU can be democratized or, more fundamentally, whether the EU can be seen as an emergent polity with an emergent "demos" that might replace the current economic and political order. Starting with economic analyses has the benefit that this approach adds much-needed content to overly formalist debates about democracy and the EU.

I argue that, in different ways, both the federalist Kaleckians and the left intergovernmentalists are utopians in the sense of Engels. The federalist Kaleckians are the most obviously utopian in that their vision presupposes the mobilization of a pan-European agency, which is quite incongruent with the socio-historical conditions of contemporary European capitalism. Their analysis is marked by the functionalist assumption of a close relation between the density of communication channels and agency that does not obtain. However, though on the surface the left intergovernmentalists seem to be more "realistic", or in Engels' parlance "scientific-materialist", they are, if anything, even more "phantastic" in their misreading of the politico-economic and geopolitical structure of world money.

The left intergovernmentalists follow rather orthodox Marxist theories of imperialism, originally applied to European integration by Ernest Mandel (1967). They see the Euro representing the interests of amalgamated capitalist groupings under German leadership, rivalling the Dollar. Their "Plan A" is based on recasting the growth model of Germany from export orientation to the strengthening of aggregate demand. Failing this, their "Plan B" advocates an exodus of member states from the Euro. The problem is that Germany does not enjoy the hegemonic contender status that Plan A implies. At the same time, the Euro is not, as Plan B implies, inconsequential for shielding member states from externalities emanating from the Dollar hegemon. Both Plan A and B underestimate the structural constraints of European states acting either in concert or alone in the context of US-led global capitalism.

A more accurate reading of the situation concludes with the bad news that Europe is caught in a Weberian iron cage. In other words, a deeply troubled situation from which there is no easy escape despite the disenchanted realization that the Celestial City will never be reached (Baehr, 2001). Such a conclusion follows from Nicos Poulantzas's prescient analysis (1974) of the emerging relation between America and Europe in global capitalism after the collapse of the Bretton Woods, which he described as one of "interiorization". Poulantzas agreed with orthodox theories of imperialism that European capitalist groupings would retain autonomy in capitalist competition vis-à-vis American ones. However, they were becoming structurally subordinate as external inter-capitalist relations in the world economy were replaced by internal ones in an integrated world economy, which was being created in the image of the particularities of the American social formation. This was because the US dominated sectors that were strategic not only in international competition but in structuring the transatlantic and global economy. This includes above all the growing significance of US-centred money capital (Panitch and Gindin, 2012). As Europe's "interior bourgeoisie" became increasingly connected with the American social formation on subordinate terms, it was also progressively alienated from the distinct character of Europe's social formation, rendering increasingly difficult the task of European states to mediate between imperatives of capital accumulation and social legitimation. The situation in which Europe finds itself after the Eurozone crisis is the apogee of this longer-term development (Cafruny and Ryner, 2007; Ryner and Cafruny, 2017). Neither the federalist Kaleckians nor the left intergovernmentalists offer answers to how this iron cage can be escaped. Instead, the increased difficulties in mediating between capital accumulation and legitimation have rendered governance in the EU increasingly authoritarian.

In pursuit of this argument, the first two sections of this chapter review the Kaleckian federalists and left intergovernmentalist positions. The third and final section elaborates on the iron cage situation that Europe finds itself as a result of interiorized and structurally subordinate transnational relations with the US and attendant difficulties in mediating between capital accumulation and societal legitimation. It is argued that the transition from a disciplinary neoliberal governance, characteristic of the Single Market and the EMU before the Eurozone crisis, to an increasingly authoritarian neoliberalism is symptomatic of these difficulties.

The federalist Kaleckians

If Europe presently lacks advocates for a socialist federation, it certainly has advocates of a Kaleckian one. Leading figures here are networks of prominent, mainly post-Keynesian economists, whose thoughts also appear in publications of organizations such as the European Trade Union Institute and the International Labour Office, as well as in the so-called Euromemorandum Group (e.g. Hein, Niechoj, Schulten and Truger, 2005; Lavoie and Stockhammer, 2013; for Euromemogroup reports, see www.euromemo.eu). Some of their research is also funded by the European Commission Framework Programmes.[1] I call these economists Kaleckian federalists because of the clear influence of Michael Kalecki on their thought and prescriptions. Together with figures such as Piero Sraffa and Joan Robinson, Kalecki was among those radical Keynesians who sought to develop a general theory of growth from Keynes' analysis of the short term, which is based on the postulates of fundamental uncertainty, liquidity preference, and a tendency in capitalism towards underconsumption because of the distributive relations between capital and labour. Kalecki is of interest here because he posed the question of aggregate demand and full employment policy in class terms. Rather presciently, in an article on political aspects of full employment published in 1943, Kalecki predicted the development of a "political business cycle" where business would only support measure to stimulate employment policies in a slump but a "rentier bloc" would resist such policies at the peak of a business cycle because of its tendency to blunt the disciplinary mechanism of "the sack". To pre-empt the development of such a political business cycle, Kalecki argued that the entrepreneur should not be the exclusive or main medium through which full employment policy is conducted. He advocated ambitious programmes of public investments, public (welfare) consumption and subsidies of private consumption, and broadly the development of social and political institutions that reflected the then increased power of the working class (Kalecki, 1943).

Central to the diagnosis of the Kaleckian federalists of the problems behind the Eurozone crisis is the post-Keynesian conception of the problematic co-constituted relationship between income distribution and capital accumulation arising from the [alleged?] tendency in capitalism towards underconsumption. According to this diagnosis, the Single Market and Monetary Union form part of a broader constellation of neoliberal finance-led capitalism, which has resulted in increased inequality and a falling wage-share (Onaran and Galanis, 2013). Aggregate demand was maintained artificially and on an unstable basis by extending private debt underwritten by the financialization and securitization of assets. The United States was the centre of such "privatized Keynesianism" (or "debt-led financialization") (Crouch, 2009). The design of the Eurozone reflects the export-oriented accommodation of Europe's strongest economy, Germany, to American privatized Keynesianism ("export-led financialization"). This model was based on wage growth rising below productivity growth (Stockhammer, 2008). The Euro protected this export orientation by removing the threat of competitive devaluations and has resulted in industrial polarization, concentrating Europe's industrial capacity in the north-western industrial core (e.g. Dunford, 2005). At the same time, "peripheral financialization" sustained growth in southern and eastern European peripheries through debt-fuelled consumption and housing bubbles. Nonetheless, this occurred without the positive network capacities of the financial centres of the United States (and the United Kingdom) (Konings, 2008; Becker, Jäger, Leubolt and Weissenbacher, 2010). The global financial crisis arose out of the ultimate unsustainability of extending debt to the poor and Minsky-style Ponzi-finance leading from euphoria to panic (e.g. Minsky, 1986). In turn, the protracted Eurozone crisis is ultimately a story of general stagnation rooted in competitive austerity and the polarization between the export-oriented and peripheral financialization models. These have brought to a head the problems of maintaining a monetary union in a non-optimal currency area without a federal financial mechanism. Current attempts to manage the crisis through a one-sided adjustment by the southern deficit countries are responsible for a catastrophic equilibrium, with some models predicting the rigid application of such a course (and other things remaining equal) resulting in the equivalent of two 1930s style depressions (Sotiropoulos and Stockhammer, 2014).

Based on such diagnoses, federal-Kaleckian alternative policies are pre-scribed. For example, the overall objective of the long-established Eurome-morandum Group is to return to a full employment, environmentally sustainable European social model. The prescribed policy package includes: A European Central Bank with true lender of last resort functions. A reduction of the size and power of the financial sector via several measures: such as the separation of commercial and investment banks; the promotion of cooperative, public sector and other non-profit banks; a ban of most derivatives; a require-ment that all securities trading take place on public platforms; a tax on all financial transactions including on foreign exchange transactions; and publicly owned credit rating agencies. It accepts that not all debt will not be repaid and advocates selective default based on a debt audit. Wealth taxes should be introduced. All remaining government bonds should be swapped for mutua-lized Eurobonds. Rather than relying on finance-led and debt-financed stimu-lus of aggregate demand, a Europe-wide common fiscal policy should boost demand to generate good work. Governments with primary deficits should be given financial support to facilitate expansive policies; public investments should be boosted and funded by mutual European Investment Bank bonds; tax harmonization should make possible higher and more progressive tax rates; and the constitutional requisites for balanced budgets should be repealed. Wage policy should be coordinated with the purpose of increasing the wage share. The basic norm in this context is that wages in surplus countries should be above productivity growth and those in deficit countries at productivity growth. Europe's structural funds should be refocused on high-tech invest-ments especially in non-renewable energy. Cooperatives should be promoted, and union rights augmented. There should be a new approach to Association Agreements and trade agreements, which should support autonomous policy making space for developing countries.[2]

It is, or should be, difficult for any European socialist not to be moved by the vision conjured up by this set of economic policy alternatives. But it raises two difficult and possibly insurmountable political questions. The first pertains to the political form through which this policy content could be delivered and legitimated. The second pertains to the political agency that may deliver on the form as well as the content.

Regarding form, the left Kaleckian vision requires a root and branch revision of European treaties and the creation of a democratic European federation. This is the project of DiEM 25, founded by Yanis Varoufakis, who, as the Finance Minister of the Greek Syriza Government, experienced first-hand the power and constraints exercised by existing EU structures. To its credit, DiEM 25 has no illusions over the prospects of an evolutionary development from existing EU structures to its desired outcomes. Hence, DiEM 25 returns to the federalist conception of European integration, which insists on the necessity of rupture in the form of a constitutional moment. Hence, a Constitutional Assembly should be formed with the view of having a federal structure in place by 2025. The vision is a "full-fledged democracy with a sovereign Parliament respecting national self-determination and sharing power with national Parliaments, regional assemblies and municipal councils".[3]

In the process towards the formation of a Constitutional Assembly, DiEM 25 envisages intermediary steps, which include increased transparency and addressing the on-going crisis through "creative reinterpretations of existing treaties and charters".[4] The "modest proposal" that Varoufakis proposed with Stuart Holland seven years ago (before he became Greek finance minister) outlined what this might entail (Varoufakis and Holland, 2011). Like the Euromemorandum Group, they advocated debt mutualization through the transfer of member state debt to the European Central Bank (ECB) and the issuing of Eurobonds, although individual national states would still service the debt (at lower rates); they endorsed the policy of refinancing of banks through the European Stability Mechanism in exchange, according to their proposal, for public equity in the banks. Finally, again in line with the Euromemorandum Group, they advocated an industrial policy pursued through a beefed-up European Investment Bank. The authors argue that all these measures are perfectly legal within existing EU treaties and, indeed, would not require any forms other than the current Outright Monetary Transactions (where the ECB may intervene on the bond market) and ECB's Long Term Refinancing Operations lending to private banks.

But who is the agency that may deliver the intermediary steps let alone the longer-term Constitutional Moment? However attractive in principle, DiEM 25's response is merely rhetorical and leaves the difficult questions unanswered: "we the people of Europe...united by different cultures, languages, accents, political party affiliations, ideologies, skin colours, gender identities, faiths, and conceptions of the good society". The only apparent power resource at hand is the symbolic appeal of the celebrity status of some members of its Coordinating Collective and Advisory Panel: Varoufakis himself, Brian Eno, Noam Chomsky, Vivienne Westwood, Julian Assange, James Galbraith, Ken Loach,

Saskia Sassen, Slavoj Žižek and, interestingly, John McDonnell, whose British Labour Party has accepted the British referendum vote on Brexit, and imposed a three-line whip on the vote to trigger Article 50.

Lacking an answer from DiEM 25 itself, one might turn to Jürgen Habermas, who has long argued for the need of a European constitution and furthering a "constitutional patriotism" to replace European communitarian nationalism (Habermas, 1992). However, his answer does not differ from the conventional neo-functionalist one of mainstream integration theory (e.g., Haas, 1958). Communicative channels as such are supposed to offer the deliverance.

> Expanding and intensifying markets or communication networks ignite a modernization dynamic of opening and closure. The proliferation of anonymous relations with "others" and the dissonant experience with "foreigners" have a subversive power. Growing pluralism loosens ascriptive ties to family, locality, social background and tradition, and initiates a formal transformation of social integration. With each new impulse toward modernization, intersubjectively shared lifeworlds open, so that they can reorganise and then close once more.
>
> (Habermas, 2001, pp. 82–83)

Yet there is scant historical evidence that communication as such has delivered the substantive outcomes that federalist Kaleckians advocate, which, after all, is a Europeanization of the social democratic welfare state. On the contrary, the prevailing axiom of political sociology remains that this is only delivered through the effective collective organization of wage earners, through unions with high union density and politico-strategic coherence, and supported by political parties committed to that cause and mobilizing attendant power resources (Korpi, 1983, 2002; Esping-Andersen, 1990). Even this is insufficient. This goal also requires a capitalist class with compromised structural power resources that finds it in its interests to bargain with such a wage-earner collective. There is very little evidence, as Streeck (2013) notes in his critique of Habermas that despite an increased density of communicative interaction, these crucial conditions obtain in Europe today.[5] The European Union is both an outcome and a generator of a structural power balance that is unfavourable to labour and favourable to capital and thereby makes the federalist Kaleckian politically implausible. This is not just a question of lack of power resources but also the lack of politico-strategic coherence among wage earners. Working class organizations in Europe, such as trade unions, are not only historically weak. They are also deeply divided, not least as a result of the uneven development and core-periphery divisions generated by the problematic structural coupling of export-led and peripheral financialization. Especially unions operating under export-led financialization – ironically historically the main socio-political carriers of Kaleckian ideas – are very reluctant to support the federalist-Kaleckian vision as they are deeply implicated in existing EU economic governance through competitive corporatism (Dribbusch, Lehndorff and Schulten, 2017).

The left intergovernmentalists

This group rejects the federalist Kaleckian position for reasons similar to those just outlined. The most articulate proponents of this position include Costas Lapavitsas and his collaborators (2012). Lapavitsas and the aforementioned federalist Kaleckian proponents of a "good Euro" agree on much in their critique of finance-led capitalism and a Euro that asymmetrically favours capital over labour. However, for Lapavitsas et al., this is still the manifestation of an inter-state alliance with Germany at its apex and an expression of uneven development. Hence, national states and inter-state relations still constitute the locus of contestation.

Absolutely central to Lapavitsas analysis is the idea of the Euro as a contender to the Dollar as "world money" and, hence, as a vehicle of the contender status of German imperialism as the leader of a broader alliance of European imperialism.[6] Above all, "it aim[s] to meet the paying and reserve requirements of large European enterprises and facilitating global operations of European states", and it is "determined by the large European banks and enterprises that primarily deploy the Euro" (Lapavitsas et al., 2012, pp. 157–158). According to Lapavitsas, the "good Euro" alternative of the federalist Kaleckians is bound to fail because they do not recognize that existing Euro policies are internally related to the credibility that the Euro needs to accumulate in world markets to secure its world money status. Hence, the "good euro" alternative may mean "no euro" (ibid., p. 67).

For Lapavitsas et al., therefore, the only alternative is a structural break and "progressive exit" from the Eurozone. It would entail a return to national currencies, allowing deficit countries to adjust through devaluations, cessation of debt payments, nationalization of banks, the introduction of capital controls, and comprehensive industrial policy. Democracy, in this context, would occur through the reintroduction of national sovereignty and representative democracy and, presumably, economic and industrial democracy too. In a text co-authored with Heiner Flassbeck, Oskar Lafontaine's former chief advisor, Lapavitsas argues that, ideally, such an alternative would proceed through European intergovernmental cooperation, including progressive and enlightened German leadership. Recognizing "the entirety of its economic policy is based on export surpluses", Germany would need to radically revise its model towards strengthening aggregate domestic demand and weakening foreign demand, restoring wage growth and increasing corporate taxes and using proceeds for public investments. Such a turn would require "an honest and serious discussion inside the country" (Flassbeck and Lapavitsas, 2015, pp. 48, 36). Acknowledging that such changes would provoke massive resistance from within Germany, Flassbeck and Lapavitsas propose two possible scenarios. First "combined political pressure by other European states, including France" might compel Berlin to accept such a leadership role. Alternatively, an EMU implosion in which one or more states moved towards exit might generate "a coalition of debtor countries" (Flassbeck and Lapavitsas, 2015, p. 49).

The merit of the left intergovernmentalist position is that it thematizes the questions of agency that the supranationalists cannot answer and, consequently, the political forms required seem at first sight less fanciful. But this is not supported by the historical record. The national state-based progressive alternatives advocated here have been tried before, most notably in the 1970s, and with very little success. Mitterand's U-turn in 1983 is exemplary here and one wonders, if austerity in the Eurozone is due to the pursuit of credibility for the purpose of the Euro becoming "world money", what constraints would national currencies face? The argument assumes that it is German obstruction that mainly constrains this alternative and that a reorientation in German agency is a possible solution. This assumption overstates the power of German agency. Furthermore, the argument rests on a questionable conception of "world money" and a corresponding neglect of the extent to which the Euro, as a successor to the European Monetary System, was all along a *defensive response* that entailed an accommodation to the vagaries of American monetary hegemony post-Bretton Woods and US dominance in financial structures.

The question can be posed in the following terms: If the Euro is world money, why should the "good Euro" supranational alternative in principle be impossible? After all, world money generally enjoys the 'exorbitant privilege' of being able to pursue expansionary policies without the international system imposing adjustments. Indeed, Lapavitsas himself states that, although this is why the status of world money is coveted, the Euro cannot exercise these privileges because it has not yet won this coveted status (Lapavitsas et al., 2012, p. 157). This strikes me as a rather economistic conception devoid of geopolitical content.

More conventional realist international political economy has a real lesson for heterodox economics in this context. After the collapse of Bretton Woods, through the structural power exercised via global financial markets and the reserve currency status of the USD, the United States was able to pursue discretionary economic policies without the need for internal adjustment, by "delaying and deflecting" adjustment requirements onto the rest of the world, including Europe (Cohen, 2006). As Randall Henning (1998) has demonstrated, every major and successful initiative towards European monetary integration has been in response to turbulence in Europe generated by this American policy. German current account surpluses have been central to protecting states participating in European monetary cooperation on the capital account. Of course, this entails accepting the Germany-imposed conditionalities and, as Lapavitsas and others show, the benefits are dubious. But that does not negate the function that the European Monetary System and the European Monetary Union (EMU) has served to shield member states from the vagaries of Dollar hegemony. The conclusions are sombre. For, while they support Lapavitsas's argument on why a "good Euro" is unlikely to work, they similarly shed doubt over any progressive alternative arising out a nation state-based exit-strategy, whether under German leadership or not.

Europe's iron cage: from disciplinary neoliberalism to authoritarian neoliberalism

An alternative reading of the situation facing the European starts with Nicos Poulantzas's (1974) interiorization thesis as defined in the introduction. This thesis has informed more concrete and contemporary analyses of American political economy, transatlantic relations, and European integration (e.g., Cafruny and Ryner, 2007; Panitch and Gindin, 2012; Ryner and Cafruny, 2017). It does not deny that European, especially German, capitalist economic groupings amalgamate to form autonomous competitive units of considerable significance in the global economy and, as Lapavitsas has noted, the euro must be seen as a product of this. However, it goes one step further by highlighting the importance of certain sectors for strategically structuring the global economy. Three such sectors are banking and finance, the military-industrial complex, and the energy sector. All three are dominated by American capital and this determines a whole series of corporate practices, know-how, modes and rituals to do with the economic sphere. While these are organic to the American social formation, they are not so to European formations – and Europe therefore remains dependent on America. The emulation of American business models, including shareholder value, must be seen in this context. This is also a decisive structural context for the endurance of the Dollar as the world currency and, a fortiori, why the Euro is not a serious contender (cf. Grahl, 2001).

Consequently, transatlantic capitalist relations are characterized by a finance-led structure that developed as a response to post-Fordist stagnation in the 1970s and the attendant fiscal crisis of the state. Streeck (2014) is one of many who argued that financial innovation has been the key mechanism through which capitalist contradictions have since been deferred (cf. Harvey, 1991, pp. 182–188). But Streeck's argument for a structurally driven transition from a "debt-state" to a "consolidation-state" only captures the specific situation in Europe. Despite passing references to American seigniorage, he, too, fails to capture the geopolitical contrast between Europe and the USA. USA is *not* a model "consolidation state" inclined to pay off (public or private) debt. This is evident from the debt-fuelled origins of the 2008 financial crisis itself or a simple stylized reading of its basic national accounts over the last 30 years. So why has this absence of consolidation policies that it seeks to impose on other indebted states or economies been feasible in the United States? This is due to the unique capacity of the US to convert debt into capital accumulation and hence secure its position at apex in the hierarchy of capitalist states because of dollar seigniorage and the "interactive embeddedness" between global finance, and domestic (corporate and retail) finance (cf. Seabrooke, 2001; Duménil and Lévy, 2004; Konings, 2011).

Streeck is more on the mark in capturing the dynamics in second and third tier of the hierarchy of capitalist states which defines the dynamics between the European core and periphery. Lacking seigniorage privileges, these are states that require fiscal consolidation as a "confidence building measure" to ensure they remain attractive to creditors on financial markets by showing they intend to service their debt (Streeck, 2016, pp. 121–122). The uneven capacity to institutionalise a consolidation state is crucial for understanding the hierarchy between the European core and the periphery in this regard and this, in turn, depends on more straightforward economic variables such as terms of trade. For that reason, the corporatist states in northern Europe, most notably Germany, have been relatively successful in this endeavour. But this does not mean they can easily behave as the first-tier hegemonic state. The states in Europe's periphery, which lack favourable terms of trade and are, in fact, increasingly caught in a middle-income trap (where they directly compete on costs with emerging markets), have much weaker capacities to institutionalize consolidation. Hence, as Henning suggests, they have drawn on EMU membership to obtain the requisite credibility. This is taking place, however, on increasingly harsh terms as, in the wake of the Eurozone crisis, the northern states, mainly Germany, is using its leverage to generalise a European a consolidation state-structure (ibid., pp. 127–141). This is done through increasingly authoritarian means through executive prerogatives and a permanent state of exception.

In its first decades, the then European Economic Community helped assign plausibility to the Cold War contention, Wilsonian in its origin, that capitalism and democracy had been reconciled and stood in stark contrast to totalitarian socialism. Together with the "embedded liberal" "double screen" of the Bretton Woods system (Ruggie, 1982), the Common Market was an essentially intergovernmental, pragmatic construct that enabled the pursuit of the economies of scale deemed essential to realizing a Fordist accumulation regime in Western Europe (Milward, 1984; Anderson, 2009, pp. 4–15). On this basis, the Common Market also helped secure the material requisites of Marshallian social citizenship, which enabled civic (property) rights to be combined with the political rights of representative democracy (Milward, 1992). The prevailing democratic order had its limitations and hypocrisies. But above all it is the stability and the limitations of the historical conditions of existence of the postwar equation of capitalism and European democracy that need to be recognised. Already the "second project of European integration" (Cafruny and Ryner, 2007), instituted through the Single Market project, the European Monetary System (EMS) and Economic and Monetary Union (EMU) significantly curtailed the scope of democratic deliberation and the content of social rights. When now also the second project of integration finds itself in crisis, Europe stands at a stark watershed.

In essence, the second project of integration constituted a system much akin to Hayek's idea of an 'inter-state federation' (Anderson, 2009, pp. 30–31; Streeck, 2016, pp. 113–141). It dealt with what neo-conservatives famously conceived of as 'excess democracy' (Crozier, Huntington and Watanuki, 1975) by constitutionalizing market relations and property rights of increasingly transnational capital whilst at the same time drawing on the disciplinary force afforded by the mobility of the same.[7] Arguably, curtailing such 'excess' had always been a central function of the European Economic Community (now the European Union) as the imprint of the German Ordoliberalism can be traced to the Treaty of Rome itself (Bonefeld, 2002). But if this is so, then the centrality and extent of the curtailing powers were of a different order after the EMS, the Single Market and the EMU. Be that as it may, this "disciplinary neoliberal" and "new constitutional" system (Gill, 1992, 1998; see also Offe, 1985; Streeck, 2014) arose in particular circumstances and was limited by its conditions of existence. The question of democracy in Europe today needs to be posed in the context of its crisis, that is, the Eurozone crisis as a particular manifestation of the global financial crisis and ultimately finance-led capitalism.

The latter is indicated by the increased use in EU governance and law of what Franz Neumann once called 'general clauses' (*Generalklausulen*) associated with increasing arbitrariness of the executive in the dying days of the Weimar Republic, which then continued and proliferated in the Nazi era. Neumann's key antagonist was, in this context, Carl Schmitt who justified the increased use of general clauses and executive power with reference to a 'permanent state of exception' (Schmitt, 1985). According to Neumann:

> General clauses. . .are not specific laws with true generality. They embody rather a spurious generality. A legal system which derives its legal propositions primarily from such principles. . .is nothing but a mask under which individual measures are hidden. . .The renaissance under the Weimar democracy of the notion of the generality of laws and its indiscriminate application. . . . was thus used as a device to restrict the power of the Parliament which no longer represented exclusively the interests of big landowners, or the capitalists, or the army, or the bureaucracy. Now the general law, within the economic sphere, was used in order to preserve the existing property system and to protect it against intervention where such was regarded as incompatible with the interests of the above-named groups.
>
> (1964)

There is a strong parallel between this development in Weimar jurisprudence and the usage of executive arbitrary power in the current European Union by the so-called Troika (The European Commission, the ECB and the IMF). From Lukas Oberndorfer's forensic analysis (2015), one can identify four key manifestations of arbitrary executive power in the New Economic Governance (consisting in the so-called Two-Pack, Six-Pack, and the Fiscal Compact) that the EU instituted as a response to the Eurozone Crisis (ibid.).

The first two illustrate Neumann's "spurious generality". First, there is an increase in the *scope* of reforms encompassed by the Excessive Deficit Procedure (EDP). In the disciplinary neoliberal phase in the Growth and Stability

Pact of old, EDP's only pertained to the return to "sound" macroeconomic variables, characterized by what Neumann called "determinate generality". But now the scope has been increased to include "structural" reforms to enhance "competitiveness", which previously was within the domain of the voluntarist Open Method of Coordination. This domain is rife with spurious generalities as the relationship between, for instance, wage policies, the degree of regulation of labour, product and service markets, and competitiveness are highly uncertain and contested and therefore open to arbitrary interpretation by the executive. Second, compared to the original GSP, there is a reduced minimal threshold for a state to fall within the EDP (0.5%/GDP structural deficit). Not only does this reduce the threshold for a "state of permanent exception" of Troika intervention to occur. The 0.5 "cyclically-adjusted" figure is highly spurious as it relies on the equally spurious concept of "reference medium-term rate of potential GDP growth". Third, there is the introduction of Reverse Majority Voting, which seriously constrains the ability of democratically elected governments in the Council of Ministers to curtail the power of the Troika. Whereas it used to be the case that EDP's were enacted through Qualified Majority Voting in the Council, the Council now requires this voting procedure to stop such enactment. This brings us to the fourth point, which is the disregard of the New Economic Governance for procedures as stipulated in EU treaties themselves. There is no legal basis for Reverse Majority Voting in EU Treaties. To the contrary, according to Article 121 of the Treaty of the Functioning of the European Union the European Commission must not adopt a decision, which consequently receives its validity through inactivity by the Council as implied by the reverse majority procedure. A particular case of procedural infringement is the de facto authority of the Eurogroup over economic affairs, though, as opposed to the Economic and Financial Affairs Council (ECOFIN), it has no legal personality in the Treaties.[8]

Conclusions

When Engels critiqued Utopian socialists like Saint-Simon, Fourier and Owen, he did not do so in a dismissive way but with the utmost respect. Indeed, for Engels it was only Philistines who were blind to the socialists' stupendous thought – and germs of thought – once they could break out through their phantastic covering (Engels, 1880 [1986], p. 403). Utopian thinking was, then, not an antimony to scientific-materialist analysis but an antithesis, which when reworked could make a profound contribution to changing the world. Similarly, the debate between federalist Kaleckians and left intergovernmentalists makes a profound contribution towards envisaging what a different and better kind of Europe could look like. As Gramsci's critical engagement with Sorel and Machiavelli suggests (1971, pp. 316–319, pp. 385–392), politics is not only the art of the possible but also of the impossible, and the immanent force of social myths are potentially productive forces in socio-political development. They must, however, be grounded in effective reality.

Here the reading of the European situation is more difficult than the one Engels thought he confronted at the end of the 19th century. In Engels' version of the socio-political dialectic there was a Euclidean relationship between the contradictions and crisis to be overcome and its solution. In many respects, though the heterodox debate reviewed here contributes to utopian imaginaries of what Europe could be and thereby help us construe Europe as an object of economic regulation and a site of contestation, they do not seem to have learned that the sad lesson of the 20th and 21st century is that Engels' Euclidean assumption was itself a "fantastic" assumption.

My Poulantzasian reading of the socio-political situation after the Eurozone crisis is more sombre and indeed disheartening. Subjects seem not to be up to the task of summoning the formidable strength required to break out of the iron cage in which Europe finds itself.[9] The key symptom of this is the current "radicalization" (cf. Oberndorfer, 2015) of disciplinary neoliberalism whereby, in the wake of the crisis, it becomes an authoritarian neoliberalism and loses its constitutional quality. As indicated by what José Manuel Barroso called the "silent revolution" of further commodification and privatizations after the financial crisis (Gill, 2016), neoliberal forces retain the political initiative. As recanted by the heterodox economists reviewed here as another speculative bubble is developing, this repeats the mistakes of the finance-led growth model. But as one of the founding fathers of integration theory suggested, power can be defined as the ability to afford not learning from mistakes (Deutsch, 1963, p. 111).

This raises the question of whether Europe has entered a curious phase of "catastrophic equilibrium" characterized by immobilism and stagnation. The idea of authoritarian neoliberalism is inspired by another concept of Poulantzas "authoritarian statism" (Poulantzas, 1978), which he argued was a rigid and therefore a weak form of state. Several authors, starting not from the articulation of "stupendously grand thoughts" of European alternatives, but with the weaknesses and rigidities of current modes of rule, have started to ask whether embryonic alternatives can be identified in "disruptive agency", and then especially "prefigurative pragmatic agency" which has arisen in the reproduction crisis of a Eurozone characterized by austerity (Bailey, Clua-Losada, Huke, Ribera-Almondoz and Rogers, 2018). A fruitful avenue of research would relate these developments to the heterodox alternatives articulated above. However, this line of investigation should also be extended to include the analysis of the "interiorised" transnational relations capitalist geopolitics. Furthermore, it should have no illusions about the formidable problems in scaling up such agency, and insofar as Syriza, Podemos and other movements have their basis in them, the ending is not necessarily a happy one.

Notes

1   A prominent example is the 2011–2016 FESSUD project (How Finance Can Better Serve Economic, Social and Environmental Needs). The Principal Investigator of

this project was the prominent post-Keynesian economist Malcolm Sawyer. http://fessud.eu/ (accessed June 4, 2017), who also plays a leading role in the Euromemorandum Group.

2 This prescribed policy-package is taken from Euromemorandum Group, *Euromemorandum 2010/11: Confronting the Crisis, Austerity and Solidarity*. With slight variations, depending on conjunctural developments, these policies reflect the group's rather consistent line over many years.

3 https://diem25.org/manifesto-long/#1455748561092-7b8f1d50-a8c2

4 Ibid.

5 This seems to be the central point made by Streeck in his debate with Habermas in the 2013 volume of *Blätter für deutsche und internationale Politik*. Adam Tooze seems to rehearse the essence of Habermas' argument in his critical review of Streeck (Tooze, 2017). But Habermas and Tooze do not meet their own burden of proof and, on this score at least, Streeck has the better of the argument.

6 As such, Lapavitsas et. al. follow in the tradition of Ernest Mandel (e.g., Mandel, 1967).

7 Stephen Gill originally proposed reading the re-launch of European integration to be essentially a response to 'excess democracy' (1992). Claus Offe's comments on the conservative ungovernability thesis advanced a similar argument earlier, albeit at a higher level of abstraction and without reference to the European Community (1985). Streeck's more recent analyses (e.g., Streeck, 2014) have been explicitly influenced by his compatriot.

8 This was famously revealed when Yanis Varoufakis queried the legal basis for excluding him, as Greek Minister of Finance, from the deliberations of the Eurogroup and he was told that it had no obligation to include him as it was not an official institution of the EU.

9 Max Weber's conception of an iron cage is a useful antidote against the teleological assumptions shared by virtually all European integration scholarship and to which the left is far from immune, namely: European integration is a largely benevolent process that unfolds to progressively represent the rational aspirations that are potential in human nature. By contrast, the iron cage denotes a deeply troubled situation from which escape is impossible, despite the disenchanted realization that the Celestial City will never be reached (see Ryner, 2015; Ryner and Cafruny, 2017).

References

Anderson, P. (2009) *The new old world*. London: Verso.

Baehr, P. (2001) 'The "iron cage" and the "shell as hard as steel": Parsons, Weber and the *Staalhartes Gehäuse* metaphor in *The protestant ethic and the spirit of capitalism*'. *History and Theory* 40(2), pp. 153–169.

Bailey, D.J., Clua-Losada, M., Huke, N., Ribera-Almondoz, O., and Rogers, K. (2018) 'Challenging the age of austerity: Disruptive agency and the global economic crisis'. *Comparative European Politics* 16(1), pp. 9–31.

Becker, J., Jäger, J., Leubolt, B. and Weissenbacher, R. (2010) 'Peripheral financialization and vulnerability to crisis: A regulationist perspective'. *Competition and Change* 14 (3–4), pp. 225–247.

Bonefeld, W. (2002) 'European integration: The market, the political and class'. *Capital & Class* 26(2), pp. 117–142.

Cafruny, A. and Ryner, M. (2007) *Europe at bay: In the shadow of US hegemony*. Boulder, CO: Lynne Rienner.

Cohen, B. (2006) 'The macrofoundations of monetary power', in Andrews, D. (ed.) *International monetary power*. Ithaca, NY: Cornell University Press, pp. 31–50.

Crouch, C. (2009) 'Privatised Keynesianism: An unacknowledged policy regime'. *British Journal of Politics and International Relations* 11(3), pp. 382–399.

Crozier, M., Huntington, S. and Watanuki, J. (1975) *The crisis of democracy: Report on the governability of democracies to the Trilateral Commission*. New York: New York University Press.

Deutsch, K. (1963) *The nerves of government: Models of political communication and control*. New York: The Free Press.

Dribbusch, H., Lehndorff, S. and Schulten, T. (eds.) (2017) *Rough waters: European trade unions in a time of crisis*. Brussels: ETUI Press.

Duménil, G. and Lévy, D. (2004) 'The economics of US imperialism at the turn of the 21st century'. *Review of International Political Economy* 11(4), pp. 657–676.

Dunford, M. (2005) 'Old Europe, new Europe and the USA: Comparative economic performance, inequality and market-led models of development'. *European Urban and Regional Studies* 12(2), pp. 149–176.

Engels, F. ((1880 [1986])) 'Socialism: Utopian and scientific', in Marx, K. and Engels, F. (eds.) *Selected works*. New York: International Publishers, pp. 399–434.

Esping-Andersen, G. (1990) *The three worlds of welfare capitalism*. Cambridge, UK: Polity Press.

Euromemogroup. Reports, Available at http://www.euromemo.eu/. (Accessed on 4 June 2017.)

Flassbeck, H. and Lapavitsas, C. (2015) *Against the troika*. London: Verso.

Gill, S. (1992) 'The emerging world order and European change', in Miliband, R. and Panitch, L. (eds.) *The socialist register 1992: New world order?* London: Merlin Press, pp. 157–196.

Gill, S. (1998) 'European governance and new constitutionalism: EMU and alternatives to disciplinary neoliberalism in Europe'. *New Political Economy* 3(1), pp. 5–26.

Gill, S. (2016) 'Transnational class formations, European crisis, and the silent revolution'. *Critical Sociology* 43(4-5), pp. 635–651.

Grahl, J. (2001) 'Globalized finance: The challenge to the Euro'. *New Left Review* 8 (March–April), pp. 23–47.

Gramsci, A. (1971) *Selections from the prison notebooks*. Translated by Q. Hoare and G. Nowell-Smith. London: Lawrence & Wishart.

Haas, E. (1958) *The uniting of Europe: Political, social and economic forces*. Stanford, CA: Stanford University Press.

Habermas, J. (1975) *Legitimation crisis*. London: Heinemann.

Habermas, J. (1992) 'Citizenship and national identity: Some reflections on the future of Europe' *Praxis International* 12, pp. 1–19.

Habermas, J. (2001) *The post-national constellation*. Cambridge: Polity.

Harvey, D. (1991) *The condition of post-modernity*. Oxford: Blackwell.

Hein, E., Niechoj, T., Schulten, T. and Truger, A. (2005) *Macroeconomic policy coordination in Europe and the role of trade unions*. Brussels: ETUI Press.

Henning, R. (1998) 'Systemic conflict and regional monetary integration: The case of Europe'. *International Organization* 52(3), pp. 537–573.

Kalecki, M. (1943) 'Political aspects of full employment'. *Political Quarterly* 14(4), pp. 322–331.

Konings, M. (2008) 'European finance in the American mirror: Financial change and the reconfiguration of competitiveness'. *Contemporary Politics* 14(3), pp. 253–275.

Konings, M. (2011) *The development of American finance*. Cambridge: Cambridge University Press.

Korpi, W. (1983) *The democratic class struggle*. London: Routledge and Kegan Paul.

Korpi, W. (2002) 'The great trough in unemployment: A long-term view of unemployment, inflation, strikes, and the profit/wage ratio'. *Politics & Society* 30 (3), pp. 365–426.

Lapavitsas, C., Kaltenbrunner, A., Labrinidis, G., Lindo, D., Meadway, J., Michell, J., Painceira, J.P., Pires, E., Powell, J., Stenfors, A., Teles, N. and Vatikiotis, L. (2012) *Crisis in the Eurozone*. London: Verso.

Lavoie, M. and Stockhammer, E. (eds.) (2013) *Wage-led growth: An equitable strategy for economic recovery*. Basingstoke: Palgrave Macmillan/ILO.

Mandel, E. (1967) 'International capitalism and 'supra-nationality', in Miliband, R. and Saville, J. (eds.) *The socialist register 1967*. London: Merlin Press, pp. 27–41.

Milward, A. (1984) *The reconstruction of Western Europe 1945-51*. London: Routledge.

Milward, A. (1992) *The European rescue of the nation state*. London: Routledge.

Minsky, H. (1986) *Stabilizing an unstable economy*. New Haven, CT: Yale University Press.

Neumann, F. (1964) *The democratic and authoritarian state*. New York: Free Press.

Oberndorfer, L. (2015) 'From new constitutionalism to authoritarian constitutionalism: New economic governance and the state of European democracy', in Jäger, J. and Springler, E. (eds.) *Asymmetric crisis in Europe and possible futures*. London: Routledge, pp. 186–207.

Offe, C. (1985) *Contradictions of the welfare state*. London: Hutchinson.

Onaran, O. and Galanis, G. (2013) *Is aggregate demand wage-led or profit-led? National and global effects*. Conditions of Work and Employment Series No. 40. Geneva: International Labour Office. Available at http://www.ilo.org/wcmsp5/groups/public/—ed_protect/—protrav/—travail/documents/publication/wcms_192121.pdf. (Accessed on 3 May 2016).

Panitch, L. and Gindin, S. (2012) *The making of global capitalism*. London: Verso.

Poulantzas, N. (1974) 'Internationalisation of capitalist relations and the nation state'. *Economy and Society* 3(2), pp. 145–179.

Poulantzas, N. (1978). *State, Power, Socialism*. London: Verso.

Ruggie, J.G. (1982) 'International regimes, transaction and change: Embedded liberalism in the postwar economic order'. *International Organization* 36(2), pp. 379–415.

Ryner, M. (2015) 'Europe's ordoliberal iron cage: Critical political economy, the euro area crisis and its management'. *Journal of European Public Policy* 22(2), pp. 275–294.

Ryner, M. and Cafruny, A. (2017) *The European Union and global capitalism: Origins, development, crisis*. London: Palgrave Macmillan.

Schmitt, C. (1985) *Political theology: Four chapters on the concept of sovereignty*. Chicago, IL: University of Chicago Press.

Seabrooke, L. (2001) *US power in international finance: The victory of dividends*. Basingstoke: Palgrave Macmillan.

Sotiropoulos, D. and Stockhammer, E. (2014) 'Rebalancing the euro area: The cost of internal devaluation'. *Review of Political Economy* 26(2), pp. 210–233.

Stockhammer, E. (2008) 'Some stylized facts on the finance-dominated accumulation regime'. *Competition and Change* 12(2), pp. 184–202.

Streeck, W. (2013) 'Vom DM-Nationalismus zum Euro-Patriotismus? Eine Replik auf Jürgen Habermas'. *Blätter für deutsche und internationale Politik* 58, pp. 75–92.

Streeck, W. (2014) *Buying time: The delayed crisis of democratic capitalism*. London: Verso.

Streeck, W. (2016) *How will capitalism end?* London: Verso.

Tooze, A. (2017) 'A general logic of crisis'. *London Review of Books* 39(1), pp. 3–8.

Varoufakis, V. and Holland, S. (2011) *A modest proposal for overcoming the Eurozone crisis.* Policy Note 2011/3, pp. 1–11. Annandale-on-Hudson, NY: Levy Economics Institute of Bard College.

8 After the crisis

Lessons on economic and political paradigms and policies

Robert Boyer[1]

As belief in the omnipotence of market mechanisms collapsed after the crisis of finance-led accumulation, it is time to reconsider the nature and dynamic of economic crises and the role of the state to govern the economy and secure social justice. I start from three lessons drawn from the structural crisis of finance-led growth and other major crises.

First, endogenous mechanisms recurrently generate crises in modern capitalism. Nonetheless, the specific type of crisis, the precise mix of mechanisms, and the affected economic spaces in each case are always distinctive. This makes it hard to generalize lessons learnt from one structural crisis to the next, even for the same kind of capitalism or the same period.[2] It is even harder when intellectual and political elites resort to magical thinking. Examples include the conviction that 'this time is different' (a recurrent error), that 'the business cycle is obsolete' (the 1970s), that 'Japan is No. 1' (1980s), that 'we are entering a new epoch devoid of crisis' thanks to central bank policies that produced the 'great moderation' (1990s), and that the Euro has proved a success after 10 years because it protected the EU from the subprime crisis (2009). Such magical thinking dramatically increases the probability of a major crisis. For it illustrates Hyman Minsky's paradox that 'stability produces instability' through complacency (Minsky, 1982), leading to what Alan Greenspan described during the dot.com bubble as 'irrational exuberance' (Greenspan, 1996).

Second, structural crises involve the breakdown of the factors that previously governed capital accumulation. This explains why it takes time for contemporaries to recognize 'this is a crisis' and give it a name. There are delays before the nature of the crisis is recognized, especially where it is denied outright, described in euphemistic terms, or expected to end quickly with a return to a mythical golden age. It is tempting to identify the symptoms of crisis as no more than turbulence amidst prosperity, a pure exception highly unlikely to return, an adverse shock, the effect of irrational conduct, and so on. Once it is seen as a structural crisis, there is radical uncertainty in economic paradigms, analyses, and policy recommendations. For, as Joseph Schumpeter (1954) acknowledged, if economic paradigms and policy models fail, their underlying macroeconomic doctrine must be wrong. Yet the initial strategies deployed by private and public actors in response to structural crises generally favour a return to the status quo ante, thus reinforcing the previous policies that led to the crisis. In the Great Depression in 1929–1932, for example, there was a return to financial orthodoxy; likewise, the initial response to the internationalization and supply-side problems that contributed to the crisis of Fordism was resort to Keynesian demand management policies. Recent examples include attempts to create a market for non-performing derivatives in the sub-prime crisis; and, for the Eurozone crisis, the adoption of the failed Washington Consensus policies of austerity. These attempts to turn the clock back mean leading actors struggle over the required strategies for overcoming the crises. and how to reduce the radical uncertainty that halts investment and accumulation by developing new economic paradigms. Policymakers must therefore make decisions without theoretical guidance or justification from the past paradigm. What is needed is a new approach that can inspire new models of development and guide state action to achieve them.

Third, turning from practical and theoretical to normative concerns, an important response to the global trend of rising inequality has been the idea of growth with equity. This emerged in Latin America a decade ago but merits application elsewhere. This invites us to reconsider the embedding of the state in the wider society, its contribution to advancing new models of development, and its potential in promoting, undermining, or reversing social justice. This requires special attention to how the state can be reorganized to reduce inequalities while promoting a sustainable growth regime.

Combining these three lessons, this chapter will address the relations among growth, employment, and equality in regulation-theoretical terms. There are six main parts. The first introduces a taxonomy of crises as a basis for reflecting on the lessons that might be drawn. Second, reflecting the origins of the regulation approach in efforts to explain the surprising crisis of the Fordist era (*les trente glorieuses*), it summarizes the evolution of economic models in Europe and the United States after the Second World War and notes how their different crises legitimized a return to the liberal theory of efficient, self-regulating markets. The third, notes how the new system of resurgent market fundamentalism later suffered a similar fate and the financial crisis has enabled several lessons to be drawn about finance-led growth regimes. Fourth, this has prompted a new paradigm that restored state intervention through a pragmatic approach to crisis management and economic policy that heeds some of the lessons from the history of past crises so the next one can be anticipated and, if it cannot be prevented, crisis management can be based on lessons about what measures work. Fifth, I introduce the trilemma of market responsiveness, the dynamics of efficiency, and social justice, and consider how a socioeconomic system can incorporate the goal of social justice. In this context, I clarify the links among the social protection system, social well-being, and the institutional forms that shape the growth regime. Sixth, these policies cannot just replicate those adopted in developed countries after the World War II (WWII) because the internationalization of trade, direct investment, financial capital, and intellectual property rights have created an unprecedented degree of interdependence among policies for economic growth are also sustainable in terms of reducing social inequality and environmental damage.

1. A taxonomy of crises

From the start, the regulation approach gave a central place to the analysis of crises. Based on observations of the crisis of the Fordist growth regime, it focused on providing historical analyses of the succession of major crises. This makes it part of the broader project of institutional and historical macroeconomics. The proliferation of crises in the 1980s and 1990s also led many mainstream economists to re-examine the history of financial crises and seek to formalize their dynamics. Yet they continued to regard crises as temporary, anomalous deviations from a self-equilibrating economy based on interdependent markets. This position is quite different from the regulation approach view that they are grounded in the crisis-prone logic of capitalism with its contradictions, uneven development, and inherent social tensions. Thus, it has its own distinctive concepts and explanatory principles (Boyer, 2015b, p. 105).

The regulation approach distinguishes five forms of crisis (see Table 8.1). First, there are crises that result from an external perturbation or shock, such as a natural or climatic catastrophe or, again, the impact of an event originating outside its economic space, such as a war. Shocks are frequent, especially in an increasingly integrated international economy. Second, there are endogenous or cyclical crises which are recurrent features of a mode of regulation and means for its re-equilibration or renewal. These crises are products of institutional forms and institutional compromise and do not directly undermine the

Table 8.1 Illustrations of the crisis taxonomy

Type	Historical examples	Contemporary period
Apparently exogenous shock	Crisis of provisioning	Petrol shocks 1972, 1979; first and second Iraq wars
Crisis as integral part of regulation	Business cycles in 19th century	Stop-and-go cycles in post-war monopoly regulation (Fordism)
Crisis of regulation	Non-reproductive cycle: 1929–1932, USA	Acceleration of inflation and claims for indexation of wages in 1960s
Crisis of accumulation regime	Intensive accumulation without mass consumption	Japanese crisis of 1990s, 1997 Asia crisis
Crisis of mode of production	Crisis of feudalism	Breakdown of soviet economy

Source: English version of Table 5.1 in Boyer (2015b, p. 84)

overall mode of regulation. Third, there are crises of the mode of regulation that are irreversible but do not, at least initially, undermine the accumulation regime which remains viable. Fourth, there are crises of the accumulation regime itself as it approaches the limit of the contradictions inherent in its most essential institutional forms – the hierarchy of which varies with each accumulation regime – and the scope of accumulation expands, escaping the space of regulation (examples are the impact of internationalization on Fordism). Fifth, there are crises of the mode of production, such as feudalism in the past or, perhaps, capitalism in the future (Boyer, 1990, pp. 50–60; 2015b, pp. 80–83).

The third and fourth crises can also be described as structural crises that affect the overall mode of development. These are not mere cyclical downturns that can be reversed. Most of them are simultaneously financial, economic, institutional, and political. This is illustrated by the collapse of the Soviet bloc; Japan's two lost decades; Italy's trajectory after joining the European Monetary Union; the effects of the financial crisis in the USA; and the Eurozone crisis. There are three ways to diagnose a structural crisis: (1) an inability of existing institutional forms to channel the accumulation regime and the everyday economic behaviour of firms and wage earners; (2) institutional forms being eroded by the very functioning of the mode of regulation, leading to the irreversible breakdown of its regularities when the mode of development is *en régulation*, rendering the accumulation regime non-viable in the long run as its prerequisites vanish; and (3) political, financial, and economic actors not agreeing on a new compromise to sustain a new development mode (Boyer and Juillard, 2000, p. 124, 134 and 136, respectively). This means it *is impossible to go back to the pre-crisis configuration.* In other words, it is dangerous to keep applying the same policies that led to a succession of crises born of careless liberalization, especially of finances, or to return to post-war policies without updating them. New goals and instruments of economic policy will be required, often discovered through trial-and-error experimentation.

2. The golden age in developed economies: Reducing social inequalities with high and stable growth

2.1. The 1950s: Equilibrium of economic efficiency and social justice

In the mid-1950s, Paul Samuelson's *Economics* (1948) was a leading mainstream introductory text. In its first chapter, he insists on the need to choose between equality and efficiency, as exemplified by the Soviet Union and the United States respectively. Indeed, Samuelson suggested that, the greater a society's equality, the weaker its economic performance. This false dichotomy surprised those familiar with the French case, where strong economic growth, surpassing that in the USA, coincided with falling inequality. The standard neoclassical theory could not explain this situation. Examining only static equilibria, it considered this positive outcome to be impossible. French regulation theory developed to explain the features of this seemingly anomalous economic order, which it labelled Fordism (Aglietta, 1979; Boyer, 1990). In Fordism, while unequal income distribution is compressed by strong wage growth and an extended social wage, profits remain relatively stable and generate high levels of productive investment and productivity as well as near full employment. The regulation approach countered neoclassical theory's focus on static equilibria by analysing a specific set of economic institutions allowing new growth models to emerge based on innovative policies.

2.2. The surprising 1960s: Symbiosis between inequality reduction and growth

The instability and stagnation that marked the inter-war period were overcome thanks to the complementarity between a cluster of structural changes and the transformation of economic institutions, neither of which, would have been a sufficient cause (see Figure 8.1). The Fordist model depicted in this figure envisages a high productive capacity, as numerous innovations had been created in the interwar period, including mass production chains, and the setbacks associated with the Great Depression and WWII were overcome by extremely high investment in new technologies. Thus, as the new system was established, there was enormous scope for boosting productivity, whose fruits were divided between wages, profits and a decline in the relative prices of the new industrially produced goods.

However, the greatest innovation was reaching a compromise with wage earners so mass production was in tune with mass consumption thanks to the

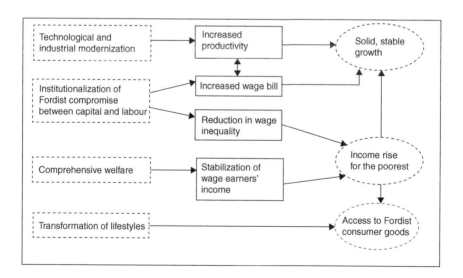

Figure 8.1 Institutional changes that favoured growth and inequality reduction after 1945

indexation of nominal wages to inflation and productivity. Previously increased output was absorbed by the social strata with higher incomes and stronger purchasing power, exported to colonies, or simply sold on the world market. This key innovation was to synchronize the domestic market with technological progress. It led to four institutional changes. First, access to education was promoted. For example, in the USA, the Servicemen's Readjustment Act (commonly known as the G.I. Bill) provided access to low-cost education for returning veterans; in France, access to education was a result of democratization; and, in social democratic states, there was a strong emphasis on human capital formation (André and Delorme, 1983). Second, an extremely progressive personal taxation system was introduced and widely accepted. In the USA, the marginal tax rate in the late 1950s for the wealthiest section of society was 83.5%, which contrasts with the current almost-flat tax rate, radically lowering the redistribution of wealth to the poorest (Piketty, 2013). Third, Keynesian policies were introduced for counter-cyclical economic management to secure the macroeconomic conditions for near full employment with limited inflation. And, fourth, increased social spending disconnected access to health services, vocational training, family benefits and housing from purely market-based mechanisms. Some countries embarked on the road to the decommodification of labour-power; others (especially in northern Europe) saw the rise of welfare capitalism (Pedersen, 2006).

In short, the socioeconomic regime was completely transformed through intensive institution-building with a view to recovering from the losses and setbacks associated with the Great Depression and WWII. This did not involve social engineering to realise a Pareto optimum but was a complex process of institutional and behavioural innovation that had largely unanticipated effects. Indeed, all political factions and governments, regardless of ideological orientation, came to see this as the start of a new era of capitalism. In France, the liberal President, Giscard d'Estaing, stated his admiration for social democratic societies; European Christian democrats and social democrats also welcomed economic integration. In the USA, Democrats and Republicans shared the same concept and practice of Keynesian economic policy and Alfred Sloan, senior executive of General Motors, was the highest-paid employee. His position contrasts starkly with today's capitalism, where investment bank Chief Executive Officers sit at the top of the income scale and no longer regard themselves as employees. Lastly, full employment was virtually achieved, giving that wage earners had strong negotiating powers. In France, which currently has about 9% unemployment and more than 2.5 million people out of work, with many others being obliged to work part-time (at the time of writing, December 2017), wage-earners' negotiating power is not so great and strategies to increase wage flexibility are being pushed.

2.3. Diversity of national socio-political compromises and plurality of capitalism

This general Fordist model followed different national trajectories. Statistical analysis has shown at least four types of capitalism co-exist in the Organization for Economic Cooperation and Development (OECD) (cf. Amable, Boyer and Barré, 1997; Amable, 2003). These types are presented in Figure 8.2.

The first type is market (or liberal) capitalism, found in the USA or United Kingdom. It makes extensive use of market mechanisms with regulatory agencies ensuring their correct functioning. After WWII, collective agreements in leading sectors and generalization of wage increases in other key economic sectors – thanks to near-full employment, achieved through active monetary and fiscal policies inspired by Keynesian theory – delivered a return to growth and a significant reduction in inequalities.

The second configuration is the social democratic model, distinguished by the permanent negotiation of new social compromises in which all economic actors have a voice in the decision-making power to effect institutional change. Moreover, given that national solidarity is expressed through universal social coverage, this model was the most effective in reconciling social justice and economic efficiency, even during the financial crises that occurred after they opened to international capital. The Nordic countries illustrate this model.

Model three is state-led capitalism. Here the central government (as in France) or regional governments (e.g., Germany's Länder) manage the economy. Under this arrangement, the previously large public sector now undertakes many interventions and high social transfers, funded from taxation and social security, allowing a significant redistribution of national income that drives domestic markets (France) or job creation in the export sector

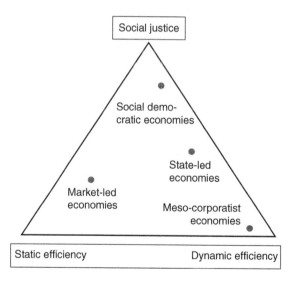

Figure 8.2 Types of capitalism and relation between efficiency and equality, until the 1970s

(Germany). In both cases, growth was compatible with falling inequality, at least until the 1970s.

The fourth model is meso-corporatist capitalism, which is structured around large business groups involved in a wide range of industries. In this model, adopted by Japan and the Republic of Korea, an initial compromise ensures job security for workers whose skills are essential to production, while the wage structure is constrained by the fact that managers are trained within and loyal to the company. This is another way to guarantee the complementarity between reduced inequality and economic performance. Traditionally, social security was provided mostly by these business groups, but the model's crisis and long-term stagnation led to an increasingly extensive social policy intervention by the State.

3. The end of the 'golden age': The success of market-led regimes and their crises

3.1. *The 1980s: A conservative counter-revolution*

The 1980s saw the emergence of a revolution that began at the level of ideas and probably would not have been so successful were it not for the exhaustion and open crisis provoked by the previous model followed by OECD countries.

First, total factor productivity in the USA was at a standstill so that, while the institutions responsible for distributing income remained in place, growth stagnated and distributive conflicts rose to the surface, creating inflation and unemployment.

Second, a wave of internationalization destroyed earlier compromises. Under Fordism, the interests of industrial capitalists and wage earners were complementary. However, when an economy's export growth passes a certain threshold, these interests grow apart: what cannot be sold domestically is exported and wages become a cost of international production, rather than a source of domestic demand. For example, German manufacturers – especially of capital goods – did not sell much on the domestic market but exported their output to the rest of the world. This broke the link between capital and labour at the national level.

Third, financial globalization exacerbated the growing disconnection between economic and political space, since capital owners could withdraw their money from financial institutions or centres and place it elsewhere, which undermined the material basis of the virtuous circle of growth based on domestic mass production and domestic consumption.

These changes led to the endogenous emergence of a new ideology, shared intellectually at least by conservative and socialist governments. This asserted that: (1) the market was far better than the state at allocating resources; and (2) inequalities favoured market incentives, given the significant efficiency gained by rewarding talent with high wages. Thus, 'the winner takes it all' became the slogan of modern capitalism. The result was a surprising return to classical macroeconomics, which holds that inequalities are positive because they incentivize work; a lean welfare state will force workers to accept wage concessions; and the wealthy benefit the economy because they generate savings and, according to pre-Keynesian theory, will invest them, thereby creating more jobs for the poor. Innovators must, therefore, be well remunerated to make the economy grow (see Figure 8.3). This figure shows the extent of the shift in the economy's core paradigm, which acts as a catalyst and justification for changes to laws, remuneration systems, and economic policies which now aim to guard against disruption to what are declared to be inherently stable market economies.

3.2. The 1990s: The failure of all alternatives to market capitalism

For this paradigm to take root, it required the failure of other alternatives that favoured the extension of the post-war institutional configurations in response to new technological and international context.

First, in the mid-1980s the socialist government of France tried to respond to the global recession by increasing public spending in a form of Keynesianism in one country. However, widening public and external deficits quickly led to the adoption of an austerity plan that had a lasting impact on economic policy in France and elsewhere. These events have been interpreted as the end of Keynesianism in the new global economic context. Since then, French capitalism has not been considered a viable alternative to the United States model.

A second episode prompted a re-evaluation of social democratic capitalism: financial globalization caused a banking and economic crisis in Sweden that led to a reform of social security coverage involving moves to privatize many

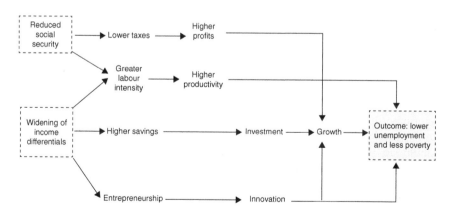

Figure 8.3 The paradigm shift of the 1980s: social inequality as an incentive for growth

services, such as health care, and to lower public spending as a proportion of GDP. Although this re-commodification of labour-power weakened the social democratic model, it still retained many of its hallmarks.

The collapse of the Soviet system had even graver repercussions. In fact, with the fall of capitalism's most serious rival, pressure for reforms in favour of workers' and citizens' rights under various forms of capitalism, dissipated. The market economy system is all that remained, with democracy as its necessary counterpart in the political sphere. This led Fukuyama (1992) to declare that the collapse of the Soviet Union marked the 'end of history'.

In the 1980s, meso-corporatist capitalism in Japan seemed to threaten the superiority of the United States' market economy model. However, opening to international capital flows created a stock market and real-estate bubble whose rupture ultimately put an end to buoyant growth. Two lost decades of near-total stagnation followed, which destroyed the prestige and appeal of Japanese capitalism. Only the economic policies of Prime Minister Shinzo Abe ('Abenomics') allowed the country to embark on a new phase.

Thus, in the 1990s – a glorious period for the US economy – a new type of capitalism seemed to triumph and became the sole international benchmark: finance-led capitalism.

3.3. 1990–2006: The triumph of finance-led capitalism

Financial innovation became the driving force at the heart of modern capitalism thanks to the shortcomings of the alternatives. This led to radical shifts in the four types of capitalism (see Figure 8.4). They all focused on the privatization of welfare, the lowering of taxes and opening to international competition with a view to arriving at the static efficiency model. Indeed, dynamic efficiency matters little in a context of strong volatility: when a fast response is required, market capitalism is the most effective regime. Thus, where it fosters volatility, the capitalist model becomes a virtuous circle for economies that follow its example, and a vicious circle for the rest. This explains why the rest of the world tried to emulate the US strategy.

The establishment of a finance-led economy was a paradoxical development, given that the Fordist model was dominated by the logic of value-added creation. The finance-led model works by anticipating future wealth – measured by stock exchange performance – which then drives the investment, production and demand process. Expectations and confidence in finances determine the regime's potential. A simulation of this system using a relatively simple model (Boyer, 2000) showed that in the 1990s the conditions for stability in the US economy had already been met. Great importance was attached to households' financial assets, which account for a large proportion of disposable income, and include the direct or indirect ownership of shares and bonds, sometimes through pension funds (see Figure 8.4). For US citizens, this model seemed to herald a period of unlimited and effortless prosperity: with the prospect of increasing wealth, individuals could seek loans to buy

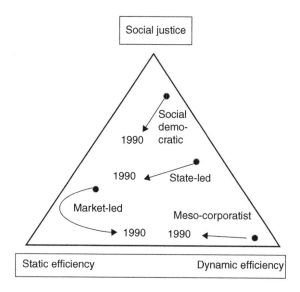

Figure 8.4 The shift to market capitalism in a context of financial instability, 1980–1990

property, which could then be pledged as security to buy a vehicle, with the value of the vehicle then used to borrow money for a holiday. In this way, it seemed possible to complete the macroeconomic circle without any drawbacks.

This apparent success explains why so many European macroeconomists have, since the 2000s, advised their own governments to adopt the United States method that employs lending and finance as the key instruments of economic activity. Such recommendations are naive because US economic structures are very distinctive – with only the United Kingdom being broadly comparable. For other countries, especially France, Germany, and Japan, the production logic of value creation in non-financial companies is far more important than financial value and the process of financialization. Growth and stability in these three economies have thus been weakened by financial liberalization and innovation, which are incompatible with other institutional forms built on the pursuit of competitiveness and industrial performance.

3.4. 2007–2008: The failure of liberalization and financial globalization

The relaxation of lending criteria and mass securitization of subprime loans in the United States caused a structural crisis. In fact, the lack of control over financial innovations created an almost unprecedented speculative bubble that gradually contaminated the domestic and international economy (Boyer, 2013a). A 1930s-style depression was avoided by mass state intervention, breaking with the orthodoxy that formerly prevailed in economic policy. The U.S. central bankers learnt from the errors committed by their predecessors in the 1930s. Instead of allowing a chain reaction of bankruptcies to develop among the financial actors, Alan Greenspan supplied abundant liquidity to insolvent banks and governments accepted the widening of the public deficit (see Table 8.2). After the event, continued growth and slight inflation were observed, instead of depression and deflation. This was the price that had to be paid for a modest recovery that proved short-lived, since the US had lost an economic driver in credit growth, and exports, consumption, and investment failed to replace it.

The 2007–2008 bubble did not occur in isolation, but in some measure responded to the crisis in the new economy and its associated financial liberalization, which in the 1980s had translated into property speculation and the savings and loans crisis (events on a smaller and more localized scale, since financial innovations were not yet widespread). The finance-led crisis immediately led to a squeeze on lending for international trade, halting of investment decisions, and plummeting production in almost every country. The system of international accumulation regime now faced a structural crisis. The centrality of the USA in international financial intermediation meant that the breakdown of confidence in the stability of the banking system relations also descended into crisis, since it had no regulations or instruments at its disposal to control the spread of excess credit, especially to emerging economies.

This was the second failure of financial liberalization. Capital accounts liberalization was intended to stabilize exchange rates and allow better distribution of capital between developed and developing countries. However, the exact opposite occurred: a 'currency war' broke out and the savings of developing countries funded the consumption of rich ones.

3.5. From 2009 to the present: The structural crisis of all growth regimes

The most severe crisis occurred in countries where governments trusted in the virtues of financial liberalization and passed the initiative to private entities: Iceland, Ireland, the UK and the USA. These countries should have adopted more heterodox policies, in other words, a total break from what was recommended by the previous theory and implemented by their respective central banks and finance ministries (Boyer, 2011c). Some analysts expected a possible repeat of the lost decade in Japan: medium-term economic stagnation with a risk of deflation. More generally, four lessons can be drawn from the crisis of finance-led accumulation.

- There are some novel features in this crisis that intensify it and make it harder to resolve. There has been a continuous process of internationalization of trade and finance over four decades; new capitalist powers have emerged; the absolute hegemony of the US has been eroded and there is a trend towards multilateral international negotiations – stopped under

Table 8.2 Types of economic policy, 1945–2014

Growth regimes and periods	Mass production and mass consumption 1945–1971	Globalization and financialization 1972–2007	New Developmentalism and State role, 2007–present
Overview of features			
1. Conceptualization of the economy	Structural instability that requires state intervention	Set of self-regulated markets	State as guarantor of financial stability and driver of development
2. Dominant theory	Keynesian macroeconomics	Neo-Classical theory	New development theories (ECLAC, China)
3. Type of socio-political compromise	Capital-labour compromise	Dominance of finance	New Deal with citizens
Economic policy			
4. Monetary policy	Optimization of the balance between employment and inflation	Stabilization of low inflation and subsequent boost for finances	Return to the lender of last resort, non-neutrality of credit and currency
5. Public spending and tax system	Automatic stabilizers	Procyclical public spending	In depressions: high multipliers
6. Income policy	Collective agreements, minimum wage, and progressive tax system	Individualization and decentralization, fixed rate system	Fight against inequality, establishment of financial norms
7. Competition policy	Limited to a group of national oligopolies	Opening to international competition and rise of global oligopolies	Softening of the policy against concentration of capital
8. Trade and exchange rate policy	Slow international opening; fixed but adjustable exchange rate	Spread of flexible currency regimes, except in the eurozone	Control of the real exchange rate to improve national development

Source: elaborated by the author based on this text

Donald Trump's presidency; and, finally, we can observe potential conflicts between continuing financialization and continued commitment to democratic principles.

- The crisis was difficult to anticipate and understand because the succession of seemingly marginal reforms (internationalization of treasury bonds, rise of pension funds, the principle of shareholder value, privatization, labour market flexibility, etc.) aiming at more efficiency and macroeconomic stability cumulated to finally generate an unprecedented institutional and political configuration that was seriously crisis prone.

- Moreover, given the new social and political polarization of most economies, the system was hard to reform through collective action and has led to populist resistance. There are two important aspects here. One is that the more mobile actors (transnational firms and financial capital) are shaping the laws, tax system, and many other aspects of the accumulation regime and economic policy. Another is that most national states are now too small to deal with crises rooted in an increasingly international economy at the same time as the Bretton Woods international organizations are growing weaker.
- This said, we have learnt to avoid repetition of the subprime crisis, we must implement integrated supervision of commercial banks, investment banks, and insurance companies. Likewise, it is not enough to make the risks linked to derivatives more transparent, we must maintain the link of responsibility between borrowers and lenders. We should also prohibit new financial products involving the transfer of risk from the better informed to the less well informed. It is also necessary to institute procedures of approval for new financial products incorporating clauses guaranteeing the absence of major negative macroeconomic externalities. Another lesson is that it is essential to recruit the best financiers for financial supervisory agencies, to reduce the asymmetry between private and public sectors in terms of market finance skills.[3]

The recession of 2008–2009 was also severe in countries that based their growth on exports and dynamic innovation: Germany, Japan, and the Republic of Korea. Governments and public opinion took note of the fragility of their development model and their extreme dependence on growth in the world economy, to the point where they considered a transition to a system based on the development of the domestic market and, particularly, consumption.

China seemed to escape the successive recessions that struck other countries in the first phase of the crisis triggered by the collapse of Lehman Brothers. In fact, thanks to credit and exchange-rate controls and an ambitious public infrastructure programme, the Chinese economy grew only slightly slower than it had previously (Boyer, 2011a, 2012a). However, the period since 2013 marked a turning point, since growth in international trade slowed and the model based on productive investment and the real-estate sector began to run out of steam. This presented an opportunity to refocus policies to transition towards the domestic market and the meeting of social and environmental needs created by the boom.

The European Union faced a different crisis: in the first phase, the magnitude of the automatic stabilizers limited the consequences of the crisis, but in 2010 the size of public deficits aroused such concern among the international finance markets and the authorities in Brussels as to provoke a return to austerity, even before economic recovery was assured (Boyer, 2012b). During this process, a structural weakness emerged that had been underestimated by the architects of the euro: the heterogeneity of Eurozone countries' specializations and regulations reflected the inconsistencies and the incomplete nature of the European Union institutions. Consequently, the financial crisis segued into an economic crisis that became a political crisis concerning European integration (Boyer, 2013b).

4. The state and economic policy: A new paradigm

4.1. The 'trilemma' of market responsiveness, dynamic efficiency, and social justice

From Paul Samuelson to theorists of the 'real business cycle', capitalism has traditionally been analysed in terms of the relation between static efficiency – the ability to react to unexpected changes, to currency crises or to downturns in world trade – dynamic efficiency – the capacity to constantly improve productivity and standards of living – and social justice – moderate economic inequality. But Fordism succeeded for other reasons. Not only did it smooth out business cycles but, more importantly, it was able to reconcile modernization, general improvements in living standards, and reductions in inequality. This was achieved through new socio-political compromises that gave meaning and legitimacy to an intense institutional constructivism. The two models that were best able to reconcile dynamic efficiency and greater social justice were, initially, social democratic capitalism and, later, state-led capitalism (see Figures 8.2 and 8.5). Indeed, at the end of the 1960s, several US experts travelled to France to witness the French miracle and take some of its lessons back home.

4.2. Lessons from the structural crises of fordism and finance-led accumulation

It is worth highlighting some of the analytical findings that emerged from the re-evaluation of the concept of the State and its aims and instruments. The following proposals are the result of two conclusions drawn from the above analysis. First, we must heed the lessons of history if we are to correct the mistakes that lead to severe economic crises. Second, the policies that countries need are likely to vary and, indeed, should be compatible and consistent with the development model and type of regulation that characterizes each national economy. Different paradigms and policies characterize different models of development and we should avoid generalizing lessons from one model to another.

4.3. Loss of belief in the efficiency and self-regulation of financial markets grants new legitimacy to state intervention

The historical record suggests a correlation between financial liberalization and the frequency and severity of crises. *A contrario*, adequate regulation and institutional forms can prevent major financial crises over an extended period of several decades. This can be seen from the post-war Golden

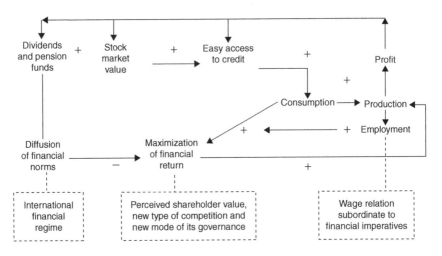

Figure 8.5 Finance-led accumulation regime

Age, and the experience of Canada and Germany despite the Lehman Brothers collapse and the risk of contagion. Therefore, a new planning mechanism needs to be invented, since corporations continue to plan their activities at the national and international levels, while States follow market patterns, in other words, the consequences of strategic decisions taken by multinationals. This model differs from the Keynesian vision in which the State sets the rules of the game, making expectations converge around a growth path agreed by all participants in decision-making and where the State controls private and social capital and companies duly adapt. Today, we are living in a period when Morgan Stanley or Goldman Sachs decide the viability of Greece's growth regime. This is clearly a question of the usurpation of the economic power conferred by the democratic system and threatens national sovereignty. It leads to a serious dilemma regarding respect for citizens' decisions versus securing international stability. Perhaps we should reaffirm, following Polanyi (1944), that the role of finance is not to control and organize society to its own benefit. Rather, it is up to collective processes, essentially of a political nature, to align the direction and intensity of innovation, including financial innovation, with the pursuit of society's well-being.

4.4. Collapse of belief in the neutrality of monetary policy

In academic circles, the triumph of neoclassical economics had finally convinced central banks and governments that monetary policy should only be used to keep inflation within strict limits with a view to protecting real activity at the macroeconomic level in the medium and long term. Important changes that could have advanced these goals were not made due to the liberalization and proliferation of financial instruments and the corresponding increase in monetary liquidity. These were the direct cause of a series of financial bubbles, which initially provided rapid growth but later plunged modern economies into a great systemic crisis. Similarly, central banks induced a crisis by stepping up the refinancing of banks in the hope that they would increase lending and thus boost investment and consumption. In Europe, for example, the mechanism whereby monetary policy is transmitted to the real economy has fallen into a liquidity trap; the fact that monetary policy has it limits does not mean that money is neutral.

To avoid repeating these episodes, monetary policy must be redesigned and recognized as a major influence on economic activity levels, although this is not enough to guarantee financial stability (Boyer, Dehove and Plihon, 2004). Other instruments are needed, such as macroprudential supervision and reform of microprudential methods.

4.5. In a depression, public spending becomes a useful tool to boost effective demand

Contrary to the prevailing theory of Ricardian equivalence – which envisages null or negative multiplier effects – the capacity to boost demand in a depression is useful. As the International Monetary Fund (IMF) eventually recognized and has demonstrated, multipliers are enhanced in periods of economic depression, which means that fiscal policy functions more effectively than monetary policy and can help stave off collapse, although there are limits to its ability to stimulate recovery, as shown by the long period of stagnation in Japan since the 1990s. The clear recessionary effect of austerity policies in Europe since 2011 provides further empirical evidence of the power of Keynesian multipliers and the errors of Ricardian equivalence when the economy is far from full employment (Boyer, 2012b).

4.6. Absolute principles of competition policy are compromised, especially to bail out large banks and manufacturers

It was once thought that competition policy was the sole tool for spurring innovation and growth. This was not the case in the European Union, whose southern economies have not reached the levels of research and development spending found in the north. Neither have significant economic and financial liberalization freed Latin America from its dependence on commodity exports or the weakness of its innovation systems. Competition is the heart and engine of capitalism, but without strong collective control – as foreseen by Marx and confirmed by economic history – it repeatedly creates oligopolies and monopolies. The Lehman Brothers crisis points to another lesson: an unprecedented concentration of financial institutions can make them 'too big to fail' or 'too connected to fail'. These changes clearly contradict neoclassical ideology, in which the system is regulated by competition between small units.

4.7. Erratic exchange-rate trends demonstrate the limitations of financial globalization: governments must have an exchange-rate policy

In today's economy, with high capital mobility and huge volumes of financial transactions in international trade, exchange rates depend on the equalization of rates of return on mobile capital. This exchange rate has no short- or medium-term connection with the real exchange rate based on each country's integration in the world economy; in other words, there is a new understanding of the exchange-rate regime (Bresser-Pereira, 2009). So, it is important to devise instruments to return to an exchange rate that permits viable international economic integration thanks to the resilience of a production system capable of supporting exports and achieving balance-of-payments equilibrium (Boyer, 2011b). For a long time, the IMF claimed that any disturbance in the equilibrium of the exchange-rate market would undermine the efficient allocation of capital. It has since learnt that capital controls can, at least partially and for a time, reduce the instability caused by sudden changes in internal and external capital flows.

4.8. A more progressive income tax system is needed to respond to the failure of trickle-down economics

The idea that allowing inequalities of wealth and income to grow would stimulate economic development has foundered. If this were true, Latin America would be a highly-developed region. Even though the richest man in the world lives in Mexico, it cannot be inferred that the country will develop as a result, since highly mobile capital and a regressive tax system make it impossible to remedy income inequalities. More generally, the exclusion of core social groups from the leading political alliance increases the probability of a major crisis (witness the exclusion of wage-earners from the dominant bloc in Italy or the hegemony of finance that preceded the subprime crisis). Conversely, the exit from a financial crisis is the shorter, the more transparent and consensual is decision-making. The contrast between Japan and Sweden is instructive here. Long-term historical studies show that progressive income and inheritance tax systems played an important role in reducing economic and social inequalities after WWII. By contrast, implementing a flat tax rate and lowering taxes on capital have contributed decisively to rising inequality since the 1980s (Piketty, 2013).

5. The welfare state, growth and social justice

Ideological and theoretical representations of welfare influence the reforms implemented in various countries. The claim that Bismarckian systems drive up labour costs and undermine competitiveness and employment is used to justify welfare cuts, while Beveridgean systems are facing the tax revolt of the middle classes and the erosion of their tax bases due to high financial capital mobility. Social security is regarded as a pure cost without any positive or significant contribution. This reductionist accounting-based vision totally neglects the fact that social security promotes well-being, generally reduces inequality and may also be the catalyst for dynamic economic efficiency. This triad was first noted in studies that sought to interpret the 'Dutch miracle' (Visser and Hemerijck, 1997) (see Figure 8.6).

5.1. Investment in health and education increases well-being

Education means nurturing citizens who can make informed decisions; effective health-care systems provide longer lives free of serious diseases; and unemployment benefits and the minimum wage reduce poverty among wage-earners. Yet while these services have improved wellbeing, current methods of calculating national accounts cannot measure this.

Where the provision of education, health and insurance against economic risks are collectively organized and financed by society-wide contributions, the welfare and tax systems exert a clear redistributive impact and can help to reduce inequality. Conversely, the individualization of insurance contracts, the decentralization of many welfare components and the rise of pension funds lead to diverging trajectories among individuals with quite similar initial characteristics.

5.2 Welfare systems: Reconciling the theories of Keynes and Schumpeter

The welfare state affects the economy in many ways and may promote innovation, growth, and economic performance. A dynamic policy of minimum wage increases might temporarily harm less productive firms, but offers an incentive for labour-saving innovations and a long-run increase in productivity. Furthermore, within societies where the economically active population mostly comprises wage-earners (*société salariale*), salaries are key determinants for consumption and global demand. Thus, they may offset the labour-saving bias of technological change through the coevolution of demand.

Hence, the conceptions of Schumpeter and Keynes are more complementary than opposed (Dosi, Fagiolo and Roventini, 2008). Health expenditures contribute to better wellbeing, less absenteeism and longer life expectancy, which in turn permits a higher return on investment in education and training. Education for the population at large, conceived as learning how to solve problems, brings a key ingredient to the dynamism of national systems of innovation. Nordic countries have built on the lessons that emerged from the 'Dutch miracle' and now recurrently adjust the complementarity between their welfare and innovation systems (Boyer, 2014a).

Both Keynes and Schumpeter proposed a similar updating concerning unemployment benefits. These do not create an 'unemployment trap'. On the contrary, it can be avoided through a generous replacement rate, complemented by an active training policy to reassign workers from obsolete

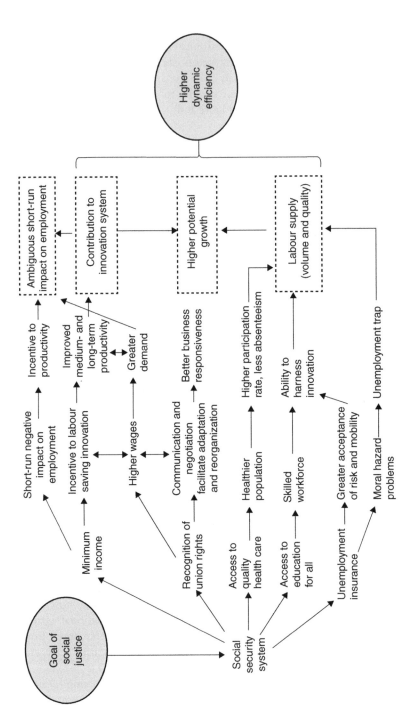

Figure 8.6 How some welfare regimes enhance dynamic efficiency

sectors to rapidly growing, high productivity ones. Yet, apart from the Nordic countries, the fundamentals of a universal welfare state in symbiosis with the national innovation system have been abandoned in favour of a crude cost-cutting approach, with complete disregard for the adverse effects on population wellbeing, long-run production capacity and the ability to innovate and explore the upgrading of international specialization (Amable, Boyer and Barré, 1997).

6. How globalization may invalidate past lessons

While the above macroeconomic analysis from post-war advanced economies and its lessons are appealing, it suffers from two important theoretical defects. First, it assumes that national economies are implicitly closed when there has been an increasing internationalization of trade, direct investment, financial capital, and intellectual property rights. And, second, it assumes that financing is determined by real factors. These assumptions are outdated in today's world.

6.1. The great danger of financial globalization

One might have thought that the spectacle of the 1997 Asian financial crisis would serve as a warning for other countries that succumbed to the charms of financial globalization and the rapid growth of loans denominated in foreign currency, in this case the dollar. Capital is attracted to emerging economies but flees when adverse events occur, leading banking and exchange-rate crises to erupt simultaneously. For, on the one hand, the former occur as credit expands faster than the economy can absorb it, causing speculative, real-estate and stock market bubbles; and, on the other hand, the inability to repay foreign-currency-denominated loans feeds widespread mistrust of the local currency. Nearly all studies of financial crises reach the same conclusion: opening the capital account and allowing domestic agents to become indebted in foreign currency is extremely dangerous, unless the utmost caution is exercised regarding prudential regulation and oversight (Boyer, Dehove and Plihon, 2004).

In the late 2000s, several countries that recently joined the international system, particularly new European Union member states from Eastern Europe, adopted the same risky strategy the Asian countries employed in the 1990s. Bulgaria, Estonia, Hungary, and Latvia all saw credit surge as a proportion of GDP, and allowed borrowing in euro-denominated loans, resulting in heightened risk (see Table 8.3). While international financial institutions were trying to diversify these countries' portfolios and attract direct investment, the national authorities settled for economic growth.

The US crisis gradually spread to the rest of the world, producing a reversal in direction as capital flowed back towards large financial centres, even though they were also in crisis, since it was believed they could provide greater

Table 8.3 Factors increasing the likelihood of twin crises, 2009

	Foreign currency loans (Percentages of the total)	Foreign currency credit (percentages of GDP)	Short-term credit (less than 1 year) (percentages)
Republic of Korea	9.5	119.0	–
India	1.4	81.0	–
Brazil	2.0	61.0	–
Czech Republic	8.0	97.3	8.8
Poland	24.0	58.3	5.6
Hungary	55.0	106.7	18.2
Slovakia	35.0	107.2	13.2
Bulgaria	53.0	90.3	28.2
Romania	54.0	66.7	19.6
Lithuania	61.0	94.7	14.8
Estonia	82.0	161.0	25.7
Latvia	86.0	134.2	33.6
Turkey	29.0	23.8	9.1
Ukraine	49.0	31.3	10.2

Source: prepared by the author on the basis of IMF data

guarantees than emerging economies. It appears the world is witnessing the re-emergence of twin financial crises in globalized countries. The only countries that seem to have learned from the Asian crisis were those that were directly affected, with emerging economies in general paying little heed to that lesson. Yet while South Korea and Brazil suffered several profound crises, the Eastern European countries did not.

6.2. Advantages and disadvantages of the growing interdependence of economies

If there is no single pattern that development models and inequality regimes follow, why are they so persistent? Boyer (2014a) shows that a rather coherent or at least internationally compatible system is gradually being formed (see Figure 8.7).

Expanding incomes under the finance-led growth regime in the USA ran parallel to the widening inequality generated by the rapid modernization of production in China. This is not the only example of co-evolution within the world economy.

Indeed, the euro crisis, the threat to extended welfare systems and the defence of social solidarity are the consequence of the joint pressure exerted by China's catching-up in most industries and the recurring global financial crises caused by the United States' promotion of liberalization and globalization in trade, capital, and finance.

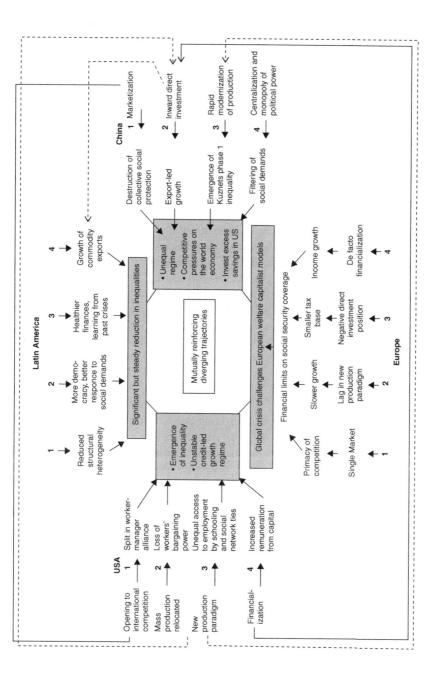

Figure 8.7 Complementarity of national inequality regimes and development models

The Latin American paradox – an atypical fall in economic inequality until the mid-2000s, albeit one starting from extreme social polarization – is also explained by the region's specialization (complementing those of China and the USA), its ability to learn from recent financial crises, and its transition to democracy. To this we can add that governments have finally responded positively to demands for social protection.

The macroeconomic imbalances driven by widening inequality within each domestic economy are symmetrical in the USA and in China; consequently, only compensating movements in international trade and finance permit the viability of socioeconomic regimes that could not be sustained behind closed borders: abundant credit to sustain living standards despite stagnant average real income in the USA; industrial overcapacity due to shrinking labour share in National Income in China; and low household saving rates in the USA compared with Chinese high savings, partially channelled back to the US financial system. Thus, the internationalization of production, capital, and finance makes it seem that contrasting inequality regimes are compatible and viable, since they are embedded into complementary development models. This also explains opposite evolutions concerning inequality: there is less inequality between countries because globalization permits a variety of finance-dominated growth regimes and those led by exports, innovation, or commodities, but each regime nurtures widening inequalities for individuals within the same national state.

7. Conclusions

Widening inequality emerged as a key challenge for most countries in the 2010s, threatening social cohesion, eroding political legitimacy, and ultimately undermining economic resilience. We must therefore question the premise of neo-classical theory that treats inequality as a positive vector of an emergent growth regime because inequality allegedly motivates workers, stimulates investment, and promotes innovation as a source of growth and jobs.

In this context, the search for alternative socioeconomic systems could learn from the USA and Europe after WWII: strict market supervision and strong public intervention simultaneously reduced inequality and promoted rapid and relatively stable growth. However, a return to these experiences is impossible owing to the new productive models, the internationalization of production, and financial globalization. Instead, the conceptual framework developed by economists from social democratic countries should be mobilized to demonstrate the conditions required for an extensive welfare state in which economic efficiency and social justice are not only compatible but even complementary.

What might be the principles of a policy for development in the 21st century? First, we have learnt that bringing inflation under control through a prudent monetary policy does not guarantee financial stability: finances must be regulated. Second, outside of full employment, unemployment is involuntary: so, monetary and fiscal policies can affect the level of activity, especially in a depression, when public spending can efficiently reduce unemployment. Third, exchange rates should not be determined solely by short-term capital movements; they should allow the national economy to participate in the international system through an efficient production model. And, fourth, if the policy game does not permit the re-institutionalization of a fair wage distribution, we need a progressive taxation of income and capital.

The world has experienced a period of radical transformation of economies, societies and international relations that can only be analysed imperfectly with the great theories inherited from the past. In the long term, capitalism and its theories should change concurrently. However, almost all economists base their analyses on outdated theories: the neoclassical school outdated by a century; Keynesianism by 50 years, and even regulation theory by a decade or so. Thus, economists should be cautious when evaluating and judging the current economic situation and advising politicians on this basis. Accordingly, this chapter set out a global vision that can be applied to theories, then abstract models and, finally, in applied models that could guide decisions on economic and social policies and long-term strategies. Today's world has experienced such profound change that past theories have lost relevance. Let us hope that a period of great theorization, like that of the 1930s, is about to unfold.

Notes

1 Based largely on a chapter, 'Growth, employment and equality: The new role of the state' (pp. 273–297), in A. Bárcena and A. Prado (eds.) (2016), *Neostructuralism and heterodox thinking in Latin America and the Caribbean in the early twenty-first century.* Santiago: Economic Commission for Latin America and the Caribbean. However, sections specific to Latin America have been cut and other material has been integrated from Boyer (1990, 2000, 2011b, 2011c, 2012b, 2013a, 2014b, 2015a, 2015b).

2 On the specificity of the crisis in South Korea and Latin America, see Boyer (2014a, pp. 94–95).

3 These lessons come from the research project, *'Crises, changes, and continuity'* (Boyer, 2014b).

References

Aglietta, M. (1979) *A theory of capitalist regulation: The US experience.* London: NLB.

Amable, B. (2003) *The diversity of modern capitalism.* Oxford: Oxford University Press.

Amable, B., Boyer, R. and Barré, R. (1997) *Les systèmes d'innovation à l'ère de la globalisation.* Paris: Economica.

André, C. and Delorme, R. (1983) '*Matériaux pour une comparaison internationale des dépenses publique*', Statistiques et Etudes Financières. No. 350. Paris: Impr. Nationale.

Boyer, R. (1990) *Regulation theory: A critical introduction.* New York: Columbia University Press.

Boyer, R. (2000) 'Is a finance-led growth regime a viable alternative to Fordism? A preliminary analysis', *Economy & Society* 29(1), pp. 111–145.

Boyer, R. (2011a) 'A new epoch but still diversity within and between capitalism: China in comparative perspective', in Lane, C. and Wood, G. (eds.) *Capitalist diversity and diversity within capitalism*. London: Routledge, pp. 32–67.

Boyer, R. (2011b) 'Aprender de las crisis financieras. ¿Como organizar sistemas financieros domésticos desarrollistas?', in Orlik, N.L. and González, T.L. (eds.) *Las instituciones financieras y el crecimiento económico en el contexto de la dominación del capital financiero*. Mexico, DF: National Autonomous University of Mexico, pp. 295–325.

Boyer, R. (2011c) *Les financiers détruiront-ils le capitalisme?* Paris: Economica.

Boyer, R. (2012a) 'The Chinese growth regime and the world economy', in Boyer, R., Uemura, H. and Isogai, A. (eds.) *Diversity and transformations of Asian capitalisms*. London: Routledge, pp. 184–205.

Boyer, R. (2012b) 'The four fallacies of contemporary austerity policies: The lost Keynesian legacy', *Cambridge Journal of Economics* 36(1), pp. 283–312.

Boyer, R. (2013a) 'Financial innovations, growth and crisis: The subprime collapse in perspective', in Yagi, K., Yokokawa, N., Hagiwara, S. and Dymski, G.A. (eds.) *Crises of global economies and the future of capitalism. Reviving Marxian crisis theory*. London: Routledge, pp. 151–173.

Boyer, R. (2013b) 'Origins and ways out of the euro crisis: Supranational institution building in the era of global finance', *Contributions to Political Economy* 32(1), pp. 97–126.

Boyer, R. (2014a) 'Is more equality possible in Latin America? A challenge in a world of contrasted but interdependent inequality regimes', Working Paper No. 67. Berlin: desigualdades.net International Research Network on Interdependent Inequalities in Latin America. Available at: http://www.desigualdades.net/Resources/Working_Pa per/67-WP-Boyer-Online.pdf (Accessed on 19 April 2018).

Boyer, R. (2014b) *'What have we learnt from the succession of crises?' Contribution to the project: 'Crises, change, and continuity.'* Institute of Social Studies, Erasmus University Rotterdam. Unpublished paper.

Boyer, R. (2015a) 'A world of contrasted but interdependent inequality regimes: China, United States and the European Union', *Review of Political Economy* 27(4), pp. 481–517.

Boyer, R. (2015b) *Économie politique des capitalismes: Théorie de la régulation et crises*. Paris: La Découverte.

Boyer, R., Dehove, M. and Plihon, D. (2004) *Les crises financières*. Paris: La documentation française.

Boyer, R. and Juillard, M. (2000) 'The wage labour nexus challenged: More the consequence than the cause of the crisis', in Boyer, R. and Yamada, T. (eds.) *Japanese capitalism in crisis: A regulationist interpretation*. London: Routledge, pp. 119–137.

Bresser-Pereira, L.C. (2009) *Pourquoi certains pays émergents réussissent et d'autres non*. Paris: La Découverte.

Dosi, G., Fagiolo, G. and Roventini, A. (2008) *Schumpeter meeting Keynes: A policy friendly model of endogenous growth and business cycles*. LEM Paper Series no. 21. Pisa, Italy: Sant'Anna School of Advanced Studies.

Fukuyama, F. (1992) *The end of history and the last man*. New York: Free Press.

Greenspan, A. (1996) *The challenge of central banking in a democratic society*. The Annual Dinner and Francis Boyer Lecture of The American Enterprise Institute for Public Policy Research, 12 December. Washington, DC: US Federal Reserve. Available at: https://www.federalreserve.gov/boarddocs/speeches/1996/19961205.htm (Accessed on 19 April 2018).

Minsky, H.P. (1982) *Can 'it' happen again? Essays on instability and finance.* New York: M. E. Sharpe.

Pedersen, O.K. (2006) 'Corporatism and beyond: The negotiated economy', in Campbell, J.L., Hall, J.A. and Pedersen, O.K. (eds) *National identity and the varieties of capitalism: The Danish experience,* Montreal: McGill-Queen's University Press, pp. 245–270.

Piketty, T. (2013) *Capital in the twenty-first century.* Cambridge, MA: Harvard University Press.

Polanyi, K. (1944) *The great transformation: The economic and political origins of our time.* New York: Rinehart.

Samuelson, P.A. (1948) *Economics: An introductory analysis.* New York: McGraw-Hill.

Schumpeter, J.A. (1954) *Economic doctrine and method: An historical sketch.* New York: Oxford University Press.

Visser, J. and Hemerijck, A. (1997) *'A Dutch miracle': Job growth, welfare reform and corporatism in the Netherlands.* Amsterdam: Amsterdam University Press.

Part IV

Fetishistic or reflexive learning?

9 The EU's competitiveness fetish

Industrial renaissance through internal devaluation, really?

Angela Wigger

Industrial policy, once a key pillar of European integration, has been outlawed during the past decades of neoliberal reign. As part of recent European Union (EU) crisis-management plans however, industrial policy seems to be reviving. The European Commission's Communication, *For a European Industrial Renaissance,* issued in 2014 is telling here, announcing that "a strong industrial base will be of key importance for Europe's economic recovery and competitiveness" (European Commission, 2014). To overcome the crisis and make the EU future proof, the goal is to reverse the process of deindustrialization, reflected in the transfer of manufacturing capacity to China and other emerging markets by boosting industrial competitiveness. The target is to increase the manufacturing share of the EU's GDP from its current 15 percent to 20 percent by 2020. Manufacturing, which accounts for 40 percent of all EU exports, is argued to be the main driver for "innovation, jobs, growth and wealth" (ibid.).

Boosting the competitiveness of EU manufacturing industries certainly sounds politically appealing, particularly against the backdrop of a rising popular fatigue with fiscal austerity. Moreover, competitiveness evokes a vision of being part of a successful and "winning" community. A cursory inspection of the EU competitiveness agenda may give the impression of a perspicacious Keynesian-type of industrial policy – one that supports knowledge-intensive sectors and tackles the persistently high unemployment in the EU since 2009. However, reforms in the spirit of competitiveness are highly deceptive. Competitiveness is primarily understood as "price and cost" competitiveness, creating favourable parameters for export-led growth. EU industries should be able to compete on global markets on the basis of lower prices (European Commission, 2016a). Because individual economies within the Economic and Monetary Union (EMU) cannot cheapen export prices by engaging in unilateral devaluation, internal devaluation has been advocated as the way forward. The suggested strategy is three-tiered: first, depreciating real wages and inducing further labour market reforms; second, intensifying inter-company competition to lower prices; and third, lowering the overall level of corporate taxation. Arguably, internal devaluation as a substitute for exchange rate adjustments has been on the agenda since Maastricht. The EMU has literally been designed to rule out Keynesian-style industrial policies through deficit spending. Moreover, far-reaching internal devaluation measures have already been employed in the context of Memoranda of Understanding and the new economic governance packages, such as the European Semester of 2010 or the Euro Plus Pact of 2011. Nonetheless, the new industrial policy is new as far as it seeks to anchor internal devaluation in a regulatory framework according to which not only the most crisis-hit member states, but the entire EU has to step up reform efforts. EU economies not only have to undercut each other's cost and price competitiveness, or corporate tax rates in a competitive, beggar-thy-neighbour fashion, but also those of the main trading partners or rivals. The suggested race-to-the-bottom has strong authoritarian aspects, whereby not only democratic institutions but also social partners are being disempowered (Wigger, 2018). Although EU member states have weakened the first set of Commission proposals for bilateral competitiveness pacts or competitiveness authorities, the democratically unelected and unaccountable Commission will still gain further discretionary powers in areas that hitherto have fallen outside the EU's competence. In addition, the powers of the European Courts are likely to be strengthened to sanction cases of non-compliance with commonly agreed competitiveness benchmarks.

Some political economists echo the message from EU institutions, repeating the claim that labour costs in the EU are too high to remain competitive (for example, Eichengreen, 2008, p. 380). In contrast, post-Keynesian and critical political economy scholars have shown that the EU's neoliberal crisis management has failed dramatically (for example, Jäger and Springler, 2015; Sandbu, 2015; Stiglitz, 2016; Stockhammer, 2016). This chapter takes this further by examining the new industrial policy strategy as the most recent crisis-management strategy. Whereas previous research labelled the EU crisis management as "muddling through" (Overbeek, 2012), or as "lacking a clear vision" (EuroMemorandum, 2013), it will be shown here that the driving coalition of EU governments, EU institutions, and organized capital have a clear and outspoken vision. This vision continues to be neoliberal in orientation and does not display a radical break with the crises measures hitherto. The new industrial policy, which is actually a disguised form of internal devaluation, rather calibrates neoliberal structural adjustments by putting the primary burden of adjustment on labour rather than capital: while wage repression, labour market reforms, and intense price competition directly and indirectly deflate labour, the reduction of corporate taxes expedites the redistribution of wealth from labour to capital. As this chapter will argue, little if anything has been learned from the previous crisis management. Internal devaluation exacerbates existing structural asymmetries and economic disintegration further, and thus will fail just as earlier forms of neo-liberal crisis-management also failed.

The chapter is organized as follows: Section one sketches the wider EU approach to crisis management since 2008 and locates the new industrial policy therein. Section two outlines and discusses the internal devaluation strategy with regard to the issue of reducing unit labour costs and intensified price competition. Section three reveals the authoritarian traits of the regulatory format, and Section four analyses the coalition of key driving political agents. The concluding section summarizes the main findings and considers the possibility that, in the name of competitiveness, the last remnants of labour rights risk being torn down in a major assault on democracy.

1. EU crisis management revisited

When major financial institutions, and particularly those with large US subprime exposure, faced a heightened liquidity shortage ("credit crunch") and the threat of insolvency in 2007–2008, many EU governments reacted quickly by bailing out banks considered of systemic importance ("too big to fail"). State aid packages took the form of massive loans or liquidity guarantees, government-sponsored mergers, corporate tax exemptions, a (partial) nationalization of banks by the acquisition of "toxic" assets and state purchase of preferential shares, and government guarantees for deposits (see Wigger and Buch-Hansen, 2014). The Commission took more than 500 decisions from 2008 to 2015 concerning 117 European banks (European Commission, 2016b). The bailouts amounted to roughly €747 billion, while another €1,188 billion was made available in guarantees on liabilities (TNI, 2017, p. 4). Soon after, when other industries in distress such as the car, steel, construction, or shipbuilding industries, also demanded emergency state aid to cope with the worsening crisis, the Commission was no longer so permissive and declared state aid to be a distortion to competition in the common market. At the time, the Commission construed the crisis as a crisis within the financial sector only, and optimistically expected the crisis to be over by December 31, 2010, the expiry date of permitted state aid schemes for the financial sector. Even though the expiry date had to be extended several times, the Commission maintained that the bailouts mitigated the course of the crisis considerably, and that the adoption of subsequent financial regulations reduced the build-up and the emergence of systemic risk across the financial system.

Bailing out the financial sector, in conjunction with overall lower GDPs and declining tax revenues, exhausted national budgets. The crisis was subsequently no longer interpreted as a crisis of the financial sector but as a sovereign debt crisis due to excessive government spending. Particularly Southern Eurozone members suffered from growing current account imbalances and rapidly accumulating public debt, facing acute difficulties to sell bonds (and thus, public debt) on financial markets. In response, the EU, together with the International Monetary Fund (IMF), provided conditional loans to governments, while, in parallel, the European Central Bank (ECB) started a series of liquidity injections to the financial system. Rather than blaming the financial sector, crisis-hit Eurozone-member governments were accused to have lived beyond their means, which served as a political legitimation for the imposition of painful austerity programmes. A range of Eurozone-specific and more general EU-28 regulatory and treaty-based measures were adopted. These comprised the European Semester of 2010; the Euro Plus Pact; the Six Pack of 2011; the Treaty for Stability, Coordination and Governance, leading to the Fiscal Compact of 2012; and the Two Pack of 2013. These measures imposed a strict EU monitoring of national budgets, limiting the capacity to run budget deficits and adopt costly social and economic policies. Tightening member states' fiscal discipline and enhancing their ability to service their debts served the purpose of regaining the trust of financial markets and their rating agencies. Austerity packages did not stabilize public finances: they merely targeted ongoing budget deficits, while protecting the accumulated stock of existing debt (Sandbu, 2015, p. 64). As a result, deficit and debt ratios stayed high, while economic contraction and depression aggravated. Even IMF economists eventually concluded that austerity did more harm than good (see for example Blanchard and Leigh, 2013). However, EU bureaucrats and politicians continued to push for strict budget rules. With EU austerity politics under mounting critique, Jeroen Dijsselbloem (2017), former head of the unelected and democratically unaccountable Eurogroup, announced, "there will be a change in the policy mix [. . .] moving away from austerity and putting more emphasis on deep reforms." Particularly, structural reform boosting economic competitiveness came to be heralded as the new strategy. In other words, the crisis's root causes came to be framed as a lack of competitiveness of European economies.

The EU has a longstanding tradition of policies justified by the rhetoric of competitiveness. Already the preambles of the Treaty of Rome of 1957 declared "a high degree of competitiveness" as a Community goal (Article 2). Indeed, competitiveness performance indexes, benchmarking best practices and scoreboards have formed the apex of the neoliberal organization of capitalism in Europe for decades. The Lisbon Agenda of 2000 and its successor strategy Europe 2020 were entrenched with notions of competitiveness. When the crisis hit, "competitiveness" moved up the agenda. In 2011, the European Commission announced:

> [w]hile fiscal imbalances are at the forefront of the current policy debate, they are by no means the only area where policy action is needed. Recent developments have highlighted the urgent need for some euro-area Member States to restore their external balances and to improve their competitiveness.
>
> (European Commission, 2011, pp. 21–22)

The Four Presidents' Report (2012) launched the idea that EU member governments should conclude annual contractual arrangements with the Commission, targeting areas where competitiveness was weak. In January 2013, German Chancellor Merkel proclaimed at the World Economic Forum in Davos, Switzerland that "Competitiveness Pacts," along similar lines to the Fiscal Compact, should create the prerequisite to get access to financial aid from EU budgets under what euphemistically had been termed the "solidarity mechanism." A month later, the Commission launched a proposal for a "Convergence and Competitiveness Instrument," which suggested a procedure according to which the Commission would make recommendations to individual member governments on how to regain competitiveness (European Commission, 2013). Almost simultaneously, the European Council committed itself to negotiate "Partnerships for Growth, Employment and Competitiveness," entailing that individual governments and the Commission would conclude bilateral reform contracts, which would be subject to approval by Council, notably in the configuration of the Competitiveness Council (European Council, 2013, pp. 17–20). In contrast to the reform requirements spelled out in the Memoranda of Understanding (MoU) between member states and the Troika or the IMF/EU, the envisaged competitiveness treaties would encompass all Eurozone members. Furthermore, in contrast to the Country-Specific Recommendations (CSRs) issued *ex ante* by the Commission under the European Semester procedure of 2011, the competitiveness treaties would be legally binding, which would make them enforceable through *ex post* litigation before the EU Courts. In the absence of political support, the Council negotiations were stalled in June 2014; yet the idea of member state-specific competitiveness reforms has persisted ever since. The Five Presidents' Report, prepared by the European Commission's President, in cooperation with the Presidents of the Euro Summit, Eurogroup, the European Central Bank, and the European Parliament, proposed establishing "National Competitiveness Authorities" entrusted with the supervision of policies and performances in the field of competitiveness (see Five Presidents' Report, 2015). To trivialise the binding character, the Commission subsequently renamed the envisaged Competitiveness Authorities, Competitiveness Boards, and in September 2016, the Council subsequently issued a recommendation calling upon Eurozone members to establish "National Productivity Boards" – a slightly weakened version of what the Commission initially proposed.

2. Industrial renaissance through internal devaluation

The Commission Communication "For a European Industrial Renaissance" (2014) prophesies a vast on-shoring of manufacturing production back from emerging markets to Europe, provided competitiveness measures were adopted. In addition to increasing the manufacturing share of the EU GDP from 15 to 20 percent by 2020, keeping pace with China, India or Brazil takes centre-stage. The Commission emphasized that EU's relative weight in world trade and share of world capital flows vis-à-vis emerging markets had both declined. The Chinese economy, for example, no longer exclusively caters for labour-intensive low value-added production but climbed the ladder towards high-quality, high value-added segments, notably in the computer and electronics sector, and became the world's largest exporter at country-level, while attracting a share of FDI equal to the EU (European Commission, 2015a, pp. 14, 98). The Communication is just one among many policy programmes. The European Fund for Strategic Investments (EFSI) established in June 2015, also referred to as the Juncker Funds, named after Commission President Jean-Claude Juncker, for example, seeks to co-finance and leverage risky "infrastructure and innovation projects" around Europe that would not otherwise be funded. Similarly, the Programme for the Competitiveness of Enterprises and Small and Medium-sized Enterprises (COSME) seeks to improve SMEs' access to credit on the basis of guarantees and counter-guarantees, as well as through using the securitization of debt-finance portfolios as leverage.

The various packages may give the impression of an active industrial policy consisting of state aid packages meant to counter the decline in Europe's industrial base as they had been employed during the stagflation crisis of the 1970s. However, as former Commissioner Almunia (2014) affirmed, the new industrial policy differed markedly from that of the 1970s. In the view of the Commission, the EU's future prosperity depends on its ability to attract investments, most notably Foreign Direct Investment (FDI) to compensate for low domestic investments. Since the 1970s, investments in the production sphere in relation to GDP have been declining, which is due to saturated markets, lingering overcapacity, slowly growing aggregate demand and a vast tertiarization. Measured in terms of gross fixed capital formation, investments decreased from 22.1 percent of GDP in 2000 to 19.3 percent in 2014, which compares to 45 percent in China or 30 percent in India (European Commission, 2015a, p. 8). From 2000 to 2014, de-industrialization accelerated in the EU: the share of manufacturing of the total EU GDP fell by 3.5 percentage points in nominal value-added terms (from 18.8 to 15.3 percent), and employment in manufacturing 16 percent, which translates in a reduction of 6 million jobs (ibid., pp. 5–7, 14). Whereas the crisis also hit the service sector hard, its impact was much heavier on manufacturing industries. De-industrialization has not affected all manufacturing sectors equally, and its national impact is also uneven, with manufacturing output dropping dramatically in Greece, Italy, Portugal, Spain, and Cyprus (ibid., p. 7). Although the debt-fuelled accumulation model in the EU's Southern periphery bolstered gross fixed capital formation from 1995 up to 2008, most investments were made in non-tradable sectors, such as construction in Spain, tourism in Greece, and other services in Ireland, which increased import dependency and worsened current accounts (Stockhammer and Onaran, 2012a, pp. 13–14; Collignon and Esposito, 2014). According to the Commission, the way to attract investments in the real economy is to boost the competitiveness of European economies.

Competitiveness is almost exclusively understood in terms of internal devaluation, which can "mimic the expenditure-switching effects of 'external' exchange rate devaluation" (European Commission, 2011b, p. 22). European economies should become more resilient through falling wages, prices and corporate tax rates. Wage moderation is expected to make "labour" less costly for business, and to translate into overall lower prices for goods and services. Likewise, more intense price competition, alongside a vast deregulation of product markets and further privatizations, is expected to lead to lower prices and hence overall lowered production costs. In addition, reduced corporate tax burdens, reduced taxes on exports, and a "revenue-neutral" shift from taxes on labour to consumption are expected to restore an attractive investment climate in Europe (European Commission, 2011b). In short, internal devaluation is expected to boost extra-EU exports and improve EU trade balances. Or, as German Chancellor Merkel (2013) declared, the yardstick of competitiveness "should be whether our products can compete in global markets." Emulating the emerging markets' comparative advantage of cheap labour and deflating labour constitutes a cornerstone of the new EU industrial policy.

Industrial renaissance through deflating labour

A central yardstick to assess and compare the evolution of competitiveness is unit labour costs, a ratio between productivity and total labour compensation (direct and indirect labour costs), indicating whether labour costs rise in line with productivity gains. The components vary, ranging from total labour cost structures, like wages or employers' contributions to social security and pension schemes vis-à-vis units of produced output or number of hours worked, whether at individual company, industry, regional or national level. Reducing unit labour costs is believed to have positive signalling effects to investors and will eventually boost economic growth and higher net exports, with a trickledown effect on employment and re-industrialization across Europe. Chancellor Merkel (2013), for example, reiterated it was vital to keep driving down labour costs to create a regulatory environment in Europe that is attractive to investors. Unit labour costs can be reduced either by increasing productivity or reducing elements of the total labour costs structure. However, since de-industrialization in the 1970s, productivity in the EU has slowed considerably, and productivity gains in the tertiary sector are limited. Consequently, labour market adjustments, notably through wage suppression or labour market flexibilization, are strongly emphasized, particularly as wages for temporary and flexible labour tend to be lower, and as social security benefits or experience-rated pay can be avoided.

Scoreboards of unit labour costs have become all-pervasive in EU crisis management. The general argument is that Greece, Ireland, Spain and Portugal have had real wage increases "far beyond of what could be justified on the basis of efficient production" (see Sandbu, 2015, p. 37). Germany's relatively low unit labour costs often serve as a benchmark to illustrate that, since 2000, unit labour costs in the Southern periphery increased 25–30 percent faster than in Germany (Stockhammer and Onaran, 2012b, p. 198). So, it should not surprise that the far-reaching internal devaluation programme, adopted under Chancellor Schroeder's Agenda 2010 is now not only considered a recipe for ailing economies in the South but also for all Eurozone economies. *Modell Deutschland* entails that job protection was lowered, job acceptance regulations for unemployed tightened (including so-called 1 euro jobs outside regular labour markets), temporary work agencies deregulated, social welfare for long-term unemployed dismantled, social contributions reduced, collective bargaining decentralized and corporate taxes cut (Stockhammer and Onaran, 2012a, p. 15, 2012b, p. 197; Collignon and Esposito, 2014). A range of EU member states have already adopted similar reforms, varying from "piecemeal although significant deregulatory measures" to "far-reaching overhauls of the whole labour code" – either voluntarily or to meet Troika imposed requirements in return for financial support (Clauwaert and Schoenmann, 2012). Moreover, in the context of the European Semester, the Commission demanded wage cuts in the non-tradable public sector, expecting private wages would follow suit; a freezing or lowering of minimum wages; a radical decentralization of collective wage-setting procedures; and labour market flexibilization, including an easing of hiring and firing, flexible working time or changes in overtime and time-off provisions through reducing or abolishing compensation (see ETUI, 2014, pp. 59, 62). The root causes of the crisis, in other words, have become re-construed in terms of inflexible labour, rising and too high labour costs, unproductive labour and implicitly, too powerful trade unions.

Experiments with internal devaluation have hitherto only fostered structural asymmetries in Europe. In Greece, where services account for 80 percent of the GDP and where productivity gains are thus difficult to achieve, unit labour costs were reduced by 20 percent on the basis of rigorous interventions in the wage bargaining process, labour market flexibilization, and a reduction of minimum wages by 22 percent and an additional 10 percent for the young (ibid., p. 10). In addition to mass dismissals and a vast exodus of Greeks seeking jobs elsewhere, 36 percent of Greeks find themselves at risk of poverty or social exclusion – the highest rate in the Eurozone, and 10 percent higher than the Eurozone average (Stiglitz, 2016, p. 226). So far, internal devaluation has increased neither employment levels nor exports. Labour costs have foremost been reduced in the public sector, which therefore left the export position unaffected. Moreover, Greek exports are concentrated in capital-intensive low and medium technology sectors, and not labour-intensive sectors. Lower wages did also not translate into lower prices. In fact, Greek export prices increased by 20 percent from 2009 to 2013 – the highest increase in the Eurozone (ETUI, 2014, p. 17). Reducing unit labour costs, in other words, merely served to improve returns on capital. These returns have not been invested in long-term productivity, or in projects that improve the structural position of existing industries. As Sablowski (2012) explains, lowering wages in Greece cannot solve the problem that Greek industries cannot keep up the competition with Germany's in high-tech manufacturing, automobile production, or the machine-tools industry, simply because such industries (or equivalents that would allow for high-value added production for export) do not exist.

Germany's internal devaluation programme is often told as a success story because, since 2000, net exports have driven three quarters of its GDP growth. However, German workers have not profited from higher wages and the growth of jobs was almost exclusively due to precarious and part-time employment (Sandbu, 2015, pp. 27–28). German manufacturers also tended not to invest in the German economy but relocated production to cheap labour areas in Central and Eastern Europe, notably Poland, the Czech Republic, Hungary and Slovakia, from where they imported components and processed material more cheaply (see Esposito and Guerrieri, 2014, p. 89). Moreover, EU economies mainly trade with each other, albeit in a highly uneven manner, and the expansion of Germany's manufacturing industry has led to a contraction of manufacturing in other EU economies. This was further spurred by the valorization of surplus capital through credit extension to the EU's periphery (and thus, what has not been paid out in wages). Cheap credit not only led to expansionary fiscal policies and household consumption as the main lever for economic growth in the South, but also further augmented the trade surplus of the EU's North.

A competitive reduction of unit labour costs cannot solve structural economic asymmetries in Europe. EU economies cannot all expand their industries and pursue an export-led growth pattern with a large trade surplus; particularly as a reduction of unit labour costs in a given member state will weaken unit labour costs in others. Wage repression, in combination with austerity, undermines not only domestic but also intra-EU consumption, while triggering deflation, all factors that make the proclaimed export-led growth strategy a chimera. The obsession with export competitiveness is premised on the presence of strong global demand; however, global demand is weak. As extra-EU exports account for a relatively small share of the EU's GDP (ranging between 12 to 15 percent, see Eurostat, 2017), internal devaluation will have a moderate effect on the EU's net-export position, if at all (Stockhammer and Onaran, 2012b, pp. 195–196). Furthermore, reducing unit labour costs does not reduce debt burdens in poor deficit countries. Instead, it leads to a growing share of "working poor" and precarious workers, hitting hard on the youth, women, and migrants, particularly non-EU migrants, and low-skilled workers (EuroMemorandum, 2013, p. 39; ETUI, 2014, p. 10).

Competitiveness measured on the basis of unit labour costs is a crude reductionist travesty that dehumanizes and objectifies commodified labour to the extreme. As Marx observed in the *Grundrisse* (1973 [1939], p. 164), under capitalism, individuals are ruled by abstractions and the character of these abstractions is a product of historic relations. The abstraction, or idea however "[. . .] is nothing more than the theoretical expression of those material relations which are their lord and master" (ibid.). Scoreboards of unit labour costs are such an abstraction. Used as a calculus for competitive comparisons, unit labour costs transpose human labour into a symbol of quantifiable and commensurable exchange value, which then underpin entire policy programmes. As will be shown in the next section, labour is not only depreciated on the basis of reducing unit labour costs, but also intensified capitalist competition, another key strategy of the EU internal devaluation agenda.

The competition–competitiveness Nexus in internal devaluation

The Commission readily admits that internal devaluation through reducing unit labour costs is not the only strategy required, as only the cost of labour is targeted, thereby neglecting variable production costs such as energy and raw materials (European Commission, 2015a, p. 57). Thus, it also advocates a strict enforcement of competition rules as one of the main levers to reduce the cost of capital, energy, raw materials and other production inputs. Particularly the prices in the non-traded intermediate sectors, like electricity and energy, are in the spotlight. In addition, a range of "pro-competition" reforms have been announced, notably reforms that remove perceived (regulatory) market barriers in product markets. Moreover, flanking regulatory packages, such as the "Regulatory Fitness and Performance Programme" (REFIT) and "Competitiveness Proofing" have already been employed to remove existing legislation and to screen future legislation regarding their impact on competitiveness.

The competitiveness agenda is premised on the idea that Eurozone economies can compete themselves out of the crisis based on an overall lowering of price levels. According to former Competition Commissioner Almunia (2012a, 2012b), competition policy is "the cheapest and most effective structural reform", "at no extra cost for the taxpayer." Competition, he argued, enhances "competitiveness and innovation, creates jobs and drives economic expansion". The Commission's unfathomable faith in capitalist competition as the backbone for economic growth builds on the axiom that positive feedback loops in the form of higher competitiveness and better performance of entire economies can be expected if a plethora of discrete companies strive to become more efficient, increase their productivity and stay ahead of rivals through lower prices. The benefits of capitalist competition are presented as inherently positive-sum, lifting society to ever-higher standards of economic wealth, or, in the words of the European Commission (2016a), "consumers, taxpayers, workers and businesses – everyone is better off overall when competition exists in our markets." Competition policy is also portrayed as a redistributive policy: through competition, prices are expected to converge towards marginal production costs, thereby reducing the portion of realized surplus value for capitalists and benefitting consumers.

Lower prices and economic growth through increased consumption might appear much-needed in times of economic slump and recession, and a strict enforcement of competition rules might seem less painful than tight austerity packages, onslaughts on social rights, labour and welfare state retrenchment. Moreover, the freedom to compete is often associated with broader notions of political freedom and individual self-determination. However, as Marx wrote in the *Grundrisse* (1973 [1939], p. 650): "[i]t is not individuals that are set free by free competition; it is, rather, capital which is set free" (Marx, 1973 [1939], p. 651). Competitive pressures can intensify to an extent that the prices of competitors can only be undercut by reducing variable production costs through a further exploitation of labour and nature (Wigger and Buch-Hansen, 2014).

To remain profitable and stay in production, capitalists constantly have to enhance the productivity of labour or cheapen labour. Internal devaluation through intensified competition rule enforcement may strike a chord among a great variety of political persuasions; however, ultimately, capitalist competition also deflates labour.

3. The authoritarian guise of internal devaluation

A range of scholars highlighted the authoritarian nature that EU crisis responses have (Bruff, 2014; Durand and Keucheyan, 2015; Oberndorfer, 2012; Sandbeck and Schneider, 2014), thereby drawing on Poulantzas's (1978, 1979) concept of authoritarian statism (see Oberndorfer, 2012; Sandbeck and Schneider, 2014) and Hall's (1979, 1985) work on authoritarian populism (see Bruff, 2014). In addition to outright violations of formal democracy, the authoritarian traits consist of constitutional and legal changes that have reconfigured EU institutions and its member states into less democratic entities. Executive, judicial, and bureaucratic discretionary powers have been strengthened, key decision-making areas insulated from the democratic control of legislative forces, *de jure* and *de facto* coercion has become more prevalent, and fewer attempts are being made to achieve consent with contesting groups through policy and/or material concessions.

The form in which competitiveness measures are being imposed is yet another domain of economic governance where we witness the removal of conventional forms of democratic contestation and accountability (see also Wigger, 2018). For example, competition rules enforcement, ensuring more intense price competition as a form of internal devaluation, has been insulated from democratic control since the beginning of European integration. The Commission, the supranational competition authority, is investigator, prosecutor, judge, jury and executioner all in one, and thus fuses legislative, executive and judicial powers. Commission decisions in competition cases can only be challenged before the European Courts. In addition to individual case decisions, the Commission often issues quasi-legislation, such as substantive notices, comfort letters, codes of conduct, and guidelines, which allow it to circumvent democratic legislative processes. There is no comparable field where the Commission enjoys such far-reaching discretionary powers and where the Council and the Parliament have so little to say (see Wigger and Buch-Hansen, 2015). Or, as incumbent Competition Commissioner Vestager (2015) has admitted herself in one of her speeches, "[t]here is simply no room to spare for political interference".

Similar authoritarian traits can be observed in the suggested governance framework for competitiveness. The initial idea of "Competitiveness Pacts" – annual bilateral reform contracts signed between individual member states and the European Commission – had to be enforceable before the Courts. Including the punishing arm of the Courts was considered pivotal as, according to Commission President Juncker, the 2011 Euro Plus Pact on Stronger

Economic Policy Coordination for Competitiveness and Convergence failed to deliver the expected results – not because of the substance of the policies but because of their non-binding intergovernmental nature (Five President's Report, 2015, p. 4). The Five Presidents' Report, which suggested establishing "National Competitiveness Authorities," no longer mentioned the involvement of the Courts in cases of non-compliance but envisaged these authorities would have functional autonomy and enjoy a statuary basis in national law so their decisions would have the authority of law. Moreover, these authorities had to be politically independent from ministries and public authorities when supervising national policies and performances of competitiveness (see Five Presidents' Report, 2015). Having national rather than supranational competitiveness authorities was meant to increase the perception of national ownership and also to leave room for national disparities and legal traditions. According to the Report, "Member States have a responsibility and self-interest to maintain sound policies and to embark on reforms that make their economies more flexible and competitive" (ibid., p. 4). What may at first glance appear as a decentralized approach is, however, highly centralized. The Commission was envisaged as the chief coordinator, entrusted with the task of supervising the national competitiveness authorities, and formulating common templates and standards. The Commission would then use the reported progress by the national authorities as a basis for the Commission's "country-specific recommendations" in the European Semester (ibid., p. 7–8). Common standards had to span the field of "labour markets, competitiveness, business environment and public administrations, as well as certain aspects of tax policy (e.g. corporate tax base)" (ibid., p. 9). Importantly, national competitiveness authorities should be mandated to "assess whether wages are evolving in line with productivity" as well as in comparison with other Eurozone members and "the main comparable trading partners" (ibid., p. 7). Furthermore, they should promote the "flexicurity" concept, the contradictory combination of flexible and reliable labour contracts, coupled with lifelong learning strategies and modern social security systems (ibid., p. 9). In October 2015, the European Commission (2015b) issued a "Recommendation for a Council Recommendation on the Establishment of National Competitiveness Boards". The preference for "boards" rather than "authorities" was probably intended to appease member governments with a much less perilous-sounding term, given the climate of growing Euroscepticism and outright anti-EU sentiments. Yet, by suggesting the Council recommend such boards, the Commission sidestepped the ordinary legislative procedure, thereby excluding any parliamentary oversight and debate, or formal democratic accountability (see European Parliament, 2015). The Council (2016) eventually weakened the Commission's suggestions but adopted the overall policy course. It renamed the competitiveness boards into productivity boards and downgraded the role of the Commission from a coordinator to a facilitator in the exchange of views among national boards. Nonetheless, the annual reports of these productivity boards will inform the country-specific recommendations in the European

Semester, while their main task will be to ensure member states "raise productivity while containing unit labour costs" and make adjustments when "cost competitiveness lags behind the euro area average" (European Council, 2017, p. 6).

Whether internal devaluation is regulated based on bilateral competitiveness pacts, national competitiveness authorities, or national productivity boards, the suggestions all constitute an assault on democracy, marginalizing not only national parliaments and the European Parliament but also the social partners. Although the Commission maintains it will not intervene directly in wage levels and collective bargaining rules, it advocated that social partners should use the annual competitiveness reports as guidance during wage-setting negotiations. Based on the European Semester, the Commission already has a foot in the door, allowing it to intervene into the wage formation process and demand labour cost adjustments, thereby intruding into policy domains that used to be a national preserve. As the European Trade Union Confederation (ETUC) has argued, "we are only a hair's breath away from setting maximum wage standard[s] for collective bargaining that are legally binding, or from questioning the validity of strike action [. . .]" (2015).

4. Driving and contesting forces internal devaluation as industrial policy

The competitiveness agenda and the internal devaluation strategy have been actively promoted and supported by organized (transnational) capital. The so-called "Captains of Industry," assembled in the European Round Table of Industrialists (ERT), were invited to a meeting in Berlin in March 2013, bringing together the German Chancellor Merkel, French President Hollande and Commission President Barroso, where it was jointly agreed that industrial competitiveness should be at the centre of EU policy making (ERT, 2013a). The fifteen ERT members present at the meeting made their position unequivocally clear: to be competitive, the EU needed more business-friendly regulations, such as tax reductions, less labour protection and more labour market flexibilization, lower wages and severance payments, further privatizations as well as the facilitation of mergers and acquisitions, or what the ERT calls "market-driven consolidation" (ibid.). In June 2014, the ERT (2014, p. 1) issued an Agenda for Action 2014–2019 for the newly appointed Commission, titled "EU Industrial Renaissance", echoing the Commission's documentation and demanding "industrial competitiveness should be mainstreamed throughout all policy areas and at all policy levels."

Already back in the 1990s, representatives of transnational industrial capital deplored the lagging competitiveness of the EU vis-à-vis Japan and the US, blaming high tax levels, high social and energy costs, and the "exorbitant" contracts between social partners and environmental legislation (Barber, 1994, p. 2). The ERT included a "Competitiveness Working Group" into its organizational structure, and suggested a Commissioner for Competitiveness at Commission level, and a Competitiveness Council at Council level. While the Competitiveness Commissioner should be entrusted with the task of scrutinizing EU legislation for its aptness to industrial interests, and preventing all kinds of directives that might harm the interests of large corporations attempting to compete on a global scale, the Competitiveness Council should have a veto right, blocking all new Commission initiatives that dilute the competitiveness of the European industry (ERT, 2014, p. 2). Basically, a "competitiveness screening" of all EU legislation had to be conducted at the proposal stage, as well as on all subsequent amendments until final adoption, while existing regulations had to undergo "fitness checks" (ERT 2011, p. 4, 2012, p. 1), or "benchmark tests", comparing the regulatory environment of EU industries with those in main competitor markets (ERT, 2014, p. 3). The ERT further insisted that competition policy be integrated into a new strategic and holistic industrial policy that would take global competition as a basis for decisions and enhance EU companies' ability to be competitive internationally (ERT, 2011, 2012, 2013b, 2014). State aid, which was previously regarded as competition distorting among EU economies, had to be reconsidered in a global context, and access to private capital, including private equity and venture capital – alternative types of finance – had to be facilitated (ERT, 2012, p. 1). Finally, the EU climate and energy policy had to be adapted to ensure that target of the industry's share of 20 percent of EU GDP by 2002 is not endangered (ERT, 2014, p. 4).

The ERT's suggested agenda was supported by nationally organized industrial capital. In a series of joint declarations, the German BDI (Bundesverband der Deutschen Industrie, Federal Association of German Industry) and Confindustria, Italy's largest employers' association, as well as the French MEDEF (Mouvement des entreprises de France or Movement of Enterprises of France), demanded that their governments put industrial competitiveness "at the core of each and every European policy" (BDI, 2014a, 2014b). These business consortia called for a fundamental change in the EU governance structure, suggesting the imposition of a "watchdog for competitiveness", such as by upgrading the competences of the Competitiveness Council, and a fast-track procedure that would allow circumvention of amendments by the European Parliament when adopting new legislation or when abolishing burdensome and costly legislation (see BDI 2014a). The BDI and Confindustria even threatened that more business-friendly measures were prerequisites of future investments in Europe, emphasizing that otherwise 90 percent of future economic growth will be generated outside Europe (ibid.). Strengthening price competitiveness was identified as a main driver for innovation, particularly in the field of electricity prices, where state policies were blamed for a rise of 37 percent since 2005 (BDI, 2014a). To achieve price competitiveness, the costs of labour, energy, finance and administrative requirements had to be reduced, while non-price competitiveness had to be fortified by an improved regulatory environment for enterprises. The outspoken demands by organized industrial capital were corroborated by the OECD (2014), which recommended that all

EU member states, including those less hard-hit by the crisis, should push forward reforms that enhance competitive pressures in both labour and product markets, lower the tax burden on corporate income and capital gains, lower unit labour costs through a significant reduction in nominal wages, and "reducing the dualism between temporary and permanent jobs" (ibid.). As the previous sections have shown, the joint articulation of national and transnational business seems to have borne fruit: internal devaluation achieved through lowering the costs of labour, reducing prices and taxes has become the most prevailing agenda point in EU crisis management. The Commission's new industrial policy embraced the demands of organized industries almost literally, while competitiveness proofing mechanisms for existing and future regulation have been put in place.

EU crisis management also led to considerable social unrest and political contestation, most notably in Southern Europe, where concerted actions, such as a series of transnational campaigns, manifestos and petitions, as well as joint strike days and weeks of action against EU austerity policies sought to chart an alternative future for European integration (see Wigger and Horn, 2014). However, whereas Europe's political Left has not managed to win the support of a vast constituency, neo-populist Eurosceptic, radical right and even neo-fascist parties successfully harness feelings of discontent and insecurity. The statist centre-left moreover seems entangled by the enthralling competitiveness rhetoric as a remedy to rising poverty and social exclusion and has not discredited and de-legitimized the prevailing narrow vision of competitiveness. Even though ETUC, the umbrella organization of national trade unions, vehemently condemned the establishment of competitiveness or productivity boards (see ETUC, 2015), the uneven manifestation of the crisis and the persistent asymmetries of economic development in Europe has led to a situation in which organized labour is fractionalized into competing confederations with different positions or at times even contradictory interests, making it difficult to achieve transnational labour solidarity (Horn, 2012). Even more striking is the disrespect of the social dialogue at EU level. None of the austerity or the hasty bailout packages has been implemented in cooperation with trade unions. As ETUC (2014) writes, in formal meetings with the Troika, trade unions could voice demands and critique in ten-minute time slots, while Troika-representatives reacted with a "set response," replying with "generalities" or in an elusive way. The exclusion of contesting forces from EU decision-making is an ongoing feature. Illustrative is the establishment of a permanent dialogue between the Commission with consumers in the form of an "Annual European Competition and Consumers Day," or the establishment of the "European Consumer Consultative Group," while for organized labour there is no equivalent. The structurally disadvantaged position of the Left is narrowing the scope for a more progressive and democratically justified EU crisis management. Decisions taken behind closed doors with the participation of financial and transnational industrial capital significantly constrain the room for manoeuvre for subaltern forces.

5. Conclusions

The prevailing interpretation of the crisis at EU level has shifted over time from a crisis within the financial system, to a crisis of sovereign debt, and more recently, to a crisis of lacking competitiveness of European economies. As German Chancellor Merkel (2013) stated: "[. . .] from a European standpoint we must aim to be so competitive that we not only stay prosperous but become even more prosperous." The question is however, who will become more prosperous on the basis of the EU competitiveness agenda. Competitiveness is now conflated with lower wages, lower prices, and lower corporate taxes, thereby construing the crisis in terms of inflexible labour markets, and high labour and production costs. What has been disguised as the new industrial policy primarily serves to maximize the freedom of capital to exploit labour, which implies that less surplus from the production sphere will have to be redistributed to wage earners. Ever since the adoption of neoliberal policies in the late 1970s, average wage shares of GDP have been on a downward trend, and so have corporate taxes. In a context where member states will have to undercut each other's internal devaluation policies in a "beggar-thy-neighbour" fashion, labour will be even further devalued. We see thus more of the same neoliberal remedies imposed in a highly authoritarian fashion, which not only insulates political decision-making from formal state democratic interventions but also marginalises any form of social dialogue. As competition disunites more than it unites, the competitiveness agenda, alias industrial policy, also risks the establishment of a solid basis for future social cohesion and pan-European worker solidarity. What is more, the competitiveness strategy is counter-productive and will only worsen the vast structural imbalances and uneven economic development in Europe, and if aggregate demand is tempered further, the propensity to invest in real production will stay weak. Thanks to the above-mentioned structural problem of overaccumulation, ever more surplus capital will be freed for circulation in the financial sphere with the prospect that the next manifestation of this crisis will again be in the financial sector; however, this time far more dramatic than what we have seen since 2007/8.

References

Almunia, J. (2012a) *The role of competition policy in times of crisis.* 6 December. Brussels: European Commission. Available at: http://europa.eu/rapid/press-release_SPEECH-12-917_en.htm (Accessed: 26 April 2018).

Almunia, J. (2012b) *Competition policy for innovation and growth: Keeping markets open and efficient.* 8 March. Copenhagen: European Commission. Available at: http://europa.eu/rapid/press-release_SPEECH-12-172_en.pdf (Accessed: 26 April 2018).

Almunia, J. (2014) *Competition policy enforcement as a driver for growth.* 18 February. Brussels: European Commission. Available at: http://europa.eu/rapid/press-release_SPEECH-14-178_en.htm (Accessed: 26 April 2018).

Barber, L. (1994) 'EU industry concerned at competition: Round Table seeks to stop drain of jobs to US, Asia'. *Financial Times* 25(November), p.2.

Blanchard, O. and Leigh, D. (2013) *Growth forecast errors and fiscal multipliers.* IMF Working Paper 13(1). Washington, DC: IMF.

Bruff, I. (2014) 'The rise of authoritarian neoliberalism'. *Rethinking Marxism* 26(1), pp. 113–129.

Bundesverband der Deutschen Industrie (BDI) (2014a) 'A call from BDI and Confindustria to the German and Italian government ahead of the Spring European Council. Joint Declaration with Confindustria', Available at: http://www.bdi.eu/bdi_english/download_content/BDI_Confindustria_Joint_Declaration_EN.pdf (Accessed: 22 April 2017).

Bundesverband der Deutschen Industrie (BDI) (2014b) 'Strengthening competitiveness and creating more Jobs in Europe our priorities for the future. A call from BDI and MEDEF to the European Council', Available at: http://www.bdi.eu/bdi_english/download_content/Joint_Declaration_final.pdf (Accessed: 22 April 2017).

Clauwaert, S. and Schoenmann, I. (2012) 'The crisis and national labour law reforms: A mapping exercise'. ETUI Working Paper 04.

Collignon, S. and Esposito, P. (2014) 'Unit labour costs and capital efficiency in the Euro Area. A new competitiveness indicator', in Collignon S. and Esposito P. (eds.) *Competitiveness in the European economy.* London: Routledge, pp. 46–72.

Dijsselbloem, J. (2017) *Remarks following the Eurogroup meeting of 20 February 2017.* 20 February. Brussels: European Council. Available at: http://www.consilium.europa.eu/en/press/press-releases/2017/02/20/eurogroup-jd-remarks/ (Accessed: 26 April 2018).

Durand, C. and Keucheyan, R. (2015) 'Financial hegemony and the unachieved European state'. *Competition and Change* 19(2), pp. 129–144.

Eichengreen, B. (2008) *The European economy since 1945: Coordinated capitalism and beyond.* Princeton: Princeton University Press.

Esposito, P. and Guerrieri, P. (2014) 'Intra-European imbalances, competitiveness and external trade: A comparison between Italy and Germany', in Collingnon, S. and Esposito, P. (eds.) *Competitiveness in the European economy.* Abingdon, UK: Routledge, pp. 82–104.

EuroMemorandum (2013) 'The deepening crisis in the European Union: The need for a fundamental change', Available at: http://www.euromemo.eu/euromemorandum/euromemorandum_2013/(Accessed: 20 April 2017).

European Commission (2011a) Quarterly Report on the Euro Area 10(3), Brussels.

European Commission (2011b) *The effects of temporary state aid rules adopted in the context of the financial and economic crisis.* Brussels: Commission Staff Working Paper.

European Commission (2013) *Towards a deep and genuine Economic and Monetary Union. The introduction of a convergence and competitiveness instrument.* Brussels: Communication from the Commission to the European Parliament and the Council.

European Commission (2014) *For a European industrial renaissance.* Brussels: Communication from the Commission to the European Parliament, the Council, the European Economic and Social Committee and the Committee of the Regions.

European Commission (2015a) *EU structural change 2015.* Luxembourg: Publications Office of the European Union.

European Commission (2015b) Recommendation for a Council recommendation on the establishment of national competitiveness boards within the Euro Area. COM (2015) 601 final: Brussels.

European Commission (2016a) 'Industrial policy', Available at: https://ec.europa.eu/growth/industry/policy/index_en.htm (Accessed: 20 April 2017).

European Commission (2016b) *EU competition policy in action*. Luxembourg: Publications Office of the European Union.

European Council (2013) *Conclusions*. EUCO 217/13. Brussels: European Council.

European Council (2016) *Recommendation for a Council recommendation on the establishment of National Productivity Boards*. ECOFIN 590, UEM 248. Brussels: European Council.

European Council (2017) *Council recommendation on the economic policy of the Euro Area*. ST 5757. Brussels: European Council.

European Parliament (2015) *European Parliament resolution of 17 December 2015 on completing Europe's Economic and Monetary Union*. 2015/2936(RSP). Brussels: European Parliament.

European Round Table of Industrialists (ERT) (2011) *Global competitive distortions on the rise: What EU policy makers should do, and what they should not do*. 12 October. Brussels: ERT.

European Round Table of Industrialists (ERT) (2012) *ERT's priorities for an integrated industrial policy*. 19 July. Brussels: ERT.

European Round Table of Industrialists (ERT) (2013a) *ERT meets with Merkel, Hollande and Barroso on Europe's competitiveness*. 18 March. Brussels: ERT.

European Round Table of Industrialists (ERT) (2013b) *Letter to the European Council Presidency: ERT recommendations ahead of the June 2013 Council*. 4 June. Brussels: ERT.

European Round Table of Industrialists (ERT) (2014) *EU industrial renaissance: ERT agenda for action 2014–2019*. 11 June. Brussels: ERT.

European Trade Union Confederation (ETUC) (2014) 'The functioning of the Troika: A report from the ETUC', Available at: https://www.etuc.org/IMG/pdf/THE_FUNCTIONING_OF_THE_TROIKA_finaledit2afterveronika.pdf (Accessed: 26 April 2018).

European Trade Union Confederation (ETUC) (2015) 'ETUC position on National Competitiveness Boards', Available at: https://www.etuc.org/documents/etuc-position-national-competitiveness-boards#_ftnref1 (Accessed: 22 April 2017).

European Trade Union Institute (ETUI) (2014) *Benchmarking Working Europe 2014*. Brussels: ETUI.

Eurostat (2017) 'International trade', Available at: http://ec.europa.eu/eurostat/ (Accessed: 21 April 2017).

Five Presidents' Report (2015) 'Completing Europe's economic and monetary union', Available at: https://ec.europa.eu/commission/sites/beta-political/files/5-presidents-report_en.pdf (Accessed: 22 April 2017).

Four Presidents' Report (2012) 'Towards a genuine economic and monetary union', 5 December. Available at: http://www.consilium.europa.eu/uedocs/cms_Data/docs/pressdata/en/ec/134069.pdf (Accessed: 22 April 2017).

Hall, S. (1979) 'The great moving right show'. *Marxism Today* 14–20 January.

Hall, S. (1985) 'Authoritarian populism: A reply to Jessop et al'. *New Left Review* 1(151), pp. 115–124.

Horn, L. (2012) 'Anatomy of a critical friendship: Organised labour and the European state formation'. *Globalizations* 9(4), pp. 577–592.

Jäger, J. and Springler, E. (eds.) (2015) *Asymmetric crisis in Europe and possible futures: Critical political economy and post-Keynesian perspectives*. New York: Routledge.

Marx, K. (1973 [1939]) *Grundrisse*. London: Penguin Classics.

Merkel, A. (2013) Speech at the World Economic Forum annual meeting. 24 January Davos, Switzerland: World Economic Forum. Available at: http://www.bundeskan zlerin.de/ContentArchiv/EN/Archiv17/Reden/2013/2013-01-24-merkel-davos. html (Accessed: 20 April 2017).

Oberndorfer, L. (2012) 'Vom neuen zum autoritaeren Konstitutionalismus'. *Kurswechsel* 2, pp. 62–67.

Organisation for Economic Co-operation and Development (OECD) (2014) *Economic challenges and policy recommendations for the Euro area*. Paris: OECD Publishing.

Overbeek, H. (2012) 'Sovereign debt crisis in Euroland: Root causes and implications for European integration'. *The International Spectator: Italian Journal of International Affairs* 47 (1), pp. 30–48.

Poulantzas, N. (1978) *State, power, socialism*. London: New Left Books.

Poulantzas, N. (1979) 'Is there a crisis in Marxism?'. *Journal of the Hellenic Diaspora* 6(3), pp. 7–16.

Sablowski, T. (2012) 'The global economic crisis: Impoverishing Europe', *Global Research: Centre for Research on Globalization*, May 16. Available at: https://www. globalresearch.ca/the-global-economic-crisis-impoverishing-europe/30863 (Accessed: 26 April 2018).

Sandbeck, S. and Schneider, E. (2014) 'From the sovereign debt crisis to authoritarian statism: Contradictions of the European state project'. *New Political Economy* 19(6), pp. 847–871.

Sandbu, M. (2015) *Europe's orphan: The future of the Euro and the politics of debt*. Princeton: Princeton University Press.

Stiglitz, J. E. (2016) *The Euro: How a common currency threatens the future of Europe*. London: W.W. Norton & Company.

Stockhammer, E. (2016) 'Neoliberal growth models, monetary union and the Euro crisis: A post-Keynesian perspective'. *New Political Economy* 21(4), pp. 365–379.

Stockhammer, E. and Onaran, O. (2012a) 'Wage-led growth: Theory, evidence, policy', Political Economy Research Institute. Working Paper Series No. 300, Amherst, MA: University of Massachusetts Amherst.

Stockhammer, E. and Onaran, O. (2012b) 'Rethinking wage policy in the face of the Euro crisis: Implications of the wage-led demand regime'. *International Review of Applied Economics* 26(2), pp. 191–203.

TNI (2017) *The bail out business: Who profits from bank rescues in the EU?* Amsterdam: Transnational Institute.

Vestager, M. (2015) 'The values of competition policy', Keynote at CEPS Corporate breakfast, 13 October. Available at: https://ec.europa.eu/commission/commis sioners/2014-2019/vestager/announcements/values-competition-policy_en (Accessed: 22 April 2017).

Wigger, A. (2018) 'The new EU industrial policy: authoritarian neoliberal structural adjustment and the case for alternatives'. *Globalizations* 17 (1) DOI: 10.1080/ 14747731.2018.1502496.

Wigger, A. and Buch-Hansen, H. (2014) 'Explaining (missing) regulatory paradigm shifts: EU competition regulation in times of economic crisis'. *New Political Economy* 19 (1), pp. 113–137.

Wigger, A. and Buch-Hansen, H. (2014) *The politics of European competition regulation: A critical political economy perspective*. London: Routleddge.

Wigger, A. and Buch-Hansen, H. (2015) 'EU competition regulation: A case of authoritarian neoliberalism?', in Hartmann, E. and Kjaer, P.F. (eds.) *The evolution of intermediary institutions in Europe: From corporatism to governance*. Basingstoke: Palgrave Macmillan.

Wigger, A. and Horn, L. (2014) 'Uneven development and political resistance against EU austerity politics', in Pradella, L. and Marois, T. (eds.) *Polarizing development: Alternatives to neoliberalism and the crisis*. London: Pluto.

10 The legitimacy crisis within international criminal justice and the importance of critical, reflexive learning

Jeff Handmaker

At a 2016 meeting of the American Society of International Law, Benvenisti and Nouwen (2016) explored whether the system of international criminal justice faced a "crisis of legitimacy." Building on an earlier debate in the *European Journal of International Law* in 2010, Nouwen and Werner argued that the deeply held, albeit erroneous, claim by legal advocates and academics that law is impartial renders it "a strong tool in political struggles" (Nouwen and Werner, 2011b, p. 1164). The authors were responding to a critique of their initial contribution, which argued that, while one may seek to "mobilise the law" in the context of a (violent) conflict, "the structure of the law itself escapes the logic of the political" (Schotel, 2011, p. 1154).

Is the system of international criminal justice truly in crisis? Is it even possible to escape the political character of the law? In their initial contribution, Nouwen and Werner argued that "(w)hile there is nothing wrong with attempts to protect the [International Criminal] Court from political interference, portraying it as fighting the political has a disadvantage: it blinds us to the politics of the ICC itself" (Nouwen and Werner, 2011a, p. 943). More specifically, they noted, international prosecutors have claimed to stand outside the realm of politics, while at the same time taking decisions that are profoundly political (ibid., p. 962).

Concerns about the legitimacy of international criminal justice institutions have, indeed, particularly focused on the work of the International Criminal Court (ICC). The serious and entirely avoidable failure of the first ICC prosecutor to reveal exculpatory and confidential evidence to the defence counsel during its first trial against Thomas Lubanga, a former military commander in the Democratic Republic of Congo who was charged, and eventually convicted of recruiting child soldiers, nearly destroyed the prosecution's case altogether (Katzman, 2009). It has also been argued that the ICC has fallen short in investigating and prosecuting gender-based crimes, for both normative and attitudinal reasons (Mouthaan, 2011). Internal challenges have also been noted, concerning "the scope of investigations and certain practices," including the way in which charges are filed and confirmed, as well as – more fundamentally – the approach of the

ICC in deferring to national jurisdictions (Amnesty International, 2012, p. 4). Even the then Vice-President of the Court, acknowledged (somewhat vaguely) that there have been challenges relating to the "internal functioning of the Court" (Kaur, 2011, p. 8). These internal weaknesses have been accompanied by a global campaign of de-legitimization led by the former US ambassador to the United Nations, John Bolton. In essence, the US campaign threatened to withdraw military and other assistance from countries that chose to ratify the Rome Statute establishing the ICC (Bolton, 2001). The initial vehemence of the Bush-Bolton era opposition to the Court by the United States gradually gave way to a cautiously supportive position in relation to referrals by the Security Council in the cases of Sudan and Libya (although statements from the Trump administration suggest a renewed, confrontational stance). Other, more recent, external challenges to the legitimacy of the ICC have come from African countries, which have accused the ICC of being biased against leaders on the continent. Consequently, several member states' parties of the Rome Statute that established the ICC have indicated their desire to withdraw (Allison, 2016).

Scholars, too, have questioned the legitimacy of the ICC, especially concerning the actions of the prosecutor, which have come under heavy fire as "steeped in controversy" and "self-defeating" (Danner, 2003; Orentlicher, 2003; Goldsmith, 2003).

However, none of these critiques on the internal functioning of the ICC, or even the external legitimacy challenges, could readily be said to amount to a *crisis*; they can all be considered as "accidental" in the sense that they refer to causes that are "varied and overdetermined" and, in any event, are subject to "well-developed routines" established for managing such crises (Jessop, 2015, p. 247). By contrast, the indeterminate character of law, which has been readily observed by critical legal scholars such as Koskenniemi (2009), elaborating on his *Apology to Utopia* thesis, is an objective limitation of international law generally, from which the international criminal justice system has emerged. Nouwen and Werner's argument reflects this critical reading of international law, which acknowledges the existence of deeper structural problems.

Hence, as I argue in this chapter, the *real* crisis of legitimacy faced by the Court and, indeed, the international criminal justice is more generally, relates not so much to the existence of international legal norms and enforcement institutions as such, but to the crude and culturally essentialist way in which the ICC prosecutor, and the NGOs (non-governmental organizations) that support the Court, regard themselves, the perpetrators, and the victims/ survivors of international crimes. The crisis, in other words, stems from how the Court itself, particularly in the discourse of the prosecutorial office, which is represented as a non-political administrator of justice in response to allegations of international crimes, is taking decisions that fail to consider the complex social, cultural and political contexts in which these crimes took place.

The system of international criminal justice, including law and legal institutions, is profoundly political. Legal scholars frequently under-estimate the extent to which legal practice involves – indeed demands – systematic, strategic reflection. By the same token, then, the crisis of legitimacy facing international criminal justice is a "moment for reflection" (Jessop, 2015, p. 255). Like Nouwen and Werner, Harmen van der Wilt (2011) has acknowledged that, in responding to the many criticisms of universal jurisdiction for international crimes, and to the work of the International Criminal Court, it is helpful to analyse the work of international criminal justice in an inter-disciplinary way.

Having set out the issues, the second part of this chapter presents a framework for analysing the liberal underpinnings of the international criminal justice system. Part three, drawing on Mutua's (2001) critical assessment of the human rights corpus, focuses on how efforts to invoke the international legal system in order to manage international criminal prosecutions have proved problematic. Part four explores the implications of a strategic approach to legal advocacy for reflexive (legal) learning and the management of crises through international criminal justice mechanisms, focusing on the dimensions of the legitimacy crisis generated by the international legal system itself, which Koskenniemi (2009, p. 12) defines as "managerialism".

The concluding part comments on the extent to which strategic legal advocacy, a critical approach to legal interpretation and an approach of critical, reflexive learning present opportunities for lawyers to engage explicitly with the politics of international law in a way that creates opportunities for "learning *from*" the legitimacy crisis (Jessop, 2015, p. 257) and thereby enhances, rather than undermines, the role of law as a mediator of crisis.

My analysis relies on various sources of data. They include the comprehensive portrayal of the international criminal justice system and, especially numerous statements made by the ICC prosecutor in the acclaimed documentary film *The Reckoning* (2003). I also rely on my extensive interactions with ICC staff members, scholars, journalists and other followers of the ICC's work over more than a decade since the Court's establishment in 2002. This material is complemented by on-the-record statements made by the initial prosecutor of the Special Court of Sierra Leone, David Crane, and other representations of international criminal justice issues, in academic commentary and in the media.

A framework for analysing legal mobilization in international criminal justice

This part provides a framework for analysing the pursuit of international criminal justice through international and national courts. This framework has three features.

First, it introduces the liberal rule of law concepts that have underpinned a civic protection charter, which has, in turn, become the legal basis upon which the international criminal justice system emerged. Second, it deploys Mutua's Savages, Victims and Saviours (or SVS) metaphor to critique liberal assumptions underpinning human rights and to evaluate the efforts of lawyers working within the international criminal justice system who struggle to come to grips with the complex social and cultural contexts in which law functions. Third, it adopts a reflexive learning approach, which I will argue below provides a more grounded basis for approaching international crises through legal approaches.

A civic protection charter based on the rule of law

From the 1940s until the 1960s, a then-small community of nation-states oversaw the creation of what I have described as a "civic protection charter" that significantly altered the relationship between civic actors and the state (Handmaker, 2009, pp. 26–29). This emerged in three phases. The first phase of the charter featured four key normative developments in international law and the development of a system of global *governance*, from the creation of the United Nations by way of the Charter of the United Nations (1945), to the establishment of human rights protection standards by the Universal Declaration of Human Rights (United Nations, 1948). Consolidation of the Charter followed, building on earlier treaties governing the conduct of war and humanitarian protection standards through the Fourth Geneva Convention of the International Committee of the Red Cross (ICRC) (1949). This included an obligation on states to prosecute combatants whose actions resulted in a grave breach of the Conventions. The second phase began in the 1960s and continued until the mid-1990s, primarily under the auspices of the United Nations, but also in different regions of the world. Covenants on civil and political rights, as well as on economic, social and cultural rights that both came into force through the United Nations (1966a, 1966b) helped develop and establish the principles of the Universal Declaration of Human Rights, and created institutions to oversee state compliance with these treaties. Other international treaties came into being, accompanied by administrative structures that aimed to ban racial discrimination, prohibit torture (United Nations, 1984) and promote and protect the rights of women, children, migrant workers and persons with disabilities, as well as the problem of enforced disappearances. Finally, a third phase of civic protection began in the mid-1990s and continues to the present day, featuring the establishment of specific, though mostly *ad hoc* efforts to prosecute international crimes through UN-created institutions and national court systems, as well as agreement in the late 1990s on the Statute of Rome, the liberal legal basis for a permanent international criminal law system.

Civic actors, both individuals and collectives, have mobilized this charter to advocate for state accountability and to promote normative entrenchment at the domestic level to protect fundamental human rights, to make claims against states and ultimately agents of a state, based on liberal-internationalist conceptualizations of the rule of law (Ignatieff, 1999; Ignatieff and Gutmann, 2001). The domestication of human rights norms has not always led to greater respect for human rights (Arts and Handmaker, 2010). Indeed, uneven implementation and sometimes reluctance by states or their institutional organs to respect, protect and fulfil human rights has triggered a growing consciousness among civic actors, and especially lawyers, that international human rights can, and should, be mobilized in various ways, whether in domestic legal argumentation, as the basis of other forms of social justice struggle (Klaaren, Handmaker and Dugard, 2011) or through *naming and shaming* (Donnelly, 1989; Korey, 2003; Risse, Ropp and Sikkink, 1999). As explained in the next section, one of the explanations for the uneven treatment of international human rights norms relates to their liberal character.

A plea for self-criticism through the SVS metaphor

In a seminal article that addressed the failings of international human rights law and the movement that accompanies it, Makau Mutua (2001) produced a stirring critique of its liberal underpinnings, concluding with a plea for self-criticism by those involved in the collective "corpus" of human rights. Departing from a classic, liberal depiction of human rights, Mutua saw the human rights movement as being characterized by a three-sided "prism" of savages, victims and saviours, which he referred to as the "SVS metaphor". He explained this prism as having pre-determined characteristics, notably barbarism (of the state), victimhood (of those subject to human rights violations), and a saviour mentality of mainly Western organizations intervening to prevent or respond to human rights abuses.

As I have argued elsewhere and develop in this chapter, Mutua's critical interpretation of the human rights corpus through the SVS metaphor also reflects problems concerning popular representations of international criminal justice and explains its crisis of legitimacy (Arnoldussen, 2011; Handmaker, 2011). Mutua's critique of the international human rights regime forms part of a radical critique of international law, which applies to a wide range of international legal vocabularies, from international human rights law, to international economic law. Known as *Third World Approaches to International Law* or "TWAIL," these approaches regard the regime of international law, particularly in relation to developing countries, as largely "illegitimate" in that it "legitimizes, reproduces and sustains the plunder and subordination of the Third World by the West" (Mutua, 2000, p. 31). Reynolds has argued that TWAIL continues to be relevant in critiquing the function of international law, which is increasingly invoked to address what he regards as a state-imposed mantra of a "permanent state of emergency" (2017, p. 7). For example, drawing on this approach, Reynolds analyses Israel as a "settler colonial state," which permits the treatment of the occupied territory of Palestine as a "space for exception" in which international law is readily set aside (ibid., pp. 195–243). Reynolds also applies this approach to analyse Australia's treatment of aboriginal people in imposing a state of emergency in the Northern Territory, which has had profound consequences for sovereignty and land ownership (ibid., pp. 244–265).

These critical approaches to international law reinforce Koskenniemi's (2009) argument that one must look beyond the normative liberal tendency that underpins the world view of many lawyers, that is, to look beyond simply the content of law and the largely techno-managerial way in which it is enforced. As discussed in the next section, this has profound implications for legal education.

Reflexive legal learning

Originally derived from Pierre Bourdieu's scholarly work in the 1980s and later incorporated into his *Reflexive Sociology* (Bourdieu and Wacquant, 1992), a substantial body of scholarly writing has emerged on the importance of "reflexive learning" in education, including legal education. Within this complex body of scholarly work, Anthony Amsterdam (1984) argued for the importance of clinic-based education as a core component of law school education. This plea related to Teubner's (1983) argument in favour of "reflexive law," which engaged with broader social considerations aimed at addressing fundamental inequalities. Thus, Teubner argued that "unlike formal law, (reflexive law) does not accept 'natural' subjective rights. Rather, it attempts to guide human action" (Teubner, 1983, p. 255). Rather than teaching merely the content of law, there was a compelling argument, he claimed, that law schools should also be involved in teaching the practice of law. Hence, legal practice involves much more than regurgitating legal norms: it also requires an understanding of how law structures society and economic relations.

The scholarly arguments in favour of clinic-based legal education continued to take hold in the 1990s, where the work of Shalleck (1995) and Quigley (1996), engaged with, among other factors, the social justice dimensions of doing clinical work. Scholarly work of the early 2000s, such as Neumann (2000), noted the largely unchanged approach to legal education in the US, which under-valued the crucial clinical dimension (and still does). Countering the unjustified resistance towards this pedagogic strategy, Voyvodic and Medcalf (2004) went a step further and emphasized the value of an inter-disciplinary approach to clinical legal education. Such a socio-legal approach to law had earlier been endorsed by Friedman (1986) in relation to law school education and by Nelken (2004), more specifically in relation to legal culture, as well as by Scheppele (2004) in relation to social rights. In other words, the economics, sociology and politics (including gender-relations) played as much, if not a greater role in the outcome of legal disputes than the content of law itself. Finally, Ashar (2016) argued that clinic education was crucial to democratic lawyering and emphasized the importance of developing knowledge bases, while Babacan and Babacan (2017) highlighted the role of accessible clinical education as enhancing civic consciousness.

The possibility of reflexive legal learning from the management of crises is directly related to the way in which legal education is organized. As Jessop has observed, a "crisis does not automatically lead to learning: cognitive capacities may be lacking ... It can also involve different degrees of reflexivity, i.e., learning about learning" (2013, p. 242). Elaine Mak confirms this dilemma in her critique of legal education, observing that the so-called "T-shaped lawyer" should be a legal professional that "is able to cope with these challenges based on deep legal knowledge and skills...with broad knowledge of other disciplines and academic skills" (2017, p. 7). Mak goes on to observe that "legal education does not sufficiently prepare law school graduates to master the competences" required of other disciplines (ibid., p. 8). In other words, most law graduates *lack the cognitive capacities for reflexive learning*, rarely possessing the knowledge to effectively manage complex economic and other crises, or even to relate to colleagues with non-legal backgrounds.

In short, appreciating the challenges, as well as the social, economic and political significance of reflexive learning in legal education are indispensable components of understanding about the *potential* of law to manage complex disputes. This resonates with the position that "learning from crisis" allows for opportunities to reflect on that crisis, and the implications this has for future crisis management (Jessop, 2015, p. 257).

Analysing the pursuit of international criminal justice

Drawing on the framework of analysis from the previous section, the emergence of an international criminal justice system as part of the global civic protection charter is assessed. This section then critiques efforts by various civic, state and intergovernmental actors forming part of the international criminal justice movement to end impunity for international crimes through international criminal law and justice institutions.

The emergence of an international criminal justice system

The development of international criminal justice as a *system* is a relatively new development, comprising the most recent component of the civic protection charter, and it is still based on liberal understandings of the rule of law. The Tokyo and Nuremburg Tribunals were established to prosecute alleged perpetrators of war crimes in Asia and Europe following the Second World War, while the International Criminal Tribunal for the former Yugoslavia and the International Criminal Tribunal for Rwanda were created half a century later to address widespread violations following civil wars in these two countries in the 1990s (Klip and Sluiter, 1999). Special and hybrid courts have also been established, including the Special Court for Sierra Leone, the Extraordinary Chambers in the Courts of Cambodia and the Special Tribunal for Lebanon. All these courts and tribunals have gradually developed their own jurisprudence. The jurisdictions of these courts, both at national and international levels, are a product of state-driven processes. It is therefore doubtful whether civil society organizations can be said to have *formed* the ICC, although the substantial contribution by NGOs has led to such claims being made (Glasius, 2006).

Following the establishment of the ICC, the exercise of national jurisdiction for international crimes received additional, normative impetus. Many countries that ratified the Rome Statute have passed implementing legislation to prosecute alleged perpetrators, regardless of the nationality of the alleged perpetrator or victims, or where the crimes took place. Because of these normative and institutional developments, individuals and corporations can be held directly accountable for international crimes in a variety of jurisdictions. Van den Herik acknowledges the value of having universal jurisdiction over international crimes. She writes that "one of the dark side effects of the phenomenon of globalization is that also criminals and crime are increasingly moving beyond borders. It is thus by necessity that extraterritorial criminal jurisdiction is and should be exercised" (Herik, 2009, p. 225).

By insisting on the *necessity* that states exercise extraterritorial jurisdiction, van den Herik implied that criminal prosecution is the most desirable direction for international criminal justice to take. Indeed, national prosecuting authorities in certain influential states that have established complementary systems for prosecuting international crimes at the domestic level, notably: Spain, the United Kingdom, Switzerland, Belgium, South Africa and the Netherlands. In the enforcement of international criminal justice, States routinely interact with NGOs, which monitor the ICC regarding its implementation, and lobby in relation to specific complaints aimed at alleged perpetrators, urging state prosecuting authorities to act (Glasius, 2006, p. 23). Accordingly, the perceived "necessity" of prosecuting international crimes at the ICC, and the interweaving relations between civic actors and states involved in enforcing international criminal justice make it difficult to recognize the crisis of legitimacy surrounding the international criminal justice system, let alone evaluate that crisis.

Critiquing the international criminal justice system through the SVS metaphor

The pursuit of international criminal justice can be usefully critiqued using Mutua's SVS metaphor. Surprisingly, critics of the ICC are rare, and have mostly confined their objections to the legal basis and external pressures facing the Court. It is therefore productive to explore the social and cultural underpinnings of the international criminal justice system, and particularly the role of international prosecutors. For this, Mutua's SVS metaphor is a useful analytical basis for critiquing the international criminal justice system, or at least the popular representation of this system.

The documentary film *The Reckoning* (2003) accurately portrays the international criminal justice system and, in particular, the functioning of the ICC prosecutor, Luis Moreno Ocampo, as engaged in legal-institutional mobilization against the alleged perpetrators of international crimes. However, in focusing on the legal functioning of the Court, the film fails to address what really underpins the conflicts addressed by the international criminal justice system, the violence that emerges from these conflicts, and the realistic prospects of fostering international criminal justice solely through institutions such as the ICC. In other words, the film successfully conveys the perspective of the ICC prosecutor, while leaving many crucial questions unanswered. While the failure to address these questions and to take a more critical line is hardly surprising, for reasons mentioned earlier in this section, the representation of the international criminal justice system and the legal advocates who are engaged in a form of politics – from the ICC prosecutor to the NGOs who support him/her – deserve a deeper, critical analysis.

The organization that produced the film, the International Centre for Transitional Justice, is part of a global network of NGOs. While the film is a mostly uncritical representation of the ICC and, especially, its first prosecutor, Luis Moreno Ocampo, the film vividly reveals how the SVS metaphor is deployed.

In its depiction of barbarism, the film shows scenes of marauding rebels, allegedly led by Thomas Lubanga (later brought to trial at the ICC), yelling and waving crude weapons as they appear engaged in the pillaging of communities. Another notable scene in the film depicts members of the government-led Sudanese militia group *Janjaweed*, galloping on horseback and brandishing what appear to be crude swords and other weapons. Numerous simplistic representations in the film of the Lord's Resistance Army (LRA) rebel group in Northern Uganda complete this picture of a "savage" African culture, and confirm my own personal impressions of attitudes held by staff members of the ICC, and especially those working in the Office of the Prosecutor.

Crane conveyed similar images of savagery in his opening statement during the trial of alleged leaders of the Revolutionary United Front (RUF) at the Special Court of Sierra Leone:

> This is a tale of horror, beyond the gothic into the realm of Dante's inferno…Their alleged crimes against humanity cannot justly or practically be ignored, as they were the handmaidens to the beast – the beast of impunity that walked this burnt and pillaged land – its bloody claw marks in evidence on the backs of the hundreds of thousands of victims in this tragic conflict.
> (Special Court of Sierra Leone, 2004, pp. 2–5)

The *Reckoning* further depicts stereotypical victims alongside the representations of the savage culture ostensibly behind their persecution. Images in the film include those of helpless women who have been viciously raped and beaten after a brutal raid by the LRA on one of their euphemistically named "protected villages," a displaced persons' camp in Northern Uganda. Images are also shown of burning corpses after an attack on a village by militias in the Congo, and there are stomach-churning scenes of a young boy whose leg is torn to shreds after the LRA forcibly tethered him to prevent him escaping. No effort is made to ask why people had been (forcibly) transferred to these villages in the first place (Dolan, 2009).

Child soldiers, both in terms of their rights and in terms of international criminal accountability, have been extensively written about (Arts and Popovski, 2006; Honwana, 2006; Wessels, 2006; Drumbl, 2012). Global campaigns, including *A World Fit for Children*, have been launched to end the recruitment of child soldiers and to prosecute individuals who have been involved in forced recruitment. However, the preoccupation of scholars, NGOs and agencies with this important topic has led to a "distorted understanding" of the conflicts in which child soldiers have been embedded (Dolan, 2002, p. 145). In addition, the understandably strong emotions generated by the recruitment of children in armed conflicts, and other violations associated with their recruitment, have been exploited by prosecutors. Crane, referring to a "lost generation" of children who had been forcibly recruited into the army of the RUF rebels, noted that:

> There is in Sierra Leone an entire lost generation of children, lost souls wallowing in a cesspool of physical and psychological torment. ...This lost generation, victim or perpetrator, are overall victims of this joint criminal enterprise that was led by Sesay, Kallon, and Gbao among others. Children will come before you and testify in effect, "I killed people! I am sorry, I didn't mean it".
>
> (Special Court of Sierra Leone, 2004, p. 11)

It is impossible not to experience emotions when confronted by such hideous examples of human rights violations, particularly when they involve children. But how do these ghastly images help us to understand the reasons why such crimes were committed, or the immense challenges faced by the governments and societies of Uganda and Sierra Leone to compensate the victims, and provide their citizens with a stable and secure future? Should the mere existence of "protected villages" not generate questions about Uganda's forced resettlement of people to these compounds – which were then targeted by LRA rebels, helping to create a humanitarian crisis? Is it helpful to refer to former child soldiers as a "lost generation," suggesting they are beyond hope or redemption?

But perhaps the most notable aspect of the *Reckoning* is its depiction of the saviours. Referring to his role as a prosecutor in 1985 against Argentinian generals accused of grave crimes, Ocampo comments: "All my life I had the idea that this was the most important work of my life...and now I feel it was just my training...to do this job". These and other statements by Ocampo, Chung and others working in the Office of the Prosecutor of the International Criminal Court reproduced in this section come from the documentary film by Yates (*The Reckoning*, 2003).

As a self-appointed saviour, Ocampo has no qualms about insisting he take decisive action, brushing aside concerns raised by his colleagues that he was moving too fast in investigating the LRA in Uganda and thereby risking further destabilising the situation there. Ocampo responded: "I knew I had to run. I had to show very quickly some outcome, some results."

The notion of helpless victims faced with a "savage" culture, awaiting the intervention of a (Western-based) saviour is reinforced by Christine Chung, an ICC principal investigator interviewed in the film, who makes it clear that her presence in the field is necessary: "In the course of the investigation it's critical to go there. You have to understand the culture, the environment and you want to meet the people that are going to be your potential witnesses."

Is it helpful to depict barbaric and savage cultures pitted against helpless victims, themselves dependent on (largely Western) intervention? Does prosecutor Crane's depiction of "gothic" horror help us to understand what led to the war in Sierra Leone, and what is needed to reconstruct the country and its society? Should a durable peace be part of the Court's calculation in any way, and is the "quest for international justice" enough? Should we not be encouraged to ask critical questions in order to strengthen the international criminal justice system? Apart from an emphatic "yes" to the last question, I do not pretend to provide satisfactory answers to these political questions. But, the debate must continue.

Legal advocacy and the potential for reflexive legal learning

In this section I elaborate on how legal learning can take place through a *strategic* encounter with legal advocacy, by reflecting on reflexive learning as an analytical lens. More specifically, I explore the extent to which strategic legal advocacy presents opportunities for lawyers to engage with the politics of international law, by connecting to the broader social considerations of law (Teubner, 1983), as it relates to the global system of international criminal justice and, in particular, to prosecutorial discretion as well as "institutional inquiries" (Jessop, 2015, p. 257) into the failings of the ICC in particular. Furthermore, I explain how strategic legal advocacy, and an approach of reflexive legal learning, depend on a close-knit coalition of not just lawyers, but various stakeholders with multi-varied, but ultimately compatible interests and expectations that engage with the social justice dimension of legal practice (Shalleck, 1995; Quigley, 1996).

Learning how to adopt a contextualized approach to prosecutorial discretion

The highly selective application of the law that gives prosecutors wide discretion is woven into the text of the Rome Statute of the ICC (United Nations, 1998); it is also entrenched in national legislation (Zegveld and Handmaker, 2012). These international and national legal norms, together with procedural and evidentiary rules, closely circumscribe the criteria for prosecuting international crimes, but still allow for a wide margin of interpretation. Such rules may be triggered by necessity, in particular the existence of limited resources. But, there is another crucial reason as well that leads to a clear structural bias and is crucial from a legal learning standpoint, namely the absence of a contextual understanding on the part of those pursuing international criminal justice.

The mission of the law and legal institutions engaged in international criminal justice is essentially twofold. First, the mission is to frame rules to ensure that consequences attach to gross violations of human rights and International Humanitarian Law (IHL). Second, it is to ensure that these rules are applied in a consistent and even-handed manner. However, politics always play a role, both in framing the rules and in implementing them. Justice is never blind and is nearly always available only to the perceived "victors" of a specific conflict.

Legal advocates, from the prosecutors who bring such cases before the courts, to the defence counsel who represent the alleged perpetrators, and even the non-governmental organizations (NGOs) who advocate for attention to specific issues, all bring their own, particular appreciation or consciousness of the law to their tasks. Many legal advocates, often without much critical reflection, seek to mobilise the law without necessarily addressing the social and political context in which such crimes have taken place. International prosecutors in particular rarely acknowledge openly the politics of what they do, with some notable exceptions, such as the former chief prosecutor of the International Criminal Tribunal for the former Yugoslavia, Louise Arbour (2008). By purporting to be neutral and impartial, these legal advocates mask the ideological basis upon which strategic decisions are taken to investigate, prosecute and punish international crimes.

The liberal ideological basis upon which decisions are taken to investigate and prosecute can be revealed through a careful examination of what cases eventually find their way to the courts and are prosecuted, accompanied by a contextual assessment of why some cases are chosen over others.

Part of the complexity in explaining the dynamics of international criminal justice through prosecution for international crimes, is that international law is not the homogenous system it once was. It has evolved into what Kosken-niemi has described as "a wide variety of specialist vocabularies and institutions" (2009, p. 12). The international criminal justice system, which was established to hold perpetrators accountable, is one of the most recent products of this evolution and is no less contested than any other specialist area of international law. As discussed by Drumbl (2005, p. 1295), there is some dispute as to whether a system of international criminal justice really exists, from an institutional and/or doctrinal standpoint. I tend to agree with Sands (2003), who indicates there is such a system of international criminal justice, particularly following the creation of the International Criminal Court in 2002. Indeed, the international criminal justice system is riddled with practical and legal obstacles, and, as I have already suggested, operates on a highly selective basis. The system also lacks a coherent policy framework. As Sieff and Vinjamuri have observed: "Despite the plethora of motivations that inspired war-crime trials historically, an international strategy for indicting war criminals cannot be justified in the absence of clear policy goals" (2002, p. 103).

Learning how to build national capacities to prosecute

In an article published nearly a decade after he presented his critique of the international human rights system through the "SVS metaphor," Mutua reflected on how the international criminal justice system, and the ICC in particular, could be improved (Mutua, 2010). He called on the ICC, and others within the system, including NGOs, to appreciate the need to build civil societies in countries being investigated by the ICC. More fundamentally, Mutua demanded a more "holistic understanding of the root causes of the culture of impunity and the seemingly intractable ethnic, social, and political problems" (ibid., p. 2). Rather than take legal action against the perpetrators of grave crimes itself, Mutua has insisted that the ICC take seriously its clearly prescribed role in supporting domestic legal procedures (ibid., p. 3). This is affirmed by Nouwen (2013) in her comprehensive study of the failings of the international criminal justice system, and especially the ICC, to realise its core function of promoting *complementary* systems to prosecute international crimes in the national court systems of Uganda and Sudan.

Beyond building national capacities to prosecute, the international criminal justice system must dispense justice in a much more even-handed (i.e. socially just) manner, not least in light of growing concerns that international criminal justice fails to take seriously basic principles of due process, including rights of the accused through what Munyard has regarded as a "blind paper shuffle" (Munyard, 2010).

Acknowledging the dangers of managerialism

Perhaps the most perplexing dimension of legal learning for both civic and state advocates who support the ICC and the complementary role of national jurisdictions is the persistent danger, frequently noted by Koskenniemi (2009), that engagement in the international criminal justice system might lead to simplistic "managerialism" solutions. More specifically, Koskenniemi warned of the common assumption that "international problems. . .should be resolved by developing increasingly complicated technical vocabularies for institutional policy-making" (2009, pp. 13–18). In other words, it would be a mistake to compensate for the failures of rules in the international criminal justice system simply by creating new rules. It is crucial to engage with the politics of the crisis of legitimacy facing the system.

Contrary to the perception of former ICC prosecutor Ocampo, who claimed to be "putting a legal limit to the politicians" and "policing the borderline" by drawing a distinction between what is political and what is criminal, Nouwen and Werner observe that "determining who is 'on the political side' or not is inherently political, especially when it involves the labelling of groups and individuals as international criminals" (Nouwen and Werner, 2011a, p. 962). Furthermore, in determining whether a "crisis" of legitimacy in criminal justice exists, one must critique the nature of the crisis itself; otherwise, the term "loses credibility" and "business seems to go on as usual, until the next 'crisis' comes around" (Benvenisti and Nouwen, 2016, p. 206).

As in any political process, legitimacy concerns will continue to be raised. The system for prosecuting persons suspected of international crimes, whether through international tribunals such as the ICC or via a national court, are far from ideal. Addressing these concerns requires a more conscious and deliberate engagement with the broader political questions surrounding international criminal justice – from the decision to investigate and eventually prosecute, to the determination of guilt or innocence – rather than merely following the bland legal content or procedures through which the law is implemented.

Managerialism concerns aside, acknowledging the politics behind international criminal justice opens the possibility that learning from the international criminal justice system is administered by legal-technocrats and ideologues only. By opening a more critical debate, advocates within the international criminal justice system may ensure that not only lessons are learned from the crisis of legitimacy faced by the system, but that new policies may be shaped. This could take the form of a "call for quick action" that is directed against "those directly affected" by the crisis – namely the closely-watching constituency of world leaders, NGOs and the victims of individual and mass atrocities – in a highly productive way (Jessop, 2015, p. 258).

Conclusion

This chapter has demonstrated that, contrary to the largely legal-doctrinal thinking of most lawyers engaged in international criminal justice, efforts by legal advocates to end impunity for international crimes are obviously a form of politics. By adopting an approach of critical, reflexive learning, lawyers are better positioned to explicitly engage with the politics of international law in a way that enhances, rather than undermines the role of law as a mediator of crisis.

Unlike the multiple external challenges posed by the USA and the Africa block of member states that have withdrawn from the system, or threatened to do so, the *real* crisis of legitimacy faced by institutions such as the ICC will deepen if the structural bias towards under-developed countries framed by an essentialized understanding of states, the victims of human rights violations and the role of international institutions and advocates as *saviours* are not addressed. In other words, the current crisis is largely of the system's own making. This perception stems from a combination of the bombastic attitude of international prosecutors such as Ocampo and Crane, the self-serving interests of states, and the uncritical stance of a large body of NGOs that have played an important role in the establishment and functioning of the international criminal justice system and to some extent reinforce its crisis of legitimacy. Consistent with Ignatieff's assessment of the human rights movement in general, the international criminal justice movement "is facing a crisis of self-doubt, not because it is failing, but because it has not dealt honestly with the implications of its success" (Ignatieff, 1999, p. 12).

By contrast, considering the "structural bias" of institutions (Koskenniemi, 2009, p. 9), including courts and tribunals established to administer international criminal justice, strategic legal advocacy can strengthen the legal mechanisms to investigate, prosecute and adjudicate international crimes in a consistent and even-handed manner. Accordingly, it may be possible to move away from a mentality of Savages, Victims and Saviours, and engage in a more honest and transparent politics as part of collective global efforts to both end impunity and address the legitimacy crisis facing the international criminal justice system.

References

Allison, S. (2016) 'African revolt threatens international criminal court's legitimacy', *The Guardian*, 27 October.

Amnesty International (2012) 'The International Criminal Court: Coming challenges, issues and conclusions', Statement presented at the Justice for All Conference, 15 February. Sydney: University of New South Wales.

Amsterdam, A. (1984) 'Clinical legal education: A 21st century perspective', *Journal of Legal Education*, 34(4), pp. 612–618.

Arbour, L. (2008) 'The responsibility to protect as a duty of care in international law and practice', *Review of International Studies*, 34, pp. 445–458.

Arnoldussen, T. (2011) '*The Reckoning*: A different perspective?', *Recht der Werkelijkheid*, 32(3), pp. 107–111.

Arts, K. and Handmaker, J. (2010) "'Cultures of constitutionalism' subsection', in Frischman, M. and Muller, S. (eds.), *The dynamics of constitutionalism in the age of globalisation*. The Hague: Hague Academic Press, pp. 57–109.

Arts, K. and Popovski, V. (eds.). (2006) *International criminal accountability and the rights of children*. The Hague: Hague Academic Press.

Ashar, S. (2016) 'Deep critique and democratic lawyering in clinical practice', *California Law Review*, 104, pp. 201–232.

Babacan, A. and Babacan, H. (2017) 'Enhancing civic consciousness through student pro bono in legal education', *Teaching in Higher Education*, 22(6), pp. 672–679.

Benvenisti, E. and Nouwen, S. (2016) 'Leaving legacies open-ended: An invitation for an inclusive debate on international criminal justice', *AJIL Unbound*, 110(3), pp. 205–208.

Bolton, J. (2001) 'The risks and weaknesses of the International Criminal Court from America's perspective', *Law and Contemporary Problems*, 64, pp. 167–180.

Bourdieu, P. and Wacquant, L. (1992) *An invitation to reflexive sociology*. Chicago: University of Chicago Press.

Danner, A. (2003) 'Enhancing the legitimacy and accountability of prosecutorial discretion at the International Criminal Court', *American Journal of International Law*, 97, pp. 510–552.

Dolan, C. (2002) 'The optional protocol: In the best interest of whom?', *Journal of Conflict, Security and Development*, 2, pp. 141–148.

Dolan, C. (2009) *Social torture: The case of Northern Uganda, 1986–2006*. Oxford: Berghahn.

Donnelly, J. (1989) *Universal human rights in theory and practice*. Ithaca: Cornell University Press.

Drumbl, M. (2005) 'Pluralizing international criminal justice', *Michigan Law Review*, 103, pp. 1295–1328.

Drumbl, M. (2012) *Reimagining child soldiers in international law and policy*. Oxford: Oxford University Press.

Friedman, L. (1986) 'The law and society movement', *Stanford Law Review*, 38(3), pp. 763–780.

Glasius, M. (2006) *The International Criminal Court: A global civil society achievement.* New York: Routledge.

Goldsmith, J. (2003) 'The self-defeating International Criminal Court', *University of Chicago Law Review,* 70, pp. 89–104.

Handmaker, J. (2009) *Advocating for accountability: Civic-state interactions to protect refugees in South Africa.* Antwerp: Intersentia.

Handmaker, J. (2011) 'Facing up to the ICC's crisis of legitimacy: A critique of the reckoning and its representation of international criminal justice', *Recht der Werkelijkheid,* 32(3), pp. 100–106.

Herik, L. van den (2009) 'The difficulties of exercising extraterritorial criminal jurisdiction: The acquittal of a Dutch businessman for crimes committed in Liberia', *International Criminal Law Review,* 9, pp. 211–226.

Honwana, A. (2006) *Child soldiers in Africa.* Philadelphia: University of Pennsylvania Press.

Ignatieff, M. (1999) *Whose universal values? The crisis in human rights.* Amsterdam: Stichting Praemium Erasmianum.

Ignatieff, M. and Gutmann, A. (eds.). (2001) *Human rights as politics and idolatry.* Princeton, NJ: Princeton University Press.

International Committee of the Red Cross (ICRC) (1949) *Convention relative to the protection of civilian persons in time of war.* United Nations Treaty Series, v. 75. Geneva: ICRC.

Jessop, B. (2013) 'Recovered imaginaries, imagined recoveries: A cultural political economy of crisis construals and crisis-management in the North Atlantic Financial Crisis', in Benner, M. (ed.), *Beyond the global economic crisis: Economics and politics for a post-crisis settlement.* Cheltenham: Edward Elgar, pp. 234–254.

Jessop, B. (2015) 'The symptomatology of crises, reading crises and learning from them: Some critical realist reflections', *Journal of Critical Realism,* 14(3), pp. 238–271.

Katzman, R. (2009) 'The non-disclosure of confidential exculpatory evidence and the Lubanga proceedings: How the ICC defense system affects the accused's right to a fair trial', *Northwestern University Journal of International Human Rights,* 8, pp. 77–101.

Kaur, H. (2011) *The International Criminal Court: Current challenges and perspectives,* Keynote address at the Salzburg Law School on International Criminal Law. Salzburg, Austria: Salzburg Law School.

Klaaren, J., Handmaker, J. and Dugard, J. (eds.) (2011) 'Public interest litigation in South Africa: Special issue introduction', *South African Journal on Human Rights,* 27(1), pp. 1–7.

Klip, A. and Sluiter, G. (1999) *Annotated leading cases of International Criminal Tribunals.* Antwerp: Intersentia.

Korey, W. (2003) *NGOs and the Universal Declaration of Human Rights: A curious grapevine.* New York: St. Martin's Press.

Koskenniemi, M. (2009) 'The politics of international law – 20 years later', *European Journal of International Law,* 20(1), pp. 7–19.

Mak, E. (2017) *The T-shaped lawyer and beyond: Rethinking legal professionalism and legal education.* The Hague: Eleven International Publishing.

Mouthaan, S. (2011) 'The prosecution of gender-based crimes at the ICC: Challenges and opportunities', *International Criminal Law Review,* 11(4), pp. 775–802.

Munyard, T. (2010) *Are these international courts, courts of justice?* Presented at the Institute of Social Studies (ISS) Development Research Seminars. The Hague: International Institute of Social Studies.

Mutua, M. (2000) 'What is TWAIL?', *Proceedings of the ASIL Annual Meeting*, 94, pp. 31–38.

Mutua, M. (2001) 'Savages, victims, and saviors: The metaphor of human rights', *Harvard International Law Journal*, 42, pp. 201–245.

Mutua, M. (2010) *The International Criminal Court in Africa: Challenges and opportunities* (NOREF Working Paper No. 3). Oslo: Norwegian Peacebuilding Centre.

Nelken, D. (2004) 'Using the concept of legal culture', *Australian Journal of Legal Philosophy*, 29, pp. 1–26.

Neumann, R. (2000) 'Donald Schön, The reflective practitioner and the comparative failures of legal education', *Clinical Law Review*, 6(2), pp. 401–426.

Nouwen, S. (2013) *Complementarity in the line of fire*. Cambridge: Cambridge University Press.

Nouwen, S. and Werner, W. (2011a) 'Doing justice to the political: The International Criminal Court in Uganda and Sudan', *European Journal of International Law*, 21(4), pp. 941–965.

Nouwen, S. and Werner, W. (2011b) 'Doing justice to the political: The International Criminal Court in Uganda and Sudan: A rejoinder to Bas Schotel', *European Journal of International Law*, 22(4), 1161–1164.

Orentlicher, D. (2003) 'Judging global justice: Assessing the International Criminal Court', *Wisconsin International Law Journal*, 21(3), pp. 495–512.

Quigley, F. (1996) 'Seizing the disorienting moment: Adult learning theory and the teaching of social justice in Law School Clinics', *Clinical Law Review*, 2(1), pp. 37–72.

Reynolds, J. (2017) *Empire, emergency and international law*. Cambridge: Cambridge University Press.

Risse, T., Ropp, S. and Sikkink, K. (1999) *The power of human rights: International norms and domestic change*. Cambridge: Cambridge University Press.

Sands, P. (ed.). (2003) *From Nuremberg to The Hague: The future of international criminal justice*. Cambridge: Cambridge University Press.

Scheppele, K. (2004) 'A realpolitik defense of social rights', *Texas Law Review*, 82(7), pp. 1921–1962.

Schotel, B. (2011) 'Doing justice to the political: The International Criminal Court in Uganda and Sudan: A reply to Sarah Nouwen and Wouter Werner', *European Journal of International Law*, 22(4), pp. 1153–1160.

Shalleck, A. (1995) 'Clinical contexts: Theory and practice in law and supervision', *New York University Review of Law and Social Change*, 21(1), pp. 109–182.

Sieff, M. and Vinjamuri, L. (2002) 'Prosecuting war criminals: The case for decentralisation', *Conflict, Security and Development*, 2(2), pp. 103–113.

Special Court of Sierra Leone (2004) *Prosecution opening statement, trial of the RUF accused*, Case No. SCSL-2004-15-PT. Freetown: Sierra Leone.

Teubner, G. (1983) 'Substantive and reflexive elements in modern law', *Law and Society Review*, 17(2), pp. 239–286.

United Nations (1945) *Charter of the United Nations*. United Nations Treaty Series, v. 1. San Francisco: United Nations.

United Nations (1948) *Universal declaration of human rights (UDHR)*. United Nations Treaty Series, v. 660. New York: United Nations.

United Nations (1966a) *International covenant on civil and political rights*. United Nations Treaty Series, v. 999. New York: United Nations.

United Nations (1966b) *International covenant on economic, social and cultural rights*. United Nations Treaty Series, v. 993. New York: United Nations.

United Nations (1984) *Convention against torture and other cruel, inhuman or degrading treatment or punishment*. United Nations Treaty Series, v. 1465. New York: United Nations.

United Nations (1998) *Rome statute of the International Criminal Court*. United Nations Treaty Series, v. 2187. New York: United Nations.

Voyvodic, R. and Medcalf, M. (2004) 'Advancing social justice through an interdisciplinary approach to clinical legal education: The case of legal assistance of Windsor', *Journal of Law and Policy*, 14, pp. 101–132.

Wessels, M. (2006) *Child soldiers: From violence to protection*. Cambridge, MA: Harvard University Press.

Wilt, H. van der (2011) 'Universal jurisdiction under attack: An assessment of African misgivings towards International Criminal Justice as administered by Western states', *Journal of International Criminal Justice*, 9(5), pp. 1043–1066.

Yates, P. (director) (2003) *The Reckoning: The Battle for the International Criminal Court* (Documentary film). Available: Skylight Pictures.

Zegveld, L. and Handmaker, J. (2012) *Universal jurisdiction: State of affairs and ways ahead: A policy paper*. ISS Working Papers Series, no. 532. The Hague: International Institute of Social Studies.

Part V

Limits to learning and the scope for overcoming them

11 Insouciance, indifference and any inspiration in the face of emergent global crises?

Des Gasper

Introduction: global transition through global crisis?

Many authors and research teams have noted serious indications and risks of an escalating multi-faceted global crisis in which various subsidiary crises – environmental, financial, economic, social, national-political, nationalist, cyber, epidemiological – will feed each other. The authors range from, for example, IT multi-millionaire James Martin (2007) and the former Dutch right-liberal party leader and Defence Minister Joris Voorhoeve (2011), through integral theorists like Ervin Laszlo (2010), the Stockholm Environment Institute and Paul Raskin et al. (2002), to critical theorists like Ulrich Beck (2009) and Nancy Fraser (2013).

Growing recognition over the past two generations of such a possibility is not matched by corresponding global precaution. The veiled and contestable nature of many of the processes that contribute to the multiple crises and of their interactions, combined with the growth imperatives of capitalism, techno-optimism and market theology, plus nationalist loyalties, ambitions and rivalries mean that denial, inattention and non-preparation prevail. Further, the risks and eventual harms are disproportionately imposed on the poor and marginal, both inter- and intra-nationally, as vividly illustrated already in the immediate impacts, crisis-response practices and long-term results of "eruptions" such as hurricanes. This allocation of risks and harms means ruling elites typically largely carry on regardless.

This chapter first explores some of the mechanisms at work, including with special reference to climate change. One family of mechanisms, the ruling myths of techno-optimism, embrace "Fear No Evil." They deny danger, thanks to a belief that technological transformations mean crisis will never arrive or it will always trigger rapid solutions. Unending economic growth will be assured through capitalist-driven innovation, as envisaged by, for example, Martin, Friedman (2016), or Diamindis and Kotler (2012). A second family of issues concerns endemic underestimation and indifference towards dangers – "See No Evil, Hear No Evil" – typically based on a tacit expectation that nearly all eventual costs can be imposed on weaker groups with the rich escaping relatively unharmed. Further, the costs and risks to weaker groups are systematically downgraded and excluded. Relevant techniques include: requiring types of quantitative data that have never been collected for poor groups (for example, on diseases particular to the poor); using monetary measures in which the poor count for little; inverting the precautionary principle to prioritize avoiding any risk of damaging the interests of the wealthy; and so on.

Given a dominant "No Worries" culture, crisis becomes an inevitable stage before any eventual response and change. The second half of the chapter considers some possible lines of response and evolutionary paths. I focus most on the complex theory of global crisis developed since 1990 by Paul Raskin and his Tellus Institute associates, including Tariq Banuri, Gilberto Gallopin and Robert Kates, and recently updated in Raskin (2016). Their *Great Transition Initiative* (GTI) series anticipates several themes considered in the present volume. It refines the characterization of crises as both threat and opportunity and shows the need for powerful alternative visions, values, proposals and networks. It presents a set of scenarios that vary according to the relation between the intensity of crisis and the relevance and effectiveness of the preparations and capacities for response. "Barbarization Scenarios," for example, will arise where severe crises are confronted by little capacity to rethink and innovate, especially where this is weakened by rigid nationalist identities.

While crisis may be a necessary step in bringing about change, it is not a sufficient basis for desirable change. It can easily provoke fear, hate and increased selfishness. Craig Murphy's work (e.g. 2005) on two centuries of efforts to build global governance arrangements identified other elements necessary for an effective progressive response. Networks must not only be formed and motivated but in addition, to be ready when crisis erupts, they must have produced practicable ideas and formed links to potentially sympathetic decision-makers. Otherwise crises will be used to enforce retrogressive change, for which ideas funded by money-power frequently sit ready and waiting, as illustrated in Naomi Klein's *The Shock Doctrine* (2007).

With reference to the requirements mentioned above for effective crisis anticipation, preparation and response suggested by Murphy and the GTI work, I evaluate the Rio+20 process through the 2012 global summit on sustainable development and the subsequent 2015 Agenda for Sustainable Development (United Nations, 2012, 2015) that includes the Sustainable Development Goals, agreed by all governments. Are there some promising signs?

"No worries"

Nexus: intersecting causes and the possible enormity of coming crisis

The infinite web of interconnected systems is routinely identified in crisis literatures as both a likely cause of eventual major crises and a barrier to consensual recognition of and response to the risks (e.g. Beck, 2009; Houtart, 2010; ISSC-UNESCO, 2013). The web of interconnection underlies the distinction between crisis as event, a relatively short-term explosion or eruption, and crisis as an unfolding process that predates and continues after the event. Focusing one-sidedly on crisis as event contributes to preoccupation with symptoms, as in the world of international disaster "relief" (Gómez, 2014). The proliferation of connections and implications underlines the importance of preparation, in terms of networks, ideology and practical capacities for response; but the hidden and uncertain character of underlying connections facilitates denial and non-prepara-tion. Nancy Fraser links these evasions and the overall inadequacy of responses to our contemporary "economic, financial, ecological, and social" crises to "a major crisis of democracy": "constituted public powers increasingly lack the capacity and the will to stand up to private powers" (2014, pp. 1–2).

Globalization theory stresses interconnections across national boundaries. In the language of the Great Transition Initiative, humankind entered a "Plane-tary Phase" in the late 20th century:

> Heretofore, the world could be reasonably approximated as a set of semi-autonomous entities – states, ecosystems, cultures, territories – subject to external interactions. Now, as a superordinate system forms and global-scale processes increasingly influence the operation and stability of subsystems, such reductive partitioning becomes inaccurate and misleading.
>
> (Raskin, 2016, p. 13)

A proto-form of this awareness was emerging from the 1960s and informed US attempts to exert global control. For example, the then US Secretary of State, Dean Rusk, wrote in 1965 that "[t]oday we can be secure only to the extent that our environment is secure" (cited in Mazower, 2013, pp. 265–266).

More fundamental still are interconnections among realms typically sepa-rated epistemically and organizationally. Together, the cross-national, cross-global, cross-sectoral connections spawn possibilities unforeseen in sectoral and discipline-bound organizational worlds. A cross-system or "nexus" approach looks for "hotspots," where multiple stresses combine and could trigger system collapse or transformation (see, for example, Owen, 2014).

> The fundamental uncertainty about our future as a species and as elements of the global socio-ecological systems (GSES) to which we belong, comes from the deeper impact of the fusion and interactions among those social, technological, economic, cultural, and environmental processes, and not just by the simple summation of those.
>
> (Gallopín, 2016)

Crisis? what crisis? – see no evil, hear no evil, fear no evil

Actors face difficulty in distinguishing quickly or reliably between accidental events and periodic fluctuations on the one hand, and system-generated crises on the other. System-generated processes are overlaid by many random or fleeting factors and fluctuations and are therefore difficult to read, easy to deny. Raskin remarks on "the full arsenal of psychological responses: discounting dangers in sweet denial, finding distraction in passing amusements and baubles, and seeking succour in the false panaceas of free markets, religious rapture, or individual beatitude" (2016, p. 2). To denial and distraction, he adds despair: "the three D's of an anxious culture."

Equally important though is a lack of despair: a blithe undistracted optimistic current that does not deny challenges but asserts they will all be vanquished if governments unshackle the genius of entrepreneurial spirit. Some believe innovation will forestall every crisis, others that it at least can or will ensure salvation when crises arise. Using a mega-version of Albert Hirschman's "The Hiding Hand" hypothesis (2014), they believe challenge will always elicit adequate response and there will be no progress if precaution is guided only by current knowledge.

Amongst the techno-optimists and apostles of invincible technical progress are many North American entrepreneurs, such as Peter Diamandis (see Diamindis and Kotler, 2012). The Reagan administration's rejection in the 1980s of environmental precaution, both domestically and internationally, was "led by optimists in the innovative adaptive power of capitalism and societal networks, like Herman Kahn, Julian Simon, and 'green' Californian Stewart Brand"; (Mazower, 2013, pp. 338–339). An important public spokesman for this "Song of Growth" is *New York Times* journalist Thomas L. Friedman (Gasper, 2012). A bullish optimism pervaded his 2005 bestseller on globalization, *The world is flat*. After somewhat more caution in *Hot, flat and crowded* (2009), on climate change, he reverts to type in *An optimist's guide to thriving in the age of accelerations* (2016).

For some authors, the choice of bullish or bearish orientation should be tactical. They argue that people "turn off" from doom scenarios alone. People must be offered a rosy prospect, not only bearish warnings, if one wants to retain their attention and involvement. In contrast, O'Hagan (2017), drawing on Marshall (2016), warns that "climate optimism has been a disaster," feeding complacency and escapism. Kingsnorth adds that the problem goes deeper than a need to cultivate optimism: "we have failed to act on [climate change] because at one level we don't want to act on it. And we don't want to act on it because we don't want to believe it's really happening" (2014, p. 17). He and Marshall cite the Nobel Prize winning psychologist Daniel Kahneman on unwillingness to change present life-habits: "no amount of psychological awareness will overcome people's reluctance to lower their [current] standard of living. So that's my bottom line: there is not much hope" (cited in Kingsnorth, 2014, p. 18). Underpinning the syndrome described by Kahneman are also factors he does not highlight: that the damaging life-habits do lower standards of living but primarily those of people far away in time or space, not of the high-living consumers.

Precaution for whom? Crisis for whom?[1]

In this volume, Jessop and Knio distinguish crises that can be managed through established crisis-management routines from crises of crisis management.

Established crisis-management routines centrally include sacrificing the weak through a disproportionate imposition of risks and eventual damage upon the poor and marginal (the "risk recipients," courtesy of the munificence of the "risk donors": see Beck, 2009, p. 30). The optimism of bearish authors often seems to rest partly on a tacit (or open) readiness to sacrifice other people, while they and the privileged groups they represent refuse to change or even introduce changes that hurt others. A set of eight interconnected features can be mentioned here.

First, different safety standards are applied for poor people in poor countries. When designing a house or a bridge in a rich country or for rich people so it will be proof against fire, earthquakes, floods and other accidents, architects and engineers apply highly demanding criteria. Chances of disastrous outcomes must be minimized because at stake are the lives and safety of valued and monied clients, cum voters, cum potential litigants and whistle-blowers. However, in climate change discussions, those who are at risk are overwhelmingly far away in space, time and socio-political location: they are especially the babies, small children and elderly (see, for example, data in International Panel on Climate Change [IPCC], 2012; WHO, 2014) in poor families in distant countries, those from future generations (especially two or more generations ahead) and, most especially, the intersection of those two populations. In particular, mainstream proposed policies aim above all to not disturb the lifestyles of today's valued and monied businesses and consumers, clients and voters, in the powerful countries from where the climate studies are undertaken or funded. This leads to distorted and selective application of the precautionary principle.

Discussion of the global carbon budget frequently proceeds in terms that would be inconceivable when designing and applying safety standards within a rich country. Sceptics about energetic measures to move away from fossil fuels take comfort, for example, from a new projection that:

> The world could emit about 750bn tonnes of carbon dioxide from 2015 onwards and still be "likely" – IPCC jargon for a two thirds chance – to keep further warming [beyond the existing 0.9°C above pre-industrial levels] below 0.6°C. . . . [So] the carbon budget lasts a few decades, not just a few years.
>
> (*The Economist*, September 23, 2017)

That such discussions proceed in terms of taking a one-third (or, often, one-half) chance of failure reveals a situation in which those pondering whether or not to modify their lifestyles and those of their voters or customers are not the people at most risk of negative effects from inaction. Instead, they feel (rightly or wrongly) confident in their own capacity to cope with climate changes. Even risk levels a tenth or a twentieth of such levels would not be remotely acceptable politically for design processes that directly affect rich country residents.

Second, human impacts, as opposed to physical impacts and monetized economic impacts, often remain simply unexamined. That some current discussions, including in the 2015 Paris accord, are now framed in terms of a 1.5°C temperature rise ceiling rather than the previous (more) politically palatable but scientifically unwarranted supposedly safe 2°C ceiling represents progress. It also hints at the political pressures and ethically challenged science that earlier generated the 2°C figure and associated work.[2] Kevin Anderson, then Director of Britain's Tyndall Centre for Climate Change Research, warned that a global *average* 2°C rise will "kill a lot of poor people" (cited by Hamilton, 2010, p. 194). The rises anticipated during this century in much of sub-Saharan Africa and South Asia, where most of the world's poorest live, are considerably higher and would devastate much of existing agriculture. In addition, they would be accompanied by much more frequent periods of extreme temperature and/or drought and/or extreme rains and winds (IPCC, 2012; World Bank, 2012). For the most vulnerable groups, notably small children and the oldest people, those extremes and their side-effects (such as floods and pathogen spread) entail seriously increased morbidity and mortality.

General neglect of such impacts is reflected in the Intergovernmental Panel on Climate Change (IPCC)'s latest general Assessment Report of 2014 (AR5), an enormous digest of the previous seven years of scientifically peer-reviewed publication. Children, especially small children, make up the bulk of those vulnerable to climate change and the associated extreme weather events and health hazards. Eighty-eight percent of the estimated deaths attributable to climate change in 2000, according to the World Health Report (WHO, 2002, p. 223) were of babies and children younger than five years, essentially amongst poorer families in poorer countries. Yet children received no special attention in the work summarized in AR5, even in its huge second volume on the impacts of climate change. Analysis of that volume's Summary for Policy Makers shows it hardly talked of "people," and it never mentioned children (Fløttum et al., 2016). Despite offering figures on GDP impact and other economic measures of climate change impact, it provided no figures on impacts in terms of lives lost, nor on health impacts more broadly. While separate attention was granted to eco-systems and to non-human species, specific vulnerable human groups remained virtually invisible in the AR5 Summaries for Policy Makers. All national governments have accepted declarations and conventions about human rights, and IPCC's work is explicitly intended to inform policymakers, yet the language of human rights is completely absent. It is not used to organize AR5's discussions of impacts or policy alternatives (ibid.). Overall, a "human lens" has not yet penetrated far in the genre of state-approved climate science, as selected and summarized by IPCC.

Third, the impersonal form of scientific gaze that predominates, and that downgrades or fails to mention human deaths and children's lives, often leads to talking of risk in a dehumanized way. The risk of an event should be considered as [probability of the event x resulting damage], with damage measured in terms of human significance. So, a low-probability of very-high-damage-for-persons can still mean high risk; this is recognized in the design process of bridges in rich countries. But the IPCC's AR5, typical of most rich country discussions of climate change, combined the conceptual inhibition about recognizing the human values at stake with an impersonal standardized language for talking about probability levels. A chance of mortalities that is below 33 percent had to be called "unlikely." This contributes to soft-pedalling of the real risks involved.

Fourth, another way of marginalizing the life interests of the poor in climate assessments involves their removal from attention because of rules about the required type of data − that, for example, the estimated impacts must be quantified and must be derived in random control quasi-experimental studies and/or have appeared in strong peer-reviewed journals. This can exclude lesser-studied health effects − notably the diseases of the poor − and many non-health effects too. For some types of extreme climate event, no specific, let alone precise and reliable, quantitative basis of estimation of their probability, intensity and impact yet exists. They are therefore omitted from projected impacts.

Fifth, some methods inherently exclude certain issues and groups. Aggregative monetized evaluations (as emphasized in, for example, the Stern Review, 2007, and the World Development Report, 2010) give less weight to the effects on poor people, since their monetary "footprint" is very small. They further allow gains for the rich to outweigh losses for the poor (now and in the future), even their loss of life; and they underplay non-monetized effects such as political instability. The business technique of discounting the future, applied in such studies to climate policy, drastically downgrades the interests of future generations (see the critique by Shue, 2006).

Sixth, many exclusions arise through an approach that seeks to estimate impacts within separate sectors, based on models that assume closed sectors, and that underplays how insecurity in people's lives is produced by the local intersections of multiple forces that cross sectoral and national boundaries and that discipline-bound research may not envisage or anticipate. For example, environmental deterioration can contribute to political instability in some poor countries, that can affect economic and health situations in those countries, their neighbours, and rich countries that are no longer unreachable, untouchable, secluded entities.

Seventh, many examples of minimizing climate change impacts on persons, especially health impacts, involve deliberately "conservative" estimation. Examples include judgements about the volume of emissions attributable to rich country consumers (lowered by excluding the emissions generated in supplier countries like China), about the length of time carbon dioxide (CO_2) will remain in the atmosphere, and about the shape of the [emissions→harm] function, assumed to be linear even though this entails underestimation. Often such conservatism is compatible with avoiding criticism from financially and politically powerful devotees of fossil-fuelled economic growth. It can also be compatible with a strategy of seeking to test whether or not estimated impacts are serious even when we make minimalist assumptions, in order not to delay identification of responsibilities for change until all uncertainties are resolved, which could be too late or never (see, for example, discussions in a themed section of *Ethics, Policy and Environment*, 2011; and the reply by Nolt, 2013). This strategy of making rock-bottom estimates is not suitable though for giving more realistic estimates of likely impacts, let alone for paying due precautionary attention to risks faced by the most vulnerable people. Even for maintaining the existing economic system, the systematic blind spots and congenital "conservatism" of current ruling ideology towards environmental change and its "business-almost-as-usual 'green economy'" approaches mean that: "they are, in the name of prudence, gambling that mega-crises will not overwhelm gradual market and policy responses" (Raskin, 2016, pp. 35–36).

Eighth, sustaining all the preceding seven forms, is indifference to, or contempt for, the weakest groups. While humanitarian disasters periodically and temporarily counteract indifference, the disproportionate exposure of the poor in such disasters reflects the secular indifference, which explains why so little is spent on prevention. "Both the World Bank and UN agencies quote dismal figures: only 3.6 percent of the disaster related financing went into prevention (World Bank, 2012), a share that is similar for official humanitarian aid (Development Initiatives, 2013)" (Gómez, 2014, p. 29).

So, in these and other ways, damage is ignored and underestimated. The eight factors listed above express the "common sense," embodied in institutionalized analytical routines, of a ruling order and this will not easily change. They were presented above largely in terms drawn from the estimation of threats related to climate change. Equivalents can be found in other contexts, such as famines, food security and health security more generally. Many famines are unreported, for they concern the remote and rejected poor and happen in slow motion. Sen (1981) demonstrated the potential significance and cost-effectiveness of competitive democracy and a free press for countering blindness to and sacrifice of the weakest groups in famines, but these offer no guarantee of sufficient counterbalance to the forces of indifference and othering, either in famines or in other crises. Competing political parties and competing media may all still ignore the weakest groups, and not only when those lie outside the national boundaries. The categories of capitalism veil violence done to many ordinary people's lives. The impacts are never described as violence, remarks Tyner, who explores "the market logics of letting die with respect to those individuals deemed redundant in [capitalist] society" (Tyner, 2016, p. 10).

Not looking and not caring are further fed and instituted through cultures of nationalism and the legacies of its history. Mazower (2013) remarks how the 19th century liberal nationalist vision of cooperating sovereign nations was for Europe only. Each European state also had the duty to engage in a supposed civilising mission globally and to colonize peoples outside Europe, where however the rules of civility would not apply to the uncivilized, who could appropriately be crushed in order to later be gradually civilised. By the time of their 20th century wars the combatant powers in Europe were ready to treat each other as brutally as they were accustomed to do with the supposed savages outside.

Indifference to the fate of others is thus not without price. Brutality spreads. Further, ignorance about what happens to the poor leads the rich to underestimate how eventual feedbacks and fight-backs will endanger them too.

The necessity but insufficiency of crises: on essential preparations

In the face of institutionalized insouciance and indifference, even antagonism, to other people(s), including through inflexible programming of identities, motivations and response patterns, as well as through instituted ignorance and megalomania, global crises seem to be an unavoidable trigger stage for forcing response, learning and change. As Gallopin notes, for "at least...the case of climate change, the time window for changing is closing faster than the typical societal response time" (2016, p. 1). Only through crisis does response accelerate.

Major change may not happen without crises, but crises fan fears and conflict. Intra- and inter-national conflicts can block reforms, contributing to deepening of the crises, as sketched in the GTI's Barbarization Scenarios. If we are fortunate, global citizens' reactions may reverse the downward spiral. If not, then we may transition to a "broken world," to use Tim Mulgan's phrase, in which some of the conditions long assumed in liberal Western philosophy to be present and that rationalize and license liberalism – notably the presence of only moderate scarcity – no longer apply. A broken climate system will mean that not all persons' basic needs can be reliably satisfied. Mulgan's *Ethics for a broken world* (2011), written in the form of an "After the Fall" moral philosophy textbook, reflects critically on the blithe assumptions in Western liberal individualist philosophy that contributed to the generation and non-prevention of the Fall.

> human development thinking stands on the assumption of an affluent world, not a broken one. They take for granted that the conditions for justice and democracy [as articulated by Hume and Rawls] remain in place, but during [and after] crisis this may be not an accurate assumption (Hume, [1777] 2010; Mulgan, 2011). Therefore, it seems limited what human development ideas can offer in this respect.
>
> (Gómez, 2014, p. 37)

In a more political analysis, Nancy Fraser sees a crisis of democracy that is, she says, "the specifically *political* dimension of a broader, multifaceted crisis... economic, financial, ecological and social... a 'general crisis'," of failure to control "financialized, globalizing, neoliberal capitalism" (2014, p. 1). For this objective crisis to become a subjective crisis and a system legitimation crisis, for people to respond in ways that seek fundamental system reform or replacement, requires many conditions to be fulfilled. People must perceive the crisis as concerning them, as serious, as avoidable and as worth trying to respond to. Does it concern them? People have to feel a sense of collective responsibility and collective membership of a shared community of fate. Is it avoidable? People "must interpret the crisis dynamics they experience as manifestations of system failures, not as fatalities, which could not be otherwise; they must, in other words, reject the neoliberal mantra of 'TINA' [There Is No Alternative]" (Fraser, 2014, p. 5).

The futures scenarios suggested in the Great Transition Initiative's work vary according to the relationship between the intensity of crisis and the nature and strength of capacities – including motivations – for constructive response (see, for example, Raskin, 2008; Kubiszewski, Costanza, Anderson and Sutton, 2017). Three pairs of scenarios are investigated. The first of the Conventional Worlds scenarios is "Market Forces:" unconstrained market forces lead and will supposedly engender and channel ample technical innovation. Response capacity is assumed to be more than adequate. In reality, suggest the GTI modellers, this pathway will generate environmental and social collapse. Hence its partner scenario, "Policy Reform," which involves the "light touch," "sustainable development" approach accepted on paper by leading governments since Rio 1992 and updated in Rio+20: a set of measures to safeguard, channel and supplement market forces. The second pair of scenarios, Barbarization, envisage as their starting-point the failure of the Conventional Worlds paths: "Breakdown" involves comprehensive collapse following the failure of "Market Forces" or "Policy Reform" paths; while, in "Fortress World," some countries manage to seal themselves off from the collapse elsewhere. The third pair, Great Transitions, conceives trajectories that avoid or effectively respond to major collapse, thanks to fundamental system transformations: a move to small-scale local "Eco-Communalism," which GTI deems unlikely except as a possible eventual evolution post-"Breakdown;" and a hoped for "New Sustainability Paradigm," that somehow innovates its way – organizationally, culturally and politically as well as technologically – to be able to mould and accommodate the aspirations worldwide within a finite planet. Central to the GTI research agenda, then, has been to consider how and under what conditions a Policy Reform path might, through successive crises and responses, feasibly lead into a New Paradigm transition and, on this basis, to inspire efforts in such a direction.

The earlier study *The Great Transition* (2002) focused on global networks of social movements that mobilize young people as the likeliest engine of system-changing response, because they were seen as the constituency with the most potential time, energy, hope and anger. But this is just one possibility, and GTI work and sister streams have looked more broadly at social movements and how they could cooperate internationally and influence and sometimes drive more powerful institutionalized formations: states and corporations. The 2016 *Journey to Earthland* posits the central role of a Global Citizens Movement or network of movements and other social forces that do not wield executive power but that experience and interpret crises and attempt to exert influence in periods when windows of opportunity open. The same concern is central to the work of Craig Murphy, mentioned in the introduction to this chapter, and is applied in my own work to the emergence and global impact of "human development" thinking, led by the Pakistani economist Mahbub ul Haq (Gasper, 2011).

Thus, while Nancy Fraser's analysis posits some required functions, the GTI and Murphy look too at possible specific mechanisms of change (see also Gasper and St. Clair, 2010). The little or no net response regarding environmental sustainability in the past two generations indicates the insufficiency of existing mechanisms. Democracies and corporations remain preoccupied with the short-term and national states have focused on narrowly conceived self-interest (Falk, 2010). Raskin is also unimpressed with the performance and potential of the other players prominent in current Policy Reform efforts:

> None of the principal characters now on the global stage are strong candidates to be trailblazers of a Great Transition. In different ways, they express concerns too narrow and outlooks too myopic for the task. Thus, the United Nations, relying on the cooperation of its reluctant member countries, ardent defenders of their own national interests, cannot mount an adequate response to the crisis and promise of the Planetary Phase; the top priority for corporations remains higher returns for shareholders, not the common good; and institutionalized civil society organizations, plowing their separate vineyards and competing for donor funds, are ill-prepared for the larger project of conceptualizing and advancing a coherent system shift.
>
> (Raskin, 2016, p. 30)

So, he concludes, a Policy Reform scenario could proceed only if driven forward by a powerful Global Citizens Movement. But he expects it will remain insufficient. The modified-business-as-usual contents of the Policy Reform path do not change the driving imperatives and dynamics of existing systems and cannot mobilize the motivational momentum needed for major redirection. As in the past two generations since the 1972 Stockholm UN Conference on the Human Environment, Policy Reform will in reality mainly remain talked about and not done.

> the contradictions between the dynamics of the standard paradigm and the requirements of the Planetary Phase [will remain]. The accumulation of wealth concentrates power and influence, while consumerism, polarization, and individualism constrain collective action. Short-termism keeps politicians focused on the next election, not the next generation; profit trumps people and the environment; and nationalism subverts common action.
>
> (Raskin, 2016, p. 44)

Given this diagnosis, a plausible change trajectory involves a long-term horizon – much of the 21st century in most GTI exercises – and, "in even the most benevolent transition from the modern to the planetary … bad things are bound to happen along the way" (Falk, 2016, p. 1). Keeping people motivated on such a long and winding road depends on the emergence of a new imaginary: a perception of and commitment to "Earthland." Raskin is optimistic though about the prospect of this happening, because:

> [Gradually, awareness of the] objective entanglement also enlarges the subjective space of consciousness. Expanding the latticework of connection brings awareness of our place in a planetary nexus, nurturing our sense of responsibility to one another, to future generations, and to fellow creatures in a vibrant planetary fabric. This historical condition nurtures emergent values – solidarity, well-being, and ecocentrism – and institutions that reflect the need for democratic global governance and economies that give priority to social equity and community cohesion, human fulfillment and the healing of nature. … The expectation that contemporary circumstances will kindle a correlative adjustment in worldview grounds the "hope hypothesis."
>
> (2013, p. 7)

The GTI website hosts a set of commentaries on *Journey to Earthland* that raise thoughtful queries, criticisms and extensions (see, for example, Falk, 2016; Tucker, 2016). Joan Cocks (2016) expresses a sceptical admiration for Raskin's Gramscian-style optimism of the will:

> To see, in local grassroots movements around the world, the shimmering signs of a world-historical collective actor – his culturally heterogeneous but politically united Global Citizens Movement – that can struggle to transform border-obsessed nation-states and predatory economic dynamics into a post-capitalist and cosmopolitan Earthland.
>
> (Cocks, J., 2016)

She fears though that what is now emerging seems often closer to Fortress World. Mische, like Murphy, emphasizes that one cannot bypass the state or corporations and that any change path must involve close interaction with them by citizen movements. Yet, in the worlds of businesses and governments there is often massive organized opposition to proposed changes; and each progressive social movement generates a countermovement.

Mark Mazower's *Governing the world*, a similar exercise to Murphy's, reviews two centuries of moves to build forms of global governance. He notes how the United States lashed back in the 1980s against the attempts to promote a New International Economic Order through the United Nations system. It led the unleashing of market powers to crush national sovereignty elsewhere, using soft power, hard power, intergovernmental and non-governmental organizations, multinational companies, and compliant agencies to achieve its goals. While it employed a language of universalism, it often exempted itself from the new rules (Mazower, 2013, pp. 422–427). Mazower concludes that the world of capital and its dependents, dominated by the US, is incapable of dealing with its collective challenges. It has hollowed-out the states that should be essential instruments for cooperation for ensuring necessary public goods, national and global.

Glimmers of hope from Rio+20 and the SDGs?

Let us now consider which elements from these discussions appear in contemporary global negotiations and preparations, whether as signs of impasse or of change, and whether as confirmed or refuted. Where is the Policy Reform agenda going? And, if and when it encounters limits and contradictions, does it offer any bases for longer-term transformations?

The 1992 Rio Summit on Environment and Development, the Earth Summit, grew out of a generation of analyses of the need to channel economic development along environmentally sustainable paths. It produced the visionary Agenda 21 but relatively little machinery for follow-up; and the tools that did exist or were added remained within disconnected policy silos. Dodds, Laguna-Celis and Thompson (2014) describe how two decades later the successor 2012 Rio+20 summit emerged in response to growing problems and also the new ambitions, capacity and coordination amongst various middle-powers and global civil society networks cooperating via a reinvigorated United Nations system.

The mismatch between available environmental analyses and actual environmental policy relative inaction, intra- and inter-nationally, led to a campaign for a Rio+20 Summit. It was initiated by the Lula government in Brazil in 2007 and gained backing from various developing countries. Acceptance was won through the UN system in 2009, with the Summit scheduled for 2012. This step reflected too the rise of the G20 in place of the G7 as the predominant "inner circle" inter-governmental coordination forum (the G7 consists of the largest rich market economies; the G20 includes in addition the BRICS (Brazil, Russia, India, China, South Africa) countries and other large "emerging economies"); which in turn reflects the growing weight and assertiveness of countries like Brazil, China, India, and Mexico, the decreasing dominance and prestige of the USA after the Iraq debacle and the 2008 financial crisis, and the need for global coordination of responses to the latter and its impacts. There was also growing realization that the global development agenda, including its anti-poverty agenda, and the global environment agenda could never be effectively managed in isolation from each other. Attention to environment had to accommodate development aspirations, and attention to development had to respect environmental threats.[3] In 2010, in response to the call for suggestions for the now approved 2012 Summit, the Colombian government proposed that the Millennium Development Goals (MDGs) for 2015 should be succeeded by a Sustainable Development Goals

(SDGs) agenda (officially and more broadly, the 2030 Agenda for Sustainable Development), that would explicitly integrate the so-called "people" and "planet" agendas.

The US administration pressed to limit Rio+20 to a short meeting that would produce a brief statement of intent (Dodds et al., 2014, p. 154). Something different emerged. The US and its closest allies, such as the UK and various leading global corporations, evidently now possessed less blocking power than they enjoyed around the Rio 1992 Summit. For not only had the G7 been largely superseded by the G20 but some middle powers, not least Mexico and Brazil, supported by many developing countries, had pushed successfully to revive and extend the roles of the UN General Assembly and the UN Economic and Social Council (ECOSOC), including through use of more flexible and participatory formats. Among the resulting changes, one may note the following, which have applied also during the follow-on stage that led to the SDGs in 2015:

- The General Assembly and its constituents, the delegations of national governments to the United Nations in New York, have become more active, generating initiatives and working with the UN Secretariat to follow these up. The President of the General Assembly (each year the leader of a different delegation) channels proposed initiatives.
- Key delegations are now convened for less formal and more flexible discussions by entrepreneurial governments such as Brazil and Mexico, in New York and elsewhere. Some of these supplementary fora for preparatory work have brokered advances that previously remained impossible for years or decades within the formal channels of intergovernmental negotiations directly involving all countries. For example, argue Dodds, Laguna-Celis and Thompson (2014), the 2011 NEXUS conference convened by Germany achieved what the UN's Commission on Sustainable Development had never been able to do: initiate cross-sectoral attention to the nexus between water, energy, and food security (Hoff, 2011; Weitz et al., 2014).
- The arrangements have reportedly allowed more effective involvement of networks of smaller states, not only powerful actors like the EU but for example even for some time the alliance of Bolivarian states (known as ALBA).
- The moribund post-Rio-1992 Commission on Sustainable Development was replaced after Rio+20 by the use of an annual focused High Level Political Forum on Sustainable Development, to get global legitimacy and commitments.
- The more flexible consultative and negotiation arrangements have also included greatly increased interaction with stakeholder networks of non-governmental organizations, business, and other groups, starting long before the large civil society days that parallel the inter-government negotiations in major conferences.
- Brokering these arrangements were reportedly a generation of energetic, confident and capable global bureaucrats from "the South," and of

entrepreneurial Southern government officials such as Colombia's Paula Caballero, initiator of the SDGs.[4] Many of these seem to be not only skilful managers, but exponents of the type of empathetic global vision and emotional-relational maturity highlighted by Lindner (2016) as central for advancing a *Great Transition*.

There remain, nevertheless, huge gaps in what was agreed at Rio+20. The outcome document was short on ambition, time-frames, goals and targets on greening economies. It excluded, for example, a sustainability reporting requirement for listed companies, even though that had already been introduced in Brazil, South Africa, and Malaysia and was in preparation for the EU (Dodds et al., 2014, pp. 190–191).

However, argue Dodds and his associates, the whole Rio+20 and Agenda 2030 processes have involved several fundamental steps of reorientation, that could lead much further. First, there was not only a shift in declared commitment, to sustainable development rather than merely GDP, and an agreement to negotiate new goals, but intensification of the institutional shifts just mentioned, in terms of who is involved and who drives the global negotiation processes. The institutional architecture is more adequate now for follow-up than after the Agenda 21 of 1992 or the 2000 Millennium Declaration, and has more capacity to integrate across numerous agencies, channels and sub-agendas. Particularly noteworthy are the revival of ECOSOC as a key UN organ, that is supported by a strengthened UN Department of Economic and Social Affairs that has merged several UN Secretariat bodies, and operates in partnership with annual High Level Political Fora attended by heads of government. These fora represent a revival also of the General Assembly. Rio+20 paved the way too for the reform and revival of the United Nations Environment Programme, which had never previously become a body with universal membership and authority.

Second, the Millennium Development Goals were produced in the years around 2000 exclusively by Northern donor-dominated agencies – notably the OECD and the World Bank – with little wider consultation and negotiation. They became central because of the predominance at that stage of international aid. Changing global relations have meant that far wider involvement was demanded for preparation of the successor global development agenda. As recounted by Dodds, Donoghue and Roesch (2016), the SDGs notion derives from the South and its negotiation was never controlled by the North. It was initiated and pushed by Colombia, together with some Southern partners including Peru and Guatemala (and later, to widen the political base, the United Arab Emirates). After the notion was accepted in 2013, a preparatory process was devised that found a workable balance between having an illegitimately small preparatory group and an unwieldy group of all nations. A working group was set up, with 30 seats but that would be open in its discussions and open to representations. After inability to agree on which 30 countries would fill the seats, they became shared by 70 members, thanks to agreements within UN regions to share seats among sets of countries. The result was a downgrading of the relative power of traditional blocs. Individual countries were more able to speak out and not only operate through blocs.

This Open Working Group (2013–14), energetically co-chaired by the Hungarian and Kenyan ambassadors to the UN, allowed an unusual combination of flexibility and yet depth of involvement, and of mutual learning and cooperation within and across countries and with stakeholder groups and specialist agencies. Thus, third, Dodds, Donoghue and Roesch (2016) describe a forest of lines of communication and arenas of consultation and lobbying – in thematic areas and via stakeholder groups, intra-nationally, regionally and globally. Many informal arenas supplemented the formal procedures, increasing trust and crossing borders; for example, a "Friends of..." group of governmental delegations was active for each thematic area, and the World Resources Institute organized many confidential informal fora to develop ideas.

These more open and flexible working methods were continued during the deliberations in and around the UN General Assembly during 2014–2015 to prepare the SDGs summit of September 2015: intensive and informal mingling of governments, agencies, stakeholder "Major Groups" and other stakeholders. The two "co-facilitators," the ambassadors of Ireland and Kenya, became de facto chairs of the process. Exceptionally, their drafting authority was never questioned, and for example their idea of including a visionary opening statement, not only writing a UN-style bureaucratic document, was adopted.

While allowing creative handling of the form, tone and details of the document, the G77 countries (including, not least, India) plus China in effect took control of the process by refusing to diverge substantially from the main points of the Open Working Group report, rejecting the pressure from high-income countries to downgrade the status of the report to being just one advisory input. The processes and efforts employed in the OWG gave its report a new legitimacy. Thus, almost uniquely for a global negotiation, agreement was reached on the draft SDGs document in New York several weeks before the heads of states summit in Rio that provided formal endorsement; there were no further gains to be had for any party by further dispute. It is, suggest Dodds, Donoghue and Roesch (2016), the most encompassing and universal policy agenda ever adopted, and was produced by the most participatory preparatory process. As claimed by the outgoing UN Special Representative on Migration, Peter Sutherland: "the Sustainable Development Goals posit that States have a collective interest and responsibility to ensure that the most vulnerable people and populations, including migrants and refugees, are not left behind by economic, social and environmental progress" (United Nations, 2017, para.10).

What does this story show? First, it is one of several processes that show some scope for advance by using mechanisms other than, and prior to, full-scale global intergovernmental negotiations: including building up of "soft law," sharing of proposed good practices and standards, and "'minilateralism', whereby small groups of interested States work together to develop and implement new ideas that can then be debated, and perhaps adopted, in more formal settings" (United

Nations, 2017, para. 89, referring to Naim, 2009). Second, though, the current detailed content of the SDGs is certainly underwhelming; and even more so for the indicators that have as yet emerged, which may dominate the active attention of many participating governments and agencies. However, third, the efforts behind Rio+20 and the SDGs seem to show, at least at the level of an extensive set of global and national elites and organizations of many types, some significant commitment to "Earthland," not just a self-interested gaming: a self-perception as global citizens while being also local, national and regional members. This offers part of a basis for moving further. It is far as yet from fulfilling many of the requirements for global reorientation proposed in the models of Raskin and Murphy; but those models do not expect instant fulfilment. The GTI work (e.g. Raskin, 2008) hopes for a progressively unfolding series of stages, in each of which the fulfilment of some of the requirements will lead on to further responses and reactions as a succession of diverse crises erupt.

Conclusion

We noted strong reasons to be pessimistic. The global power-system that is gestating global crisis is embedded in myriad minds and institutions and subsidiary power-systems, not only through the open pulls of money power in a primarily money-dominated world. Our review of the frames and channels by which the interests of poor people are downgraded in climate change analyses illustrated how difficult reform is likely to be. Ignorance of other people, indifference and even antagonism and malice towards them, plus insouciance and wishful thinking, all render more difficult the cooperative arrangements and preparations necessary for a sustainable world. Crisis theorists suggest persuasively that only crises will bring major response, while warning that crises are liable to exacerbate some of the problems and causes.

We noted also some bases for hope. Crises can be prepared for. Many relevant resources for response and reform exist already. The creation of the 2030 Global Agenda shows a growing global infrastructure of governmental, private and civil society actors, networks and values, that are active in various ways to reform the global power-system and to restrain its destructive and damaging tendencies. This may provide stepping-stones to mitigate and navigate the series of crises that can unfold. How far can the SDGs in particular grow into an effective focus for attention and mobilization? Dodds, Donoghue and Roesch propose that: "The SDGs have been framed as a 'we the people[s]' document, rather than using only a state-centric approach. Its achievement will lie in their ability to inspire people around the world" (2016, p. 128). Whether this ability grows seriously over time, as happened with the Universal Declaration of Human Rights, remains to be seen, and worked on. Global developments since the emergence of the SDGs accord and the Paris climate accord in 2015 have been largely negative. Phases of retrogression are expected, however, in the crises-and-transition literatures. Retrogressions and the crises they will promote can be part of the mechanisms of change.

Notes

1 This section extends and amends ideas in Gasper (2015).
2 See Drijfhout et al. (2015) on abrupt shifts in climate systems that are projected to emerge from temperature rises even below 2°C.
3 Correspondingly, Tariq Banuri of Tellus/the Stockholm Environment Institute became director of the Rio+20 secretariat. The work of the Global Sustainability Panel in 2010–2012, led by Kevin Rudd (Australia's Foreign Minister) and Jairam Ramesh (India's Environment Minister), helped to spread the realization that little progress could be made in managing climate change without approaching this as part of a global development pact, argue Dodds et al. (2014).
4 Sha Zukang (China), as head of the UN's Department of Economic and Social Affairs, authorized an open process for Rio+20 conference preparations; all important conference materials were online for registered stakeholders (Dodds, Laguna-Celis and Thompson, 2014, p. 117). His deputy Nikhil Seth (India) headed the conference secretariat and ensured cross-agency cooperation via joint task teams. Mohamed Khalil (Egypt) led the negotiations on Resolution 67/203 for implementation of Rio+20. Farrukh Khan (Pakistan) led negotiations that created the UN Environment Assembly linked to UNEP.

References

Beck, U. (2009) *World at risk*. Cambridge: Polity Press.

Cocks, J. (2016) 'Reflection on *Journey to Earthland: The great transition to planetary civilization*', Great Transition Initiative. Available at: http://www.greattransition.org/reflection/jte-joan-cocks (Accessed: 25 April 2018).

Development Initiatives. (2013) *Global humanitarian assistance report 2013*. Bristol: Development Initiatives.

Diamindis, P. and Kotler, S. (2012) *Abundance: The future is better than you think*. New York: Free Press.

Dodds, F., Donoghue, D., and Roesch, J.L. (2016) *Negotiating the SDGs*. London: Routledge/Earthscan.

Dodds, F., Laguna-Celis, J., and Thompson, L. (2014) *From Rio+20 to a new development agenda*. London: Routledge/Earthscan.

Drijfhout, S., Bathiany, S., Beaulieu, C., Brovkin, V., Claussen, M., Huntingford, C., Scheffer, M., Sgubin, G. and Swingedouw, D. (2015) 'Catalogue of abrupt shifts in intergovernmental panel on climate change climate models', *Proceedings of the National Academy of Sciences of the United States of America (PNAS)* 112(43), pp. E5777–E5786.

Falk, R. (2010) 'A radical world order challenge: Addressing global climate change and the threat of nuclear weapons', *Globalizations* 7(1–2), pp. 137–155.

Falk, R. (2016) "Reflection on *Journey to Earthland: The great transition to planetary civilization*", Great Transition Initiative. Available at: http://greattransition.org/reflection/jte-richard-falk (Accessed: 25 April 2018).

Fløttum, K., Gasper, D. and St. Clair, A.L. (2016). 'Synthesizing a policy-relevant message from the three IPCC "worlds": A comparison of topics and frames in the SPMs of the Fifth Assessment Report', *Global Environmental Change* 38, pp. 118–129.

Fraser, N. (2013) *Fortunes of feminism: From state-managed capitalism to neo-liberal crisis*. London: Verso.

Fraser, N. (2014) 'Transnationalizing the public sphere in the context of crisis', *Dies Natalis Lecture*, 7 November, Erasmus University Rotterdam.

Friedman, T.L. (2009) *Hot, flat and crowded: Release 2.0*. New York: Picador.

Friedman, T.L. (2016) *Thank you for being late: An optimist's guide to thriving in the age of accelerations*. New York: Farrar, Straus & Giroux.

Gallopín, G. (2016) 'Reflection on *Journey to Earthland: The great transition to planetary civilization*', Great Transition Initiative. Available at: http://www.greattransition.org/reflection/jte-gilberto-gallopin (Accessed: 25 April 2018).

Gasper, D. (2011) 'Pioneering the human development revolution: Analysing the trajectory of Mahbub ul Haq', *Journal of Human Development and Capabilities* 12(3), pp. 433–456.

Gasper, D. (2012) 'Climate change: The need for a human rights agenda within a framework of shared human security', *Social Research* 79(4), pp. 983–1014.

Gasper, D. (2015) 'Precautionary? Principled?', in Di Paola, M. and Kamal, D. (eds.), *Climate change and human rights: The 2015 Paris conference and the task of protecting people on a warming planet*. London: Wiley-Blackwell (Global Policy).

Gasper, D. and St. Clair, A.L. (eds.) (2010) *Development ethics*. Farnham: Ashgate.

Gómez, O.A. (2014) 'What can the human development approach tell us about crisis?', *International Journal of Social Quality* 4(2), pp. 28–45.

Hamilton, C. (2010) *Requiem for a species: Why we resist the truth about climate change*. London: Earthscan.

Hirschman, A. (2014) *Development projects observed*. Washington, DC: Brookings Institution Press.

Hoff, H. (2011) *Understanding the nexus*. Background Paper for the Bonn 2011 Conference on the Water, Energy and Food Security Nexus. Stockholm Environment Institute, Stockholm.

Houtart, F. (2010) 'The multiple crisis and beyond', *Globalizations* 7(1–2), pp. 9–15.

IPCC (2012) *Managing the risks of extreme events and disasters to advance climate change adaptation: A special report of working groups I and II of the Intergovernmental Panel on Climate Change*. Cambridge: Cambridge University Press.

ISSC-UNESCO (2013) *World Social Science Report 2013, changing global environments*. Paris: OECD and UNESCO.

Kingsnorth, P. (2014) 'The four degrees', *London Review of Books* 36(20), pp. 17–18.

Klein, N. (2007) *The shock doctrine*. Harmondsworth: Penguin.

Kubiszewski, I., Costanza, R., Anderson, S., and Sutton, P. (2017) 'The future value of ecosystem services: Global scenarios and national implications', *Ecosystem Services* 26 (A), pp. 289–301.

Laszlo, E. (2010) *The chaos point: The world at the crossroads*. London: Piatkus/Little, Brown.

Lindner, E. (2016) 'Reflection on *Journey to Earthland: The great transition to planetary civilization*', Great Transition Initiative. Available at: http://www.greattransition.org/reflection/jte-evelin-lindner (Accessed: 25 April 2018).

Marshall, G. (2016) *Don't even think about it*. London: Bloomsbury.

Martin, J. (2007) *The meaning of the 21st century*. London: Eden Project/Random House.

Mazower, M. (2013) *Governing the world: The history of an idea, 1815 to the present*. Harmondsworth: Penguin.

Mulgan, T. (2011) *Ethics for a broken world: Imagining philosophy after catastrophe*. Montreal: McGill-Queen's University Press.

Murphy, C. (2005) *Globalization, institutions and development*. London: Routledge.

Naim, M. (2009) 'Minilateralism', *Foreign Policy*, 21 June.

Nolt, J. (2011) 'Themed section on: How harmful are the average American's greenhouse gas emissions?' *Ethics, Policy and Environment (2011)*, 14(1), pp. 3–42.

Nolt, J. (2013) "Replies to critics of 'How harmful are the average American's greenhouse gas emissions?'", *Ethics, Policy & Environment* 16(1), pp. 111–119.

O'Hagan, E.M. (2017) 'Climate optimism has been a disaster', *The Guardian*, 21 September. Available at: https://www.theguardian.com/commentisfree/2017/sep/21/climate-optimism-disaster-extreme-weather-catastrophe.

Owen, T. (2014) 'Human security mapping', in Martin, M. & Owen, T. (eds.), *Routledge handbook of human security*. London: Routledge, pp. 308–318.

Raskin, P. (2008) 'World lines: A framework for exploring global pathways', *Ecological Economics* 65(3), pp. 451–470.

Raskin, P. (2013) 'Game on: The basis of hope in a time of despair', *Development* 56(1), pp. 86–92.

Raskin, P. (2016) *Journey to Earthland: The great transition to planetary civilization*. Boston: Tellus Institute.

Raskin, P., Banuri, T., Gallopín, G., Gutman, P., Hammond, A., Kates, R. and Swart, R. (2002) *Great transition: The promise and the lure of the times ahead*. Boston, MA: Stockholm Environment Institute and Tellus Institute.

Sen, A.K. (1981) *Poverty and famines*. Oxford: Clarendon.

Shue, H. (2006) 'Ethical dimensions of public policy', in Moran, M., Rein, M. and Goodin, R.E. (eds.), *The Oxford handbook of public policy*. Oxford: Oxford University Press, pp. 709–728.

Stern, N. (2007) *The economics of climate change: The Stern review*. Cambridge: Cambridge University Press.

The Economist (2017) 'Breathing space', September 23, pp. 67–68.

Tucker, M.E. (2016) 'Reflection on *Journey to Earthland: The great transition to planetary civilization*', Great Transition Initiative. Available at: http://www.greattransition.org/reflection/jte-mary-evelyn-tucker (Accessed: 25 April 2018).

Tyner, J. (2016) *Violence in capitalism: Devaluing life in an age of responsibility*. Lincoln: University of Nebraska Press.

United Nations (2012) *The future we want*, A/RES/66/288. New York: United Nations.

United Nations (2015) *Transforming our world: The 2030 agenda for sustainable development*, A/RES/70/1. New York: United Nations.

United Nations (2017) *Report of the special representative of the Secretary-General on migration*, A/71/728. New York: United Nations.

Voorhoeve, J. (2011) *Negen plagen tegelijk: Hoe overleven we de toekomst?* Amsterdam: Atlas Contact.

Weitz, N., Nilsson, M. and Davis, M. (2014) 'A nexus approach to the Post-2015 agenda: Formulating integrated water, energy, and food SDGs', *SAIS Review of International Affairs* 34(2), pp. 37–50.

World Bank (2010) *World Development Report 2010: Development and Climate Change*. Washington, DC: World Bank.

World Bank (2012) *Turn down the heat: Why a 4°C warmer world must be avoided*. Washington, DC: World Bank.

World Health Organization (WHO) (2002) *The World Health Report 2002*. Geneva: WHO.

World Health Organization (WHO) (2014) *Quantitative risk assessment of the effects of climate change on selected causes of death, 2030s and 2050s*. Geneva: WHO.

12 The permanent crisis of development aid

Wil Hout

The thinking about development is permeated by notions of crisis, which derive from the awareness that there is an immense – and unacceptable – inequality in life chances between people born in different parts of the world (Selwyn, 2014, pp. 10–13). Many people in rich countries understand the development crisis in terms of a moral obligation to come to the assistance of fellow human beings living in poor countries. Development assistance has thus been an important component of the development project ever since the end of World War II (cf. McMichael, 1996).

It is ironic that development assistance, which has been inspired by the perceived crisis in development, has itself shown signs of crisis during most of its existence. Despite spending several trillions of USD in aid, the United Nations (2016) estimated that the number of extremely poor people had risen to 836 million by 2015. Seven decades after World War II ended, the adoption of the Sustainable Development Goals was deemed necessary to end global poverty, among other goals. Various observers have voiced scepticism not only about the achievements of aid in fighting global poverty, but also about its impact in other domains. Migration may serve as a useful example: in a review of research evidence accumulated over 45 years, Clemens (2014) showed that aid programmes and trade agreements have not curbed migration flows. Development assistance seems to have had almost the opposite effect from that intended because, by stimulating growth, aid practices may actually have stimulated migration.

The perceived failure of aid to make a difference in ending poverty has led to repeated crises of legitimacy. At various moments over the past 70 years, critical analyses emphasizing the perverse effects of aid became quite popular. Writing on aid since the 1960s, development economist P.T. Bauer was adamant in his criticism. He claimed:

> Foreign aid does not affect the major factors behind the material backwardness of underdeveloped countries; the continued poverty of the recipient countries is therefore not surprising. The policies of the recipient countries have on the whole served to retard or obstruct possible advance.
>
> (Bauer, 1966, p. 58)

Contemporary aid critics emphasize that the crisis of development assistance is inherent to the notion of aid itself. A staunch critic, Dambisa Moyo, suggests that aid is caught in a vicious cycle:

> With aid's help, corruption fosters corruption, nations quickly descend into a vicious cycle of aid… This is the … cycle that chokes off desperately needed investment, instils a culture of dependency, and facilitates rampant and systematic corruption, all with deleterious consequences for growth. The cycle that, in fact, perpetuates underdevelopment, and guarantees economic failure in the poorest aid-dependent countries.
>
> (Moyo, 2009, p. 49)

Not only aid sceptics, but also supporters of aid, recognise that giving aid carries inherent risks. Former Dutch Minister for Development Cooperation, Bert Koenders, was aware of such risks but emphasized that the legitimacy of development assistance should be enhanced by developing tools for risk management. In his policy note, *Our Common Concern*, Koenders suggested:

> Active involvement in fragile states certainly entails risks when it comes to achieving results and accounting for expenditure. However, neither the international community nor the Netherlands can afford to do nothing. The price is simply too high. This requires a flexible approach that allows considered risks to be taken. It is however important that risks be properly identified and managed as far as possible.
>
> (MFA Netherlands, 2007, p. 43)

This chapter reviews the permanent crisis of aid as a failure to learn *from* the crisis (Jessop, 2015, p. 257). Instead of drawing lessons that question the legitimacy of aid, which would require a reflexive attitude and an analysis of deeper causes of the difficulty to address development problems, the aid industry usually responds to doubts regarding aid effectiveness by highlighting the *symptoms* of crisis and measures to remove them. Accounts about corruption in aid-receiving governments are normally approached with routinized crisis management techniques, aimed at curbing the practices of corrupt officials (cf. Jessop, 2015, p. 247). Common responses include the temporary cessation of aid flows, the choice for different aid-delivery channels and/or the support to "public integrity" agencies, but these generally fail to address the underlying problem.[1]

The aid industry typically responds to development crises with new schemes that are aimed at solving the previous crisis. As Mosse (2011, p. 4) has put it aptly, policy making on development assistance has become characterized by "a technicalization of policy and the centralization of expertise." Based on their technical understandings of development issues, policy-makers focus on the symptoms of crisis, and typically adapt existing aid schemes to deal with emerging realities. Innovations, which reflect the attempt to learn *about* crises, remain within the parameters set by the dominant aid paradigm, and fail to address fundamental causes such as increasing global inequality. Accordingly, I seek to interpret the major innovations introduced into the aid architecture since the rise of the Post-Washington Consensus in the mid-1990s (cf. Fine et al., 2003) as elements of the permanent crisis of aid. The innovations, embodied in projects on the Millennium and the Sustainable Development Goals, were responses to the legitimacy crisis that affected development assistance. The MDG and SDG projects can both be understood as responses by the aid community to the crisis construals regarding development assistance that had become influential in public debate.

The evolution of development aid

The evolution of development aid can be interpreted in terms of the *thinking about* and *practices in* development policies. Although these two elements are closely interconnected, it makes sense to distinguish them for analytical purposes.

Thinking about development

The history of development thinking has often been narrated as a sequence of "paradigms" or schools of thought. Starting at the end of the 1940s, with the advent of decolonization, "development" became the central feature of the policies adopted by international organizations and Western governments. Inspired by the success of the Marshall Plan for the reconstruction of Europe, development aid was provided to the governments of countries in the global South. The identification of "gaps" between the existing and desired situation in the developing world became a hallmark of development thinking. Early scholars, such as Rosenstein-Rodan (1943), emphasized industrial investment in countries with a large agricultural surplus workforce as the key element of a "big push" to industrialization. This idea was later generalized into the persistent notion of the financing gap between required investment and available resources, which development assistance could help to fill and thereby contribute to economic growth (cf. Easterly, 1999). Other scholars offered their own disciplinary explanations. Modernization theorists identified an institutional gap created by the difference between social mobilization and participation (cf. Sangmpam, 2007); education economists highlighted the human capital deficit (cf. Hanushek, 2013); and scholars of science and technology noted the existence of a knowledge and technology gap (cf. Cherlet, 2014). An "interventionist paradigm" (Reusse, 2002, pp. 6–7), which interpreted the task of development agencies as gap-filling, became dominant in the thinking about development and aid.

The most recent incarnation of the thinking about development aid has been shaped by the World Bank, which was the driving force behind the so-called Washington Consensus and Post-Washington Consensus. Both emphasized the role of the market in development. While the Washington Consensus was aimed at eliminating the state in the development process through liberalization, privatization, and deregulation, the Post-Washington Consensus stressed the building of institutions for markets under the guidance of a regulatory state (Williamson, 1993; World Bank, 2001).

Practices in development[2]

Development professionals are the day-to-day shapers and implementers of policies that are devised against the background of the paradigmatic divide between strands of development thinking. Interpretations of aid practices have stressed that development practitioners operate as an "epistemic community," a "network of professionals with recognized experience and competence in a particular domain and an authoritative claim to policy-relevant knowledge within that domain or issue-area" (Haas, 1992, p. 3). Their world is one of "travelling rationalities" (Mosse, 2011, p. 3) or even "travelling orthodoxies," where "development policy remains resolutely optimistic about the power of its favoured approaches and institutional solutions, overplaying the impact and blurring the distinction between normative representations and actual outcomes" (ibid., p. 7).

Development professionals are generally motivated to improve the lives of people in poorer countries, and wish to contribute to poverty reduction or eradication. They share a set of understandings of and values about development, acquired as part of their (academic) training. Yet, they work in agencies subjected to a principal-agent logic (Killick, 1997; Gibson et al., 2005, pp. 43–44). The agencies, who are the "agents" of policy implementation, may have preferences that differ from those of their "principals" (ministers or senior civil servants at the helm of a department). Typically, development agencies are interested in maintaining their budget, while their principals may be more concerned about the efficient implementation of aid programmes or the avoidance of risks.

Development agencies are operating in complex and risk-prone environments, where development outcomes depend on many different factors beyond their control. The agencies have great difficulty in measuring their organizational outputs and the performance of their staff. For this reason, staff assessments rely on the success of disbursing allocated aid funds (the practice of "moving money" as described by Easterly, 2002, p. 228), the quality of project and programme management, and the production of reports and memorandums (Carlsson et al., 1994, p. 5; Gibson et al., 2005, pp. 134–135, 154–156). Evaluations are common features of the cycle of aid projects and programmes, but they take much time in preparing and their conclusions tend to get published long after the end of the evaluated activities so their contribution to learning is quite limited (Gibson et al., 2005, pp. 151–154).

The fact that development agencies assess staff mainly based on observable outputs has generated a technical outlook on development, where bureaucratic measurements take precedence over engagement with the local situation in the aid-recipient countries (cf. Eyben, 2011, pp. 153–156). Although staff of the aid agencies realise that the political realities in target countries have an important influence on the impact of their programmes, the "institutional ethos" of their organization leads them to focus on narrow development targets rather than broader social transformation (Unsworth, 2009, p. 890).

The sense of a continuing crisis in the development project, epitomized by the persistence of poverty despite the spending of billions on aid, has led the donor community to embrace the notion of "aid effectiveness." With the accompanying trend of "managing for results," which is an important component of New Public Management, the adoption of the aid effectiveness agenda has induced aid agencies to specify what results they are achieving with the national aid budget (cf. Cooke and Dar, 2008; Gulrajani, 2011). A prime example of this trend has been the UK's Department for International Development (DFID), which specifies its objectives in the so-called Single Departmental Plan (Department for International Development, 2015). DFID's report to Parliament 2015–2016 provided a quantitative estimate of how many people were supported by DFID's assistance across eight sectors: wealth creation; poverty, vulnerability, nutrition and hunger; education; health; water, sanitation and hygiene; governance and security; humanitarian assistance; and climate change (Department for International Development, 2016, p. 5).

The technocratic outlook in the epistemic community of aid practitioners leads them to focus on how immediate problems with aid delivery can be remedied (learning *about* crisis) rather than reflect on what are the more fundamental causes of the legitimacy crisis of development aid (learning *from* crisis). Over the past decades, learning about the crisis of aid has resulted in two responses: expansion and connection. The first response has led to attempts to *expand* the agenda beyond a narrow understanding of aid, by getting away from projects targeting concrete development outcomes. The second element has been to *connect* the goals of development policy to other policy priorities, in order to make aid more palatable to popular constituencies.

Expansion and connection of the aid agenda

Learning from the crisis of the 1990s

The mid-1990s were, in many respects, a high point in the permanent legitimacy crisis of development aid. As a first sign of this crisis, spending on development assistance by donor countries and multilateral agencies experienced a decrease in real terms as of 1992, and reached the 1990 level again only in 2003 (see figure 12.1). Next to this, the World Bank, which had been at the vanguard of the Western development project since the end of World War II, came under increasing attack because it had become obvious that its development precepts, rolled out over the developing world since the oil crisis of the late 1970s, had not worked. On the contrary, a decade and a half of

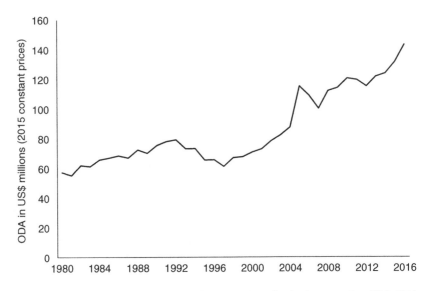

Figure 12.1 Official development assistance from OECD to developing countries, 1980–2016
Source: Organisation for Economic Co-operation and Development 2017b.

structural adjustment policies, implemented as part of the Washington Consensus, resulted in increased poverty in many countries across the global South. The most obvious challenge to the World Bank was the "50 Years is Enough" campaign, which was a protest movement of a great number of international NGOs against the policies of the Bretton Woods institutions. Targeting the annual meeting of the Boards of Governors of the World Bank and IMF in Madrid in 1994, the campaign questioned the legitimacy of the policies implemented by the two international financial institutions, and resulted in a clear sense of crisis at these institutions (Fox and Brown, 1998, pp. 7–9).

Both the Organisation for Economic Co-operation and Development (OECD) and the World Bank demonstrated their ability to learn *from* the crisis of development aid experienced in the 1990s (Jessop, 2015, p. 257) by contributing to a paradigmatic change in development assistance policy. The new mantra that was introduced by the two organizations emphasized *poverty reduction* and *aid effectiveness*. The attention to poverty reduction took the place of economic growth, as it was recognised that "the complexity and diversity of growth experiences are not amenable to simplistic policy prescriptions" (World Bank, 2005, p. xiii). In his first year as President of the World Bank, James Wolfensohn called for "a broader, more integrated approach to development – a new paradigm, if you will." To this he added that "[p]overty reduction remains at the heart of everything we do" (Wolfensohn, 2005, p. 51). The emphasis on aid effectiveness was an attempt to offer an alternative for the output-oriented focus that had characterized much of the aid agenda since the adoption of the 0.7 per cent target for official development assistance by the United Nations General Assembly in 1970. Thus, the OECD's Development Assistance Committee (DAC) started to stress the need for a results orientation in development assistance (Development Assistance Committee, 1996, pp. 2–3).

The two elements of the revised approach to aid were expressed in two key policy initiatives: the DAC Ministers' statement on Development Partnerships in the New Global Context (Development Assistance Committee, 1996, pp. 19–20) and the World Bank's Comprehensive Development Framework (Wolfensohn, 1999). The DAC Ministers adopted the report *Shaping the 21st Century*, which had a set of international development targets at its core that were to become the basis for the Millennium Development Goals. In doing so, the DAC Ministers chose to expand the development agenda to include explicitly agendas on social protection and sustainable development, which would go beyond traditional development targets. The report formulated the following targets for development assistance policies that would need to be reached by 2015 (Development Assistance Committee, 1996, pp. 9–11):

* Reduce extreme poverty by one-half;
* Achieve universal primary education and gender equality (by eliminating gender disparity in primary and secondary education), improve basic health care (to reduce infant, child and maternal mortality) and create universal access to reproductive health services; and
* Implement national policies for sustainable development.

The tools for achieving the new international development targets also demonstrate the expansion of the development assistance agenda beyond traditional donor-recipient interactions. *Shaping the 21st Century* introduced "ownership" as a key principle for aid delivery: development programmes should henceforth be based on "agreement and commitment from developing country partners, through their own national goals and locally-owned strategies" (Development Assistance Committee, 1996, p. 9). Further, the DAC Ministers argued that the broader context of aid would require that "development co-operation and other policies must work together" and that external development partners must coordinate their activities among each other (Development Assistance Committee, 1996, pp. 14–15).

The Comprehensive Development Framework, which the World Bank adopted during Wolfensohn's term as President, contributed to the expansion of the aid agenda. As Wolfensohn put it in a speech to the World Bank's Board of Governors in 1998:

> While focusing on the macroeconomic numbers or on major reforms like privatization, we have ignored the basic institutional infrastructure, without which a market economy simply cannot function. ...Too often we have focused too much on the economics, without a sufficient understanding

of the social, the political, the environmental, and the cultural aspects of development.

(Wolfensohn, 2005, p. 115)

The framework Wolfensohn (2005, p. 116) advocated is illustrative of the expansion of the development assistance agenda. It included a focus on five distinctive elements: a "good governance" agenda, targeting transparency, voice, anti-corruption and government effectiveness; the regulatory framework of a market economy, including property rights, competition law and legal protection; social policies focused on inclusion in sectors such as health and education; public services and infrastructure; and policies for environmental sustainability.

An important addition, and in many senses a catalyst in terms of agenda-setting, was the work done on aid effectiveness at the World Bank's Development Research Group, led by staff such as David Dollar and Lant Pritchett (see World Bank, 1998). The World Bank's Chief Economist at the time, Joseph E. Stiglitz, was clear about the intention of the Bank's key publication on the issue:

> Foreign aid is as much about knowledge as it is about money. Helping countries and communities generate the knowledge that they need for development is a prime role of assistance. And aid itself is a learning business that continually evolves as lessons of success and failure become clear. *Assessing Aid* is a contribution to this ongoing learning process. It aims to contribute to a larger "rethinking of aid" that the international community is engaged in – a rethinking in two senses. First, with the end of the cold war, there is a group that is "rethinking aid" in the sense of questioning its very existence in a world of integrated capital markets. In response to this trend, we show that there remains a role for financial transfers from rich countries to poor ones. Second, developing and developed nations alike are reconceptualising the role of assistance in light of a new development paradigm. *Effective aid supports institutional development and policy reforms that are at the heart of successful development.*
>
> (World Bank, 1998, p. ix, italics added)

The "powerful narrative" that resulted from the World Bank's Development Research Group (Court and Maxwell, 2005, p. 721) was summarized in the conclusion that "aid works" (World Bank, 1998, p. 2). This conclusion was taken up quickly in the epistemic community of professionals working on development assistance (cf. the examples mentioned in Hout, 2007). According to a former Director General at the UK's Department for International Development, it was crucial that "the story line was presented simply and clearly: move to the poverty efficient aid allocation model by supporting countries where people were poorer and where good policies ensured better returns on the aid dollar" (Ahmed, 2005, p. 767). Apart from pointing out the

World Bank's success in promoting the lessons on aid selectivity drawn from the research by Dollar and his team, Ahmed argued that the researchers were highly motivated to get their lessons across within the donor community: "it was clear that their objective was not simply to add to the stock of human knowledge about aid effectiveness, it was to change the way aid was allocated in practice" (ibid.). The success of the new narrative that "aid works" implied that the aid agenda had been connected effectively to the neo-institutionalist agenda of the Post-Washington Consensus, whose main protagonist was Joseph Stiglitz (see Stiglitz, 1998).

The DAC and World Bank's initiatives coalesced ultimately into the main initiative of the global development community, the Millennium Development Goals, which were contained in the United Nations Millennium Declaration of September 2000 (United Nations, 2000), and took on board notions of governance-based aid selectivity. The Millennium Declaration expanded the development assistance agenda by specifying a series of broad-based objectives across seven elements: peace, security and disarmament; development and poverty eradication; protecting our common environment; human rights, democracy and good governance; protecting the vulnerable; meeting the special needs of Africa; and strengthening the United Nations. The MDG agenda revolved around eight operational targets, to be achieved by 2015, in most cases taking the situation in 1990 as a benchmark (United Nations, 2017):

1. Eradicate extreme poverty and hunger (halve the proportion of people in extreme poverty; achieve full employment and decent work; and halve the proportion of people suffering from hunger);
2. Achieve universal primary education;
3. Promote gender equality and empower women (by eliminating gender disparity in education);
4. Reduce child mortality;
5. Improve maternal health (reduce maternal mortality by three quarters; and achieve universal access to reproductive health);
6. Combat HIV/AIDS, malaria and other diseases (halt and reverse the spread of HIV/AIDS; achieve universal access to HIV/AIDS treatment; and halt and reverse the incidence of malaria and other major diseases);
7. Ensure environmental sustainability (integrate principles of sustainable development into country policies and reverse the loss of environmental resources; reduce biodiversity loss; halve the proportion of people without access to safe drinking water and basic sanitation; and improve the lives of at least 100 million slum dwellers); and
8. Develop a global partnership for development (develop an open and non-discriminatory trading and financial system; address the needs of least developed and landlocked countries and small island developing states; deal with the debt problems of developing countries; provide access to affordable drugs in developing countries; and make available benefits of new technologies).

Learning from the MDG experience

The adoption of the Millennium Development Goals seems to have served the purpose of the international development aid community to get development higher on the political agenda. As is evident from Figure 12.1, the overall level of official development assistance from OECD member countries more than doubled in real terms between 2000 and 2016. The MDGs also seem to have instilled new dynamism among politicians and leading civil servants, witness the attention given to a series of high-level meetings following the Paris Declaration on Aid Effectiveness (2005). The Accra Agenda for Action (2008) and the Busan Partnership for Effective Development Co-operation (2011) were agreed as follow-up to the Paris Declaration and, since the meeting in Busan, the Global Partnership for Effective Development Co-operation (GPEDC) has served as a platform for discussions among representatives from governments, business, private foundations and civil society. Since 2011, the GPEDC has held high-level meetings in Mexico (2014) and Nairobi (2017).

When judged on its own merits, as documented in the UN's final report on the implementation of the MDGs, the MDG project seems to have achieved good results.[3] Yet, the report concluded:

> Despite enormous progress, even today, about 800 million people still live in extreme poverty and suffer from hunger. Over 160 million children under age five have inadequate height for their age due to insufficient food. Currently, 57 million children of primary school age are not in school. Almost half of global workers are still working in vulnerable conditions, rarely enjoying the benefits associated with decent work. About 16,000 children die each day before celebrating their fifth birthday, mostly from preventable causes. The maternal mortality ratio in the developing regions is 14 times higher than in the developed regions. Just half of pregnant women in the developing regions receive the recom-mended minimum of four antenatal care visits. Only an estimated 36 per cent of the 31.5 million people living with HIV in the developing regions were receiving ART in 2013. In 2015, one in three people (2.4 billion) still use unimproved sanitation facilities, including 946 million people who still practise open defecation. Today over 880 million people are estimated to be living in slum-like conditions in the developing world's cities.
>
> (United Nations, 2015a, pp. 8–9)

The UN's MDG report can be interpreted as a political attempt to provide a discursively selective reinterpretation (see Jessop, 2015, p. 257) of the gains made between 2000 and 2015. The return to the crisis rhetoric seems to have been useful in legitimizing the search for a follow-up to the MDG project, as a way of stressing that the MDGs were unfinished business, and a new phase was necessary to continue addressing the development crisis.

Already in 2011, four years before the end date of the MDG project, UN Secretary-General Ban-Ki Moon established the UN System Task Team on the Post-2015 UN Development Agenda. In its report, the task team pointed to several trends that characterise the persistent development crisis: the growth of global inequalities in income, wealth and knowledge; the continuing pressure on food, land, health and education systems as a consequence of continuing population growth; environmental degradation and natural disasters; conflict and insecurity; and deficits of governance and accountability (UN System Task Team on the Post-2015 UN Development Agenda, 2012, pp. 12–19). The task team's conclusion was that, "[g]oing forward, greater interdependence among countries and the global challenges ahead will require a truly global agenda for development, with shared responsibilities by all countries" (ibid., p. 19). This approach is clearly in line with the type of learning described above: the task team attempted to expand the agenda to include issues apart from aid, and connect the development agenda to issues of sustainability, conflict and governance.

The outcome of the discussion on the post-2015 agenda was the embrace of the Sustainable Development Goals (SDGs) as successors to the MDGs. The SDGs comprise 17 broad goals and 169 targets. Next to focusing on the objectives already included in the MDGs, such as those related to poverty, hunger, decent work, education, health and sustainable development, the SDGs also concern access to energy, the reduction of inequalities, use of the oceans and seas, as well as peace, justice and strong institutions (United Nations, 2016). The preamble of the General Assembly's resolution on the so-called 2030 Agenda for Sustainable Development illustrates the expansive nature of the SDGs, as well as the attempt to connect development goals to objectives in other domains. In the first place, the preamble indicates the SDGs are meant to be global and universal: "All countries and all stakeholders, acting in collaborative partnership, will implement this plan." Next, the preamble connects "sustainable development" across many policy domains, by specifying that the SDGs "are integrated and indivisible and balance the three dimensions of sustainable development: the economic, social and environmental" (United Nations, 2015b).

The response embodied in the adoption of the SDGs has expanded the development agenda almost beyond recognition. As the quote from the preamble to Agenda 2030 makes clear, the responsibility for implementation of the agenda has been spread over "all countries and all stakeholders." Making "all" responsible for action may amount to making no one clearly accountable. Diffusing responsibilities may easily give rise to collective action problems. The risk of making "all" responsible is that the inevitably political nature of decision making on which countries and groups should contribute most to realising the SDGs has been obscured. Further, the "solution" of connecting the development goals to the fundamental transformation of the economic, social and environmental system has made the SDG agenda so broad that it is difficult to see how specific responsibilities towards developing countries should be implemented.

Conclusions

This chapter discussed some changes in the international development agenda that were introduced since the mid-1990s. It argued that development aid has been permeated by a sense of crisis, which is the consequence of the nature of the project's agenda. The main objectives of the project, which are understood in terms of improvements in the quality of life of the world's poor and disadvantaged, are not easily achievable, and often appear to be receding as real achievements are being reported.

The awareness of the crisis of development assistance has led to a dual approach. On the one hand, the aid agenda has been expanded to practices and approaches that go beyond the narrow understanding of development assistance. On the other hand, the response to the feelings of crisis resulted in connecting development objectives to policy priorities in other domains.

Over time, the development industry has shown clear practices of learning about the legitimacy crisis affecting aid. This form of learning has focused on the symptoms rather than the deeper causes of the legitimacy crisis. One domain-specific response to the sense of crisis is manifested in the search for new and successful narratives. Over the past two decades, the narratives have tended to focus on seemingly "new" development goals. Thus, the rediscovery of poverty in the mid-1990s led to the focus of the MDGs on objectives related to social protection. The awareness of increasing problems of environmental sustainability and biodiversity resulted in the addition of a wide range of objectives as part of the SDG agenda. The expansion of the development agenda and its connection to other policy priorities seems to have produced a narrative that was successful in the short run, witness for instance the Make Poverty History campaign that mobilized millions of people in 2005 (cf. Harrison, 2010). While this way of learning about crisis may solve immediate issues related to the perceived legitimacy of aid, it does not address more fundamental causes related to the persistence of global poverty, which are related to the power differences characterizing international political and economic relations.

The technocratic orientation of the epistemic community of development professionals has limited its reflexive potential. The focus on short-term solutions (expressed in the learning *about* crisis) seems to stand in the way of more fundamental reflection, which would be the prerequisite to systemic learning *from* crisis. The introduction of new global development narratives – embedded in the MDGs for the 2000–2015 period, and the SDGs for 2015–2030 – may have been a proper response to the scepticism about aid at the beginning of the twenty-first century. Given the limited attention to the structural barriers to reform of the international trade and financial system, it is unlikely such initiatives may offer a long-run solution for the legitimacy crisis of aid.

Notes

1 A well-documented case was the corruption scandal involving the Office of the Prime Minister of Uganda in 2012. Budget support was suspended in response to allegations about the misuse of funds that were allocated to support post-war reconstruction of Northern Uganda (Tran and Ford, 2012). Compared to previous years, the total of official development assistance provided to Uganda was somewhat lower in 2012 and 2013, but returned to its previous level in 2014 (Organisation for Economic Co-operation and Development, 2017a).

2 Parts of this section draw on Hutchison et al. (2014, Chapter 3).

3 The analysis of the effects of globalisation by Milanovic (2016, p. 11) have shown, however, that there are huge global inequalities in gains in real per capita income since the late 1980s. Moreover, the analysis of Fukuda-Parr et al. (2014, p. 5) of the "power of numbers" of the MDGs show that, although the MDG project appears to have generated much attention to certain development issues, the framing of the goals has had unintended consequences of simplification and support for techno-cratic strategies, which meant a reversion in development thinking away from more human-development oriented approaches.

References

Ahmed, M. (2005) 'Bridging research and policy', *Journal of International Development*, 17 (6), pp. 765–773.

Bauer, P.T. (1966) 'Foreign aid: An instrument for progress?', *Foundation for Economic Education*. Available at: https://fee.org/articles/foreign-aid-an-instrument-for-pro gress/ (Accessed: 25 April 2018).

Carlsson, J., Köhlin, G. and Ekbom, A. (1994) *The political economy of evaluation: International aid agencies and the effectiveness of aid*. New York: St Martin's Press.

Cherlet, J. (2014) 'Epistemic and technological determinism in development aid', *Science, Technology & Human Values*, 39(6), pp. 773–794.

Clemens, M.A. (2014) 'Does development reduce migration?', in Lucas, R.E.B. (ed.) *International handbook on migration and economic development*. Cheltenham: Edward Elgar, pp. 152–185.

Cooke, B. and Dar, S. (2008) 'Introduction: The new development management', in Dar, S. and Cooke, B. (eds.) *The new development management: Critiquing the dual modernization*. London: Zed, pp. 1–17.

Court, J. and Maxwell, S. (2005) 'Policy entrepreneurship for poverty reduction: Bridging research and policy in international development', *Journal of International Development*, 17(6), pp. 713–725.

Department for International Development (DFID) (2015) *Single departmental plan: 2015 to 2020*. London: DFID.

Department for International Development (DFID) (2016) *Annual report and accounts, 2015–16*. No. HC329. London: DFID.

Development Assistance Committee (DAC) (1996) *Shaping the 21st century: The contribu-tion of development co-operation*. Paris: OECD.

Easterly, W. (1999) 'The ghost of financing gap: Testing the growth model used in the international financial institutions', *Journal of Development Economics*, 60(2), pp. 423–438.

Easterly, W. (2002) 'The cartel of good intentions: The problem of bureaucracy in foreign aid', *Journal of Policy Reform*, 5(4), pp. 223–250.

Eyben, R. (2011) 'The sociality of international aid and policy convergence', in Mosse, D. (ed.) *Adventures in Aidland: The anthropology of professionals in international development.* New York: Berghahn, pp. 139–160.

Fine, B., Lapavitsas, C. and Pincus, J. (2003) *Development policy in the twenty-first century: Beyond the post-Washington consensus.* London: Routledge.

Fox, J.A. and Brown, L.D. (1998) 'Introduction', in Fox, J.A. and Brown, L.D. (eds.) *The struggle for accountability: The World Bank, NGOs, and grassroots movements.* Cambridge, MA: MIT Press, pp. 1–48.

Fukuda-Parr, S., Yamin, A.E. and Greenstein, J. (2014) 'The power of numbers: A critical review of Millennium Development Goal targets for human development and human rights', *Journal of Human Development and Capabilities,* 15(2–3), pp. 105–117.

Gibson, C.C., Anderson, K., Ostrom, E. and Shivakumar, S. (2005) *The Samaritan's dilemma: The political economy of development aid.* Oxford: Oxford University Press.

Gulrajani, N. (2011) 'Transcending the great foreign aid debate: Managerialism, radicalism and the search for aid effectiveness', *Third World Quarterly,* 32(2), pp. 199–216.

Haas, P.M. (1992) 'Introduction: Epistemic communities and international policy coordination', *International Organization,* 46(1), pp. 1–35.

Hanushek, E.A. (2013) 'Economic growth in developing countries: The role of human capital', *Economics of Education Review* 37, pp. 204–212.

Harrison, G. (2010) 'The Africanization of poverty: A retrospective on "Make Poverty History"', *African Affairs,* 109(436), pp. 391–408.

Hout, W. (2007) *The politics of aid selectivity: Good governance criteria in US, World Bank and Dutch foreign assistance.* London: Routledge.

Hutchison, J., Hout, W., Hughes, C. and Robison, R. (2014) *Political economy and the aid industry in Asia.* Basingstoke: Palgrave Macmillan.

Jessop, B. (2015) 'The symptomatology of crises, reading crises and learning from them: Some critical realist reflections', *Journal of Critical Realism,* 14(3), pp. 238–271.

Killick, T. (1997) 'Principals, agents and the failings of conditionality', *Journal of International Development,* 9(4), pp. 483–495.

McMichael, P. (1996) *Development and social change: A global perspective.* Thousand Oaks: Pine Forge Press.

Milanovic, B. (2016) *Global inequality: A new approach for the age of globalization.* Cambridge, MA: Harvard University Press.

Mosse, D. (2011) 'Introduction: The anthropology of expertise and professionals in international development', in Mosse, D. (ed.) *Adventures in aidland: The anthropology of professionals in international development.* Oxford: Berghahn, pp. 1–31.

Moyo, D. (2009) *Dead aid: Why aid is not working and how there is another way for Africa.* London: Allen Lane.

MFA Netherlands (2007) *Our common concern: Investing in development in a changing world.* Policy Note Dutch Development Cooperation 2007-2011. The Hague: Ministry of Foreign Affairs of the Netherlands, Development Corporation.

Organisation for Economic Co-operation and Development (OECD) (2017a) 'Aid (ODA) disbursements to countries and regions (DAC2a)', OECD.Stat. Available at: http://stats.oecd.org/Index.aspx?datasetcode=TABLE2A (Accessed: 25 September 2017).

Organisation for Economic Co-operation and Development (OECD) (2017b) 'Disbursements of ODA in constant prices of 2015', Query Wizard for International Development Statistics (QWIDS). Available at: http://stats.oecd.org/qwids (Accessed: 25 September 2017).

Reusse, E. (2002) *The ills of aid: An analysis of third world development policies.* Chicago: University of Chicago Press.

Rosenstein-Rodan, P.N. (1943) 'Problems of industrialization of Eastern and South-Eastern Europe', *Economic Journal*, 53(210/211), pp. 202–211.

Sangmpam, S.N. (2007) 'Politics rules: The false primacy of institutions in developing countries', *Political Studies*, 55(1), pp. 201–224.

Selwyn, B. (2014) *The global development crisis.* Cambridge: Polity.

Stiglitz, J.E. (1998) *More instruments and broader goals: Moving toward the post-Washington consensus.* Helsinki: UNU World Institute for Development Economics Research.

Tran, M. and Ford, L. (2012) 'UK suspends aid to Uganda as concern grows over misuse of funds', *The Guardian*, 16 November.

United Nations (2000) *United Nations millennium declaration.* A/RES/55/2. New York: United Nations.

United Nations (2015a) *The Millennium Development Goals report 2015.* New York: United Nations.

United Nations (2015b) *Transforming our world: The 2030 agenda for sustainable development.* A/RES/70/1. New York: United Nations.

United Nations (2016) 'Sustainable development goals', Available at: http://www.un.org/sustainabledevelopment/sustainable-development-goals (Accessed: 25 September 2017).

United Nations (2017) 'We can end poverty: Millennium Development Goals and beyond 2015', Available at: http://www.un.org/millenniumgoals (Accessed: 25 September 2017).

United Nations System Task Team on the Post-2015 UN Development Agenda (2012) *Realizing the future we want for all: Report to the Secretary-General.* New York: United Nations.

Unsworth, S. (2009) 'What's politics got to do with it? Why donors find it so hard to come to terms with politics, and why this matters', *Journal of International Development*, 21(6), pp. 883–894.

Williamson, J. (1993) 'Democracy and the "Washington Consensus"', *World Development*, 21(8), pp. 1329–1336.

Wolfensohn, J.D. (1999) 'A proposal for a comprehensive development framework. A discussion draft', World Bank, January 21. Available at: http://web.worldbank.org/archive/website01013/WEB/0__CO-87.HTM (Accessed: 25 September 2017).

Wolfensohn, J.D. (2005) *Voice for the world's poor: Selected speeches of the World Bank president James D. Wolfensohn, 1995-2005.* Washington, DC: World Bank.

World Bank (1998) *Assessing aid: What works, what doesn't, and why.* New York: Oxford University Press.

World Bank (2001) *World Development Report 2002: Building institutions for markets.* Washington, DC: World Bank.

World Bank (2005) *Economic growth in the 1990s: Learning from a decade of reform.* Washington, DC: World Bank.

13 Crisis, common sense and the limits to learning in EU external governance

Zuzana Novakova

On EU external governance

In general, governance aims to coordinate relations of complex interdependence through continuing dialogue to promote negotiated consent, resource sharing, and concerted action without excessive reliance on markets or top-down command. Inside the European Union (EU), it mainly takes the form of multi-level governance based on continuing efforts to identify mutually beneficial joint projects from a wide range of possible projects, redefine them as circumstances change, monitor progress in relation to agreed objectives, mobilize resources controlled by different actors, and organize the material, social, and temporal conditions required to achieve them. In its external relations, EU governance occurs in the shadow of hierarchy in the sense that the relation is asymmetrical and EU institutions and member states hold the upper hand in setting the terms for inclusion of other economies or access to benefits from the EU. In many ways, the EU's development has been a project to transform the geostrategic dynamics in post-war Europe by converting the troubled relations between rival states and economies from one of political enmity and zero-sum competition into forms of partnership. Two key steps in this regard concern transforming the domestic regimes in post-dictatorial Southern Europe and transforming the regimes in Central Eastern Europe following the fall of the Berlin wall. The key mechanism in both cases was conditional inclusion, i.e. integration based on meeting specific criteria and targets. The same public philosophy has underpinned the EU's external policy – especially in its immediate "neighbourhood" – with a view to including external partner countries into the EU's internal policy framework based on their commitment to, and implementation of specific reforms. This would be a stepwise process as partner countries are drawn more closely into concentric circles of EU governance (Zielonka, 2006). The policy umbrella for conducting relations between the EU and sixteen of its neighbours in Eastern Europe as well as in Southern Mediterranean, the European Neighbourhood Policy, became the most ambitious "external governance project" (Lavenex, 2004; Lavenex and Schimmelfennig, 2010) or "governance export" policy (Gänzle, 2009). Depicted in the famous phrase of "sharing everything but institutions" (Prodi, 2002), which in practical terms foremost refers to shared market space, shared regulatory framework and political dialogue. At the core of this form of relations remains the EU single market: the biggest carrot offered to partner countries being a stake in the common market, which implies trade liberalization while adopting the norms, rules and regulations of EU's complex acquis communautaire (Buschle, 2014).

Analogous to EU relations with other neighbouring countries, the bilateral relations between the EU and Ukraine envisioned a deep and comprehensive free trade area based on Ukraine's adoption of norms and regulations of EU's complex acquis communautaire. In this sense, "sharing everything but institutions" (Prodi, 2002) refers mostly to market liberalization: around 80% of the Association Agreement is formed by trade-related provisions (van der Loo, 2016) and the (legislative, human, financial and technical) resources dedicated to this area by far outnumber any other field of cooperation. Nonetheless, although governance is supposed to provide better ways of dealing with complex problems and to avoid issues of market and state failure, it is not immune to its own crisis tendencies. I illustrate this from the crisis in and/or of EU-Ukraine relations. This challenged the inherited policy approach to governance based on conditional, stepwise inclusion.

When "crisis in" meets "crisis of": EU external governance and the Ukrainian crisis

"The world will never be the same again" said Herman van Rompuy, European Council President in reacting to events in Ukraine (ECFR, 2014). Indeed, the eruption of what came to be labelled as the "Ukraine crisis" opened a range of challenges for the established order on the European continent. It threatened the security order, called the prevailing ideational hegemony into question, and highlighted critical issues about the model(s) of economic and political integration in the region. The EU leadership was quick to label it "the gravest threat to the European security order in decades," one in which the "stability of the European house itself was at stake" (van Rompuy, 2014d). In the words of the head of the European Commission, this particular crisis "threatens the very security of Europe internally and the very idea of what Europe stands for internationally…The situation in Ukraine is a test of [EU] capability and resolve to stabilise our neighbourhood" (Barroso, 2014a, 2014d).

The events in Ukraine challenge the EU's modus operandi in the region, expressed in the European Neighbourhood Policy (ENP), leading to a review of the EU's core policy and strategy in the aftermath of this crisis. This initially took the form of an external crisis moment – a crisis in its neighbourhood – to which the EU needed to develop an appropriate but more or less routine foreign policy response. It quickly threw established procedures into question, triggering a crisis of governance regarding Europe's neighbourhood policy as a situation in which the EU leadership is not only unsure about how to achieve its aims but even about what their aims should be in a situation of radical uncertainty. As such it opens space for a review of the established routines of

ENP, of EU's external governance policy, in broader terms that went well beyond EU-Ukraine relations. In other words, rather than being a mere crisis in, the recent governance and security crisis in Ukraine largely speaks to the general crisis of EU external governance vision and practice vis-à-vis its neighbourhood.

This is precisely our interest here: how the need to manage the crisis in Ukraine speaks to a structural crisis of EU policy in the region. In this sense, the "Ukraine crisis" highlights some symptoms of an internal crisis of EU's external governance project, a project embodied in the so-called ENP. The core assumptions upon which this vision builds were already in crisis before it faced the situation in Ukraine – in a structural crisis fostered by the disparity between an ideational persistence within the policy approach on one hand and a changing materiality of the political economy in wider Europe on the other. This said, the "Ukraine crisis" simply highlighted and exemplified this crisis within EU's policy.[1]

It should perhaps be remarked here that the Ukraine crisis remains only one among a series of crisis moments within the spatial-temporal scope of EU's external governance. There is little doubt that previous crisis situations, such as the events of the Arab spring, presented a massive challenge to the models and beliefs at the heart of the ENP and that lessons from such previous crises found their way into the recent policy and strategy review. In this sense, what makes the Ukraine crisis distinct is that it led to the longest and most public review of the framework for EU's engagement in the neighbourhood (European Commission and High Representative of the EU for Foreign Affairs and Security Policy, 2015a) and that, as such, it opened ground for an analogous review of the whole of EU's security strategy and its principles of external action.

This chapter looks at the encounter of these two crises. It moves thematically from how the EU institutional leadership interpreted the *crisis in* Ukraine and how the learning from this crisis was converted into new policy guidelines, to the deeper level of a structural *crisis of* the EU external governance project. Conceptually this case-study sheds light on how meaning-making limits the scope for thinking about policy measures in crisis response. Distinguishing between "crises in" and "crises of" a system, we approach the Ukraine crisis both as a *crisis in* EU foreign policy and as the *crisis of* a particular form of EU foreign policy in the region (i.e. crisis of the EU external governance project). The first section unpacks the contested meaning-making about the Ukraine crisis, as documented in the communicative discourse of key EU institutional players. Which symptoms of the crisis were in focus and how these were interpreted speaks to learning in and about the crisis. Section two focuses on two core policy and strategy guidelines that have undergone a major review in the aftermath of the Ukraine crisis. Has any learning from the crisis been reflected in these reviews? How and on what level? Together, these two sections narrate a story of how the learning in, about and from the crisis is shaped by deeply ingrained imaginaries which emerged from the past materiality. While those past conditions might be gone forever, the imaginaries continue to shape the EU crisis management up to today through sediments of thoughts which they left behind in the hegemonic common sense in the social domain of EU's policy for near abroad.

Meaning-making in the EU institutional terrain: Ukraine as a crisis in EU's external governance

It is precisely in reaction to these crisis-like events in neighbouring countries that the role of ideas in EU policy can best be observed. As the EU needs to respond to these changing realities, sense-making comes to the forefront as "the processes through which events and phenomena are noticed, interpreted, and reacted to as crisis events" (Gephart, 2007, p. 127). It is crucial to the process of managing radical uncertainty. Gephart (2007) highlights two types of interruptions that trigger sense-making and changes in cognition: a new event that is not expected and an expected event that does not occur.

From the perspective of EU's neighbourhood policy, the events in Ukraine demanded interpretation on both fronts. Starting with a much-anticipated event that did not occur, namely, the failure of the Ukrainian administration to sign the Association Agreement with the EU despite years of preparation in anticipation for that event. In terms of EU's prestige, this association agreement was conceived to be one of the biggest success stories of its policy in the region. When a partner country backtracked on the agreement, it challenged the core idea and the whole finalité of EU's policy towards the region: the core EU assumption about the attractiveness of its free trade offer.[2] On the other hand, the crisis was further stirred by events that were totally unexpected: first, the annexation of Crimea by Russia, a breach of the liberal international order on the European continent, and the outbreak of open conflict in Eastern Ukraine, involving domestic separatist forces with military support from Russia.

Sense-making is about imposing labels on these events in ways that suggest plausible acts of managing the crisis (Tsoukas and Chia, 2002, p. 573, cited in Weick, Sutcliffe and Obstfeld, 2005). It involves a range of diverging narratives brought forward inside a policy domain in a situation when the diverse players are unsure about how to read the situation and unsure what their interest is therein. Sense-making is thus crucial to synthetizing what is going on in Ukraine, what is the part the EU should react to, how the EU should react to it. In effect, its outcomes constrain action.

The next stage in meaning-making is that, from the variety of interpretations at hand, only one or a few are retained and, in consequence, shape crisis communication and policy (re)action. As highlighted in the first part of this book, "a crisis is never a purely objective, extra-semiotic event or process that automatically produces a definite response or outcome. This objective moment of crisis in itself becomes socially and historically relevant through the moment of subjective indeterminacy" (Jessop, this volume). There is "no one-to-one relation between event and symptom" (ibid.), the role of ideas comes to the forefront in interpreting the crisis. It is these ideas, narratives and imaginaries[3] that in turn shape the crisis response by selectively focusing on or ignoring elements of the situation. The narratives on what constitutes the (symptoms of the) crisis are at the core of any crisis-management efforts, often involving crisis displacement. The processes of meaning-making within the social domain of EU's neighbourhood policy can delineate the scope of imaginable responses that will get considered by the ultimate decision-takers. Hence, to a large degree, meaning-making delineates the boundaries for the subsequent policy action and the related policy learning from the crisis.

Schmidt (2008) distinguishes two types of discourses in policy making: coordinative discourse, which involves the internal – often closed-door – coordination among policy-makers about a policy issue, and communicative discourse about the issue to their external counterparts. While the former involves a range of conflicting narratives and processes of deliberation, the latter often reflects the framing which builds up on those deliberations. The coordinative discourse, which occurs among the diverse players within the domain of the respective EU policy, contains a variety of crisis readings that surge in the messy initial stage of sense-making: at the outbreak of the crisis in Ukraine, a variety of (sometimes conflicting) narratives and imaginaries could be traced in the social domain of EU's Ukraine policy, or EU's neighbourhood policy at large. This comprises the EU executive institutions and their ecosystem: the world of think-tanks, umbrella organizations of different organized interests (unions, committees and platforms), political parties and European party fractions. The core of formal coordination happens among the policy makers in the European Council, reflecting the range of narratives across the whole social domain.

Given the scope of this chapter, I cannot follow the whole initial range of interpretations here. Rather, I am interested in critically examining "only" those elements from the initial sense-making that were selected and retained in the way that elites frame and narrate the crisis to a wider audience. That is the communicative discourse emanating from relevant EU institutions, to their external partners, or to the general public, which documents outcomes of meaning-making. As this initial variety was narrowed down into a common interpretation of the crisis, communications from EU institutions to various audiences indicate how the key institutional players in Brussels interpreted and construed these events. The communicative discourse (Schmidt, 2008) from the EU institution to the outside audiences reflects, in particular, those ideas that were selected and retained from the initial range of interpretations. To insulate the official narrative of the crisis events, we followed all the statements and speeches by the representatives of the EU-level executive institutions:[4] the head of the European Commission, the President of European Council, the EU Commissioner for Neighbourhood, and the head of European External Action Service. Our focus here is on the institutional representatives as "elites [who] are a rarefied embodiment of their society's culture" (Bruff, 2008). This is not to suggest that the discourses they bring forward are necessarily formulated from within the confines of their institutional environment. Rather these discourses "traverse all parts of the social world – including state and society" (Bruff, 2008, p. 9), i.e. they are diffused in the culture of the wider society in which these institutions are embedded. This is the social field of Europe's policy in the near abroad.

This discourse coming from these institutions suggests the formation of a widespread agreement on the need to distinguish two stages of Ukraine crisis. First the crisis *of* the political regime that followed the U-turn of president Yanukovic on the trade agreement with the EU is, at its core, a conflict between European values and post-soviet despotism. The mass protests on Maidan square were read as "an expression of the *majority* of the people in Ukraine in favour of European values" (van Rompuy, 2014a), or even more as a "political and cultural shift" following "a clash of two political cultures" powered by the "yearning for a European way of life" (van Rompuy, 2014c). That the popular uprisings were an expression of a widespread aspiration of Ukrainian people to be part of the EU, to Europeanize the country. As narrated by the EU Commissioner for Enlargement and European Neighbourhood "the Vilnius Summit[5] is continuing on the streets and squares of Kiev" (Füle, 2013). The EU institutional leadership even labelled the civilian protests a "civilization choice" that brings the country on "right side of history" (van Rompuy, 2014b).

Such understandings reaffirm by default the appropriateness of the EU's external governance policy: in response to the perceived mass demands in Ukraine, the EU's leadership emphasized that the union "believes in close political ties and in the power of shared prosperity" (van Rompuy, 2014e). "The Ukrainian people stood for freedom, democracy and rule of law. These are precisely the values which are the core of the European Union. And, Europe will always stand with countries willing to engage in this path" (Barroso, 2014c). In light of such interpretations, the association agreement with the EU is "an attractive strategic vision" (Barroso and van Rompuy, 2013), which provides the "blueprint for political and economic reforms" (Ashton, 2013).

Second, the security crisis on the Ukrainian territory was seen as a crucial symptom of the outdated thinking of other actors, in particular the obsolete way of reading the world in terms of Cold-war style geopolitics of sphere of influence, to which the Russian leaders and administration allegedly still cling. Russian leadership is portrayed as "trying to turn the Eastern Partnership into something it is not: a zero-sum game, a battle for the creation of past centuries' spheres of influence in the neighbourhood. This has never been the case. We will not adopt this mind-set" (Füle, 2014). The self-perception of the EU representatives posits the Union as the contrary to this logic, where the EU is about choice and freedom. "The outdated logic of the balance of powers is dangerous and wrong and we need to replace it with a logic of cooperation and dialogue" (Barroso, 2014a).

This perceived disparity between the geopolitical focus of Russia and the value-based orientation of the EU has been a recurrent theme in the communicative discourse at various occasions. Following from the first premise above, the people in Ukraine opted to be like the EU. Therefore, the interference by

Russia is an act of "bullying, and then outright aggression" which "would mean the explicit return of spheres of influence or limited sovereignty to the European continent" (Barroso, 2014d), which has no space in today's world and should be discouraged. Hence negative conditionality is imposed on Russia in the form of sanctions, aiming to socialize Russia into EU's vision of international order through the means of economic pressure. A series of sanctions and a reassessment of cooperation all aim at "bringing Russia to the conclusion that it is better to have a positive, constructive relation with Ukraine and the EU" (Barroso, 2014b). "Russia needs to choose if it wants to be a strategic partner or a strategic rival. If Russia chooses the latter path, to be a rival, we would all collectively have to take the political, economic and security consequences" (ibid.).

As such, the elite discourse is an "expression of a conception of the world" (Gramsci, 1996, p. 384), a reflection of how they conceive the context in which the events of Ukraine crisis unfold. Such narratives of the Ukraine crisis provide a necessary background for understanding which crisis construal guided the subsequent EU attempts at crisis management. In other words, why the EU reacted to these events the way it has reacted. Such a reading of the Ukraine crisis through the terms and expectations set by EU policy paradigm formulated back in early 2000s[6] has persisted despite many acknowledgements of the changing global context. It is worth noting that these interpretations have not been affected at all by the change in the EU institutional leadership[7] in late 2014.

Ukraine and the crisis *of* EU's external governance

Faced with the developments in Ukraine, the limits of the EU's policy were highlighted – putting a range of question marks over the external governance projection as such. By challenging the established routines and "normal responses," the crisis in Ukraine provides a peek into crisis of EU's policy in the region. It opened a Pandora's Box of challenges to the root ideas of EU's external governance, to the model of extending the EU common market beyond its own borders as the main stability measure in its neighbourhood, the idea of shared security and prosperity through the extension of EU's acquis communautaire into the states and markets surrounding the EU external borders. The Ukraine crisis is, in this sense, the latest in a series of crises in the socio-spatial area that the EU calls its neighbourhood. The most ambitious policy of EU's external governance has been repeatedly faced with its own in structural crisis, where the need for reform kept coming back to the table in ever-shorter intervals. The metaphor of "ring of friends" so inherently characteristic of the EU's policy approach (European Commission, 2003) needed to face the reality of the "ring of fire" in the neighbourhood (Hahn, 2015). The notion of constant crisis proved to be the new normal in Europe's neighbourhood (Dennison and Witney, 2015). The need for constant policy reviews highlighted there is something inherent in this policy that might not be best suited to deal with the processes unfolding in the region – these mostly get noticed as crisis events. Over the last 13 years, the policy has been undergoing review after review, each of which reacted to changing realities in the neighbourhood. Yet there has been little change in this policy of external governance projection. The ENP of today remains a product of an era in which it was conceived, namely, the time of EU's big-bang enlargement in 2004 and colour revolutions in Eastern Europe. The same policy ideas that characterized the world back then keep defining today's ENP, despite the numerous strategic reviews and relaunches. In 2008 new elements were added, including the Eastern Partnership to promote cooperation and enhance the transformation of the six countries at Europe's Eastern border. In 2011 two reviews of the policy rapidly followed each other in reaction to the events of the so-called Arab spring. What connects all these review topics is, above all, radical uncertainty.

For the EU policy in the region, its encounter with the crisis in Ukraine brought a wide-ranging process of reflection,[8] reconsidering the established routine of conducting EU's neighbourhood policy in this region, hence the review of its policy. With growing recognition that it was not a crisis that can be managed through established crisis-management routines in EU's external action and the numerous calls for a deeper rethink of EU policy approach, strategy and even security doctrine. What was initially perceived as an external crisis becomes also a prime example of an internal crisis of established routines: a situation of great ambiguity in which actors' perceptions of their own self-interest become problematized (Blyth, Seabrooke and Widmaier, 2007). Faced with the unfolding events, the EU's institutional agents were not only unsure about how to achieve their interests but unsure of what their interests are in a world that is not directly observable. Such fundamental uncertainty makes the institutional terrain more favourable to ideational contestation: ideas become both object and resource of political power struggles over different forms of interpretation of the situation, over knowledge in the construction of political realities. Faced with the events of "Ukraine crisis," the EU institutional terrain becomes a battleground for framings of the situation which might in turn shape all subsequent policy responses.

At the same time, a formal change in the EU leadership occurred in late 2014, coinciding with the height of crisis in Ukraine and providing a prime opportunity for critical reflection and a rethink of previous attempts at crisis management. The new leadership acknowledged the urgency of addressing the crisis of EU policy in this respect. The new Commission President Juncker made a promise to reassess the ENP in the first year of his mandate, in order to equip the EU foreign policy (FP) with a vision and tools to better manage the crises in the neighbourhood.

What followed was a major review of strategy and programmatic documents, a process of reflection unprecedented in the history of EU FP, with a consultation opened to a wide range of stakeholders including the general public. "The ENP has not always been able to offer adequate responses to these recent developments, nor to the changing aspirations of our partners.

Therefore, the EU's own interests have not been fully served either," states the consultation paper (European Commission and High Representative of the EU for Foreign Affairs and Security Policy, 2015b). "The sense of a process of review is evaluating what didn't work. Self-criticism will be part of it" (Gotev, 2015). A year later, a review of the overall global strategy for the EU's foreign and security policy was launched in an analogous manner and similar rhetoric from the EU institutional leadership.

The announcements of both strategy reviews referred to the Ukraine crisis and acknowledged the internal insufficiencies of the pre-crisis EU policy in addressing it. If we search for reflections of learning from this crisis on the institutional level, the new strategic policy guidelines resulting from these reviews are the best starting point to examine how this learning speaks to the troubled ideational structure of EU's external governance project. Following Peter Hall's classification, three levels of generalization of (cognitive) ideas are relevant to the dynamics of EU response to the crisis in Ukraine: (1) policy solutions fostered by policy makers, (2) programmes as more general frames of reference allowing actors to situate the policy measures (these basically define the problems to be solved by policies), (3) public philosophies or worldviews (*Weltanschauungen*) that organize ideas, values and principles of knowledge and society and hence undergird the policy solutions and programmes but often remain as unarticulated background knowledge (Hall, 1993). While specific policy measures and tools reflect the first order of ideas (the policy instruments); the crisis communication speaks to second and third order ideas (to the programmatic level and the *Zeitgeist*, the paradigm within which such policy is shaped).

The more we move up Hall's classification, the more does past learning that has been thrown into the crisis tend to persist intact. Comparison of the discourse in the relevant strategy formulations from 2003–2004 versus 2015–2016[9] reveals that changes in approach and established routines were limited to the level of policy instruments. The further we move up the ladder of generalization of ideas, the more do policy visions remain self-similar, despite all the rhetorical claims about changing context. If the new security strategy and the new neighbourhood policy do reflect any institutional learning from the crisis, then this learning remains heavily influenced by the past learning thrown into these crises.

Table 13.1 depicts the ideas that form the core of EU external governance under ENP, classified in terms of Hall's three levels of generalization. The ideas that dominated the ENP at the time of its conception in the early 2000s are retained at the core of the EU's "new" neighbourhood policy "reformed" and "reviewed" in light of the Ukraine crisis. The paradigmatic idea of transformation through EU external governance remains untouched. It is essentially embodied in market integration and translated into the programme of association for neighbouring countries. Amid a declared shift of aims from transformation to stabilization,[10] however, the strategy to achieve the aim remains broadly the same. In practical terms, the programmatic framework of neighbourhood relations remains one of extensive adoption of acquis

Table 13.1 Shifts in European Neighbourhood Policy

ENP 2004 (building upon EUSS 2003)	ENP 2015 (opening way to EU GS 2016)

Paradigm:
 Transformation through EU external governance and security through interconnection
 How:
 . . .based on market integration (harmonization with EU internal market rules) and good governance type of reforms (efficiency, extension of market mechanisms, transparency and "watchdog" type of civil society)
    Ultimate aim: building an area of shared stability and prosperity based on shared values ("safer Europe in a better world")
	Paradigm:
	 Stabilization through EU external governance in cases where the regime is interested in such cooperation (i.e., the Ukraine case) and inside-out perspective
	 How:
	 . . .based on market integration (harmonization with EU internal market rules) and promotion of good governance (efficiency, extension of market mechanisms, transparency and "watchdog" type of civil society)
	    Ultimate aim: security through interconnection, specifically in areas of interest to EU domestic security ("security starts at home")

(Overarching) programme: Association (extensive adoption of acquis communautaire, with the finalité of implementing deep and comprehensive free trade agreements with neighbouring countries)	**(Overarching) programme**: Association remains the key programme No change in finalité for those willing to move forward with association, but more space for flexible sectorial cooperation with those disinterested in association

Policy instrument:
 Conditionality ("more for more": more trade and aid for more reform)
    Tools: political dialogue, conditional financial aid, technocratic action plans
	Policy instrument:
	 Conditionality with updated principles for those pursuing association. Less conditionality and more flexible forms of cooperation with those disinterested in association
	    Tools: political dialogue, conditional financial aid, technocratic action plans now centred on implementation of Association Agreement

Sources: Communication from the European Commission, European Neighbourhood Policy: Strategy Paper, COM(2004)373 final versus the Review of the European Neighbourhood Policy (JOIN(2015) 50), A Secure Europe in a Better World: European Security Strategy (DOC78367/2003) versus the new A Global Strategy for the European Union's Foreign and Security Policy (June 2016)

communautaire, with the finalité of "sharing everything but institutions" through a deep and comprehensive free trade area between Ukraine and the EU.[11] Such policies highlight the reaffirmation of inherited policy measures, which build upon inclusion of Ukraine into the concentric circles of EU's external governance.[12]

In this sense, the EU response to the Ukraine crisis remains confined within the programmatic and paradigm scope of the much earlier EU policy of external governance, even though the logic of this approach has been blamed for triggering the Ukraine crisis[13] in the first place. Put bluntly, while the EU leadership labels it the biggest existential crisis for Europe as we know it and concedes that the world is not the same after Ukraine crisis (ECFR, 2014), the policy paradigm of the EU is to maintain the same approach as back in the early 2000s when Europe faced no existential crisis of this scale.

The comprehensive review of EU's strategy reflects limited institutional learning, where the higher order ideas remain intact. In the Ukraine crisis, which was a point of fundamental insecurity for EU policy in the region, there was clearly more space for ideational contestation than ever before. It is all the more remarkable, therefore, that there has been such strong ideational continuity underpinning the EU external governance policy. The processes of meaning-making remained confined within the overall paradigm that guides EU's external governance vision, even as the Ukraine crisis opened grounds to fundamentally challenge this paradigm. And this all occurred despite a growing recognition that the strategy and policy were crafted within a different context and seem no longer suitable for today's realities.

What we see here is this ideational continuity despite changing materiality: some social imaginaries persist intact and guide interpretations of the Ukraine crisis,[14] albeit rooted within the past material relations no longer applicable to explanation of the world today. In narrating their own version of the crisis, as diverse players strive to render their version hegemonic, they need to somehow speak to the hegemonic common sense and engage with the residues of thoughts left behind by past versions of common sense that remain sedimented in the particular social domain of EU's neighbourhood policy. Any social groups seeking to render their version of the events, their vision hegemonic "must engage with these sediments of thought ingrained in existing policies and institutional arrangements" (Bruff, 2008, pp. 10–11).

The need to interact with the sediments of thoughts left behind by past common sense narrows down the possible scope of compossible interpretations of Ukraine crisis, forms a predisposition for highlighting certain symptoms while interpreting them from within a particular paradigm. Sedimented ways of thinking limit the scope for new readings and restrict the space for learning from the crisis. Some inherited ways of thinking are noticeably "naturalized" and taken for granted as interpretative frames that they become the anchors for subsequent interpretations of the situation. As legacies of past common senses, such sedimented thoughts speak to and represent past materiality. While the material (constellation of) relations that gave rise to these ideas might have changed, some of the ideational elements related to those past constellations persist.

Thus, even as past learning is thrown into crisis, the organizing frames are re-invoked as different social forces seek to make sense and attribute meaning to the crisis and hegemonize the debate of its significance and consequences. Thinking in terms of the ideational as system(s) of meanings in which ideas are embedded, the EU communicative discourse on the events in Ukraine shows how the terrain in the Brussels bubble has been pre-disposed for certain interpretations of this crisis. The already accumulated sediments of thoughts in the domain of EU's neighbourhood policy were predisposed to better accommodate certain discourses over others. Most notably, the EU institutional elites in their communications around the crisis speak to such anchors, such sediments of thought from the past (material and ideational) conditions of time of the launch of a single European common market, i.e. a time when the process of European integration met the process of neoliberalism. Three distinct lines of sedimented thoughts remain "naturally" ingrained in the discourse:

1 *Stability through interconnection.* Notions of transforming relations through inclusion largely speaks back to the particular materiality of the need for post-war economic reconstruction while containing the development of a former aggressor in a controlled way, with the transatlantic interest in stabilizing European industries deeply rooted at the heart of EU integration processes. This sediment of thought was (re)articulated within a subsequent range of common senses, including those on transforming the post-dicta-torial Southern Europe, the post-communist regimes in Central Eastern Europe, as the basis of EU's neighbourhood policy, now also rearticulated in the "inside-out" perspective within the renewed Global strategy on foreign and security policy.

2 *Interconnection through market integration,* relating back to the intertwining between the process of European integration and the process of global neoliberalism around the time of the launch of a single market by the European Community. The EU common market in its particular form of embedded neoliberalism, anything to do with the social model came to be redefined through the auspices of the market. This is a legacy from the times when neoliberal political economy was gaining ideational hegemony globally, when the European Commission was looking for a way to advance European integration and embedded the neoliberal logic in its social democratic type of network (van Apeldoorn, 2000, 2003). A product of the materiality of its own era, of time when actors like the European Roundtable of Industrialists came together to define their interests transna-tionally. This common-sense assumption remains at the heart of EU's external governance: interdependence and inclusion, foremost through integration into the EU market is the area where the EU has invested most time and channelled much of the external assistance.

3 *Reification of liberal regimes,* which speaks back to the era of perceived liberal victory (early 1990s as famously depicted in Fukuyama's end of history). An underlying assumption about an ultimate (liberal) endpoint for all transitions[15] inherited from the era when the liberal economic and political model came to be coined as the only game in the town, in a system of global governance construed around a material and ideational hegemony of the Western economies. The Ukraine crisis for the EU from this perspective was a crack leading to a breakdown of a regime, opening up to democratiza-tion. Through such lenses a range of social processes on the ground remains ignored or unrecognized. Every transition in the neighbourhood is treated as

if potentially in transition to democracy, where the EU's role is to act as a transformative partner in this respect. The liberal democratic regime is reified and objectified within EU's policy documents, conceived as the ultimate endpoint, the final station, the desirable state of affairs.

These ideational anchors survive insulated from challenges by their "natural" appearance (Cox, 1996) and thus remaining one of the key mechanisms that account for the EU's limited learning in and from the Ukraine crisis. While sense-making and meaning-making are inherently political processes, as this case study shows, it is harder to challenge higher level common sense than specific policies or their modalities. The higher we move up Hall's (1993) levels of generalization of (cognitive) ideas, the less space there seems to be for contestation. At the level of paradigms upon which policies are built, that unarticulated background knowledge and its legitimating public philosophy, the need to speak to sedimented common sense widely limits the scope for meaning-making in the crisis as well as for reflection about the crisis. In this way, the hegemonic common sense sets limits to the scope for lesson drawing from crises and policy failures and, hence, the extent of policy change.

As the diverse players strive to render their narrative and their vision part of the dominant discourse, they must engage with the sediments of thought left behind by past versions of common sense, entrenched within existing policies and institutional arrangements (Bruff, 2008). Thus, they are retained within each compossible narrative of the crisis and in so doing limit the scope of imaginable policy response. The ideational terrain in the social domain of EU's neighbour-hood policy, filled with the already accumulated sediments of thought, was predisposed to better accommodate certain interpretations of Ukraine crisis over others. This is not to say these sediments prevent change in institutions or policies overall, but as "they acquire a durability which can be difficult to overcome" (Bruff, 2008, p. 10), they are a helpful element of explaining continuity.

The case-study of Brussels' response to the contemporary conundrum of crises in Ukraine strongly speaks to the limits of learning about, in and from a crisis within the EU external governance. The ENP, which is the umbrella for all EU action in Ukraine and the most ambitious EU external governance project, has undergone four (mostly reactive) reviews, including the recent one responding to what the EU leadership labels the biggest existential crisis for Europe as we know it, one after which "the world is not the same" (ECFR, 2014). Nevertheless, the policy paradigm of the EU is to maintain the same approach as when Europe faced no existential crisis of this scale: confined within the programmatic and paradigmatic scope of the much earlier EU policy of external governance. In their communications around the Ukraine crisis, the EU institutional elites speak to sediments of thought left behind by the past material and ideational conditions. While the material relations that gave rise to these ideas might have changed, some of the ideational elements related to those past constellations persist and shape the current foreign policy wisdom, the legitimating public philosophy or worldview underpinning EU external governance paradigm. Further research endeavour is needed to conceptualize "how alternative conceptions of the world are, in effect, foreclosed by this depoliticized common-sense assumption" (Bruff, 2008, p. 97).

Notes

1 The EU's policy towards Eastern Europe, based on a Eurocentric reliance on inclusion, has been cited as a trigger for the outbreak of crisis in Ukraine. By requiring the Ukrainian elite to make a clear choice between two mutually incompatible trading blocs: (1) joining the EU's trading block through a deep and comprehensive free trade area or (2) deepening relations with its traditional partners in the region. Being required to choose between two rival geopolitical projects triggered the first in the series of events labelled as "Ukraine crisis." Dragneva and Wolczuk (2016) attributed this to negligence or misconception; conversely, Burlyuk (2017) interprets it, as an unintended consequences of EU action.

2 The provisions for establishing a so-called deep and comprehensive free trade area are at the heart of the Association Agreement, with around 80% of the heads of agreement relating to FTA regulations. Access to the EU market has traditionally been the biggest carrot offered to those neighbors who fulfill the EU's conditionality in various areas.

3 Imaginary here "refers to sets of cultural elements common to a given social group (or groups) that shape 'lived experience' and help to reproduce social relations" (Jessop, this volume)

4 For present purposes, we focus on the role of these institutions in formulating a shared understanding of the Ukraine crisis, negotiating the lowest common denominators of what the crisis is about and what it means for the EU.

5 Signing of the association agreement between the EU and Ukraine was initially planned to occur at the Vilnius Summit of the European Union in late 2013. Ahead of this summit, the Ukrainian presidential administration announced that Ukraine will not sign this agreement, due to too many conflicting interests.

6 COM(2003)104 final entitled Wider Europe – Neighbourhood: A New Framework for Relations with our Eastern and Southern Neighbours, which laid the building blocks for the EU external action in the near abroad; also COM(2004)373 final entitled Communication from the European Commission, European Neighbourhood Policy: Strategy Paper.

7 Following the 2014 elections to the European parliament, the key executive posts of President of European Commission, the President of the European Council and the High Representative of the European Union for Foreign Affairs and Security Policy/Vice-President of the European Commission.

8 Some critics even accuse the EU approach of prompting the outbreak of this crisis, because the incorporation of neighbouring states into EU's concentric circles of governance fails to take into account contextual sensitivities (see footnote 1 for further reference).

9 In particular the following: EU security strategy: A Secure Europe in a Better World: European Security Strategy (DOC78367/2003) versus the new A Global Strategy for the European Union's Foreign and Security Policy (June 2016)

EU neighbourhood strategy: Communication from the European Commission, European Neighbourhood Policy: Strategy Paper, COM(2004)373 final versus the Review of the European Neighbourhood Policy (JOIN(2015)50)

10 Following from the 2015 ENP review "the new ENP will take stabilization as its main political priority in this mandate" (JOIN(2015)50 final: 2)

11 The main changes introduced pertain to application and deepness of integration in different geographical contexts, partly a function of willingness of partner countries to move forward in flexible sectorial cooperation, though none of these affect the EU approach to Ukraine.

12 In practical terms, at the level of policy solutions, the EU re-action to the events in Ukraine is practically materialized in a roadmap for pursuing more of the same routines: signing of the Association Agreement and its (provisional) entry into force, concerted aid flows, adding some symbolic actions such as visa liberalization for Ukrainian citizens visiting the EU.

13 For this discussion see Burlyuk (2017), Dragneva and Wolczuk (2016).

14 These cannot be fully attributed to mechanical notions of institutional path-dependencies. First, because such explanations would imply undue commitment to institutions at the expense of the society in which they are embedded (see, e.g., Bruff, 2008). Even if one decided to play upon the institutional primacy which we do not subscribe to, one would have to justify such notions vis-à-vis the changing social content of EU institutions (even within the short timeframe of Ukraine crisis there was a change of social democratic to centre-right leadership). Likewise, in such case the explanation would still require an embedding in wider societal context: the process of review by the EU institutional players were conducted with an unprecedented level of public participation where besides the traditional institutional actors, civil society organizations and interest groups got actively and officially involved.

15 These involve state-building processes with consolidation of power by a regime at the expense of wider democratic governance; as well as potentially explosive processes such as aggressive nation building based on exclusion, victimization and detachment; or increased radicalization among others. In the recent past of EU's neighbourhood policy, a good example of the limits of such thinking where liberal regimes are reified and objectified at the expense of attention to context-specific processes, were visible in 2011. When the wave of mass protests swiped through the Arab world, all subsequent events were interpreted as potentially democratizing, where the EU can play a role of a transformative partner, often ignoring or reinterpreting the actual socio-spatial realities.

References

Ashton, C. (2013) *Remarks by EU high representative Catherine Ashton upon arrival at the Foreign Affairs Council.* 16 December. Brussels: Foreign Affairs Council. Available at: http://eeas.europa.eu/statements/docs/2013/161213_01_en.pdf (Accessed: 20 October 2015).

Barroso, J.M. (2014a) *Remarks by President Barroso on Ukraine.* 5 March. Brussels: European Commission. Available at: http://europa.eu/rapid/press-release_SPEECH-14-184_en.htm (Accessed 1 November 2015).

Barroso, J.M. (2014b) *Statement by President Barroso following his meeting with President of Ukraine.* 12 September. Kiev: European Commission. Available at: http://europa.eu/rapid/press-release_SPEECH-14-595_en.htm (Accessed: 1 November 2015).

Barroso, J.M. (2014c) *Working together for a united Ukraine in a united continent.* 12 September. Kiev: European Commission. Available at: http://europa.eu/rapid/press-release_SPEECH-14-598_en.htm (Accessed: 1 November 2015).

Barroso, J.M. (2014d) *The European Union in the new world order.* 21 September. Brussels: European Commission. Available at: http://europa.eu/rapid/press-release_SPEECH-14-612_en.htm (Accessed: 21 October 2015).

Barroso, J.M. and van Rompuy, H. (2013) 'Article by President of the European Council Herman van Rompuy and President of the European Commission José Manuel Barroso published on the occasion of the 3rd Eastern Partnership summit in Vilnius', 27 November. Available at: http://www2.consilium.europa.eu/media/25901/139972.pdf (Accessed: 21 October 2015).

Blyth, M., Seabrooke, L., and Widmaier, W. (2007) 'Exogenous shocks or endogenous constructions? The meanings of wars and crises', *International Studies Quarterly*, 51(4), pp. 747–759.

Bruff, I. (2008) *Culture and consensus in European varieties of capitalism: A "common sense" analysis*. Basingstoke: Palgrave Macmillan.

Burlyuk, O. (2017) 'The 'oops!' of EU engagement abroad: Analysing unintended consequences of EU external action', *Journal of Common Market Studies*, 55(5), pp. 1009–1025.

Buschle, D. (2014) *Exporting the internal market: Panacea or nemesis for the European neighbourhood policy? Lessons from the energy community*. EU Diplomacy Paper 2/2014. Bruges: College of Europe.

Cox, R.W. (1996) 'Multilateralism and world order', in Cox, R.W. and Sinclair, T. (eds.), *Approaches to World Order*. Cambridge: Cambridge University, pp. 494–523.

Dennison, S. and Witney, N. (2015) *Europe's neighbourhood: Crisis as the new normal*. London: ECFR.

Dragneva, R. and Wolczuk, K. (2016) 'Between dependence and integration: Ukraine's relations with Russia', *Europe-Asia Studies*, 68(4), pp. 678–698.

ECFR (2014) *Audio: The global consequences of the Ukraine crisis*. Audio recording published on 10th July. Available at: http://www.ecfr.eu/europequestion/entry/audio_the_glo bal_consequences_of_the_ukraine_crisis (Accessed 24 October 2015).

European Commission (2003) *Wider Europe: Neighbourhood: A new framework for relations with our eastern and southern neighbours*. Communication From the Commission to the Council and the European Parliament, COM(2003)104final. Brussels: European Commission.

European Commission and High Representative of the EU for Foreign Affairs and Security Policy (2015a) *Review of the European neighbourhood policy*. Joint communication by European Commission and High Representative of the European Union for foreign affairs and security policy, JOIN(2015)50 final. Brussels: European Commission.

European Commission and High Representative of the EU for Foreign Affairs and Security Policy (2015b) *Towards a new European neighbourhood policy*. Joint consultation paper by European Commission and High Representative of the European Union for foreign affairs and security policy, JOIN(2015)6. Brussels: European Commission.

European Commission and High Representative of the EU for Foreign Affairs and Security Policy (2016) *Shared vision, common action: A stronger Europe: A global strategy for the European Union's foreign and security policy*. Joint communication by European Commission and High Representative of the European Union for foreign affairs and security policy. Brussels: European Commission.

Füle, S. (2013) *EU-Ukraine: Standing ready to help and support*. 10 December. Strasbourg: European Commission. Available at: http://europa.eu/rapid/press-release_SPEECH-13-1054_en.htm?locale=en (Accessed: 20 October 2015).

Füle, S. (2014) *Eastern partnership reached important historic milestone*. 17 July. Vilnius: European Commission. Available at: http://europa.eu/rapid/press-release_SPEECH-14-555_en.htm (Accessed 20 October 2015).

Gänzle, S. (2009) 'EU governance and the European Neighbourhood Policy: A framework for analysis', *Europe-Asia Studies*, 61(10), pp. 1715–1734.

Gephart, R. (2007) 'Crisis sense-making and the public inquiry', in Pearson, C.M., Roux-Dufort, C. and Clair, J.A. (eds.), *International handbook of organizational crisis management*. Berkeley: Sage, pp. 123–160.

Gotev, G. (2015) 'Mogherini's timid "mea culpa" on EU neighbourhood policy', *EurActive.com*, 4 March. Available at: https://www.euractiv.com/section/europe-s-east/news/mogherini-s-timid-mea-culpa-on-eu-neighbourhood-policy/ (Accessed: 9 November 2015).

Gramsci, A. (1996) *Prison notebooks*. Vol. II, Ed. and Trans. J.A. Buttigieg. New York: Columbia University Press.

Hahn, J. (2015) 'European Neighbourhood Policy reloaded', *European Commissioner Blog*, 1 April. Available at: https://ec.europa.eu/commission/commissioners/2014-2019/hahn/blog/european-neighbourhood-policy-reloaded_en (Accessed: 20 October 2015).

Hall, P.A. (1993) 'Policy paradigms, social learning and the state: The case of economic policy-making in Britain', *Comparative Politics*, 25(3), pp. 275–296.

Lavenex, S. (2004) 'EU external governance in "wider Europe"', *Journal of European Public Policy*, 11(4), pp. 680–700.

Lavenex, S. and Schimmelfennig, F. (2010) *EU external governance: Projecting EU rules beyond membership*. London: Routledge.

Prodi, R. (2002) *A wider Europe: A proximity policy as the key to stability: Speech at the Sixth ECSA–World Conference*. 5-6 December. Brussels. Available at: http://europa.eu/rapid/press-release_SPEECH-02-619_en.htm (Accessed 20 October 2015).

Schmidt, V.A. (2008) 'Discursive institutionalism: The explanatory power of ideas and discourse', *Annual Review of Political Science*, 11, pp. 303–326.

Tsoukas, H. and Chia, R. (2002) 'Organizational becoming: Rethinking organizational change', *Organization Science*, 13(5), pp. 567–582.

van Apeldoorn, B. (2000) 'Transnational class agency and European governance: The case of the European Round Table of Industrialists', *New Political Economy*, 5(2), pp. 157–181.

van Apeldoorn, B. (2003) 'The struggle over European order: Transnational class agency in the making of embedded neo-liberalism', in Brenner, N., Jessop, B., Jones, M., MacLeod, G. (eds.), *State/Space: A Reader*. Oxford: Blackwell, pp. 147–164.

van der Loo, G. (2016) *The EU-Ukraine Association Agreement: A new legal instrument for EU integration without membership?* Leiden: Brill/Nijhoff.

van Rompuy, H. (2014a) *Remarks following the extraordinary meeting of EU Heads of State or Government on Ukraine*. 6 March. Brussels: European Council. Available at: http://www.consilium.europa.eu/workarea/downloadAsset.aspx?id=18101 (Accessed: 20 October 2015).

van Rompuy, H. (2014b) *Speech at the European People's Party Congress*. 7 March. Dublin: European Council. Available at: http://www.consilium.europa.eu/workarea/downloadAsset.aspx?id=18103 (Accessed: 20 October 2015).

van Rompuy, H. (2014c) *"Europe: A continent in a changing world" Speech for the Foreign Policy and United Nations Association of Austria*. 8 April. Vienna: European Council. Available at: http://www.consilium.europa.eu/workarea/downloadAsset.aspx?id=18187 (Accessed: 20 October 2015).

van Rompuy, H. (2014d) *Speech to the 69th General Assembly of the United Nations*. 25 September. New York: European Council. Available at: http://www.consilium.

europa.eu/workarea/downloadAsset.aspx?id=40802192216 (Accessed: 20 October 2015).

van Rompuy, H. (2014e) *Remarks by President of the European Council Herman van Rompuy after his meeting with Prime Minister of Poland Donald Tusk.* 25 January. Warsaw: European Council. Available at: http://www.consilium.europa.eu/uedocs/cms_Data/docs/pressdata/en/ec/140790.pdf (Accessed: 20 October 2015).

Weick K.E., Sutcliffe K.M. and Obstfeld, D. (2005) 'Organizing and the process of sensemaking', *Organization Science*, 16(4), pp. 409–421.

Zielonka, J. (2006) *Europe as empire: The nature of the enlarged European Union.* Oxford: Oxford University Press.

Part VI

Conclusions

14 Critical realism, symptomatology and the pedagogy of crisis

Bob Jessop and Karim Knio[1]

The concluding chapter reviews our arguments in Part One in the light of the other contributions to this volume. The general significance of these contributions was explored in Chapter 1 and, rather than repeat that exercise, we focus here on specific lessons. Likewise, we will not return to the important question posed by Jane Roitman regarding whether it is scientifically and practically appropriate to treat the modern period in general as crisis prone and/or to assume that specific events and processes can best be defined as (symptoms of) crisis to the neglect of alternative ways of interpreting them. For we are not interested in highlighting crisis as a description or self-description of modern times as if this captures the *Zeitgeist* (spirit of the times) nor do we consider crisis can be the taken-for-granted form of *Zeitdiagnostik*, an approach that privileges crisis as an explanandum and/or explanans for historical and contemporary analyses of the modern period. Similarly, we do not consider the conditions of possibility of a general theory of crisis. For, while accepting that there are *real* crisis tendencies and *actual* crises, we are not interested in developing a general theory of crises or identifying the features of crisis in general. Indeed, there is no crisis in general or general crisis: only particular crises in and/or of particular sets of social relations and the totality of crises in a given conjuncture.[2] Thus, any serious approach to crises must define the specific mix of crisis tendencies that create the abstract conditions of possibility for a given type of crisis and the specific features that define the specificity of a particular crisis, whether considered as an event and/or as a process. This is illustrated by the diversity of the case studies in this volume.

Critical realism

The argument that crises are objectively overdetermined and subjectively indeterminate owes much to a critical realist (CR) philosophy of science[3] that is also informed by social scientific concerns with the dialectics of structure and agency together with the dialectics of path-dependency and path-shaping. In short, this argument invites the critical realist question: "What must the world be like for these specific symptoms of crisis (if such it be) to have emerged when, where, and how they did?" Part of the answer may be to identify the abstract possibility of crises in specific sets of social relations. But this does not provide the answer to the specific CR retroductive question we have just posed. Indeed, as Marx wrote in *Theories of Surplus-Value* and developed elsewhere:

> The general possibility of crisis is [inherent in] the formal metamorphosis of capital itself, the separation in time and space, of purchase and sale. But this is never the cause of the crisis. For it is nothing but the most general form of crisis, i.e., the crisis in its most generalized expression. But it cannot be said that the abstract form of crisis is the cause of crisis. If one asks what its cause is, one wants to know why its abstract form, the form of its possibility, turns from possibility to actuality.
>
> (Marx, 1969, p. 515)

Explaining why the abstract form of crisis turns from possibility to actuality (or not, as the case may be – and both need explanation) is a key challenge, not only in a Marxist approach to the critique of political economy (where it has received diverse answers, both theoretical and historical) but also in other accounts of crisis that seek to penetrate beneath empirical indicators and surface appearances (symptoms) to explain the objective overdetermination of the crisis. As Boyer writes above in more institutionalist terms: "endogenous mechanisms recurrently generate crises in modern capitalism. Nonetheless, the specific type of crisis, the precise mix of mechanisms, and the affected economic spaces in each case are always distinctive" (Boyer, this volume, p. 139). This is less of a challenge in explaining "accidental" crises, of course, than crises generated in and through emergent systemic properties. For, whereas the former readily lend themselves to a mechanical, additive approach to explanation, the latter are overdetermined through the structural coupling and co-evolution of various kinds of complex, open systems that operate at different sites and scales of social relations. A generic CR philosophy cannot explain this because it has an "underlabouring" role in both the natural and social sciences (Bhaskar, 1998, p 18). In other words, its purpose is philosophical clarification, identifying negative heuristics (meta-theoretical and theoretical mistakes to avoid), and facilitating conceptual development. But a generic CR cannot provide the specific theoretical concepts, explanatory principles, and detailed logic of explanation even for the abstract possibility of crises in specific fields of social relation, let alone the concrete historical explanations of particular cases of crisis in all their contingently necessary objective overdetermination. For this depends on using suitable substantive theories that are compatible with the general principles of a meta-theoretical critical realism and on elaborating a detailed historical analysis of the conditions that led to the actualization of abstract possibilities of crisis.

This argument applies to the scientific analysis of crises – analyses whose scientificity depends on adherence to particular models of scientific investigation and are inherently fallible. Specific explanations are also shaped by particular explananda, which rarely extend to the full complexity of crisis events or processes but almost inevitably highlight some aspects, elements or moments for detailed inquiry. Differences in how best to specify explananda are a fertile source of scientific disagreements, especially where incommensurable scientific paradigms are adopted (see, for example, the critical reflections on this problem in the contributions by Matthew Watson and Robert Boyer). The nature of scientific explanation depends on specific theoretical paradigms and scientific protocols. Chapters 1 and 2 illustrated this point from the extensive literature in the fields of organizational studies and organizational learning, which, as noted, have a wider significance for crises, crisis construals, and crisis lessons thanks to the crucial, typically contested and often conflictual, agential and mediating roles of organizations (and social movements) in diagnosing and responding to crises.

A further set of problems arise when we consider the *narrative plausibility* of crisis diagnoses and prognoses. Here other criteria come into play (see Chapter 3). Indeed, simplifications and strategic essentialism (knowingly reducing the complexity of a crisis in order to be able to react quickly and to mobilize social forces behind a simple message or vision) may be crucial for effective intervention into a crisis. While disinterested observers may take the time to describe and explain a crisis in detail, participants with the power to act quickly may already have developed crisis narratives and acted upon them with path-shaping consequences and other actors may already have settled on their own accounts, blamed the usual suspects, and acted on them too. Moreover, just as there are rival scientific paradigms, there are multiple entrypoints and standpoints that can be adopted in developing narratives about crisis, reflecting different social positions, identities, and interests (on the role of identities, see Nishimura, 2011). A further set of problems is grounded in the often urgent, practical question: what is to be done? The need to take emergency action may pre-empt more effective long-term solutions (see Gamble, this volume) and will have path-shaping effects that may prevent such solutions in future.

Developing a self-reflexive critical realist approach poses three sets of theoretical and practical issues. The first set of issues concerns the genesis or genealogy of crises, i.e., the objective overdetermination of crises. Over-determination refers to the condensation of several crisis tendencies and counter-tendencies into a causal nexus that is more than the sum of its parts. This notion, derived from Freudian theory and much favoured in structural Marxism, can be contrasted with multi- or pluri-causality, both of which refer to the multiplicity or plurality of different causal influences that bear upon a given effect. Neither multi- or pluri-causality as these concepts are typically deployed implies more than simple, additive causation. This may be appropriate in some cases (e.g., accidental disasters) where it would be sufficient to remove, block, or counteract one cause to prevent a disaster; it is less suited to systemic crises that originate in the causal mechanisms and emergent properties of complex open systems and causal interactions are complex and multi-channelled. Des Gasper's analysis of climate change illustrates these complexities and the veiled and contestable nature of resulting diagnoses. As noted earlier, overdetermination can be examined by observers or participants in scientific terms but, from the viewpoint of crisis construals and crisis management, this approach is more often combined with one or more competing and selective narrative accounts of the origins of the crisis and the current situation. These may draw on facts to lend them credibility; but imagination, phantasy, vision, and strategy are also important factors shaping the rhetoric of crisis narratives, which may also be differentiated according to the intended audience (on this aspect, see the chapters by Magnus Ryner and Des Gasper).

A second, related, set of issues concerns symptomatology, i.e., how to construe the symptoms of crisis in a way that enables organic responses rather than ones that are arbitrary, rationalistic and willed (Gramsci, 1971, pp. 376–377; cf. 1975, Q7, §19; see also Ryner, this volume) or involve significant elements of fantastic or magical thinking (Boyer, this volume; Wigger, this volume). Chapter 3 discussed this topic at length. The objective causal nexus that connects an invisible entity and its visible signs is not immediately transparent or self-evident but requires interpretation and evaluation. This is because there is no one-to-one relation between event and symptom since this relation is *underdetermined*. There is no algorithm that can establish *the* cause (though expert systems with fuzzy logic may attempt to narrow down possible causes on the assumption that present crises are similar to previous crises).[4] Thus, if we read symptoms as signifiers, we can ask what is being signified and, equally importantly, what is its referent? (cf. Bhaskar on the semiotic triangle, 2008, pp. 207–209; Sum and Jessop, 2013). This excludes thin constructivism, which fails to consider why only some construals have performative effects in constructing reality and seems to ignore the manner and extent to which the "real" world limits capacities to translate construals into the preservation or transformation of social relations.

A concern with signifier, signified, and referent fits the critical realist "depth ontology", which distinguishes the real (the invisible entity or entities), the actual (an "event" or "process"), and the empirical (visible signs). In these terms, as Karim Knio argued in Chapter 2, crises can be seen as stratified. They are generated by *real mechanisms*, are *actual events* or *processes*, and can be observed and assessed in terms of qualitative and quantitative *empirical evidence*. However, as the CR approach emphasizes, there is no neat one-to-one relation between these levels. Thus, the challenge is to relate the empirical symptoms, actual crisis, and underlying mechanisms as a basis for possible decisive interventions. Explicitly, but more often implicitly, symptomatological reflection is the practical response to this challenge. It is based on trial-and-error observation and construal that draws on past experience but may also require forgetting as a basis for "correct" intervention. Jeff Handmaker addresses this issue explicitly in his analysis of reflexive learning in relation to the "legitimacy crisis" of international criminal courts. Moreover, while not all the contributions are explicitly concerned with "symptomatology", they all address, in one way or another, the problems of construing symptoms and relating them to diagnosis, treatment, and prognosis.

The third set of issues concerns the possibility of learning, especially about crisis anticipation, crisis prevention, crisis management, and transcending the conditions in which crisis occurs. This was the focus, for organizational learning and various phases of crisis management, in Karim Knio's survey of the literature in Chapter 2. But the possibility of learning far exceeds the field of organizations or organizational ecologies. Our approach to learning can be described as crisis theoretical, i.e., we are interested in crises as opportunities to study learning and as incentives to learn.[5] Accordingly, we draw lessons about learning *in, through, about,* and *from* crisis. Importantly, this also covers the obstacles and limits to learning and various forms of failed learning. Lesson-drawing has been a key theme in all chapters, whether in terms of non-learning (especially on the part of the powerful), fantasy learning (reinforcing fantastic or arbitrary, rationalistic and willed ideologies and beliefs), fetishistic learning (returning again and again to pursue fetishized objectives, such as the goal of enhanced competitiveness, against evidence this objective is misperceived or simply mistaken), resilient learning (or learning to become resilient in the face of continuing but diverse crises), or reflexive learning (learning how to learn and to apply lessons based on sharing experiences collectively). It is another matter entirely, of course, as several chapters have demonstrated, whether any lessons learnt, even if adequately grounded in objective analysis of underlying causes, current conjunctures, and possible futures, can be applied. This is particularly problematic where there are powerful vested interests that oppose such solutions. Fields of application include: policy learning, political learning (defined to include governance learning and covering lessons about the politics, broadly defined, of crisis management), institutional learning (covering issues of institutional design to prevent crises, modify their forms, or manage them differently), and strategic learning (concerned with reading conjunctures, periodization, and strategic interventions to shape the future). Chandler's analysis of resilience as a mode of governance that exploits crisis illustrates how all four kinds of learning can be combined into an overall approach to managing a period where increasingly complex, interdependent social relations generate innumerable unexpected shocks, each of which has its own idiosyncrasies.

The rationale for organizing the seminar series from which this volume derives and thereby adding to the already extensive and diverse literature on learning is that previously there had been neglect of the interrelations (and potential disjunctions) between objective overdetermination, symptomatology and the pedagogy of crisis. All the chapters offer new insights into this topic. In this sense, they reject one-sided constructivist approaches, while recognizing the performative effects of those construals among many possible alternatives that come to be selected and retained in struggles around policy, politics, and strategy. They also reject one-sided, structuralist analyses that focus on the objective overdetermination of crises without recognition that crises are also moments of subjective decision-making rather than triggers for automatic, algorithmic crisis management or resolution.

Because learning is both *semiotically mediated* and *socially situated,* its investigation could begin either with the problematique of sense- and meaning-making (crisis construal) *or with* that of structuration (the asymmetries that make it easier for some actors to construe crises and act upon their construals than others). This points to the need to study the structural/strategic, discursive, and technical-cum-technological conditions of political, policy, and strategic learning (cf. Sum and Jessop, 2013, pp. 214-19). Agency plays a key mediating role in all three conditions and types of learning because the trial-and-error learning in the face of crisis (especially crises of crisis management) leads to actors in different social positions may draw different lessons and because different agents and social forces will have different capacities to act on lessons – including, in the case of the powerful, the ability to "carry on regardless" and impose the costs of their mistakes on less powerful social forces, more marginal spaces, or future generations. This indicates the scope (and, often, need) to link learning with *Herrschaftskritik*, i.e., the vertical dimension of learning. This involves the classic "who/whom" question. Who gets to define the crisis, whose construals get acted upon, which lessons become hegemonic or get imposed, and who gains and who loses from the manner in which a crisis is managed or its underlying causes removed? Different kinds of answer to this question are appropriate depending on the site, scale and kind of crisis. In no case, however, does learning occur in an ideal speech situation of undistorted communication but in circumstances characterized by structural and strategic asymmetries that bear on capacities to engage in reflexive policy and political learning, translate lessons into effective, performative crisis responses, and to pass lessons on. A related issue concerns *Ideologiekritik*. Learning is not purely cognitive but occurs – or not (see Watson, above) – in ideologically contested fields with ideological effects. Even where personal or collective lived experience is the most direct basis of learning, experience is not "ideology-free" but always shaped by pre-existing and/or reflexively modified frames of meaning, subject positions, and standpoints. In his contribution to this volume, Jeff Handmaker provides a powerful analysis of the effects of such framing in his discussion of the "SVS" (Savages, Victims, Saviour) model of human rights infractions and seeks to overcome it by offering an alternative framing based on new methods of teaching human rights law (legal clinics), reflexive learning by legal theorists and practitioners, and the further development of reflexive law.

Theoretical and methodological lessons on crisis dynamics

The concept of crisis dynamics is inherently temporal. The core definition of crisis is that of a turning point, a moment of decisive intervention, a critical juncture. As shown in Part One, a crisis can be seen as (1) an historical event; (2) a feature of a conjuncture (critical juncture); (3) a process with a past, present and future that unfolds and is triggered by a specific event that creates an *urgence*, a need to make a path-shaping decision; or (4) as a manifestation in specific conditions of an abstract possibility of crisis where the balance between crisis tendencies and counter-tendencies tips in favour of crisis, albeit always with historically specific, singular features. It can also be (construed as) a crisis "in" or a crisis "of" the ensemble of social relations that generated it or is affected by it. Moreover, as Zuzana Novakova shows in her chapter, these possibilities can be combined. For her, the Ukraine crisis is both a *crisis in* EU foreign policy and the *crisis of* a particular form of EU foreign policy in the region. This shapes the temporal forms and approaches to crisis management in the European neighbourhood. More generally, the temporality of crisis is not so much concerned with the time-space *coordinates* of crisis events, conjunctures, processes, etc., as it is about the temporal or temporalized aspects of crisis – how processes with different spatio-temporal rhythms interact to produce crises, how different actors respond to crises over different spatio-temporal horizons, and how actors are able to learn in, through, about, and from crises.

One might describe this as a "path-shaping" rather than "path-dependent" position. To the extent it means something more than the banal observation that "history matters", path-dependency characterizes a situation where disruptions lead to – or cannot prevent – the restoration of the *status quo ante,* a pre-established path. This is clearly inappropriate as an account of crises. Even where crises do result in such a return, this is not because of automatic, self-equilibrating structural mechanisms but due to the specific policies and strategies adopted in the crisis conjuncture (cf. Boyer, this volume). David Chandler identifies an interesting paradox here when he notes that crisis is now seen as a means and mode of governance oriented towards resilience. This goes beyond Tancredi's comment in Giuseppe di Lampedusa's Sicilian novel, *The Leopard*, that, "[i]f we want things to stay as they are, things will have to change" (1960, p. 31). For it goes beyond a strategic, long-term passive revolution to manage change conservatively and encompasses constant tactical resilience and flexibility in the face of frequent, ever-changing shocks, *urgences*, emergencies, and crises in order that "things can stay as they are". In other words, what appears as path-dependency in the sense of reversion to a previous path after a disturbance is not a quasi-automatic effect of structural constraints but the result of tactical and strategic action to be encouraged, institutionalized, and governed in the face of opposition and other countervailing forces.

Conversely, path-shaping involves action (or inaction) that can redirect historical pathways. In crisis conjunctures, social forces may be able to intervene to re-articulate structures, discourses, technologies of power and discipline, and the balance of forces in order to effect change. This possibility is implicit in the notion of crisis as "threat" and "opportunity" (see Chapter 3). Whereas the past matters more for path-dependency theorists, for path-shaping theorists what matters is the future. How this develops depends, in part, on choices made in the crisis conjuncture. This is a key theme in the chapters by Gamble, Ryner, and Boyer in terms of how actions make a difference; and, in negative terms, namely, the failure to learn or act in the face of continuing problems, it can be seen in the chapters by Handmaker, Gasper, Hout, and Novakova. How much difference these choices make depends on how the dialectics of path-dependency and path-shaping is mediated by overdetermined conjunctures, the shifting correlations of forces mobilized behind the efforts to implement one or another "pragmatically correct" response, and the limits of feasibility.

Table 14.1 The temporal dimension of crises

	Genealogy	*Chronology*	*Periodization*
Time	Evolutionary time of variation-selection-retention and/or time of active bricolage	Time as neutral metric to distinguish succession of events in past and present	Evolutionary time with attention to temporalities of different processes and social relations
Time Scale	Can be unilinear or multiple – depends on the object of the genealogy	Orders events and actions in unilinear clock, calendrical, or geological time	Multiple time scales to order events and actions in terms of plural time horizons
Time Frame	Essentially retrospective	Simple coincidence or succession in time	May be linked to future scenarios
Temporal Horizon	Traces origins back in time and requires view on how to avoid infinite regress	Succession of "present" times if made in real time or reconstructs past from perspective of present	Differential sets of constraints/opportunities for social forces over different horizons and action sites

Type of Explanation	Variation-selection-retention
	    Chance encounter or discovery
	      Assemblage, bricolage
		Simple narrative with beginning, middle, and end
		    Oriented to causal and/or moral lessons
			Complex narratives or explanations based on contingent necessities and a dialectic of path-dependency and path-shaping

Source: elaborated by the author from this text

The temporal dimension of crises can be approached through chronicle, chronology, or periodization (see Table 14.1). Chronicling is the least interesting approach. It involves no more than a listing of relevant events and actions in conventional calendar time. History is reduced to the passage of time, i.e., it is treated as "one damned thing after another". A chronology orders selected actions and events in unilinear time (e.g., clock times ranging from nano-seconds through the calendar to glacial time and beyond to light years). It divides the temporal development into successive stages according to the simple temporal succession or coincidence of a single series of actions and events in and across time periods (with periods being defined simply through the calendar and/or some other socially relevant marker such as business cycles, intervals between elections, or significant environmental events). This lends itself to a simple narrative of how a crisis event or process developed, an idiographic explanation (focused on the unique unfolding of a series of events), or their subsumption under a covering law explanation. In this sense, history-as-account becomes a story about history-as-event (on this distinction, see Stanford, 1994, p. 11).

Periodization is more complex than chronology and is inherently critical realist in its approach. It relates one or more series of historical events to other significant events or interests and seeks to explain them without relying exclusively on a narrative. It operates with several time-scales. It orders actions and events in terms of multiple time horizons (e.g., the event, trends, the *longue durée*; the time-frame of economic calculation vs the time-frame of political cycles; or past futures, present pasts, and the future present[6]). Thus, periodization focuses on locating crises in more or less complex conjunctures that have ontological depth and breadth, involve multiple temporalities, spatialities, etc. It divides actions and events into stages based on their conjunctural implications (as specific mixes of constraints and opportunities) for different forces over different time horizons and/or for different sites of social action. It seeks to explain the contingently necessary interaction of many factors that produced the objectively overdetermined crisis event (or process). This supports a complex rather than simple narrative. This would show how multiple time horizons and conjunctures lead to complex sets of differential constraints and opportunities for diverse social forces to act with a view to shaping the future by attempts to actualize what exists *in potentia*. It also supports a more differentiated analysis of constraints and opportunities on different kinds of learning for different actors over different spatio-temporal horizons of action. One way to explore potentialities is the development of alternative scenarios (on those proposed by the Great Transition Initiative, see Gasper, above). For further discussion, including the strategic implications of conjunctural analyses for social movements and political parties, see Jessop (2012).

Both chronology and periodization lend themselves to a recursive, reflexive use of "history-as-account" to make "history-as-event" (cf. Gosden, 1994). This practice is usefully described as historicity. Anthony Giddens defined this as:

> the use of the past to help shape the present, but it does not depend upon respect for the past. On the contrary, historicity means the use of knowledge about the past as a means of breaking with it – or, at any rate, only sustaining what can be justified in a principled way.
>
> (Giddens, 1990, p. 50)

Historicity is especially relevant during crises or other exceptional periods that disrupt established routines and habits and create opportunities to shape the future. It is also linked, as readers of this volume will already have gathered, to the pedagogy of crisis, where lessons are deployed rhetorically to shape present responses to current crises. In this context, we can distinguish at least four modes of historicity.

The first mode of historicity is *preventive learning*. At stake here are cautionary narratives that warn about cumulating crisis tendencies, especially in the face of arguments that "this time is different" (cf. Boyer, this volume). Such narratives may derive from (1) learning based on a directly experienced crisis after "it" ends; (2) learning from a crisis that has been observed in real time after "it" ends; (3) learning from a crisis through institutionalized inquiries, based on reports of those who experienced it, observed it, and seek/sought to describe, interpret, and explain it; and (4) learning from crises identified and reconstructed from other times and/ or places, although relevant comparators are typically contested and can be variously construed. These forms of preventive learning are evident in the vast literature on disaster and crisis management (partly reviewed by Karim Knio in Chapter 2) that focuses not only on how to deal with disasters and crises but also on how to prevent them, if possible, and how to minimize their fallout (whether just for the organizations involved, for the wider public, for institutions and institutional orders, or society more generally) where they cannot be prevented. They are also discussed in other chapters where failures in preventive learning, whatever their causes, are highlighted (e.g., Watson, Gasper, Hout, and Novakova).

Second, there is learning about crisis based on *identifying analogies and parallels* between past crises and the current set of symptoms. This may involve drawing on knowledge – scientifically valid, pragmatically adequate, fetishistically ritualized, or simply delusional – of famous (or notorious) historical, iconic, high profile, or benchmark crises, whether clearly relevant or not. Historicity has a key role to play here in typically contested attempts to establish the dominant construal, scientific or narrative, in a time of subjective indeterminacy. This is illustrated in the weird and wonderful diversity of historical referents in accounts of the North Atlantic Financial Crisis demonstrate (cf. Samman, 2015). This category overlaps in part the first mode of historicity. The difference consists in whether a simple search process is being undertaken to guide crisis prevention and management (preventive learning) or whether the analogies and parallels are explicitly cited in a contested process of crisis construal so that history is invoked to make history. Attempts to teach lessons *in* a crisis are often opportunistic and focus on its phenomenal forms, using an emerging crisis to advance pregiven lessons about the world. Neoliberalism provides many contemporary examples and is also associated, as Andrew Gamble notes (this volume), with efforts to redefine the causes and the blame for a crisis as it unfolds. This leads to attempts to use a continuing crisis as an object lesson in order to advance preconceived ideas about its causes, how best to resolve it, and so on. It also illustrates Jamie Peck's claim that neoliberalism fails regularly – but "fails forward", using crises to regenerate itself (Peck, 2010, pp. 6–7). This can be related, in turn, to Chandler's arguments on resilience in the face of crises as the "new normal".

Third, there is learning from crisis based on *post hoc* investigations into the origins of a crisis, its unfolding, and the success or failure (for whom, over which spatio-temporal horizons, with what medium- to long-term effects, etc.) of attempts at crisis management. None of the contributions to this volume provide examples of this kind of investigation but some do integrate the results from such inquiries into proposals on how to respond to crisis. The difference between this and the first type of learning is whether lessons are aimed at prevention (linked, perhaps, to establishing crisis prevention and management routines) or concerned with crisis management (linked, perhaps, to crises of crisis management where crises were not prevented and pose new challenges because previously learnt routine responses have failed). Andrew Gamble illustrates this from the successful intervention in the North Atlantic Financial Crisis to prevent a return to Great Depression conditions but adds that, while short-term responses and quantitative easing rescued financial institutions, a return to the pre-crisis growth trajectory did not occur. Zuzana Novakova shows how the continuing crisis in the Ukraine and its repercussions on EU foreign policy have led to policy reviews to assess where things have gone wrong and how strategy and policy might be changed to address them. Likewise, Wil Hout shows how the World Bank's Development Research Group and other agencies reconsidered the aims and means of development aid following persistent failures, leading to new goals in the form of the millennium development goals and sustainable development goals. His analysis also illustrates the case of the fast policy transfer of ready-made answers to generic problems – a policy realm of what he describes, citing Mosse (2011), as "travelling rationalities" or even "travelling orthodoxies". This reappraisal of policies to be transferred anywhere and everywhere could also be related to the transition from Consensus period to the Post-Washington Consensus period. In both periods the capacity for fast policy transfer depends on existing policy networks and power structures (Peck and Theodore, 2014).

These policy lessons are often conveyed in more or less codified terms and may either by "internalized" or "imposed" from outside and above. The former case is illustrated by internalization of the neo-liberal mantra that there is no alternative (TINA). This case is explored in different ways in the chapters by Angela Wigger, on the competitiveness imperative, Des Gasper on the difficulties of challenging the logic of capitalist development and international rivalries in relation to climate change; and Wil Hout on neoliberal solutions to lagging development and global poverty. In turn, imposition can be illustrated from the role of structural conditionalities as a *quid pro quo* for financial aid in the case of financial crises, as seen in the case of the International Monetary Fund, World Bank, or, again, the Troika in the Eurozone crisis (see Ryner, this volume). This raises issues of asymmetries of power and the mediation of policy transfer as well as affecting the kinds of lesson that might be transferred – some being easier to transfer than others. This often reinforces patterns of domination and marginalizes those without ready access of such networks and power structures.

Finally, fourth, and also relatedly, there are frequent efforts to teach lessons from the past or present. In some cases, these examples are historically grounded (but still contested), in others, the outcomes of crisis management may still be open. A link back to the previous point about structural conditionalities is worth noting. For the IMF later conceded (in a form of learning after crisis) that its insistence on neo-liberal measures in response to the Asian (or "IMF" crisis in 1997) was mistaken and that capital controls oriented to the absorptive capacity of real economy and restrictions on hot money flows would have been more appropriate. The IMF research section has admitted, against the prevailing neo-liberal wisdom in the European Union, that the austerity imposed on Greece was counter-productive, finally recognizing that debts that cannot be paid, will not be paid (cf. IMF, 2015, 2017). Another example is the attempts by theorists and political forces of various stripes to draw lessons from how the Icelandic and Irish authorities handled their financial crises after 2007–2008. Both countries were heavily exposed to this crisis because of neoliberal regime shifts that actively promoted and, in Iceland, celebrated hyperfinancialization. Iceland's crisis was more severe, given the size of its domestic economy and the level of financial indebtedness racked up by deregulated banks. However, whereas Ireland bailed out its indebted banks, Iceland nationalized them; and, this is where pointed lessons are identified, whereas the Icelandic economy is often proclaimed to have emerged from the financial crisis relatively quickly with a stronger real economy, Ireland has continued to suffer debt-default-deflation dynamics for years. It will be no surprise, of course, that this comparison of lessons about crisis management is contested.[7]

In a nutshell, theoretical and methodological lessons on crisis dynamics are intertwined with a host of contextual, material, semiotic and conduct-based selectivities. Grosso modo, while technological and discursive selectivities speak to learning in and from crises, structural and agential selectivities evoke the contours of learning about crises.

Lessons on symptomatology

As objectively overdetermined moments of subjective indeterminacy, crises can produce profound theoretical and practical disorientation. Absent this subjective indeterminacy, there can be no crisis as conventionally understood. This prompts different construals that simplify and interpret the complexities of crisis symptoms and their underlying mechanisms in different ways. As noted in Chapter 3 and above, such symptoms should be seen as *signa naturalia,* i.e., construed as *empirical* signs of *actual* events and/or processes that are contingently necessary outcomes of *real* mechanisms, rather than being themselves *signa data* and hence construed as no more than socially constructed signals. This is an important stake in the debates between thin and thick constructivists and those who adopt, explicitly or implicitly, a more critical realist position (cf. Knio in Chapter 2). From a symptomatological viewpoint, then, crisis symptoms are *signa naturalia* that need to be construed for the meaning to emerge and relevant decisions to be made and acted upon. *Signa naturalia* induce subjective indeterminacy about how to act. Sound construals have formal/material adequacy to the multiple underlying causes. Unsound construals focus on symptoms rather than underlying causes and then attempt to remove the symptoms, thereby reproducing the conditions that caused them (for an example of this in development aid practice, see Hout, this volume). This said, crisis management, resolution, or transcendence are not purely technical: they involve the articulation of an objectively overdetermined situation *and* a subjectively indeterminate moment with its prevailing correlation of forces and its changing construals. As few of the contributions to this volume are directly concerned with the challenges of symptomatology – their focus is more on crises as events, the dynamics of crises considered as processes, and the scope and limits of crisis management – readers are referred to Chapters 1 and 3 for further discussion.

Lessons on crisis learning

In exploring construals and the types of lesson that can be drawn, we need to distinguish among disinterested observers, passive victims, active participants, and those with authority or power to enact or act on lessons (e.g., legislators, regulators, judges, arbitrators) and their specific types of learning. For "outside" observers, learning about crisis occurs when they focus on real causes, dynamics, effects and observe actors' trial-and-error attempts to solve crisis and/or how other "outsiders" seek to shape its course, costs, outcome. For actors directly affected, this occurs when attention turns from phenomenal forms to deeper causes and dynamics and their relevance to crisis management. As preceding chapters illustrate, not all actors or observers can or do move to this stage; it is typically highly selective, partial, and provisional; and it is often mediated through forms of representation.

Crises can challenge past lessons and ways of learning; and open space for new lessons and ways of learning. For some actors (not always benign ones), whether those directly affected or "informed outsiders", crises can trigger a search for new forms of learning. This is where reflexive learning (Handmaker, this volume) and "double loop" learning, i.e., learning about learning, enter the picture. In other cases, we find a more ritualistic, ineffective learning, focusing on reinterpreting changing symptoms without looking to underlying causes (cf. Gasper's discussion of the continuing crisis *of* development aid in response to the crisis *of* development). However, developing new forms of learning takes time; and this typically means new forms of learning usually emerge *after* the crisis. This is where lesson-drawing from crisis has a potential role to play provided post hoc inquiries are set up with the intention of drawing serious lessons rather than, in the now legendary words of the UK Prime Minister, Harold Wilson, "take minutes and last years", thereby postponing and/or burying details about a crisis, its causes, the attribution of blame, and relevant lessons.

The relation between crisis and learning is interesting: (1) crises of a given system throw *learning into crisis* as proven lessons and learning practices are disoriented; (2) this initiates *learning in crisis*, i.e., efforts to interpret the *signa naturalia*, initially on the basis of superficial, visible features, occur with lags in real time as a crisis unfolds, often in unexpected ways and as routine crisis-management procedures prove or seem to be inadequate or inappropriate, with the result that policy-making and implementation take an experimental form; (3) then comes *learning about crisis*, i.e., trial-and-error crisis resolution leads to discoveries about the complexity and contingently necessary causes of the crisis; (4) *learning from* crisis occurs when lessons are drawn for future use once a crisis is resolved to the satisfaction of key actors or recovery takes place for other reasons, and actors reflect on the crisis and its import for future crises and crisis management. The third and fourth types of learning may lead to invocation of *lessons from the past* that involve "historicity", i.e., the use of history to make history or, put differently, the effort to define appropriate historical parallels as a basis for responding effectively to the crisis in real time. It is also possible, of course, that learning from crisis highlights the failed attempts to resolve a crisis so that these failures become a negative reference point for crisis management. The case of the Great Depression, or Japan's "lost decades", were certainly influential in shaping elite responses to the North Atlantic Financial Crisis (see the chapters by Gamble and Boyer above). In this sense, disasters and crises can also be *teachable* moments, i.e., events or processes that can be narrated to draw important lessons. The Grenfell Tower fire in London is significant in this regard because it condenses so many factors and enables many lessons to be taught about neoliberalism.

Learning has different temporal as well as spatial dimensions and involves different levels and capacities for reflexivity on the part of different social agents. Together, learning and reflexivity mean the past is transformed in understanding as the basis for present and future action. It does not follow that learning and reflexivity must lead to attempts at change (reflection on the past could lead one to believe that conservation is an appropriate response to current or anticipated future conditions). We should also note that reflexive learning may not occur. Gasper's chapter illustrates the insouciance with which elites can approach crises when their costs fall on the poor and other subaltern groups. This is also evident in the North Atlantic Financial Crisis as the powerful sought to impose the costs of their mistakes onto others, who must adapt and learn suitable lessons.

Finally, we should note that there are many ways in which learning may be ineffective. These include (1) simplistic conclusions that ignore the complexities of a crisis – learning may address only certain social, spatial and temporal aspects of a crisis; (2) fantasy lessons that lead to "magical thinking", including the belief that "this time is different", that key forces have now learnt how to avoid crises or that the underlying crisis tendencies have been tamed through new policies or weakened, if not eliminated, by structural changes (cf. Boyer, this volume); (3) falsely generalized lessons, where success in a specific instance leads to excess optimism – or failure in a single instance leads to excessive fatalism or pessimism; (4) correctly drawn lessons that are rendered irrelevant because of a turbulent policy or strategic environment such that, like generals fighting the last war, those who seek to manage or instrumentalize a crisis orient their actions to a previous crisis, rather than the present one (this is also illustrated by Boyer, Chapter 8); (5) politicized lessons where construals, narratives, and crisis responses are shaped by prior ideological, policy or political commitments – as illustrated by Watson (Chapter 4), Handmaker (Chapter 10, in relation to the savages, victims and saviours framing of international crime), and Hout (Chapter 12); and (6) non-learning due to social barriers and rigidities that block active learning, including through the sharing of experiences across various social and geographical divides, overcoming "confirmation bias" in mutually isolated social media silos, and so on.

Learning and fast policy

Normal politics "takes time", creating pressures to decide based on unreliable information, narrow or limited consultation and participation, etc., even as key actors think that policy is taking too long to negotiate, formulate, enact, adjudicate, determine, and implement. This has created a global demand for "fast policy", especially for "new *policy* ideas, especially those highly sought-after 'ideas that work'" (Peck and Theodore, 2014, p. xv, italics in original). This is an important aspect of policy learning and has prompted the rise of a "'social infrastructure' … around 'best practice' codification, practitioner conferences, learning exchanges, knowledge transfer, and communities of practice, a world that is populated by a mobile class of policy gurus, entrepreneurs, consultants, bloggers, evaluator-advocates, and model peddlers" (ibid.). Wil Hout (this volume) provides an interesting example of this policy consultant circuit – together with its adverse impact on effective policy learning. He explores how aid policies are churned regularly as each is seen to fail and shows that this is related to a focus on the symptoms of the legitimacy crisis of international aid rather than its deeper causes. This is typical of "one-size-fits-all" fast policies. So is the role of new narratives tied to new goals even as the underlying problems remain the same.

Fast policy and its social infrastructure have important effects on policy transfer across different sites and scales of policy-making, including, *a fortiori*, disaster and crisis-management. They also shape decision-making structures and processes and the form and content of policies in different areas. An emphasis on speed affects the choice of policies, initial policy targets, sites where policy is implemented, and criteria adopted for success. It leads to shorter policy development cycles, fast-tracking decision-making, rapid programme rollout, continuing policy experimentation, institutional and policy Darwinism (a constant churning of institutional innovation and policies as each measure is held to have worked or failed), constant revision of guidelines, etc. It also discourages proper evaluation of a policy's impact over various spatio-temporal horizons, including delayed and/or unintended consequences and feedback effects. The process of neoliberalization is replete with examples (see also the chapters by Gamble, Boyer, and Ryner; more generally, see Peck, 2010; and Jessop, 2013).

More generally, William Scheuerman (2000) notes a trend to "economic states of emergency" linked to a decline in the power of the judiciary (which looks to past precedent) and the legislature (which legislates for the future) and leads to enhanced power for the executive (which can take fast decisions). This is often associated with the intensification of the general recent trend towards authoritarian statism (cf. Ryner, this volume). And it can also lead to new forms of populist backlash as there is a growing disaffection from markets and states as modes of governance and crisis management (cf. Gamble, this volume).

Conclusions

Our summaries of the contributions in Chapter 1 relates them to some of the key themes of crisis dynamics, crisis construals, and crisis lessons. This concluding chapter has not repeated that task. Instead, it has offered some more general theoretical lessons on how to develop this research agenda based on critical realism, the strategic-relational approach, the interaction of objective overdetermination and subjective indeterminacy, and the role of sense- and meaning-making in the pedagogy of crisis. Likewise, in relation to issues of pedagogy, it has considered the asymmetric structuration of drawing policy lessons, securing the hegemony or domination of some lessons over others, and translating lessons into effective political, policy and strategic responses to crises. At least five empirical lessons, among others, can be derived from this closing discussion and the preceding contributions.

First, as crises are objectively overdetermined and subjectively indeterminate, learning in times of crisis takes different forms (in, about, from). So, one must study the dynamics of the lessons of crisis and how these unfold in, through, and after crises. Second, learning, like crises, whether as events or processes, have important temporal moments. These have significant implications for empirical research, especially as they interact with "spatial" dimensions, such as policy transfer across different fields, sites, levels, and scales of policy-making. They are particularly relevant for research on *policy learning* from a governance viewpoint concerned with the "instrumental" (or, perhaps, "performative") role of learning on capacities to manage crises. They also have indirect implications for *political learning*. This involves lessons about institutional design – whether at the level of the polity or politics (policy being covered under policy learning). In a broader perspective, that of critical governance studies, political learning can be extended to include the design of modes of governance and metagovernance, i.e., the governance of governance.

Third, learners' roles differ greatly (e.g., observer, participant, policy-maker) and make a difference to the nature and effects of lesson drawing. So, we need to specify the genres deployed in lesson-drawing and the purposes to which they are put in real time and subsequently. Historicity is an interesting aspect of this process. Fourth, social imaginaries, modes and techniques of learning, crisis-management routines, power asymmetries, and ideologies all condition learning. This is not a purely cognitive, technical exercise but one that is typically contested, conflictual, and asymmetric in its outcomes. These selectivities must be considered in dealing with learning and policy transfer. Fifth, this poses derived research questions: what lessons are drawn and taught on crisis prevention, crisis management and crisis performance; why do only some translate into policy? This is a topic raised in Chapters 1 and 2 and posed in different ways in all the subsequent chapters.

More broadly, and in theoretical terms, the preceding contributions *taken together* make six key innovations in the crisis literature compared with the usual state of the art:

1   They distinguish crisis as event and crisis as process and, relatedly, crises as accidental events from crises as system-generated processes.
2   They distinguish crises that can be managed through established crisis-management routines from crises of crisis management – in other words, between "crises in" and "crises of" an organization, institutional order, system, or social order.
3   They focus on the symptomatology of crisis, i.e., the challenge of moving crisis symptoms to understanding underlying causes as a basis for decisive action.
4   They go beyond the cliché that crises are threat and opportunity by distinguishing valid accounts of the origins and present nature of a crisis, whether as event or process, from more speculative accounts of what exists *in potentia*, i.e., as so many opportunities to be realized through appropriate path-shaping action.
5   They explore how crises may disorient conventional wisdom, throwing past lessons into crisis, provoking efforts to interpret crisis symptoms, learn about crises by trying to manage them, and drawing lessons after a crisis has ended. This leads to important insights into the pedagogy of crisis, a theme that runs throughout the book.
6   Compared with the conventional focus on executive authorities and disaster management agencies, attention turns to how other social forces, including sub-hegemonic or counter-hegemonic forces, such as unions, social movements, construe crises and attempt to learn lessons from them.

Notes

1   This chapter was written by Bob Jessop, with comments and input from Karim Knio.
2   This is a paraphrase of Marx's remarks in the 1857 Introduction to the Critique of Political Economy, that there is no production in general or general production (Marx, 1973, p. 101).
3   It would be wrong to describe Régis Debray as a self-identified critical realist both in terms of anachronism (the term came into currency after he wrote his essay on "Time and Politics", which was published in English in 1973 in his prison writings) and because Debray's theoretical position is better described as [structural] Marxist with clear recognition that agency makes a difference; however, Marx's later work can be described as critical realist *avant la lettre* (cf. Jessop, 2001).
4   This can itself be a source of crisis, as evidenced in the collapse of Long-Term Capital Management and, more recently, in the meltdown of sub-prime mortgages and other derivatives (see Kolb, 2011; Oneil, 2016)

5 Obviously, we are not claiming that learning occurs only in and through crises.
6 This last distinction derives from Niklas Luhmann's work on time: noting that the temporal referent of past, present, and future inevitably changes with the passage of time, he suggests that one can study the past, present, and future in the past, present, and future. This would generate a three-by-three matrix. This suggestion highlights the complex relationship between history-as-account and history-as-event (cf. Luhmann, 1982).
7 On the Icelandic case, see, for example, Aliber and Zoega (2011); Thorvaldur et al. (2010); Wade and Sigurgeirsdottir (2010); Roberts (2016), with these differences partly reflecting the time of observation as well as the theoretical perspective.

References

Aliber, R.Z. and Zoega, G. (eds.) (2011) *Preludes to the Icelandic Financial Crisis.* Basingstoke: Palgrave-Macmillan.

Bhaskar, R. (1998) *The Possibility of Naturalism.* 3rd ed. London: Routledge.

Bhaskar, R. (2008) *Dialectic: The Pulse of Freedom.* London: Routledge.

Debray, R. (1973) *Prison Writings.* London: Allen Lane.

Di Lampedusa, G. (1960) *The Leopard: A Novel.* London: Collins and Harvill.

Giddens, A. (1990) *Consequences of Modernity.* Cambridge: Polity.

Gosden, C. (1994) *Social Being and Time.* Oxford: Blackwell.

Gramsci, A. (1971) *Selections from the Prison Notebooks.* London: Lawrence & Wishart.

Gramsci, A. (1975). *Quaderni del carcere.* Turin: Einaudi.

International Monetary Fund (2015) *Greece. An Update of IMF Staff's Preliminary Public Debt Sustainability Analysis.* IMF Country Report no. 15/186. Washington, DC: International Monetary Fund.

International Monetary Fund (2017) *Greece: Staff Report for the 2016 Article IV Consultation.* Washington, DC: International Monetary Fund.

Jessop, B. (2001) 'Capitalism, the regulation approach, and critical realism', in Brown, A., Fleetwood, S., and Roberts, J.M. (eds.), *Critical Realism and Marxism.* London: Routledge, pp. 88–115.

Jessop, B. (2012) 'Left Strategy', *Transform!*, 10, pp. 9–17.

Jessop, B. (2013) 'Putting neoliberalism in its time and place: A response to the debate', *Social Anthropology*, 21(1), pp. 65–74.

Kolb, R.W. (2011) *The Financial Crisis of Our Time.* Oxford: Oxford University Press.

Luhmann, N. (1982) *The Differentiation of Society.* New York: Columbia University Press.

Marx, K. (1969) *Theories of Surplus Value.* Volume 2. London: Lawrence & Wishart.

Marx, K. (1973) 'Introduction', in Marx, K. (ed.), *Grundrisse: Foundations of the Critique of Political Economy (Rough Draft).* Harmondsworth: Penguin, pp. 81–114.

Mosse, D. (2011) 'Introduction: The anthropology of expertise and professionals in international development', in Mosse, D. (ed.), *Adventures in Aidland: The Anthropology of Professionals in International Development.* Oxford: Berghahn, pp. 1–31.

Nishimura, K. (2011) 'Worlds of our remembering: The agent-structure problem as the search for identity', *Conflict and Cooperation*, 46(1), pp. 96–112.

Oneil, K. (2016) *Weapons of Maths Destruction. How Big Data Increases Inequality and Threatens Democracy.* New York: Crown.

Peck, J.A. (2010) *Constructions of Neo-Liberal Reason.* New York: Oxford University Press.

Peck, J.A. and Theodore, N. (2014) *Fast Policy.* Minneapolis: University of Minnesota Press.

Roberts, M. (2016) *The Long Depression: How It Happened, Why It Happened, and What Happens Next.* Chicago, IL: Haymarket Books.

Samman, A. (2015) 'Crisis theory and the historical imagination', *Review of International Political Economy*, 22(5), pp. 966–995.

Scheuerman, W.E. (2000) 'The economic state of emergency', *Cardozo Law Review*, 21, pp. 1869–2011.

Stanford, M. (1994) *A Companion to the Study of History.* Oxford: Blackwell.

Sum, N.L. and Jessop, B. (2013) *Towards a Cultural Political Economy: Putting Culture in Its Place in Political Economy.* Cheltenham: Edward Elgar.

Thorvaldur, G., Holmström, B., Korkman, S., Söderström, H.T., and Vihriälä, V. (eds.) (2010) *Nordics in Global Crisis: Vulnerability and Resilience.* Helsinki: The Research Institute of the Finnish Economy. Online at http://www.etla.fi/files/2427_nordics_in_global_crisis_(kannet).pdf

Wade, R. and Sigurgeirsdottir, S. (2010) 'Lessons from Iceland', *New Left Review*, 65, pp. 5–29.

Index

For Product Safety Concerns and Information please contact our EU
representative GPSR@taylorandfrancis.com Taylor & Francis Verlag GmbH,
Kaufingerstraße 24, 80331 München, Germany

Printed and bound by CPI Group (UK) Ltd, Croydon, CR0 4YY
01/05/2025
01858389-0004